Discovering Successful Pathways
in Children's Development

THE JOHN D. AND CATHERINE T. MACARTHUR FOUNDATION

Series on Mental Health and Human Development

DISCOVERING SUCCESSFUL PATHWAYS

in Children's Development

Mixed Methods in the Study of
Childhood and Family Life

EDITED BY Thomas S. Weisner

The University of Chicago Press
Chicago and London

Thomas S. Weisner is professor of anthropology in the Center for Culture and Health (NPI/Department of Psychiatry), and Department of Anthropology, University of California, Los Angeles.

The University of Chicago Press, Chicago 60637
The University of Chicago Press, Ltd., London
© 2005 by The University of Chicago
All rights reserved. Published 2005
Printed in the United States of America

14 13 12 11 10 09 08 07 06 05   5 4 3 2 1

ISBN (cloth): 0-226-88664-6

Library of Congress Cataloging-in-Publication Data

Discovering successful pathways in children's development : mixed methods in
   the study of childhood and family life / edited by Thomas S. Weisner.
       p.   cm. — (The John D. and Catherine T. MacArthur Foundation series
   on mental health and human development)
       Papers presented at a conference.
       Includes bibliographical references and index.
       ISBN 0-226-88664-6 (alk. paper)
       1. Child development—Research—Congresses.   2. Socialization—
   Research—Congresses.   3. Ethnicity in children—Research—United States—
   Congresses.   4. Immigrant children—Research—United States—Congresses.
   5. Children with social disabilities—Research—United States—Congresses.
   6. Home and school—Research—United States—Congresses.   7. Educational
   anthropology—Research—Congresses.   8. Social ecology—Research—
   Congresses.   9. Evaluation research (Social action programs)—Congresses.
   I. Weisner, Thomas S., 1943–   II. John D. and Catherine T. MacArthur
   Foundation series on mental health and development.
       HQ767.85.D57   2005
       305.231'072—dc22   2004011327

Contents

Acknowledgments

Preparation of this volume, and the conference at which papers were presented and discussed, have been generously supported by the John D. and Catherine T. MacArthur Foundation Research Network on Successful Pathways through Middle Childhood. The members of this network took an active role in inviting and organizing some of the panels at the conference, as well as preparing their own research for the volume. The members are Phyllis Blumenfeld (University of Michigan), Catherine Cooper (University of California at Santa Cruz), Greg Duncan (Northwestern University), Jacquelynne Eccles (University of Michigan), Cynthia Garcia-Coll (Brown University), Robert Granger (WT Grant Foundation), Jennifer Greene (University of Illinois—Urbana-Champaign), Aletha Huston (University of Texas—Austin), James Johnson (University of North Carolina at Chapel Hill), John Modell (Brown University), Diane Scott-Jones (Boston College), Deborah Stipek (Stanford University), Barrie Thorne (University of California at Berkeley), and Heather Weiss (Harvard University). Thanks to Dr. Helen Davis for editorial and conference support and to Dorre Street and Faye Carter for their excellent editorial assistance in preparing chapters.

Introduction

Thomas S. Weisner

Development along Pathways

Human development is about children and families engaged in activities within a cultural and community context. Development occurs along pathways that are given to us by culture and society and that are actively chosen and engaged in by parents and children within some particular cultural ecology. Imagine these pathways as consisting of everyday contexts and activities (getting ready for bed, sleeping, having breakfast; going to church; sitting in classrooms; visiting relatives; playing video games; doing homework; hanging with friends; going to the mall; dating; "partying"; watching TV). Those activities and their cultural and ecological contexts are the "stepping stones" we traverse as we move along a pathway through the day and the day's routine. These activities make up the life pathways that we engage in each day. Not only is this activities-on-a-pathway conceptual framework useful for thinking about human development, but it certainly encourages the use of multiple methods. How can one conceptualize development as such a journey on a pathway consisting of activities in some specific cultural-ecological context and imagine that we could use only *one* method to find out about it (Weisner 2002)? Using mixed methods is the current best practice for understanding development in such contexts, and this volume offers some of the latest and best efforts in the field.

Our focus is on what children and families *do* in those varied contexts. Kessen (1993) observes that somehow we have too often neglected a fundamental question in human development: what are children actually doing and why? Discovering successful pathways involves understanding what children do when they engage in activities along some pathway, what their experiences and the meaning of them are, and why they have those experiences. This focus on diverse contexts, pathways, and behavior certainly encourages (or requires, as the authors in this volume would say) mixed methods. A pathways framework requires understanding what children do in their everyday activities, grasping the personal experiences of parents and children in those contexts, and knowing the cultural psychology — the shared beliefs, motives, and scripts organizing behavior and thought — of the communities the parents and children are in. Children not only actively and joyously engage in those activities but also resist them (Goncu 1999; Weisner 1996, 1998; Whiting and Edwards 1988).

Children's daily engagement in these routines is an important part of child development. Communities share patterned features of daily routines and a cultural psychology (though of course there are local, familial, and individual variations). These are the "population-specific" patterns that shape the local pathways of life that children engage in: "No account of ontogeny in human adaptation could be adequate without the inclusion of the population specific patterns that establish pathways for the behavioral development of children" (LeVine et al. 1994, 12). LeVine describes the socialization of children as "the intentional design of psychologically salient environments for children's development" (LeVine 2003, 1). Population-specific, shared patterns are a powerful way in which environments are designed. Multiple methods bring us closer to the goal of situating human development in the population-specific, intentionally designed everyday worlds and paths through life. These provide the cultural careers (Goldschmidt 1992) that families and societies afford us.

The developmental pathway approach to human development and the use of mixed methods for their study come at an important time. New conceptions of development and new methods are being called for in many fields, but there are as yet few examples of findings based on those concepts and methods. Journals and research funders are looking for better ways to include mixed methods as the standard for research rather than as an occasional add-on—but are unsure how to evaluate such work if made standard. Diversity in the United States and elsewhere is increasing and demographic "majority minorities" are emerging in states throughout the country, yet ways to understand these communities are lagging behind. Schools and other institutions that support families are looking for better ways to train and assist children and their families but are struggling to find policies that work. Each of these topics is considered in the present volume.

Most studies in our volume search for *successful* pathways in development—those that can lead to increased well-being and better outcomes for children and families. Hence, many of the following chapters reflect an interest in policy and its applications. How can we enhance the chances for success in youth development—that is, the provision of supports and opportunities that can guide children onto successful pathways and help keep them there—unless we fully and holistically study those pathways in the first place? The conception of development occurring along pathways in a cultural ecology drives the use of multiple methods for policy and practice as well as for basic science.

Eccles and Gootman (2002, 9–10), summarizing a national panel report, provide a list of eight broad domains that should characterize successful settings for youth and promote well-being:

- Physical and psychological safety
- Appropriate structure
- Supportive relationships
- Opportunities to belong
- Positive social norms
- Support for efficacy and mattering
- Opportunities for skill building
- Integration of family, school, and community efforts

It is not that parents and children, along with researchers, do not share a general list for what successful pathways are. Indicators of how to assess children's well-being are available across many domains (child health, education, childcare, economic security) and levels of analysis, using a wide variety of methods (Hauser, Brown, and Prosser 1997). However, as the Eccles and Gootman report emphasizes, communities vary in how they define and live out the achievement of these kinds of goals in their everyday lives and activities. The specific content and nature of the activities that make up successful pathways can vary enormously in cultures around the world and in communities in the United States. The Eccles and Gootman synthesis suggests a broad framework of perhaps universal parental and social goals for families and children, and the domains these will be in. But communities differ in their own, local, intentional designs for defining and achieving "positive social norms" or "appropriate" structure.

Well-being for children can be viewed as the engagement by children and parents in everyday routines and activities, part of a life pathway of such activities, that are deemed desirable by them and their community. These kinds of engagement produce the positive psychological experiences (effectance [White 1959], pleasure, attachments, flow, competence) that go along with sociocultural well-being. Empirical study of how to promote the supports and opportunities for children that contribute to successful pathways requires integration across the methods in the social sciences. In chapter 10 Harkness and her colleagues review their own developmental niche model for understanding cultural context and relate this work to the history of cultural ecological studies. My colleagues and I have developed a fieldwork and interview procedure, the Ecocultural Family Interview, that provides a common template for understanding the family daily routine of activities and also ensures that content specific to the community being studied is incorporated into the interview (Weisner 2002; Lieber, Weisner, and Presley, 2003).

Methods and Epistemology for Studying Children's Pathways in Context

The chapters in this volume bring together studies of successful pathways in children's development using multiple methods. Many of the studies are relevant to the policy and applied-research community as well as to the basic sciences. These studies use innovative designs, methods, and theories that bring us closer to understanding successful pathways. The different methods needed to study development in context help us to understand the "steaming green Hell" of the naturalistic, organic, ecocultural (ecological plus cultural) world of the developmental pathways of children, as well as the Newtonian icy-cold precision of the many variables floating in an imagined space that influence those pathways. These ecological and meteorological metaphors are used by Goldenberg, Gallimore, and Reese in chapter 1, quoting Sechrest and Figuerede. There certainly is analytical utility just to be content to stay in the organic, contextual, lived worlds of children and families, or to remain in the mathematical spaces of variables, logical reasoning, and social address categories (e.g., race, gender, socioeconomic status). But it is the purpose of this collection to show how invigorating the climate is (neither too steaming nor too icy) when multiple methods are used in the study of children's and families' lives.

The questions organizing the empirical studies are: What are the findings, how were they obtained, in what ways are they believable, and in what ways do they matter? If there is a debate to have about using mixed methods, then those are the questions we believe are the ones to ask. The studies in this book focus on significant findings that would not have been discovered and confirmed without the use of multiple methods of inquiry and innovative designs. The chapters combine empirical findings regarding children's developmental pathways using mixed methods; show the added value gained by using mixed methods; highlight what was learned about discovery procedures important in understanding successful developmental pathways; and feature researchers' candid experiences, both frustrating and enlightening, in using mixed methods in their work.

Although specific methodological and epistemological topics are discussed in many of the chapters, our volume is not organized around epistemology (positivism, interpretive frames), technical issues (ways of doing fieldwork, causal inference, and design), or kinds of methods (quantitative, qualitative). These topics are extensively considered already in the methods and theoretical literature in the social sciences. As Greene also comments in the final chapter, the "technical level" regarding mixing methods, appropriate designs, and techniques has an extensive literature. Handbooks on mixed methods and qualitative methods for example are available (Bernard 1998, 1999; Creswell 2002; Denzin and Lincoln 2000; Tashakkori and Teddlie 2003; Werner and Schoepfle 1987). But research using such methods to explore issues that matter for children and communities, to better understand the practical difficulties in conducting such work, and to study policy implications is much less available.

Coherence and Skeptical Realism

Broadly speaking, the great naturalistic, empirical lineage of the social sciences provides the context and tradition for much of our work. In this tradition, knowing the world is not a straightforward, direct empirical problem easily solved or left untheorized. Historical periods, cultures, communities, and individuals differ and understand the world differently. Methods arise in those very communities. Historical and political contexts are important for every topic in our volume: the study of race or identity, understanding childhood stages, how children and parents position themselves in their particular sociohistorical context, children's own sense of family and social history, and the varying contexts shaping research on children. Are different methods thus incommensurate, and are different cultures or minds or historical periods also ultimately unknowable? As Campbell frames the problem, we can know about the world through a kind of cautious, skeptical holism and realism. This holistic inquiry can create coherent, believable research knowledge.

> Those who make knowing the other problematic are correct. Those who regard it as impossible to any degree are wrong. We need an epistemology and methodology which explains how, and to what degree, knowing the other is possible, as well as the common errors made in the attempt. Mainstream postpositivist philosophy of science points the way both in its holistic coherence-based strategy for belief-revision, and in its principle of charity for the radical translation problem. (Campbell 1996, 169)

The studies in the present volume demonstrate the value of holism and contextualism in knowing and understanding and also the benefits of varied, mixed methods for discovery. Mixed methods improve ways to describe and account for coherent patterns in the worlds of families and children and then to make that knowledge as plausible and believable as one can. This is the "multiplist" approach to understanding (see chap. 1, this volume) in which one assumes that complicated matters require multiple explorations to grasp them, and where the values, goals, and agency of the individuals, families, communities, and larger institutions are part of the world to be understood (Shweder 1996).

Using varied methods encourages being inclusive, not exclusive. The debate about methods should not be framed by pitting one method (standardized assessments, questionnaires, structured interviews) against supposedly "lesser" or "better" others (observation, ethnography, historical analysis, conversational interviews). We start with the fact that all methods are incomplete and have biases. To help reduce the weaknesses of any one method taken alone, why would one not use several if possible and useful? But this does not routinely happen. Hence this observation from Webb et al. is still justified nearly four decades after it was written:

> Today, the dominant mass of social science research is based upon interviews and questionnaires. We lament this overdependence on a single, fallible method. Interviews and questionnaires intrude as a foreign ele-

ment into the social setting they would describe, they create as well as measure attitudes, they elicit atypical roles and responses, they are limited to those who are accessible and will cooperate, and the responses obtained are produced in part by dimensions of individual differences irrelevant to the topic at hand.

But the principal objection is that they are used alone. No research method is without bias. Interviews and questionnaires must be supplemented by methods testing the same social science variables but having *different* methodological weaknesses. (Webb et al. 1981 [1966], emphasis in original)

Five Topics in Development: Summary of Chapters

The chapters in this volume are organized around findings from mixed-methods research on children, families, and developmental pathways in five topical areas:

- Pathways through classrooms, schools, and neighborhoods
- Ethnicity and the development of ethnic identity in childhood
- Culture and developmental pathways
- Social experiments
- Family and intervention studies

The five areas combine basic social science with applied and policy work. Several discussions expand on how to combine methods in work of these kinds (Scott-Jones and Cross on race and identity; Huston and Brock on poverty and social experiments; Pollock on race and schooling and on mixing professions and practitioners as well as research methods; Greene on reasons to use mixed methods).

Pathways through Classrooms, Schools, and Neighborhoods

In chapter 1, Claude Goldenberg, Ronald Gallimore, and Leslie Reese summarize a remarkable multiple-method exploratory journey in their longitudinal research program of studies of Latino children's literacy development and academic attainment. Their focus is on findings that mattered for understanding contextual influences on literacy. The chapter is organized around features of community cultural ecology that mattered (demography, history, parental employment, daily routines and childcare, home-school-church connections, parental beliefs about literacy and school, community diversity). To give just one example, a finding early on puzzled the team: special "Libros" books sent home to parents in an experimental intervention, which were expected to lead to higher kindergarten literacy, did not do so, compared to sending home phonics worksheets. The team turned to their qualitative work on parental literacy beliefs to look for reasons: most parents had learned in Mexico that "to study" meant repeating words in books to learn them, so parents seldom actually discussed the text in the Libros books, which was what the experiment was intended to encourage. But parents varied in these literacy beliefs and practices. This finding in turn led to a field study of parental origin communities in Mexico. Latino parental variations in literacy practices were in part sociohistorical in origin. Town/city background (more home reading to children if parents were schooled in cities) or rural/rancho background (more reading if parents were schooled in ranchos) were related to how parents used Libros books. The subsamples on which this work was done provided hypotheses which were then confirmed using path analysis on their larger $n = 120$ sample. And this is just one reflexive back-and-forth chain of findings blending multiple methods (ethnography, qualitative interviews, questionnaires, school records and assessments, intervention/experiments) and analytic techniques in their research program. The team justifies their blend of methods by its pragmatic value in encouraging constant, questioning curiosity about their own findings, and by the fact that their findings can matter for the educational achievement of the immigrant families and children. They point out that interventions, no matter how promising, that are not fitted to the ecocultural context of those involved (whether parents, teachers, or children) will not be effective without inquiry into those contexts using multiple research methods.

In chapter 2, Heather Weiss and colleagues show how to go beyond what "everyone knew" based on survey/questionnaire data. Supposedly, maternal work will inevitably pose obstacles to school involvement. They describe the team process through which they discovered the strategies used by low-income working mothers who stayed involved in their children's education, even if working and even if the involvement in their children's education was not always directly at school. Mothers built a network of family and friends to complement what they could not do while working; used workplaces as home bases from which to make calls and for kids to do homework and learn about work skills; obtained resources from their jobs (supplies, advice, computers); and did creative multitasking between work and home settings. Part-time working mothers were most involved in school, but full-timers used many strategies to enhance learning when they could. This chapter is also about the authors' process of discovery as they moved back and forth between quantitative and qualitative findings and across the years of their longitudinal data collection. Schools could restructure policies to capitalize on what mothers were doing by better scheduling, as could employers.

In chapter 3, Lois-ellin Datta describes an evaluation study of the Comer school reform program in Detroit and how a blend of quantitative analyses (which did not show particularly strong impacts) and qualitative work (showing that well-implemented programs were effective) provides a fuller, truer picture of the impacts than either analysis alone. Information on both control and Comer schools was used, a design strategy employed in other studies in our volume (e.g., the New Hope evaluation and the Moving to Opportunity study). Although randomization was not possible, the evaluators obtained as much information using the design as possible. Datta finds this evaluation exemplary because the policy recommendations offered clear suggestions regarding what features of the Comer approach were better implemented and linked to gains for schools and students—rather than stopping with quantitative impacts that did not take account of changes in Detroit and variations in implementation that mattered over time.

All three of these school studies share a core principle: get closer to the experiences, institutions, and people in the schools and families that we are trying to study. Do not settle for one voice (only the teachers), one level of analysis (only school level or only home practices), or one social address category (e.g., only the generic category "Mexican immigrant families").

Ethnicity and the Development of Ethnic Identity in Childhood

In chapter 4, Deborah Johnson explores racial socialization and racial-coping outcomes for children in the United States using the Racial Stories Task (RST). To explore how children cope with racial barriers and prejudice while protecting their sense of self, she compared findings across three studies that used the RST in different ways: work on parenting processes, school influences, and perceived violence as a community-level influence. Johnson also compares different versions of the RST (open- or closed-ended) and where and how data were collected. Each version of the RST has advantages and disadvantages, which Johnson weighs carefully. Johnson comments that although RST measures and the use of social address proxies were useful, "it is the thousands of daily interactions that children have in school with their peers, on the way to school on the bus, on the way home walking past the police station, or talking with the teacher during lunch" that create the set of "actions and experiences" that make up the child's world and influence racial socialization and coping.

In chapter 5, Rubén Rumbaut explores definitions of the situation of the self among children of immigrants. This work is unusual from our mixed-methods perspective in that it first explores longitudinal survey questions on ethnic self-identity and then turns to qualitative interviews and other methods as ways to further explore the rich survey findings. Rumbaut explores ethnic identities in youth from varied national origins, not as inevitable outcomes of a linear process, but as "complex products of people's ongoing efforts to interpret, understand, and respond to the social structural, cultural, and historical situations in which they find themselves, within their sets of resources and vulnerabilities." Rumbaut's focus on consonant, dissonant, and selective acculturation patterns and the influences of language use, racialization, and discrimination experiences all pointed to the importance of subjectivity and situationality for understanding ethnic self-definitions. Rumbaut then turns to a follow-up using 150 in-depth qualitative interviews with young adults at one site from the survey (San Diego). This work shows how often ethnic identifications were expanded or changed by youth in this sample due to the relational experiences and the social and historical contexts that youth were now were engaging (college, work, marriage, politics). The youth themselves were pluralists, as they constantly were translating and incorporating "what is 'out there' into what is 'in here'" and through those processes crystallizing a sense of who they were.

Two discussion commentaries, by Diane Scott-Jones and William Cross, put these studies in context. Scott-Jones points out the trade-offs in methods in Johnson's series of studies and wishes for more rich descriptive data from both Johnson and Rumbaut. Cross adds a historical perspective on the use of mixed methods to study black identity and points out the blend of group identity and personality measures. He points out that although valuable new constructs were added over time in the research on black identity, the same method (self-report questionnaires) typically continued to be used to assess them. Multiple ethnic identities and situational and developmental changes in identity are clearly important, and so a true mixing of methods is needed to understand identity (considered as cognitions, feelings, and behavior) across contexts.

Culture and Developmental Pathways

In chapter 6, Tom Fricke blends survey and demographic research with ethnography. He sees the two activities as very different but not opposed. Ethnography is of course itself a suite of many techniques to study a locale, a cultural place, or a pathway. Surveys complement the ethnographic data on local experience in that cultural ecology and world of meanings. Fricke uses examples from his field research in Taiwan, Pakistan, Nepal, and North Dakota to weave together demographic data from surveys and vignettes from fieldwork that provide meaning, context, purpose, and the mechanisms to arrive at a deep understanding of what those survey data might signify. He considers findings on education, household formation, in-laws and family, marriage, residence patterns, economic decisions, fertility, and other topics. He describes, for example, the emotions surrounding a father's communication with his daughter, who has left her father's farm in North Dakota. He shows where and how fieldwork led to greatly improved survey questions and where puzzles in survey findings led to better ethnographic inquiry to understand those puzzles. Among the greatest strengths of the chapter, perhaps, is its own reflexivity, as Fricke includes his own letters and notes about doing fieldwork.

In chapter 7, Debra Skinner, Stephen Matthews, and Linda Burton describe the "structured discovery" methods of qualitative fieldwork among working poor families with children with disabilities in Boston, San Antonio, and Chicago. They describe the extensive efforts parents are making to find resources and services and make ends meet, and then use Geographic Information Systems (GIS) mapping methods for visualizing the distances traveled for services and intensity of use across months of parent involvement with those services. Neighborhood constraints and opportunities are linked to family mobility, access, and utilization of services; such linkages would not have been as clear without the use of mixed methods. The chapter also describes the debates among the research team about how and even whether to use GIS, and its merits for both analysis and policy use — merits available, however, only if GIS is used in combination with ethnographic insights and case materials.

Using Mixed Methods in Social Experiments

In chapter 8, Jeffrey Kling, Jeffrey Liebman, and Lawrence Katz offer a fascinating analysis of the Moving to Opportunity (MTO) random-assignment experiment. MTO offered vouchers to some public housing residents that allowed them to move to private apartments in lower-poverty neighborhoods. What difference did such moves make in the lives of children and parents? Qualitative interviews suggested that fear of violence led parents in public housing projects to monitor their children for sheer safety (parents and kids had to "live life on the watch") and that parents who accepted the vouchers and moved indeed were able to reduce such monitoring. Listening closely to these parents revealed the pervasive fear of violence parents experienced in the public housing projects and the importance for their lives of leaving much of that fear behind when they moved. This proved to be a main effect of "moving to opportunity." The team also better understood how MTO and public housing operated. This implementation knowledge helped them interpret quantitative findings and improve policy recommendations. MTO movers did not have higher earnings or use welfare less (as hypothesized by labor economists), but MTO did have impacts on safety and child behavior and health (as suggested by data from the parent interviews). The principal investigators did the interviews themselves, which led to improvements in later surveys, and they designed a reference frame for the team to use for interpreting the quantitative findings, including how to interpret the experimental impacts or lack of them in different domains.

In chapter 9, Christina Gibson and Greg Duncan report on another random-assignment social experiment, the New Hope antipoverty effort in Milwaukee. New Hope offered working poor families an income supplement, childcare vouchers, health care subsidies, and a community service job "if needed" to participants who worked at least 30 hours a week. Did such a relatively rich suite of benefits affect parents' and children's well-being? Both "narratives and numbers" were essential to understand the impacts. For example, acceptance (or "take-up") of the New Hope offer was selective. Boys seemed to benefit in school achievement more than girls based on teacher reports. For each of these findings, the research team could offer ethnographic evidence to guide survey analyses and interpretation of results. Further, Gibson and Duncan provide some innovative decision criteria for thinking about making inferences from a small qualitative data set drawn from a larger survey sample and for estimating parameters in the larger survey based on a much smaller qualitative subsample. These criteria work where the qualitative data are a random sample of both the experimental and control groups, as in the New Hope study. There are also some telling examples of where the ethnographic data, no matter how contextually rich and valid, could *not* be scaled up to assess *overall* program impacts. This is a useful reminder to keep in mind when reading all the clear examples in our volume of how and when such mixed methods *do* work in concert with survey data!

Aletha Huston and Thomas Brock offer commentaries from the perspectives of research on parents and children in poverty and efforts to implement programs that address policy. Huston is surprised that some researchers still see qualitative and quantitative methods as competitors and points out the many ways to blend methods: measures are on a continuum, participants and researchers should set the content for interviews, person- and variable-centered approaches are typically complementary, analysis and collection of data can be qualitative or quantitative, and observation can complement verbal reports. Brock suggests that qualitative and quantitative methods are needed for both impact research (what happened?) and implementation (why did it happen this way, or why did it not happen?) in social interventions. He points to gains for practitioners through using mixed methods for operating a program better, targeting the right beneficiaries better, finding gaps in services, and helping to determine what funds are actually needed where. He argues, from a social policy perspective, that mixed methods are essential.

Family and Intervention Studies: Mixing Research and Practice Roles

The next set of chapters has many connections to the school studies; these chapters, however, focus on interventions and on the reflexive, more inclusive blending of fieldworker, advocate, and research participant roles. In chapter 10, Sara Harkness and colleagues use their influential developmental niche model to frame their study of home-school connections. Their model looks outward from the child toward three subsystems: the child's physical and social setting, the customs and practices organizing those settings, and the psychology and cultural belief systems of those interacting with children. They review the intellectual history of the cultural-contextual and mixed-methods approaches, as well as point out that cross-cultural work requires mixed methods, since the "same" topic (home-school connections, the daily routine) can and will have very different meanings and normative patterns around the world. They then describe the process of becoming active participants in the lives of children in homes and schools (with their interlocking developmental niches) as part of a school-improvement program, GEAR UP, in Connecticut. Theirs is a mixed-methods intervention report not only because their work was holistic in its conceptions of the child developmental niche but also because of the intense participation of the team in the lives of children, parents, and school—roles that mixed research, clinical, and personal relationships.

In chapter 11, Catherine Cooper and colleagues search for ways to help immigrant youth bridge their multiple worlds and stay on "good pathways." Like Harkness et al., they focus on the process of inclusion and mixing of researcher, intervention, and participant roles in work with Latino immigrant families in California. This team describes their "interpretive cycle" of research partnerships (with families, schools, and programs) across two research studies and many years of engagement with families. In one project, for example, the team followed a group of 30 students from the time they entered a program for youth on into high school, searching, among other things, for math and English school course trajectories that showed pathways that would or would not get children into higher education. Children moved off—and back on—such pathways; there were several paths that ended up pointing the way to a college option.

Mica Pollock (chapter 12) is also interested in assisting immigrants and the poor in educational advancement. Pollock understands that mixed-methods research in the policy world has to include thinking like and using the concepts and methods of other professions—in her example "thinking like a lawyer" in the civil rights field, "like an educator" regarding classrooms, or "like a researcher" regarding contexts. One of her methods was to bring together disparate professions interested in educational equality and ask them all to make their criteria and definitions for educational equality concrete and measurable. She makes the case that ultimately all parties interested in educationally good pathways have to not only think in holistic terms but think in terms of the single, broadest remedy of all: "mapping, planning, and monitoring the academic path of each individual child of color toward universal academic ends."

Synthesis: Futures for Mixed Methods

Jennifer Greene concludes the volume with a synthesis chapter on the future of mixed methods. Greene's reprise ties the chapters to the field of evaluation and methods research generally. She describes four themes across the chapters, which also are themes in the mixed-methods tradition more generally: getting it right, doing work better, unsettling the settled (i.e., the settled categories that organize research and the institutions that fund and house and make use of research, as well as the personally unsettling experiences that can go along with blending methods), and foregrounding the political and value dimensions of research so as to better engage differences in approaches. She comments on the particular way each chapter contributes to one or more of these themes and the assumptions behind the themes. Greene points out how the themes make different epistemological assumptions: Is the world out there or constructed or both? Is the goal to describe or explain or prove cause? She says that deploying mixed methods effectively depends on the right conditions (very much in evidence in this volume but not always elsewhere): methods have relatively equal status; there is respectful understanding of these methods; there is openness to new ways of knowing; there is a value placed on pragmatism and empiricism.

Conclusion

The use of mixed methods can amplify good developmental research and have it better and more broadly read and understood than that research otherwise might have been. It is undeniable that studies that have no qualitative or ethnographic component, or no case materials, are simply less likely to enter the discourse in anthropology, history, or related fields. If they do, they may be less valorized than they might otherwise deserve to be. Similarly, research that does not have a clear design or does not have some normative or standardized assessments or has small and selective samples is less likely to be heard by economists or psychologists or those in policy and other fields. Such studies may have important findings, but they are unlikely nonetheless to influence nearly as broad an audience than if they used mixed methods. In the case of New Hope, for instance, the inclusion of a randomly sampled ethnographic sample, drawn from both the control and the program-recipient groups, not only produced new findings but drew in broader research and policy audiences who might not have paid the same attention otherwise (Weisner et al. 2002). Some may have been first drawn to New Hope because there was an experimental design, others because there were rich family ethnographic narratives, and others because there were standard child assessments and teacher ratings. It is fair to say that the combination was richer than any of its parts. The MTO, Latino Literacy, and Fricke's international survey research also are studies that clearly show this kind of value-added amplification of findings.

Methods are personal, reflexive acts as well as research tools having a technical literature and requiring instruction in their use. As Devereux (1978) pointed out long ago, methods also exist in part to help defend us against our own anxieties and amplify our personal strengths while avoiding our weaknesses. If someone feels uncomfortable in fluid and perhaps unfamiliar interpersonal situations, or situations where they do not understand the cultural scripts and norms for conduct, they are not going to like fieldwork in the green steaming jungle of everyday lived experiences in life's pathways and activities and are unlikely to choose to use methods that put them there. If researchers are comfortable in using mathematics and statistics, they are more likely to favor methods that use those tools to understand floating variables in that cold Newtonian space. The same can be true for the topics we decide to study. If we are asked to study poverty or sexuality or racial identity, and if those topics or situations make us uncomfortable, then we are less likely to want to engage those topics using methods that might put us closer—maybe too close—to them.

But mixed methods can be done by teams where one person's anxieties are another's chance for self-fulfillment. Several of the studies in our volume show the value of bringing our varied personal preferences for research practice together in teams. Not everyone can personally combine skills at multiple methods, but they do not need to, so long as they partner with others who complement their own preferences. Datta points out that there can be "methodologically multilingual" fieldworker/data analysts assisting methodologically monolingual team members, and examples of these strategies in the personal equation of fieldwork are to be found throughout this book. Most of the New Hope fieldwork team also did quantitative data analyses of the survey, for instance, to the benefit of the findings and their less multilingual colleagues.

Time and money are as always, important constraints in the cultural ecology of our own research careers and pathways. Several contributions to this volume suggest specific metrics of sampling, teamwork, theory, or policy analysis to help decide more effectively how to allocate resources. Issues of how to allocate always scarce research resources are explicitly discussed in several chapters. Some of the chapters offer specific illustrations of how relatively modest extensions of studies using a survey or questionnaire method, for example (such as through using nested case study designs or subset analyses), can produce significant gains in understanding.

Discovering Successful Pathways in Children's Development is in a research tradition that combines contributions to basic science with a drive to solve societal problems. Stokes (1997) describes Pasteur as the exemplar of a researcher in that tradition (and Einstein as the exemplar of basic science and theory seemingly without practical benefit, and Edison as the master of practical benefit unguided by basic science theory). Goldenberg et al. argue that mixed methods provide the more open, eclectic field of inquiry optimal for discovering findings that matter in Pasteur's tradition.

Burton (2000) suggests another aspect of this tradition. Children and youth themselves need and want to "matter," to feel needed, wanted, and cared about not only by those close to them but by society. Mattering in this sense provides mirroring, validation, and recognition from society and is an important nutrient in successful youth pathways. At some point, our research and our methods of conducting that research should matter to society as well. It is a considerable achievement for families and communities to attain well-being for their children, which always includes a sense of mattering, and it is a research and policy program worthy of continued scientific study to discover how more families and communities might achieve well-being along a meaningful life pathway. The kinds of innovative research programs and methods in this collection are ways to achieve this goal.

Acknowledgments

I thank the Center for Culture and Health, Department of Psychiatry and Biobehavioral Sciences, Neuropsychiatric Institute, University of California at Los Angeles.

References

Bernard, H. R. 1999. *Social Research Methods: Qualitative and Quantitative Approaches.* Thousand Oaks, CA: Sage Publications.

———, ed. 1998. *Handbook of Methods in Cultural Anthropology.* Walnut Creek, CA: Altamira Press.

Burton, L. M. 2000. "Learning to Labor: Adolescent Kinwork in Multigeneration Families." Roberta Grotberg Simmons Memorial Lecture, presented at the biennial meeting of the Society for Research on Adolescence, Chicago, March.

Campbell, D. T. 1996. "Can We Overcome Worldview Incommensurability/Relativity in Trying to Understand the Other?" In *Ethnography and Human Development: Context and Meaning in Social Inquiry,* ed. R. Jessor, A. Colby, and R. Shweder, 153–172. Chicago: University of Chicago Press.

Creswell, J. 2002. *Research Design: Qualitative, Quantitative, and Mixed Method Approaches.* Thousand Oaks, CA: Sage Publications.

Denzin, N. K., and Y. S. Lincoln, eds. 2000. *Handbook of Qualitative Research.* 2nd ed. Thousand Oaks, CA: Sage Publications.

Devereux, G. 1978. "The Works of George Devereux." In *The Making of Psychological Anthropology,* ed. G. D. Spindler, 361–406. Berkeley and Los Angeles: University of California Press.

Eccles, J., and J. A. Gootman, eds. 2002. *Community Development Programs to Promote Youth Development.* Washington, DC: National Academy Press.

Goldschmidt, W. 1992. *The Human Career: The Self in the Symbolic World.* Cambridge, MA: Blackwells.

Goncu, A., ed. 1999. *Children's Engagement in the World: Sociocultural Perspectives.* Cambridge: Cambridge University Press.

Hauser, R. M., B. V. Brown, and W. R. Prosser, eds. 1997. *Indicators of Children's Well-Being.* New York: Russell Sage Foundation.

Kessen, W. 1993. "Rubble or Revolution: A Commentary." In *Development in Context: Acting and Thinking in Specific Environments,* ed. R. H. Wozniak and K. W. Fischer, 269–279. Hillsdale, NJ: Erlbaum.

LeVine, R. A. 2003. *Childhood Socialization: Comparative Studies of Parenting, Learning and Educational Change.* CERC Studies in Comparative Education 12. Hong Kong: University of Hong Kong Press.

LeVine, R. A., S. Dixon, S. LeVine, A. Richman, P. H. Leiderman, C. H. Keefer, and T. B. Brazelton, eds. 1994. *Child Care and Culture: Lessons from Africa.* Cambridge: Cambridge University Press.

Lieber, E., T. S. Weisner, and M. Presley. 2003. "EthnoNotes: An Internet-Based Fieldnote Management Tool." *Field Methods* 15 (4): 405–425.

Shweder, R. A. 1996. "*Quanta* and *Qualia:* What Is the 'Object' of Ethnographic Method?" In *Ethnography and Human Development: Context and Meaning in Social Inquiry,* ed. R. Jessor, A. Colby, and R. Shweder, 175–182. Chicago: University of Chicago Press.

Stokes, D. E. 1997. *Pasteur's Quadrant: Basic Science and Technological Innovation.* Washington, DC: Brookings Institution Press.

Tashakkori, A., and Teddlie, C., eds. 2003. *Handbook of Mixed Methods in Social and Behavioral Research.* Thousand Oaks, CA: Sage Publications.

Webb, E. T., D. T. Campbell, R. D. Schwartz, L. Sechrest, and J. B. Grove. 1981[1966]. *Nonreactive Measures in the Social Sciences.* 2nd ed. Boston: Houghton Mifflin.

Weisner, T. S. 1996. "Why Ethnography Should Be the Most Important Method in the Study of Human Development." In *Ethnography and Human Development: Context and Meaning in Social Inquiry,* ed. R. Jessor, A. Colby, and R. Shweder, 305–324. Chicago: University of Chicago Press.

———. 1998. "Human Development, Child Well-Being, and the Cultural Project of Development." In *Socio-emotional Development across Cultures,* ed. D. Sharma and K. Fischer, 69–85. New Directions in Child Development, vol. 81. San Francisco: Jossey-Bass.

———. 2002. "Ecocultural Understanding of Children's Developmental Pathways." *Human Development* 174:275–281.

Weisner, T. S., C. Gibson, E. D. Lowe, and J. Romich. 2002. "Understanding Working Poor Families in the New Hope Program." *Poverty Research Newsletter* 6 (4): 3–5.

Werner, O., and G. M. Schoepfle. 1987. *Systematic Fieldwork.* Vols. 1–2. Newbury Park, CA: Sage Publications.

White, R. 1959. "Motivation Reconsidered: The Concept of Competence." *Psychological Review* 66:297–333.

Whiting, B. B., and C. P. Edwards. 1988. *Children of Different Worlds: The Formation of Social Behavior.* Cambridge: Harvard University Press.

PART I

Pathways through
Classrooms, Schools,
and Neighborhoods

1

Using Mixed Methods to Explore Latino Children's Literacy Development

Claude Goldenberg, Ronald Gallimore, and Leslie Reese

A Newtonian image of an inalterable, mechanical universe biased social scientists toward avoiding the messy aspects of humanity. [It mentally prepared them] for a bold exploration of the icy depths of interplanetary space. Instead, they found themselves completely unprepared for the tropical nightmare of a Darwinian jungle: A steaming green Hell, where everything is alive and keenly aware of you, most things are venomous or poisonous or otherwise dangerous, and nothing waits passively to be acted upon by an external force. . . . The sweltering space suits . . . had to come off.

Sechrest and Figueredo 1993, 647–48

Using less colorful metaphors but no less forceful arguments, Bronfenbrenner (1979) chided the developmental research community more than 20 years ago for neglecting the everyday contexts in which children develop and learn. As a result of this neglect, "our ability to address public policy concerns regarding contexts of child rearing is correspondingly limited" (1979, 844). Much has changed since 1979, and attention to context is no longer a novelty. In addition to Bronfenbrenner's "circle of influences" as a metaphor of contextual influence, other perspectives have also flourished—for example, a "woven fabric" of ecological/cultural features (Cole 1996; Weisner 1984). From the work of many research communities, over the past four decades much has been learned about context and development, including effects of cultural, community, neighborhood, family, and school factors.

Taking account of the "steaming green Hell" of context effects demanded rethinking of the methodologies that dominated psychology and related disciplines for half a century (Cronbach 1975). Since Bronfenbrenner's admonitions, a wider range of methodological and conceptual tools has come into use, although much debate accompanied his challenge and continues to this day. Many remain uncomfortable because so many of the data generated by contextual studies do not live up to the traditional methodological requirements of their disciplines. Others argue for turning away from conventional methods toward interpretive branches of the social sciences and toward the humanities for methodological foundations (Cole 1996, 4).

As epistemological debates continued, and dualistic rhetoric escalated, some concluded that the methodology wars were not likely to be ended in our lifetimes and that a purist approach would not get much research done (Miles and Huberman 1985; Greene and Caracelli 1997). A more ecumenical or "multiplist" approach suggested mixing methods from intense local observation to random-assignment experiments (e.g., Campbell 1974; Cook and Reichardt 1979; Cronbach 1975; Houts, Cook, and Shadish 1986; Sechrest, Babcock, and Smith 1993; Webb et al. 1966). The multiplist approach rejects single methods in favor of juxtaposing multiple probes using heterogeneous methods to seek stable and convergent results and interpretations across contexts, times, populations, data sets, analytic strategies, and perspectives. It assumes that all research is affected to varying degrees by values and preferences and that "individual passion and intellectual commitments provide the life force of science," which are best minimized by "trying to represent multiple preferences and values in a research program" (Houts, Cook, and Shadish 1986, 62–63).

Included in those individual preferences and values are choices of methods. Multiple, competing approaches provide one way to estimate the degree of convergence of findings and interpretations, as well as to force out conflicting assumptions. Multiplist approaches are claimed to be especially helpful for problems where little is yet known or understood (Cook and Reichardt 1979): they can reveal unsuspected relationships; suggest unanticipated variables and effects; provide a basis for more ambitious and expensive undertakings; and ground "defensible interpretations of what may be true about the world" (Houts, Cook, and Shadish 1986, 61).

Our research team has been influenced by Campbell, Sechrest, Cook, and others, and we have been purposefully ecumenical, mixing methods to study an understudied population: Spanish-speaking children of immigrant Latino parents. We chose this approach also because the existing research literature seemed markedly inconsistent with our own professional and personal experiences in Latino communities. These inconsistencies were especially marked regarding Latino children's literacy development and academic attainment.

Some inconsistencies were directly related to questions of how to help Latino children succeed in American schools in general, and how to assist their literacy development in particular. The importance of the questions we confronted could hardly matter more to the children and their parents and to the school personnel who try to serve them. Latino children are a large and growing portion of the U.S. school-age population. Despite progress and the narrowing of gaps between majority- and minority-group students, Latinos continue to be at risk for poor school attainment (Goldenberg 2001). In this chapter we will focus on the family part of the equation and review some of what we have learned about factors that influence Latino children's educational outcomes, most especially in literacy. Over the past 15 years we have tried many combinations of research methods to uncover family and school factors influencing the academic development of Latino children of immigrant parents.

What literature there was on this population often asserted that Latino parents devalue formal education either because of economic circumstances or because experiences with discrimination against Latinos have led them to conclude that education will not help their children get ahead (e.g., Ogbu and Matuti-Bianchi 1986; Suárez-Orozco and Suárez-Orozco 1996). Another perspective, no longer so common in the research literature (although still heard informally), attributed Latino children's school failure to traditional values—family ties, honor, masculinity, and immediate gratification (Heller 1966, 33–34). These perspectives, different as they are, have at least one thing in common: they attribute the difficulties Latino youngsters have in U.S. schools to discrepancies, or discontinuities, between family values and beliefs about schooling and the values and beliefs assumed to be important for school success in this country.

However, based on personal and professional experience, we were skeptical about the validity and comprehensiveness of these characterizations of Latino students and family. For example, we had observed that despite differences in cultures and outlook between Latino immigrant parents and educators in the schools their children attended, there were also considerable commonalities in their values and beliefs. Both parents and teachers want children to do well and succeed in school; both parents and teachers see formal schooling as important for economic and social mobility. Moreover, and despite attempts to maintain links with their native cultures, some immigrant parents made self-conscious attempts to move away from the educational values espoused by their parents and provide greater educational opportunities for their children than they felt they themselves had. At the same time, most of the children did not come from homes that afforded a wealth of literacy experiences. Although literacy (and other academic learning) opportunities were not nonexistent, neither were they as plentiful as they tend to be in middle- or upper-middle-class homes. The reality lay somewhere in between. In short, a complex portrait of commonalities and differences, continuities and discontinuities, seemed more plausible than the widely held stereotypes about this population (Goldenberg and Gallimore 1995).

Using several samples and mixed methods, our findings eventually converged on several broad ecocultural categories of contextual influence on children's literacy experiences and literacy development. These influences included family history and community demography, job-related constraints and enablers, domestic routines and roles, institutional influences, natal cultural schemas, and exposure to alternative cultural schemas. In the following, we summarize what we learned in our longitudinal studies about literacy learning opportunities in low-income Spanish-speaking households, including some of the ecocultural factors that either constrain or enable those opportunities. We provide illustrations of how we have used quantitative and qualitative methods reflexively and interactively to pursue questions about home influences on Latino children's literacy development. Finally, we give a brief indication of how we are currently attempting to gain comparable understanding of home influences on these children's mathematics attainment.

Routines, Settings, and Ecocultural Niches

An important theoretical assumption of our work is that influences on children's development (interactions with others, playing, watching television, reading, counting, etc.) are embedded in the routines of family life that themselves are embedded in a larger ecological and cultural (hereafter "ecocultural") niche. Our qualitative studies therefore nearly always employ as a unit of analysis some variable that is directly or indirectly linked conceptually to the routines of family life.

Use of the daily routine as the unit of analysis results in the focus on whom a child is with during various times of the day, what they are doing, what kinds of purposes organize and structure their interactions, and what kinds of rules govern their interactions. We have referred to these as the characteristics of "activity settings." Activity settings are regular scenes (e.g., doing homework, watching TV, attending mass) that represent the playing out of the family's ecocultural milieu. They represent the way families can and do structure their time based on the traditions handed down to them, the orientations provided by culture, and the strictures of the socioeconomic system within which they live. Activity settings provide the diet of communication, activity, and structure that plays an all-important role in the child's cognitive development (Gallimore, Goldenberg, and Weisner 1993). Conceptualizing influences on children's development in terms of daily routines and ecocultural niches helps provide a measure of structure and predictability to what is naturally a complex and dynamic landscape.

The use of activity settings and daily routine as units of analysis is guided by a related consideration. For research findings to be of practical value in the design of effective interventions (a complementary aspect of our work), changes induced by interventions must be fitted to the context of the lives of the individuals involved. Otherwise, the changes will not survive. A promising program of instruction can be identified, for example, but it is doomed if teachers do not have the materials, time, training, or support from other professionals—in other words, the appropriate settings—to carry it out. Similarly, mothers can be trained in innovative home reading practices, but if the assumed activity settings that permit these practices to take root do not exist and are not created (e.g., if sibling child-minding is common), the intervention program faces a formidable implementation challenge. For these reasons, knowledge of family routines, settings, and niches is vital for the sort of applied social science research to which we aspire.

Ecocultural Context Enablers and Constraints on Literacy: Opportunities and Development

Table 1.1 summarizes the results of more than a decade of studies of ecocultural features related to literacy experiences and development. The findings are organized using an "ecocultural framework" of children's literacy development, which assumes that a wide range of social, cultural, and historical factors are distilled through children's proximal experiences in the home and other developmental settings (Gallimore et al. 1989; Gallimore, Goldenberg, and Weisner 1993; Goldenberg, Reese, and Gallimore 1992; Reese and Gallimore 2000; Weisner 1984). These dimensions and others sketched in table 1.1 describe a child's "ecocultural niche"—the constellation of proximal influences in the child's day-to-day life that shape developmentally significant child experiences (Gallimore et al. 1989; Weisner 1984). "Ecocultural niche" is a useful way of conceptualizing the context of the home and of organizing and interpreting diverse forms of empirical findings. It is one way to "unpack" proxy variables correlated with reading achievement, such as socioeconomic status (SES), which highlight problems but offer limited information on specific, concrete remedial steps. The focus in this approach is on an empirical analysis to identify specific niche features that influence everyday routines in family, school, and other settings and that affect child learning opportunities, such as exposure to literacy-learning activities. Such a model has guided our more than 15 years of longitudinal studies of at-risk Spanish-speaking children and their families and provides a useful means to organize diverse and complex findings. It is an alternative way of studying "cultural effects" on development, in contrast, for example, to proxy research that compares the effects of culture- or ethnic-group membership on developmental processes and outcomes.

As table 1.1 indicates, a number of contextual factors are perhaps redundantly influencing Latino children's home literacy experiences, literacy development, or both. Obviously, some covary, which is expected within an ecocultural perspective since it is assumed that the various dimensions of the niche are interrelated, mutually supportive, and redundant.

We elaborate a few findings from the table.

Connections between Home and School

School entry has a strong effect on children's home literacy experiences. Although parents do not see promoting early literacy as part of their role during the preschool years (Reese, Balzano, et al. 1995; Reese and Gallimore 2000), once children enter school, parents are highly responsive to teachers' attempts to enlist their support to help children's literacy development. In one study, we found that children's literacy experiences and literacy materials at home nearly doubled as a result of kindergarten entrance (Goldenberg, Reese, and Gallimore 1992). One reason is that children's literacy

Table 1.1. Summary of Selected Contextual Factors Affecting Literacy Development and Achievement

Ecological/cultural niche features[a]	Selected findings
Family history and community demography (family cultural and literacy background, neighborhood context)	Grandparents' and parents' literacy correlated with children's reading achievement (Reese et al. 2000). Family literacy practices predicted by grandparents' education in home culture (Reese and Gallimore 2000). Perception of neighborhood danger increases constraints on children's activities, sometimes increasing frequency of literacy-learning opportunities (Reese, Kroesen, and Gallimore 2000). Commitment to the traditional cultural values correlated with teacher ratings at beginning and end of kindergarten and end of first grade (Reese, Balzano, et al. 1995).
Job-related constraints and enablers (hours available for children, on-the-job learning)	Father's job-related literacy and education correlated with ratings of home literacy environment & child's reading achievement (Reese, Gallimore, and Goldenberg 1999). Father's job-related literacy correlated with frequency of home literacy learning opportunities (Reese et al. 2000; Reese, Gallimore, and Goldenberg 1999).
Domestic routines, roles, and childcare	Frequency of reported reading by parents correlated with higher reading achievement (Reese, Goldenberg, et al. 1995). Mother & father participating in literacy activities with the child in first grade correlated with home literacy use rating (Reese, Gallimore, and Goldenberg 1999). Father's participation in home learning in family life in general significantly correlated with kindergarten teacher ratings (project files). Home literacy practices predict early Spanish literacy development, which predicts seventh-grade English reading scores (Reese et al. 2000).
Institutional connections and familiarity (e.g. home-school connections, home-church)	Children's literacy experiences and literacy materials at home nearly doubled as a result of kindergarten entrance (Goldenberg, Reese, and Gallimore 1992). Church attendance correlated with early reading achievement (Reese, Goldenberg, et al. 1995). Familiarity with the university system through the experience of relatives was correlated with kindergarten and first-grade achievement & teacher ratings (project files).

continued

Table 1.1. *continued*

Ecological/cultural niche features[a]	Selected findings
Cultural schema (parents' literacy theories and beliefs, attitudes toward formal schooling)	*Educación* cultural schema: child "becoming a good person" as prerequisite to doing well in school (Reese, Balzano, et al. 1995). Parents value formal schooling and aspire to high levels of education for children but believe attainment dependent on child's moral development (Reese, Gallimore, et al. 1995). Parents see themselves as playing important supporting, but not leading, role in their children's academic development (Goldenberg 1987). Parents see literacy development as beginning when children begin formal schooling; consequently, they do not typically create preschool literacy opportunities for children. Parents have "bottom-up" view of learning to read (Goldenberg, Reese, and Gallimore 1992). Parents conduct home reading sessions by focusing on accurate reading of letters and words (Gallimore and Goldenberg 1993). Parents' expectations do not enable or constrain children's achievement; rather, expectations reflect child's school performance (Goldenberg et al. 2001).
Community heterogeneity (exposure to alternative cultural schema, English, diverse groups)	Parents incorporate into natal cultural schema new features as a result of contact with U.S. model of literacy development (Gallimore and Reese 1999). Parents' years in United States predict child's English proficiency at kindergarten entry, which predicts seventh-grade reading achievement (Reese et al. 2000). Children who attended preschool had higher English proficiency, prekindergarten Spanish literacy, and seventh-grade English reading (Reese et al. 2000). Mother taking classes correlated with kindergarten achievement (project files).

[a]Adapted from Weisner 1984 and Gallimore et al. 1989.

experiences were relatively sparse before they began school. School entry therefore had a substantial positive effect—if teachers sent home literacy materials on a regular basis. In a separate analysis, we found a strong and direct link between teachers' explicit attempts to engage parents in promoting children's literacy growth and children's literacy development during kindergarten (Goldenberg and Arzubiaga 1994). However, we also found that the type of material sent home made a difference—home use of code-oriented materials (sent from school) that focused on letters, sounds, and syllable reading was strongly associated with kindergarten literacy attainment, whereas home use of meaningful "little books" was not (Goldenberg, Reese, and Gallimore 1992). All materials were in Spanish since children were learning to read in Spanish in a transitional bilingual education program.

Community Safety

Another important finding with a direct bearing on the role of family and community context is the effect of neighborhood safety on family child-rearing practices. Reese, Balzano, et al. (1995) reported that neighborhoods with high rates of gang activity, delinquency, and crime were considered by parents to be dangerous for their children in both the physical and the moral sense. Parents often responded by keeping their children close to home and closely monitoring their activities and friendships. With young children, high levels of protectiveness sometimes resulted in higher levels of children's involvement in literacy activities, as parents sought ways to keep their children entertained in reduced home areas (Reese, Kroesen, and Gallimore 2000). Reese (1998) found that this "protective" strategy was seldom employed by relatives of families under study who resided and raised their children in Mexico. The rural and semirural towns and villages in which the sample's relatives lived were unlikely to be perceived as dangerous, suggesting it was the U.S. context that produced the response.

In the United States, as children grew older, they were occasionally prevented from participating in learning activities such as the school's outdoor camp, extracurricular activities at school, or an accelerated math program at a nearby high school because of parental concerns for their safety. Furstenberg (1993) noted a similar "lock-up" strategy used by Puerto Rican parents in the high-crime neighborhoods of Philadelphia, and Jarrett (1995) described "stringent parental monitoring strategies" used by African American parents in dangerous neighborhoods. Her findings also reveal the differential use of community services by families of different SES backgrounds: middle-income families are more likely to involve their children in activities (sports, classes, teams, clubs) outside the neighborhood, whereas low-income families are dependent to a much greater degree on the availability of these resources within their immediate communities.

Cultural Schema about Literacy and Schooling

Another set of niche features we have explored has to do with cultural schema or models (Gallimore and Goldenberg 2001) in the form of parental attitudes and beliefs about children's literacy development and, more generally, formal schooling.

The immigrant Latino parents in our studies share a "bottom-up" cultural schema of literacy development: children learn to read by learning the letters, corresponding sounds, and how the letters combine to form words. Reading and writing is to be taught explicitly, in school; informal preschool literacy experiences are not accorded great importance. Children's attempts at pretending to read and write are interpreted as "making things up" and "pure scribbling" (*puros garabatos*). This model probably has its origins in parents' native countries, where reading and writing instruction followed a strict and linear sequence of learning vowels, consonants, consonant-vowel combinations, and finally learning to read words (Gallimore and Goldenberg 1993; Goldenberg 1987, 1988; Goldenberg and Gallimore 1995; Goldenberg, Reese, and Gallimore 1992; Reese and Gallimore 2000).

Parents highly value literacy for moral, religious, personal, vocational, and economic reasons. Indeed, much of the literacy activity in the homes of the immigrant families that we have visited over the years centers on sharing stories based on the Bible or with a strong moral content. The importance of reading or retelling stories with a moral, and the advice (*consejos*) that stems from these, has been noted in other studies as well (Valdés 1996). Parents also value their children's academic attainment, in part because they see it (along with English proficiency) as key to economic and social mobility. Although parents' understanding of the U.S. educational system and its "pipeline" to higher education varies considerably, virtually all parents hope that their children will attain at least some college education. But while parents' *aspirations* rarely diverged from hoping that their child would attend college, their *expectations*—what they thought was likely— varied considerably as children progressed through elementary school. We saw little evidence that expectations influenced children's achievement, however, as the traditional "expectancy model" suggests. To the contrary: Parents' expectations themselves (in particular, parents' perceptions of how interested and motivated children were) were influenced by how well their children were doing in school.

Parents take a broad view of their children's education; indeed, the Spanish cognate —*educación*— includes moral and behavioral dimensions in ad-

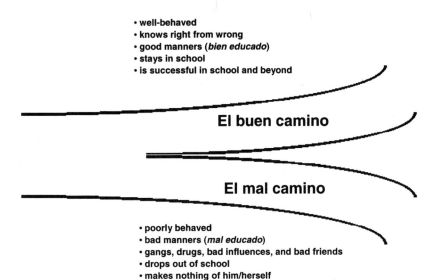

Figure 1.1. *El camino de la vida.* Moral development is the basis for academic development. Morals support and encompass academics.

dition to academic ones. Ultimately, parents want their children to stay on the "the good path" (*el buen camino*), meaning that they become responsible, respectful, morally upright individuals. One indication of being on the good path is staying in and being successful school. But although highly desirable, formal degrees (high school, college) are not seen as absolute requirements for remaining on *el buen camino* (fig. 1.1).

Examples of Mixed-Methods Investigations

We have employed a diverse set of methods—for example, survey questionnaires, open-ended interviews, participant and ethnographic observations, literacy testing, standardized test results, teacher and parent ratings—to try and understand key aspects of Latino children's academic development, particularly in the area of literacy. Analytically, we have used quantitative and qualitative methods as complementary, each providing the basis for inferences and conclusions the other could not. Quantitative methods permit the use of inferential statistics to test hypotheses about generalizable findings. Qualitative methods permit more nuanced exploration into what people say, do, and think and the meanings they ascribe to their words, deeds, and thoughts. We will illustrate this premise, and how we have used it to understand Latino children's literacy development, by describing in more detail some strands of our investigations.

Hypothesis Generation from Case Study Observations of Home Literacy

During the 1980s, many elementary schools in California were moving toward language- and literature-based approaches to literacy instruction (California State Department of Education 1987). In coordination with district teachers and administrators, Goldenberg (1990, 1994) designed a quasi-experimental study that included two types of classrooms. The first type were bilingual kindergarten classrooms that used and sent home language- and meaning-based literacy materials (Libros, literally "books"). The second type of classrooms used the readiness and phonics approach to Spanish literacy instruction employed at their schools. The readiness/ phonics classrooms also sent home packets of phonics materials with the same frequency as the Libros that were sent home in the first type of class- rooms, approximately once every three weeks. The project was designed to answer two basic questions: (1) Will the children receiving the language- and meaning-based instruction and materials outperform those receiving the traditional readiness and phonics instruction? (2) When sent home, what is the influence of the contrasting literacy materials on children's home literacy experiences and literacy development?

In order to answer the first question, we conducted standard quantita- tive comparison of student performance in the two conditions (Libros vs. readiness). At the end of the school year, randomly selected children from each group were given an individual battery of early literacy measures in Spanish (including concepts about print, letter/sound recognition, story comprehension, word recognition, and ability to write words). The students in the Libros group outperformed their peers in the readiness/phonics group (Goldenberg 1990, 1994).

To answer the second question, we used a different set of methods that combined qualitative and quantitative techniques (Goldenberg, Reese, and Gallimore 1992). Because of our focus on families' daily routine, we were interested specifically in the role of the home in children's reading perfor- mance. We wanted to know if and how parents made use of the different types of materials, and if home use was correlated with performance on end-of-year literacy measures. To this end, five students from each group were randomly selected to be observed both at home and in school. Each student was observed at home after school for 2 hours every other week, with approximately 12 visits over the course of the school year (for a total of about 220 hours of observation). Spanish-speaking observers described and timed all activities of the child, with particular focus on any activity that made use of literacy materials or skills.

We were particularly interested in use of school materials at home. The observations were coded using activity category and duration of activity. These categories were both theoretically derived a priori (e.g., use of materials from school and activities involving use of print) and empirically derived over the course of the study (e.g., children "playing church" and using the Bible in their play). In some cases, use of school materials had been observed only infrequently or fleetingly; therefore, on the final visit, parents were asked to demonstrate for the observer how they normally used the materials. This session was videotaped. Also during the final visit, parents were interviewed about their and their children's literacy practices, in an effort to capture descriptions of activities which might take place in the home but had not been observed. Finally, students were observed in their classrooms in order to detect any visible carryover of home use of materials in the class setting. (For a more detailed description of the findings of this part of the study, see Reese, Goldenberg, et al. 1995.)

Transforming qualitative data into quantitative data yielded surprising findings. The frequency and duration of Libros use at home was unrelated to literacy achievement in kindergarten. In contrast, the use of phonics worksheets was strongly and positively associated with kindergarten literacy achievement (Goldenberg, Reese, and Gallimore 1992).

In order to tease out why this unexpected finding might be true (recall that in the classroom evaluation, the Libros classrooms had outperformed the readiness classes), field notes were analyzed qualitatively and interpretively. For example, all instances in which the children used Libros materials from the school were studied in terms of what parents and children were doing and saying as they used the materials. In the following field note excerpt, Fernando is reading a Libro with his mother.

> Fernando's mother calls him over, "Ven a estudiar este libro." [Come and study this book.] He stands beside her as she sits on the bed with the baby on her lap. She reads a page and has Fernando repeat it. She is reading upside down, so when she reads "miles de melones" [thousands of melons] as "melones de melones" [melons of melons], that is how he repeats it.

On the next page, Fernando reads what he knows. When he hesitates on a word, his mother tells him and he repeats it. This form of word-by-word repetition continues for the rest of the book.

> They finish the book, and Mother says, "Otra vez." [Again.] She has him start again and they continue word by word as earlier. On one page, Fernando looks at the picture of the melons in the tree and asks, "Mamá, ¿por qué se metieron aquí los melones?" [Mama, why did they put the melons here?] She responds, "¿Sabe?" [Who knows?] and immediately says the next word to cue him to continue with the repetition.

Fernando's mother initiated the activity and referred to it as "study." Reading was practiced as a repetition of words. There is no reference to or discussion of the text of the story. On the single occasion when the boy tries to call attention to the text's meaning, his mother does not respond. The activity is rather lengthy, with the motivation to continue provided by the mother's prompting. When all of the episodes in which Fernando uses Libros are compared, they consistently share these traits.

A similar analysis of all instances of Libros use by the five children revealed overall patterns. Libros were used more frequently and for longer periods of time when the use was initiated by the parents rather than the children. When parents guided the use of the Libros, they tended to use them in ways which were similar to the ways that phonics worksheets were used. Children were encouraged to repeat or sound out words; sometimes they were told to copy sections of the books in order to practice them. Although each book had questions at the end for parents to ask children, these were never observed to be used, nor were parents observed to engage in discussion of the meaning of the text or pictures at all. On occasion parents did discuss texts with children. However, this interaction was not stimulated by reading homework but rather tended to occur when parents shared Bible stories or stories with a moral with their children.

These qualitative findings suggested the hypothesis that parents may be more successful in their use of phonics materials because they conform more closely to the parents' beliefs about literacy development. Because they see the process of reading as a "bottom-up" activity, in which students are taught first letters, then syllables, then words (Goldenberg 1988), they tended to convert the whole-text materials to this type of use. Because learning is believed to occur through repetition until the new information becomes "recorded" in the brain, parents had their children copy the books over and over. Since early reading is seen as learning to break the code of the syllables on the page, there is little attention to the meaning of the text when the purpose of the activity is perceived to be "learning to read." (We should note that parents' beliefs about the importance of "cracking the code" are in many respects consistent with current understandings in the professional literature. See Snow, Burns, and Griffin 1998.) On other occasions, for example, when the purpose of reading was to impart a moral, parents did discuss the meanings and implications of texts with children. This implies that inviting parents to participate in school-initiated literacy activity needs to take into account the parents' cultural model of what reading is and how it is taught, as well as scientifically based principles and practices.

Hypothesis Confirmation with a Larger Sample

This "cultural model" explanation for our paradoxical findings provided a hypothesis for a subsequent study (Reese and Gallimore 2000). Our case studies of 10 families had suggested the hypothesis that parents' cultural view of reading influences how literacy materials are used at home, but to confirm it a study of more cases was undertaken.

Reese and Gallimore (2000) made use of a randomly selected subset of case study families nested in the sample of 120 immigrant Latino families in our longitudinal study. These families participated in 14 in-depth home interviews over the course of the first four years of the longitudinal study, corresponding to the children's kindergarten, first-, second-, and third-grade years in school. The open-ended case study interviews took the form of guided conversations in which we sought information on family literacy activities. We probed for parents' understandings about how reading proficiency develops, about the age at which reading aloud to children is feasible, as well as how they reported reacting to children's early attempts at making meaning from print. Parents were not only asked to describe home learning experiences, activities, and values but were also asked on occasion to comment on the experiences and opinions of others.

Analysis of narrative interview data across the 32 cases confirmed the effect of parents' cultural models on home literacy practices. However, in confirming this hypothesis, we also made an additional unexpected discovery that linked parents' literacy beliefs and practices to their sociohistorical origins: literacy behaviors on the part of parents (e.g., reading aloud to preschool-aged children) were associated with parents' home country experiences. Although most parents had initially shared a common cultural model of literacy, longitudinal evidence showed changes over time in some of the families. Parents reared in towns or cities were more likely to read to children early (before formal schooling at age five) after exposure to that practice through American schooling (as a result of the school experiences of older siblings or experience with American preschools). Nearly two-thirds (65%) of the town parents began reading to their children before their children entered school. In contrast, only one of the five reared in *ranchos,* or rural hamlets, began reading to children at age four or earlier. A possible explanation is differences in parents' education levels: town mothers averaged 8.7 years of education, compared to 4.3 years for *rancho* mothers ($p < .003$).

Rancho and town life were also associated with different levels of schooling for the parents' own parents (the grandparent generation). Many of the grandparents had lived as children in *ranchos* and at that time had little access to education beyond the rudiments of reading and counting. Others, however, had moved to towns and cities and had access to formal schooling, at least through elementary school. These data suggest that parents (and grandparents) reared on *ranchos* employed practices consistent with a cultural model of reading that assumes that literacy develops after children enter school and that before that age they are not able to understand texts. Although parents in the sample shared a cultural model of how literacy develops, those with higher levels of education and urban life experiences tended to more quickly adopt the practices encouraged by American teachers. One key implication of these findings is that the school can have a substantial impact on literacy practices at home in the early school years, but this impact is likely to differ across the families. Even though all families were part of the same nominal "culture/ethnic" group, there is important variability within the group. This variability, in turn, influenced how families responded to school-based interventions. Findings also demonstrate the flexibility of cultural belief systems. Cultural models guide behaviors, but they are not unchanging; they can be modified in response to demands of the environment.

Path Analysis Confirmation of Qualitative Findings

The findings that emerged from thematic coding of narrative case material generated hypotheses that could be tested statistically with the larger longitudinal sample. These findings prompted us to collect data from all 120 families on where parents were schooled (urban /rural) and on grandparent educational levels. In addition, because of evidence of the continuing effects of home country experiences on current literacy practices in the

United States, we adjusted our SES variable to include home country occupational status as well as U.S. occupational status (choosing whichever status was higher for the composite SES variable).

Reese et al. (2000) employed path analysis to confirm that grandparents' level of education (in the home country) predicted family socioeconomic background, which in turn predicted family literacy practices. Family literacy practices predicted both children's emergent Spanish literacy and oral English proficiency, which in turn predicted seventh-grade English reading achievement. Grandparents' level of education also predicted the child's attendance in preschool, which in turn predicted oral English proficiency. Higher grandparent education directly predicted that children would attend preschool and indirectly predicted home literacy practices through higher family SES. Higher levels of both English proficiency and initial Spanish literacy performance uniquely and significantly predicted higher English reading achievement in grade 7.

These findings demonstrated variability in this population that had direct implications for children's home literacy experiences and attainment. Settings, routines, and ecocultural niches were all influenced by identifiable sociohistorical factors going back to the children's grandparents' generation. Changes in parental literacy practices occurred over time. These changes were associated both with encouragement from the school to read to children at home and to help with homework and with parents' own home country education and experiences. Taken as a whole, our findings illustrate why "one-shot" parent training sessions, in which parents are exhorted to read aloud to children or are taught how this reading should take place, are seldom successful. Without sustained activity as part of a daily routine (e.g., the school regularly requiring home reading as part of homework) and without a cultural model of literacy development that sees reading proficiency as beginning to emerge early on through repeated contact with texts, the teachings of these sessions can go unheeded by many parents.

Diverse and Recursive Mixing of Methods: The Case of Mathematics

These studies illustrate a mixed and recursive process of qualitative and quantitative analysis, data collection, and hypothesis generation and testing. So far, we have illustrated a flow from the bottom up, as trends that emerge from "messy" and often contradictory qualitative data, rooted in the daily routines of a small number of families, are confirmed through quantitative analysis of the larger sample. However, this is only one of the ways in which qualitative and quantitative methods have been combined in our work over the years. Currently, a new line of research essentially employs the sequence in reverse. In current studies of children's math performance through middle school, many of the variables constructed for the literacy analysis were utilized to develop path analyses. Correlations between early math performance and family literacy practices have led to a reexamination of case data to unravel the ways in which home literacy and numeracy practices play themselves out in children's lives in ways that have implications for their subsequent academic performance.

These data suggest that in some families numeracy activities that could be expected to better prepare children for formal instruction once they enter school are incorporated into daily routines. For example, the mother in one family is a cashier. Her children observe her making change and counting money at work. Because of their interest, the father bought a toy cash register and play money, which the children use to create activities that involve counting and making change. In another case, a mother responded to information from the school that her son might be held back a grade by working with him at home on counting activities. She reported that when she sees him counting on his own, she steps back and observes. Current research plans include a reexamination of the "academic pipeline" model of the Latino achievement gap in mathematics using the ideas about connections between numeracy and literacy development that the analysis of quantitative and qualitative data has generated.

Concluding Comments

The broad consensus that children's development occurs in a complex context, a mix of interpenetrated ecological and cultural factors that challenge even the most sophisticated and richly funded research design, provides the basis and justification for mixed-methods investigations (Greene and Caracelli 1997). We no longer have to argue, as Bronfenbrenner did a generation ago, that context matters. Nor do we have to argue that social research requires both qualitative and quantitative designs and methods. As Riggin observes, "The need to argue for the interdependence of qualitative and quantitative methods is over" (1997, 87). Our investigations and those of others contributing to this volume demonstrate that developmental pathways are more likely to be illuminated if we use a combination of empirical methods. Our interpretivist methods, such as open-ended interviews that are essentially guided conversations, led us to understand the role that formal schooling plays in the minds of Latino immigrant parents. They also helped us understand how *educación* is different from *education,* but then how the concepts relate to each other when parents talk about the developmental pathways they hope their children will follow. Our objectivist methods, such as surveys and structured observations, allowed us to test hypotheses probabilistically and led us to discover that grandparents' education and origin had a significant impact on the literacy environment and the literacy development of their United States–born grandchildren, a clear instance of developmental influence across the generations. Table 1.1 summarizes some of our most significant findings across the range of methodologies we have used; it illustrates the value of multiple methods for gaining insights into children's development and the factors influencing it.

Our research team has been enriched by multiple methodological and conceptual perspectives, but there have been times when some of us have wondered whether ecumenism was such a blessing. The following story illustrates both sides of the methodological coin.

One of the questions we posed at the outset of our longitudinal study was "What is the relationship between children's school achievement and parents' aspirations and expectations for children's eventual school attainment?" It is an important question, not just for Latino children and families but for the field of motivation more generally. The conventional wisdom is that performance is influenced by expectations (what someone thinks will happen) and aspirations (what someone hopes will happen). Numerous correlational investigations have shown a link between parents' expectations and/or aspirations and children's school performance (e.g., Coleman 1988; Duran and Weffer 1992). However, no one had ever studied the issue longitudinally throughout elementary school and on into middle school, observing aspirations and expectations over time and relating them to children's achievement. Our hypothesis was that children's school performance would influence parents' expectations and, possibly but not as strongly or as directly, parents' aspirations. We did not think that aspirations and expectations would influence children's achievement. Based on our previous work with this population (e.g., Goldenberg 1987), we expected aspirations to be uniformly high when children began formal schooling, so that there would be no correlations with attainment. Immigrant Latino parents very much want their children to attain high levels of formal schooling since they see schooling as key to social and economic stability and mobility. We also expected expectations to be consistently high, although not as high as aspirations (Laosa 1982). Our prediction was that as patterns of school performance among the children began to emerge, parents would adjust their expectations: parents of children who were doing well in school would adjust their expectations upward, whereas parents whose children were not doing very well would adjust them downward.

Testing these hypotheses required that we ask parents repeatedly (at least once a year) what their aspirations and expectations were for their children's eventual school attainment. This turned out to create some problems among members of our research team. Fieldworkers noticed that sometimes parents did not respond to the questions in ways that the interviewers had intended. For example, some parents did not seem to distinguish between expectations and aspirations. Parents were asked, "How far do you expect your child to go in school?" Some parents refused to answer, saying they were not sure. When pressed, most would make a selection from the set of choices presented, but some of the interviewers got the distinct impression that these did not represent highly meaningful answers. Indeed, we always had a subset of parents who answered "don't know." Other parents answered the expectations question using the same terminology as they had for the preceding aspirations question ("How far do you hope your child will go in school?"). For example, some said, "Well, as I already told you, I hope she'll. . . ." This again suggested to some of the fieldworkers that these were not meaningful or comprehensible questions for the parents.

In order to represent our story's conclusion, we will borrow a device from John Fowles (1969). In the celebrated novel *The French Lieutenant's Woman,* Fowles wrote two conclusions, leaving the reader to decide which ending best fit the novel and, more likely, the reader's worldview.

Ending 1

Aside from some heated discussions during project meetings ("Are these meaningful questions?" "Do we have to ask them *again?*"), we got an indication of how our mixed methodological perspectives created empirical turmoil when the number of "don't knows" spiked one year. It turned out that one of the fieldworkers, instead of trying to probe parents' thinking and trying to encourage them to select an answer to the expectations and aspirations questions, decided to offer "don't know" as a choice. From an anthropological perspective, it could be argued that she was being responsive to the parents' cultural schema, in which these questions did not seem to fit very neatly — or at all. From the more "objectivist" perspective, her attempt at responsiveness threatened the internal validity of this portion of the investigation. Nevertheless, we still collected sufficient data to test our hypothesis that children's school performance throughout elementary school is not influenced by parents' educational aspirations and expectations. Instead, the converse is true: school performance influences parents' expectations (but not their aspirations) for children's future educational attainment (Goldenberg et al. 2001).

Ending 2

As a result of some heated discussions during project meetings ("Are these meaningful questions?" "Do we have to ask them *again?*"), we reexamined our data, with its increasing percentages of "no sé" (I don't know) answers to expectations questions. This analysis resulted in a more "emic" understanding of how immigrant parents were viewing their children's academic and occupational futures, not simply how they were responding to the aspirations/expectations protocol. What we termed more broadly parents' "future orientations" (Reese, Gallimore, et al. 1995) were interpreted using the path-of-life metaphor discussed above. Parents are clear about the path that they hope that their children will follow in life and try to orient their young children in ways that will keep them on the good path. However, the choice of paths is one that the children will ultimately make for themselves, and parents are unsure of the choices their children will make, including how far they will go in school.

This story, with its ambiguous two-option ending, illustrates the outcome of a choice we made at the inception of this research program. Our methodological ecumenism led us to seek out colleagues and fieldworkers with diverse empirical perspectives, and we encouraged the intellectual diversity this produced. This choice both benefited our research and led to tensions that endangered portions of it.

Nonetheless, we remain committed to the belief that the study of children's developmental pathways and the contexts of children's development require multiple and complementary methodologies. Our challenges now are to discern how context matters and to refine the conceptual, analytical, and methodological tools to permit further understanding of contextual influences on development. From our perspective, there is no alternative to mixing methods if we want to develop comprehensive understandings of complex social phenomena such as child development, childhood, and family life. We have no choice but to shed our space suits and wade into the steaming green hell.

Such pronouncements are easy to make but leave many questions dangling. We may declare a liberal and democratic open-mindedness in which no approach or paradigm is presumptive king or queen and where we invite multiple methods to hack away at thorny and complex problems. But methodological pluralism surely has perils of its own, as our own experiences and those of others suggest (Houts, Cook, and Shadish 1986; Sechrest, Babcock, and Smith 1993). What about standards? How do we evaluate the validity of one or another method or combinations of methods? Certainly, each methodological tradition has its canons of rigor and standards of practice. This is appropriate, but we suggest it would be fruitful to develop at least some unified standards and criteria, cutting across methods and paradigms. We will leave treatment of this topic for another occasion but would like to conclude by suggesting that one criterion must be what Gage (1989) called "old-fashioned pragmatism": a methodological or paradigmatic approach—purist or hybrid—is validated when it can be shown to lead to findings, insights, conclusions, or concepts that lead to social improvement of some sort. Conversely, we can be rightly skeptical of approaches that generate much data and ink but little in the way of amelioration. While this might be seen as simply trading in one set of unanswered questions for another, we suggest that such an orientation will help us make progress in advancing and refining methods to permit greater understanding of complex social phenomena.

In his fanciful treatment of the "paradigm wars" in educational research, Gage imagined a pluralistic future where previously competing perspectives (and, of course, their attendant methods) declared a truce and vowed to judge the validity of their efforts on the basis of the good they could demonstrate: "Thus, from the jungle wars of the 1980s, educational researchers. . . . [e]merged onto a sunlit plain—a happy and productive arena in which the strengths of [various] paradigms were abundantly realized" (1989, 9).

This volume can be seen as a validation of Gage's vision, the basic premise being that mixed methods, perhaps even multiple paradigms, are essential to advancing our respective fields. This is all to the good.

We must now go the next step and ask ourselves, "Why do the results of this investigation matter?" Herein lies methodological validation; this should be our standard, or at least one of them. Some might see this perspective as too "applied" or, worse, hopelessly naïve. We make no apologies, believing as we do that the legitimacy of social science partly depends on its contributions to social improvement.

More important, we reject the notion that basic and applied research are necessarily incompatible. Stokes (1997) identified an investigative environment he called Pasteur's Quadrant, a space where use-inspired ("applied") research is combined with the pursuit of generalized knowledge ("basic research"). Rather than pitting one against the other, Stokes proposed a two-dimensional alternative exemplified by the work of Louis Pasteur. In pursuit of solving real-world problems, and superbly prepared to discover nature's secrets, Pasteur made fundamental contributions both to industry and medicine — applied fields — and to biological science. If the legitimacy of social science partly depends on its contributions to social improvement, some must commit to work in Pasteur's Quadrant. Absent such a commitment, no method or mixture of methods will, in the end, much matter.

References

Bronfenbrenner, U. 1979. "Contexts of Child Rearing: Problems and Prospects." *American Psychologist* 34:844–850.

California State Department of Education. 1987. *English-Language Arts Model Curriculum Guide, Kindergarten through Grade Eight.* Sacramento: California State Department of Education.

Campbell, D. T. 1974. "Qualitative Knowing in Action Research." Kurt Lewin Award Address, Society for the Psychological Study of Social Issues, meeting with American Psychological Association, New Orleans. (Revised version, "Qualitative Knowing in Action Research," published in *The Social Contexts of Method,* ed. M. Brenner, P. Marsh, and M. Brenner [New York: St. Martins, 1978].)

Cole, M. 1996. *Cultural Psychology: A Once and Future Discipline.* Cambridge: Harvard University Press.

Coleman, J. 1988. "Social Capital in the Creation of Human Capital." *American Journal of Sociology* 94, Supplement: S95–120.

Cook, T. D., and C. S. Reichardt, eds. 1979. *Qualitative and Quantitative Methods in Evaluation Research.* Beverly Hills, CA: Sage Publications.

Cronbach, L. J. 1975. "Beyond the Two Disciplines of Scientific Psychology." *American Psychologist* 30:116–127.

Duran, B., and R. Weffer. 1992. "Immigrants' Aspirations, High School Process, and Academic Outcomes." *American Educational Research Journal* 29:163–181.

Fowles, J. 1969. *The French Lieutenant's Woman.* Boston: Little, Brown.

Furstenberg, F. 1993. "How Families Manage Risk and Opportunity in Dangerous Neighborhoods." In *Sociology and the Public Agenda,* ed. W. Wilson, 231–258. Newbury Park, CA: Sage Publications.

Gage, N. L. 1989. "The Paradigm Wars and Their Aftermath: A 'Historical' Sketch of Research on Teaching since 1989." *Educational Researcher* 18 (7): 4–10.

Gallimore, R., and C. Goldenberg. 1993. "Activity Settings of Early Literacy: Home and School Factors in Children's Emergent Literacy." In *Contexts for Learning: Sociocultural Dynamics in Children's Development,* ed. E. Forman, N. Minick, and C. A. Stone, 315–335. Oxford: Oxford University Press.

———. 2001. "Analyzing Cultural Models and Settings to Connect Minority Achievement and School Improvement Research." *Educational Psychologist* 36:45–56.

Gallimore, R., C. Goldenberg, and T. Weisner. 1993. "The Social Construction and Subjective Reality of Activity Settings: Implications for Community Psychology." *American Journal of Community Psychology* 4:537–559.

Gallimore, R., and L. Reese. 1999. "Mexican Immigrants in Urban California: Forging Adaptations from Familiar and New Culture Sources." In *Culture, Ethnicity, and Migration,* ed. M. C. Foblets and P. C. Lin, 245–263. Leuven, Belgium: Acco.

Gallimore, R., T. S. Weisner, S. Z. Kaufman, and L. P. Bernheimer. 1989. "The Social Construction of Ecocultural Niches: Family Accommodation of Developmentally Delayed Children." *American Journal of Mental Retardation* 94 (3): 216–230.

Goldenberg, C. 1987. "Low-Income Hispanic Parents' Contributions to Their First-Grade Children's Word-Recognition Skills." *Anthropology and Education Quarterly* 18:149–179.

———. 1988. "Methods, Early Literacy, and Home-School Compatibilities: A Response to Sledge et al." *Anthropology and Education Quarterly* 19:425–432.

———. 1990. "Evaluation of a Balanced Approach to Literacy Instruction for Spanish-Speaking Kindergartners." Paper presented at the annual meeting of the American Educational Research Association, Boston, April.

———. 1994. "Promoting Early Literacy Achievement among Spanish-Speaking Children: Lessons from Two Studies." In *Getting Reading Right from the Start: Effective Early Literacy Interventions,* ed. E. Hiebert, 171–199. Boston: Allyn and Bacon.

———. 2001. "Making Schools Work for Low-Income Families in the 21st Century." In *Handbook for Research in Early Literacy,* ed. S. Neuman and D. Dickinson, 211–231. New York: Guilford.

Goldenberg, C., and A. Arzubiaga. 1994. "The Effects of Teachers' Attempts to Involve Latino Parents in Children's Early Reading Development." Paper presented at the annual meeting of the American Educational Research Association, New Orleans, April.

Goldenberg, C., and R. Gallimore. 1995. "Immigrant Latino Parents' Values and Beliefs about Their Children's Education: Continuities and Discontinuities across Cultures and Generations." In *Advances in Motivation and Achievement: Culture, Ethnicity, and Motivation,* vol. 9, ed. P. R. Pintrich and M. Maehr, 183–228. Greenwich, CT: JAI Press.

Goldenberg, C., R. Gallimore, L. Reese, and H. Garnier. 2001. "Cause or Effect? A Longitudinal Study of Immigrant Latino Parents' Aspirations and Expectations and Their Children's School Performance." *American Educational Research Association Journal* 38 (3): 547–582.

Goldenberg, C., L. Reese, and R. Gallimore. 1992. "Effects of School Literacy Materials on Latino Children's Home Experiences and Early Reading Achievement." *American Journal of Education* 100:497–536.

Greene, J. C., and V. J. Caracelli. 1997. "Defining and Describing the Paradigm Issue in Mixed-Method Evaluation." In *Advances in Mixed-Method Evaluation: The Challenges and Benefits of Integrating Diverse Paradigms,* ed. J. C. Greene and V. J. Caracelli, 5–17. New Directions for Evaluation, vol. 74. San Francisco: Jossey-Bass.

Heller, C. 1966. *Mexican-American Youth: Forgotten Youth at the Crossroads.* New York: Random House.

Houts, A. C., T. D. Cook, and W. R. Shadish. 1986. "The Person-Situation Debate: A Critical Multiplist Perspective." In "Methodological Developments in Personality Research," ed. S. G. West. Special Issue, *Journal of Personality* 54 (1): 52–105.

Jarrett, R. 1995. "Growing Up Poor: The Family Experiences of Socially Mobile Youth in Low-Income African American Neighborhoods." *Journal of Adolescent Research* 10:111–135.

Laosa, L. 1982. "Families as Facilitators of Children's Intellectual Development at 3 Years of Age: A Causal Analysis." In *Families as Learning Environments for Children,* ed. L. Laosa and I. Sigel, 1–45. New York: Plenum.

Miles, M. B., and A. M. Huberman. 1985. "Drawing Valid Meaning from Qualitative Data: Toward a Shared Craft." *Educational Researcher* 13 (5): 20–30.

Ogbu, J., and M. Matuti-Bianchi. 1986. "Understanding Sociocultural Factors: Knowledge, Identity, and School Adjustment." In *Beyond Language: Social and Cultural Factors in Schooling Language Minority Students,* 73–142. Los Angeles: Evaluation, Dissemination, and Assessment Center, California State University, Los Angeles.

Reese, L. 1998. "Parental Strategies in Contrasting Cultural Settings: Families in México and 'El Norte.'" Paper presented at the annual conference of the American Anthropological Association, Philadelphia, December.

Reese, L., S. Balzano, R. Gallimore, and C. Goldenberg. 1995. "The Concept of *Educacion:* Latino Family Values and American Schooling." *International Journal of Educational Research* 23 (1): 57–81. (Reprinted in *Cultural Diversity: Curriculum, Classroom, and Climate,* ed. J. Q. Adams and J. Welsch [Macomb: Western Illinois University and Curriculum Developers Association, 1999].)

Reese, L. J., and R. Gallimore. 2000. "Immigrant Latinos' Cultural Model of Literacy Development: An Evolving Perspective on Home-School Discontinuities." *American Journal of Education* 108 (2): 103–134.

Reese, L., R. Gallimore, and C. Goldenberg. 1999. "Job-Required Literacy, Home Literacy Environments, and School Reading: Early Literacy Experiences of Immigrant Latino Children." In *Negotiating Power and Place at the Margins: Selected Papers on Refugees and Immigrants,* vol. 7. Washington, DC: American Anthropological Association.

Reese, L., R. Gallimore, C. Goldenberg, and S. Balzano. 1995. "Immigrant Latino Parents' Future Orientations for Their Children." In *Changing Schools for Changing Students,* ed. R. Macias and R. G. Ramos, 205–230. University of California Linguistic Minority Research Institute Publication. Santa Barbara: Regents of the University of California.

Reese, L., H. Garnier, R. Gallimore, and C. Goldenberg. 2000. "A Longitudinal Analysis of the Antecedents of Emergent Spanish Literacy and Middle-School English Reading Achievement of Spanish-Speaking Students." *American Educational Research Association Journal* 37:633–662.

Reese, L., C. Goldenberg, J. Loucky, and R. Gallimore. 1995. "Ecocultural Context, Cultural Activity, and Emergent Literacy of Spanish-Speaking Children." In *Class, Culture, and Race in American Schools: A Handbook,* ed. S. W. Rothstein, 199–224. Westport, CT: Greenwood Press.

Reese, L., K. Kroesen, and R. Gallimore. 2000. "Agency and School Performance among Urban Latino Youth." In *Resilience across Contexts: Family, Work, Culture, and Community,* ed. R. Taylor and M. Wang. Mahwah, NJ: Erlbaum.

Riggin, L. J. C. 1997. "Advances in Mixed-Method Evaluation: A Synthesis and Comment." In *Advances in Mixed-Method Evaluation: The Challenges and Benefits of Integrating Diverse Paradigms,* ed. J. C. Greene and V. J. Caracelli, 87–94. New Directions for Evaluation, no. 74. San Francisco: Jossey-Bass.

Sechrest, L., J. Babcock, and B. Smith. 1993. "An Invitation to Methodological Pluralism." *Evaluation Practice* 14:227–235.

Sechrest, L., and A. J. Figueredo. 1993. "Program Evaluation." *Annual Review of Psychology* 44:645–674.

Snow, C., Burns, M. S., and Griffin, P. 1998. *Preventing Reading Difficulties in Young Children.* Washington, DC: National Academy Press.

Stokes, D. E. 1997. *Pasteur's Quadrant: Basic Science and Technological Innovation.* Washington, DC: Brookings Institution Press.

Suárez-Orozco, C. M., and M. Suárez-Orozco. 1996. *Transformations: Immigration, Family Life, and Achievement Motivation among Latino Adolescents.* Stanford, CA: Stanford University Press.

Valdés, G. 1996. *Con Respeto: Bridging the Distances between Culturally Diverse Families and Schools.* New York: Teachers College Press.

Webb, E. J., D. T. Campbell, R. D. Schwartz, and L. Sechrest. 1966. *Unobtrusive Measures.* Skokie, IL: Rand McNally.

Weisner, T. S. 1984. "Ecocultural Niches of Middle Childhood: A Cross-Cultural Perspective." In *Development during Middle Childhood: The Years from Six to Twelve,* ed. W. A. Collins, 335–369. Washington, DC: National Academy of Sciences.

2

Working It Out: The Chronicle of a Mixed-Methods Analysis

Heather B. Weiss, Holly Kreider, Ellen Mayer, Rebecca Hencke, and Margaret A. Vaughan

This chapter chronicles our early process of mixed-methods analysis in the area of family educational involvement using School Transition Study (STS) data. The STS is a large, multimethod, three-cohort study that began in 1995–1996 and followed approximately 400 ethnically diverse children in low-income families from kindergarten through fifth grade. The STS uses an ecological approach to understand low-income children's successful pathways through middle childhood and the school, family, and community contexts in which they live and learn. Such an approach is especially critical to the study of child development (Bronfenbrenner 1979).

The STS features a mixed-methods approach in its study design, data collection, and analysis. Quantitative data include, among other things, annual surveys of children's primary caregivers and teachers. In-depth case study qualitative data were collected on a subset of 23 children when they were in first and second grades. These data include interviews with children's teachers, other school personnel, parents or other primary caregivers, and the children themselves, as well as participant observations in schools and classrooms.

Our initial team of four researchers at Harvard Family Research Project (HFRP) managed the design and data collection for the qualitative case study component. Then, when the early stages of STS data collection were complete, we set out to purposively conduct a mixed-methods family involvement analysis with these early data, hoping to learn not just about family educational involvement, but also about the process of mixing methods. Although trained primarily as qualitative researchers, we were eager to embark on this mixed-methods journey. To assist us in this new direction, we added a quantitative analyst and a graduate research assistant to our team.

Listening to the Qualitative Case Study Data

> We don't even have a PTA at this school . . . primarily it's because parents are working hard. You know, I have often wondered if PTA will become a thing of the past, because parents are too busy just trying to make ends meet and get dinner on the table, and occasionally wash a pair of socks.
>
> —Second-grade teacher

> I think every parent should have time for their kids, no matter how much work you have? I think it's important to have at least one day a month. . . . When I want to talk to [my child's teacher], I just fax him something to school, from my job, or I call him.
>
> —Mother of a second grader

> [Parents] have one and two jobs, and both parents, if there are both parents. . . . But just more parent involvement [would help students succeed more]—sitting down, maybe taking them on the weekend to, if there is time, to something that doesn't have to cost money.
>
> —Elementary school principal

Our interview protocols focused primarily on family educational involvement issues, with no questions that directly explored parental work and its relationship to family involvement. Yet no matter who we asked, whether teacher, parent, or principal, and no matter what aspect of involvement we asked about, whether it was a question about the level of parent involvement at school, parent-teacher communication, or what could help children succeed, we heard reference to parents' work. In short, we were repeatedly confronted with the importance of parents' work.

Exploring an Unexpected Finding

As we listened to this recurring theme of parental work, we also revisited our earlier analyses of family involvement and discovered that this issue had been lurking in the background all along. The salience of work first arose in a teaching case on the broader dilemma of who is responsible for tending to children's nonacademic needs (Kreider 1999). We identified one case study child whose mother worked a swing shift and was unable to attend her child's school, communicate easily with his teacher, or ready her child for school. Changing her work shift with the help of the school guidance counselor improved her child's school performance and demeanor.

Additional references to parental work filled our early analyses. In a paper on home-school communication patterns, the communication actually occurred between the work and school domains. One case vignette described a process by which the teacher called her student's mother at work when he misbehaved and put the student on the phone, which immediately settled him down (Weiss et al. 1998). Issues of time demands and timing of parental work also appeared in an STS research brief on parent strategies for managing time (Mayer, Kreider, and Vaughan 1999).

However, now the issue of parents' work struck us in a new light. As we intentionally shifted our focus onto this topic, we seized on this unexpected discovery much the same way as other researchers have been pulled in unexpected directions (Rabinow 1977; Skinner 1956).

Heeding the Prior Literature and Current Policy Climate

To inform our pursuit of this unexpected and interesting finding we turned to the literature and found that a substantial gap existed in both the work-family and school-family research on the relation between parental work and family involvement. The little research that did exist focused primarily on the negative associations between work and involvement, especially for low-income mothers. Most existing literature also lacked a strong empirical base, relying on theory, advice, single methods (e.g., quantitative surveys), anecdotal information, or opinion polls (for a full review see Weiss et al. 2003).

We also considered the current policy climate to understand the relevance of our proposed analysis for informing policy. Indeed, the policy implications of an analysis on parental work and family involvement seemed timely, given the entry of many low-income mothers into the workplace due to welfare reform and current debates about extending the provisions of the Family Medical Leave Act. The results of a mixed-methods analysis could be particularly forceful talking points in such policy discussions, as combining accessible case study stories with more technical statistical findings might be especially compelling for nonresearchers.

Gauging Mixed-Methods Analysis Potential

As our STS design demonstrates, we believe strongly in the added value of mixing methods. This approach can, among other things, enhance validity through data triangulation, delineate overlapping but distinct aspects of a phenomenon, elaborate one set of findings with data from another, expand potential findings, and uncover paradoxes and contradictions between results based on different methods (Greene, Caracelli, and Graham 1989).

However, in considering the issue of parental work, we also had to think through the mixed-methods potential of this particular line of analysis. Specifically, we considered the phenomenon we were studying in order to weigh the added value of a mixed-methods approach in comparison to a single method. Greene has argued persuasively that "social phenomena are so complex and social problems so intractable [that] all of our methodological tools are needed for understanding and for action" (Greene 1996, 5). Indeed, the issue of family educational involvement seemed to be an intractable arena that could be better understood by a mixed-methods approach, and the limited understandings of the connections between work and family involvement in prior research could be especially strengthened through a mixed-methods analysis.

We also had to consider a more pragmatic issue: the availability of data to analyze. We had completed case study qualitative data collection prior to conceiving of this analysis, but STS quantitative data collection was still ongoing. Of the annual quantitative surveys of primary caregivers, only those from the kindergarten year were completely ready for analysis. We drew from these first primary-caregiver surveys (which were actually face-to-face interviews), as well as from surveys filled out by children's kindergarten teachers. We decided to use only the middle cohort because it was the largest cohort, the one from which our case study families were drawn, and would control for cohort effects of welfare reform.

Our quantitative sample consisted then of the 216 children who were in kindergarten at the time of the first wave of STS data collection. Items on the primary-caregiver survey included general work status questions, such as whether parents worked and, if so, how much. Our case study sample consisted of the 21 primary caregivers who were working (20 mothers and 1 grandmother caregiver, hereafter referred to as mothers). Because mothers constituted the vast majority of both of our samples, we narrowed our analytic focus from primary caregivers to mothers.

After considering these data constraints, our unexpected discovery still appeared to be a topic waiting to be explored, and one that could benefit from a mixed-methods analysis.

Developing Our Research Questions

To explore the connection between work and family involvement, we next articulated two questions:

1. How does maternal work influence low-income mothers' involvement in children's education?
2. What strategies enable low-income working mothers to become or stay involved in their children's education?

We shaped these questions with several considerations in mind. First, we began with a broad ecological definition of "family involvement" as participation in any activities that support children's education, whether at home, in school, or in the community. Although our quantitative data addressed a limited, school-centric set of family involvement practices like those generally measured in prior studies, we wanted a definition that could encompass any new understandings emerging from our grounded qualitative analysis. Our definition followed other broad definitions in the field (e.g., Chavkin and Williams 1985). We also wanted to pursue the positive influence of work on involvement in line with HFRP's long-standing strengths-based approach to understanding families and as suggested by early case study observations—like the second-grade mother who faxed over paperwork to the school from her workplace. Finally, we wanted a set of questions with mixed-methods analysis potential and decided that these particular research questions would require us to reach down into both our quantitative and qualitative data sets for answers.

Making Plans for Working in Concert

The mixed-methods notion of iterative, or "crossover-tracks," analysis guided our initial analytic planning and analysis (Li, Marquart, and Zercher 2000). In this approach, an intentional and iterative interplay exists between the separate analyses of qualitative and quantitative data sets, such that mixing and integration happen throughout the analysis.

Clear team procedures, such as regular team meetings, supported this approach, and we also set up procedures to facilitate reflection on our process. The team kept two detailed logs: one tracking substantive findings, the other tracking our mixed-methods process. Reading through the shared logs kept team members in close touch with the work of others, and revisiting and later analyzing the logs helped give retrospective coherence to our process.

Extensive and respectful dialogue also facilitated our work together. A stance of openness and discovery is inherent in mixed-methods work, which actively seeks multiple routes to enhanced understanding (Cook 1985). This openness to other views and perspectives includes not just rival explanatory hypotheses but more profoundly rival ways of thinking and valuing (J. C. Greene, pers. comm., November 7, 2000). Indeed, as qualitative and quantitative researchers we approached our work together with openness and curiosity about the others' methodology, learning from and embracing one another's findings. The interdisciplinary nature of our team, which brought together disparate disciplines of psychology, education, and sociology, also made open dialogue critical.

In addition, we developed structured analytic exercises to honor each other's ways of knowing and generate hypotheses. After clarifying our research questions, we each explored the core construct of work by scouring a particular quantitative or qualitative data source and generating a list of knowledge claims about work. We then reconvened to discuss these claims. This led us — as a team — to understand work as linked to economic, familial, and other supports for mothers' work and family lives. The importance of resources, support, and parent initiative emerged. For example, the notion of parental efficacy (Hoover-Dempsey and Sandler 1997) or executive function (Davis-Kean and Eccles 1999) emerged as important for mothers' strategies in balancing work and family involvement.

Turning to the Quantitative Data

Guided by clear research questions, some of us now turned to the kindergarten quantitative data. We addressed our first research question in four phases: descriptive analyses of key variables, data reduction analyses, univariate analyses relating work status to educational involvement, and a multivariate analysis on the effects of mothers' work status on forms of family involvement.

First we looked at family involvement descriptors for our sample and discovered varied and high levels of involvement to further explore. The majority of mothers, regardless of work status, reported attending at least one parent-teacher conference in the last year and/or attending an open house (80%). About half reported visiting the class (55%), attending a performance (61%), or participating in a social event (46%). A third reported helping with a field trip (33%) or volunteering in the classroom (33%). Most reported helping with children's homework (75%), having more than 10 books in the home (76%), and reading to the child (72%). Fewer than half reported reading to their children more than three times a week (40%) or other family members helping the child with homework (fathers/partners, 25%; siblings, 21%; and grandparents, 10%).

Descriptive analyses also showed parental work as a perceived barrier to family involvement, especially through the time demands it imposed. When asked, "What barriers to parent involvement do you see among your parents?" 89.5% of 154 kindergarten teachers surveyed named parents' work schedule as somewhat of a problem or a serious problem — citing work schedule more frequently than, for example, inadequate language (42%) or literacy (61%) skills. Additionally, teachers reported making significantly fewer suggestions about their students' discipline, physical or emotional care, or math or reading practice to mothers who worked full-time than to those who worked either part-time or not at all ($\chi^2 = 14.62$, df $= 6$, $n = 216$, $p < .05$).

Staying Open to Divergent Findings

While early quantitative analyses suggested that parents' work constituted an obstacle to involvement, qualitative analyses revealed a different picture. We began our qualitative analysis using within-case portraits of case study mothers, focusing on the 21 mothers who worked. Analytic techniques leading to these portraits included field notes review and analytic memos, as well as systematic coding of interviews using a taxonomy of codes that included setting and action codes for "work" and "working." Overall, our data, with some four thousand pages of interview transcript, were well suited for the creation of "thick" descriptions of social interactions and environments and actors' perspectives (Geertz 1973) and for a focus on cultural patterns and social processes within and across social and ecological settings, that is, schools and families (Hammersley and Atkinson 1995).

In emerging case portraits, several working mothers described work as a *resource* for parenting, child learning, and family involvement (described more fully in the later section on developing a cross-case qualitative typology). Surprisingly, some mothers even took their children to work on a regular basis. One mother of a second grader explained the benefits of this practice for her daughter: "It's really helping her a lot. She's like learning the computer and all that stuff."

This final qualitative picture took longer to arrive at than the quantitative findings. However, we had other stores of qualitative knowledge to inform all early mixed-methods conversations, as qualitative researchers had been deeply immersed in the case study data from the start of data collection and were known to recall anecdotes about a parent-teacher conference or a struggle over difficult math homework as though discussing their own children.

Conducting More Complex Quantitative Analyses

Moving ahead with data reduction, we created a key composite variable reflecting the combined time demands of mothers' employment and mothers' educational training (which we called "work/school" status) for use as a predictor of family involvement. Two family involvement variables — school involvement and home teaching — were also created through exploratory factor analysis, drawing from primary-caregiver survey items on attendance at school functions and on ways that mothers supported their children's education at home, respectively. School involvement consisted of volunteering, visiting the classroom, and attending curriculum events, field trips, open houses, school meetings, social events, performances, and parent-teacher conferences. Home teaching consisted of teaching math, frequency of reading, preparing one's child for the next school year, and number of books in the home.

The school involvement variable was created by dividing the continuous factor score for school involvement reported in the chart into four percentiles, reflecting low, modest, moderate, and high levels of involvement. We recorded this as an example of "qualitizing" (Tashakkori and Teddlie 1998) purely quantitative data to facilitate its use in mixed-methods research.

Univariate analyses of parent reports showed that full-time working mothers reported attending significantly fewer events at their children's schools (conferences, open houses, curriculum presentations, school meetings, visits to class, and performances) than those who were not employed or employed part-time ($\chi^2 = 19.02$, df $= 9$, $n = 216$, $p < .05$). Part-time working mothers reported the most involvement of any group, suggesting that the time demands of full-time work may interfere with involvement in school activities, but that work in general may provide opportunities for selective involvement.

Finally, a multivariate analysis of variance examined associations between mothers' work/school status and the two family involvement outcomes identified through the factor analysis (i.e., school involvement and home teaching). Results of this analysis expanded univariate findings and showed that maternal work/school status was significantly associated not only with school involvement but also with broadly defined family involvement, which included both school and home activities (Pillai's trace $= .067$, $F = 4.24$, $p < .05$).

Going with the Flow

Studying different analytic models in advance and setting up collaborative team processes did not prepare us for the messiness and pragmatically driven nature of our analysis (Mark and Greene 1997). Our analytic tracks crossed over as frequently as expected but not when we thought they would nor how we thought they would nor for the same reasons as anticipated.

As we continued to work with the data, we shifted from our early structured exercises to a more evolving and fluid analytic process, exemplified by our data reduction analyses. For example, qualitative analysts had identified work as a context related to parents' time demands in early analyses (Mayer, Kreider, and Vaughan 1999), leading our quantitative researcher to conceptualize a composite variable representing time demands (consisting of time devoted to work and/or their own education). This proved to be a stronger predictor of family involvement than education or employment alone.

In another example of this iterative enterprise, qualitative analysts relied increasingly on their stores of internalized qualitative case study knowledge to inform quantitative analysis. The quantitative analyst brought her factor analysis results to qualitative team members for interpretation and validation. Qualitative analysts drew from their internalized qualitative knowledge to see if the factors passed the grounded "this makes sense" test and whether revised factor analyses were appropriate or necessary. The interactive, back-and-forth exchanges and turn-taking of our two methodologies supported our inquiry and our progress (Greene et al. 1995).

Developing a Cross-Case Qualitative Typology

What strategies enabled low-income working mothers to become or stay involved in their children's education? To answer our second research question the qualitative analyses progressed from within-case portraits of maternal work strategies and family involvement to cross-case reading and analysis. The result was a typology of maternal strategies (Miles and Huberman 1994).

First, working mothers oversaw and managed a complex support system to support their children's learning, *promoting a kith and kin network* for help with transportation to school, behavioral monitoring at school, homework, home-school communication, and other involvement activities. Involvement helpers included extended family members, neighbors, children's older siblings, mothers' partners, babysitters, and coworkers. For example, one case study mother had her daughter walk to school each morning with her grandfather who lived nearby and also directed the grandfather to request materials from the teacher.

Mothers built strong family partnerships, distributing involvement activities among household members. One mother shared attendance at school events and home-school communication tasks with her husband, leveraging his flexibility to leave work during the day and her ability to receive calls at work from the teacher. Finally, mothers constructed a family learning culture, in which learning was valued and practiced daily among all family members. One mother who attended school timed her classes to overlap with her children's school schedules; another did her homework at the same time as her children.

Mothers also *used their workplace as a home base* for a variety of involvement activities typically performed in other settings, such as home, school, or community. A surprising number of mothers took their children to work as an intermediate or stopgap childcare location, opting to do this for reasons of enrichment as well as convenience even when other acceptable childcare was available. For example, one day a week a Latina student in the second grade went to work with her mother at a small department store. The mother saw this as a good learning experience for her daughter, who had access to a computer at the store and could learn responsibility through small, paid "work" chores. The mother also thought her daughter could observe and understand her mother's work life better, thus making the connection between education and later work options. Mothers also described using their workplace as a communications hub, making and receiving calls at work to monitor their children at home and communicating via fax or phone with school personnel. This was often the case for emergency or intensive problem-focused reasons, but also for routine conveyances like scheduling meetings. Finally, two parents working in service occupations actually had informal parent-teacher conferences at the workplace, discussing their children's progress at length when their children's teachers dropped by to pick up developed film or receive other services.

Mothers intentionally *garnered resources from work* such as direct educational opportunities for their children or indirect support for their own involvement. They accessed nonmonetary material resources like recreational supplies, books, and computer access and made use of instructional resources like educational advice, new informational networks (which often crossed class lines), tutoring or homework help, and child-focused activities in the workplace. Mothers also gained access to social resources for parenting and involvement by interacting with supportive coworkers and supervisors, many of whom were also parents.

Finally, mothers described *conquering time and space challenges* by negotiating transitions and adaptively finding time to be directly and indirectly involved in their children's education. Negotiations of time included multitasking—coordinating their own work or school attendance with their child's schedule—and taking advantage of the weekend for time with their children. One mother helped her child with homework in the family van while waiting for the child's softball game to start. A few mothers also manipulated space creatively, selecting jobs near or even in their children's school, and maximized this proximity by interacting frequently with their children and the teachers. Mothers also requested flexibility from employers and their children's teachers to allow for direct and indirect family involvement. One mother took her lunch break at the day's end to check in on her children when they arrived home from school, and one who worked a swing shift asked her son's teacher for a daytime parent-teacher conference.

Working with What You've Got

Sometimes these unexpected and nuanced practices described by case study mothers were simply not picked up in the quantitative data and thus were not amenable to direct mixed-methods analyses. For example, quantitative items did not address the issue of children at work, and quantitative coding of open-ended survey responses further obscured this dimension. A question on the 1996 primary-caregiver survey on the location of the child's out-of-school activities had been coded with categories that masked the workplace as a possible location (i.e., home, school, other person's home, day care, other).

Sometimes, however, desperation drove us into new mixed-methods territory, as captured in our mixed-methods log (8/18/00): "In some ways, mixing methods was a necessity to fully explore the salience of work to better understand family involvement, because this particular analysis was not planned for in the design of either quantitative or qualitative instruments. This drove us to comb through every data source we had in the study to be able to develop this emergent strand."

For example, we had hard copies of the completed quantitative surveys administered for later waves of data collection for our 23 case study families (as well as some of the transcribed survey interviews). We knew that a question about work and family involvement had been posed in the 1997 telephone survey with primary caregivers (owing to an interest in work/family issues by a steering committee member). Specifically, primary caregivers were asked: "How does (working/not working) make a difference in how much you are involved in [CHILD]'s school and in (his/her) learning?" As we read through the interview transcriptions for responses to this question, we found additional rich information, such as this response by the mother of a first grader: "I was able to say [to the principal and teachers], 'Hey, listen, not everyone works nine to five. Not everyone can just show up for one of these things in the evening. We need, as evening workers, to be informed of these events ahead of time' . . . I was very adamant about getting these notices more in advance. And they've . . . worked very well with that as far as changing that."

As a pilot exercise, we also read through entire transcripts of the primary-caregiver surveys for two of the case study children over three waves of data collection (1996–1998), mining these quantitative data for their qualitative representation. In many instances, we found a wealth of data on topics that, at face value, seemed unrelated to work from open-ended questions or in the spontaneous talk surrounding closed-ended questions. For example, in an unrelated question on "things your school could do to make you feel more welcome and comfortable there," we heard how one mother used her work-based informational networks to acquire important school information. She described how as a hairdresser she learned about the quality of her daughter's school by talking to her clients ("I speak to a lot of professionals"). Other similar examples bolstered our qualitative finding about the workplace as a source of education information.

This exercise and other exercises that examined our quantitative data in narrative form opened up new avenues of data to examine later systematically, addressed our limited access to all the study data at this time point, and demonstrated compelling added value for understanding the relationship between work and family involvement. It also begged the questions: What is quantitative? What is qualitative?—a fuzzy distinction that others have identified as problematic (Campbell 1974; Light 2000).

Interpreting Findings through Convergence and Divergence

The mixing of methods yielded converging findings, which aided our interpretations in complementary ways. For example, in an iterative and complementary process, time emerged as a central aspect of the association between work and family involvement. It emerged first in prior qualitative analyses on involving busy parents, then through the strength of our combined work/school status predictor compared to work status alone. Time and timing were implicated as both a barrier to and an opportunity for involvement in our quantitative finding that full-time mothers were less involved at school than part-time or unemployed mothers but that part-time mothers were the most involved, as well as in our qualitatively identified maternal strategy of "managing time and space" to coordinate work and family demands. Such complementary functions of mixed methods underscore the interdependence of quantitative and qualitative methods for asking questions and understanding meaningful processes and themes (Greene and Caracelli 1997).

Mixing methods also yielded divergent findings, which led to a more expansive and complete understanding of educational involvement among low-income working mothers. Specifically, quantitative analyses revealed

negative associations between maternal work and educational involvement, while qualitative analyses showed more subtle positive connections.
This has led us to an expanded conceptualization of work as both an obstacle to and an opportunity for involvement. Survey items, for instance,
asked closed-ended questions about work as a barrier to family involvement and defined family involvement in common but narrow ways (e.g.,
conference attendance). In contrast, our broad definition of family involvement and our grounded and exploratory qualitative methods allowed the
subtle positive effects of work on family involvement to emerge through
the qualitative data.

Feeding Early Analysis Back into Subsequent Data Collection

Many of the compelling contextual dimensions of work identified through
our analysis of the qualitative case study data were used to inform the
development of items on later quantitative primary-caregiver surveys.
Specifically, our case study findings here led us to add more work-related
questions for the year 2000 primary-caregiver survey that was still under
development. This unexpected benefit points to an added value of a mixed-
methods approach in longitudinal research (Stipek and Weiss 2000) and is
referred to as "developmental" mixed-methods work by Greene, Caracelli,
and Graham (1989).

Conclusion

Work and Family Involvement for Low-Income Mothers

This early exploratory analysis revealed that the relationship between
low-income mothers' work and family involvement is complex, consisting
of both negative and positive associations between maternal work and
family educational involvement. Patterns of interference between work
and school involvement were present, especially through the time demands
imposed by work. Mothers who worked full-time were less likely to be involved in the school than mothers who worked part-time, yet work also
appeared to open opportunities for maternal involvement. Part-time working mothers were the most involved of any group. In addition, working
mothers used four sets of strategies to generate and maintain involvement

in their children's learning: promoting kith and kin networks, garnering resources from work, using the workplace as a home base, and conquering time and space challenges. These strategies helped mothers overcome barriers imposed by work and create new involvement opportunities out of work and workplaces.

Lessons about Mixed-Methods Analyses

Through this process we learned to be open to discovery. We learned to impose structure on our mixed-methods process but also to be pragmatic and tolerate complexities. For example, faced with the constraints of unavailable data in a large project with very complex data sets, we learned that mixed-methods approaches could only be rough guides and that intentional designs might have to give way to real-world problems of data availability and deadlines. Accordingly, we developed a sense of our mixed-methods work as a dynamic hands-on process, guided only very generally by mixed-methods analytic models.

The Added Value from Mixing Methods

Our contrasting findings about maternal work as a barrier and an opportunity for family involvement underscored the value of mixing methods, specifically its potential to expand and make more complex our understanding of phenomena of interest. The contrast led to new learning beyond what "everyone knows"—that work poses obstacles to involvement—to an understanding that work can also facilitate some involvement. Specifically, this led to learning about conditions under which work can support involvement at school, open up new avenues for family involvement, and contribute to children's learning beyond school walls. On a different level, this mixed-methods analysis helped HFRP in its mission to reframe the conceptualization of family involvement, by expanding consideration of the ecological domains and relationships that influence family involvement to include a focus on parental workplace as a new ecological domain.

The fostering of creativity and flexibility in our analysis proved to be an unexpected added value of mixing methods, as we adopted unplanned and creative approaches to overcome challenges at particular points in our analysis. For example, we dealt with the unavailability of data by exploiting what data we did have: exploring survey transcripts and codebooks for hidden qualitative data. This "qualitizing" of quantitative data and structured mixed-methods analytic exercises were among the procedures that yielded new discoveries about the relationship between family involvement and maternal employment.

Mixing methods also yielded valuable implications for policy. Public policy needs to address the current work–family involvement dilemma generated by the increasing percentage of mothers entering the workforce and the new welfare-to-work transitions being made by many low-income mothers, coupled with a persistently high social value placed on family involvement in children's education. Our mixed-methods findings suggest, for example, that schools should consider how to structure themselves to relate to parents as workers, and employers should consider how to structure themselves to relate to workers as parents. Policy needs to support the articulation between work and school systems, such as through consideration of scheduling and the flexibility of employees and school personnel to move across work and school domains.

We hope this chronicle provides a glimpse into the real work of an early mixed-methods analysis and inspires others to seek the added value that we believe this kind of analysis confers. We have tried to make transparent for others some of the tools our team developed for mixed-methods analysis and some of the big and little lessons that we learned along the way.

The mixed-methods process described in this chapter represents only the beginning of our analysis of maternal work and low-income mothers' family involvement. Readers should consult Weiss et al. 2003 for our final substantive findings.

Acknowledgments

The School Transition Study was supported by a grant from the John D. and Catherine T. MacArthur Foundation Research Network on Successful Pathways through Middle Childhood, with supplementary funds from the W. T. Grant Foundation. Principal investigators for this study are Heather Weiss and Deborah Stipek. Other steering committee members are Jennifer Greene, Penny Hauser-Cram, Jacquelynne Eccles, and Walter Secada. In-depth qualitative data were collected and initially analyzed by ethnographers Kim Friedman, Carol McAllister, Jane Dirks, Jane Wellenkamp, and Gisella Hanley. We thank Kristina Pinto for a research review informing this chapter and Jennifer Greene and Eric Dearing for editorial assistance.

References

Bronfenbrenner, U. 1979. *The Ecology of Human Development: Experiments by Nature and Design.* Cambridge: Harvard University Press.

Campbell, D. T. 1974. "Qualitative Knowing in Action Research." Kurt Lewin Award Address, Society for the Psychological Study of Social Issues, meeting with American Psychological Association, New Orleans.

Chavkin, N., and D. L. Williams. 1985. *Executive Summary of the Final Report: Parent Involvement in Education Project.* Austin, TX: Southwest Educational Development Laboratory.

Cook, T. D. 1985. "Postpositivist Critical Multiplism." In *Social Science and Social Policy,* ed. R. L. Shotland and M. M. Mark, 21–62. Thousand Oaks, CA: Sage.

Davis-Kean, P. E., and J. S. Eccles. 1999. "It Takes a Village to Raise a Child: An Executive Function and Community Management Perspective." Unpublished manuscript.

Geertz, C. 1973. *The Interpretation of Cultures: Selected Essays.* New York: Basic Books.

Greene, J. C. 2001. "Mixing Social Inquiry Methodologies." In *Handbook of Research on Teaching,* 4th ed., ed. V. Richardson, 251–258. Washington, DC: American Educational Research Association.

Greene, J. C., and V. J. Caracelli. 1997. "Crafting Mixed-Method Evaluation Designs." In *Advances in Mixed-Method Evaluation: The Challenges and Benefits of Integrating Diverse Paradigms,* ed. J. C. Greene and V. J. Caracelli. New Directions for Evaluation, no. 74. San Francisco: Jossey-Bass.

Greene, J. C., V. J. Caracelli, and W. F. Graham. 1989. "Toward a Conceptual Framework for Mixed-Method Evaluation Designs." *Educational Evaluation and Policy Analysis* 11 (3): 255–274.

Greene, J. C., M. B. Geisz, D. Seigart, and G. Shrestha. 1995. "The Paradigm Issue in Mixed-Method Evaluation: Towards an Inquiry Framework of Bounded Pluralism." Unpublished draft. Cornell University.

Hammersley, M., and P. Atkinson. 1995. *Ethnography: Principles in Practice.* New York: Routledge.

Hoover-Dempsey, K. V., and H. M. Sandler. 1997. "Why Do Parents Become Involved in Their Children's Education?" *Review of Educational Research* 67 (1): 3–42.

Kreider, H. 1999. "Tim Kelly: A School Responds to a Family in Need." Harvard Family Research Project, Cambridge, MA. Available online: http://www.gse.harvard.edu/hfrp/projects/fine/resources/teaching-case/timkellyfull.html.

Li, S. M., J. M. Marquart, and C. Zercher. 2000. "Conceptual Issues and Analytic Strategies in Mixed-Method Studies of Preschool Inclusion." *Journal of Early Intervention* 23 (2): 116–132.

Light, R. 2000. "Combining Qualitative and Quantitative Approaches in Evaluating College Experiences of Harvard Undergraduates." Lecture, Harvard Graduate School of Education, Cambridge, MA, February 16.

Mark, M. M., and J. C. Greene. 1997. "Mixed-Methods Evaluations: Point/Counterpoint." Unpublished manuscript. Evaluators Institute Course, Baltimore.

Mayer, E., H. Kreider, and P. Vaughan. 1999. *How Busy Parents Can Help Their Children Learn and Develop.* Washington, DC.: National Institute on Early Childhood Development and Education.

Miles, M. B., and A. M. Huberman. 1994. *Qualitative Data Analysis.* Thousand Oaks, CA: Sage Publications.

Rabinow, P. 1977. *Reflections on Fieldwork in Morocco.* Berkeley and Los Angeles: University of California Press.

Skinner, B. F. 1956. "Case History in Scientific Method." *American Psychologist* 11: 221–233.

Stipek, D., and H. Weiss. 2000. "Integrating Qualitative and Quantitative Approaches to Research on Early Childhood." Paper presented at Head Start's Fifth National Research Conference, Washington, DC, June 29.

Tashakkori, A., and C. Teddlie. 1998. *Mixed Methodology: Combining Qualitative and Quantitative Methods.* Thousand Oaks, CA: Sage Publications.

Weiss, H., H. Kreider, E. Levine, E. Mayer, J. Stadler, and P. Vaughan. 1998. "Beyond the Parent-Teacher Conference: Diverse Patterns of Home-School Communication." Paper presented at the American Educational Research Association annual conference, San Diego, April 14.

Weiss, H. B., E. Mayer, H. Kreider, M. Vaughan, E. Dearing, R. Hencke, and K. Pinto. 2003. "Making It Work: Low-Income Working Mothers' Involvement in Their Children's Education." *American Educational Research Journal* 40 (4): 879–901.

3

Mixed Methods, More Justified Conclusions: The Case of the Abt Evaluation of the Comer Program in Detroit

Lois-ellin Datta

Current research suggests that the early months of life may be even more important for child development than previously thought. Schools, however, have to take children as they find them: some will have received appropriate developmental support, others not. The struggle to make a positive difference for high-risk children during middle childhood has been long. It generally has not been crowned with enormous success. Do we give up, try harder, or try something different? Some policy analysts argue for a focus on increasing the well-being, independence, and work capacity of the parents, preventing if possible dysfunctional family stresses, rather than attempting interventions with schools or individual children. Some conclude that waiting until school age is too late, so policy should refocus on the earliest years of life. Some argue for different specific programs, such as phonics. Some, such as the National Science Foundation–funded science and mathematics program, emphasize statewide systemic initiatives. Still others, such as the Chicago School Reform initiative, see the best unit of change as the school district itself. And others see the world as improvable "one school at a time."

The Comer program is perhaps one of the most well known of those as-
suming that although everything is important (employment, family functionality, statewide changes, district-level initiatives, and more), schools
are where the children are for many waking hours of their day and thus the
best place to begin. The program focuses on making individual schools
work better for individual children (Anson et al. 1991; Comer et al. 1996).

It is among the initiatives being tried fairly widely. In 1995, about
563 schools (433 elementary; 85 middle; 45 high schools) in 80 districts
and 22 states were involved with the Comer approach. Probably considerably more were added after 1998, when it was selected as among the "exemplary programs that work" for special federal initiatives (Cook, Murphy,
and Hunt 2000).

A recently completed study of the Comer program in one site (Detroit)
by Abt Associates (Millsap et al. 2000) is significant for several reasons. The
Abt study is among the first third-party evaluations of the program (see also
Cook et al. 1999; Cook, Murphy, and Hunt 2000). Further, it is important
because of the scale of the study, its findings, and its interesting application
of multiple methods. For example, conclusions from only the quantitative
analyses would have suggested that the program did not achieve the intended results. However, merging qualitative and quantitative data indicated that the Comer principles *were* effective, when the approach was well
implemented. The next sections present an overview of the Comer principles, a description of their implementation in Detroit, the findings from the
Abt evaluation, and then a discussion of what, methodologically, makes the
study an example of how different conclusions were reached because qualitative and quantitative methods worked together.

The Comer Schools

Almost 20 years ago, Dr. James Comer at Yale University concluded that
making a major difference in student development required a comprehensive change in the schools and the school system. That in itself was hardly
news. Many educational theorists at the time had reached similar conclusions. What differentiated Comer's approach is that he swung into action
and tested his model in New Haven's schools—and it seemed to work.

Specific elements of the Comer approach are described by Millsap
et al.: "It consists of structures, principles and operations, all designed to
foster child development, improve relations with parents and in turn create a school climate conducive to improving the educational achievement

Table 3.1. Brief Introduction to the Comer Approach

Structural elements	Composition	Task
School improvement team (SIT)	Representatives of all adults in the school: teachers, administrators, parents, support staff, other professional staff	Develop a long-range improvement plan including staff development activities
Student support team (SST)	Classroom teachers, school administrators, mental health professionals (guidance counselors, psychologists, school social workers)	Provide appropriate services to individuals and attend to global mental health concerns for the school as a whole, informed by understanding child development and interpersonal relations
Parent program	Parent representatives	Increase parent involvement and responsibility in school: shaping policy, participating in activities supporting the program, attending school events

of children" (2000, chap. 1, p. 1). Table 3.1 summarizes the three elements and what each does.

Millsap et al. write:

> The school development plan fosters such task-centered approaches as developing and adhering to agendas circulated in advance of meetings; routinizing team meetings so they become an ongoing part of school operations; ensuring coordination across teams through cross-team membership; and monitoring progress toward achievement of goals through internal assessments. The ongoing attention to the processes of change provides checks and balances, and allows for revision in schools' implementation of the SDP [School Development Program] philosophy. (2000, chap. 1, p. 2)

Conceptually, the focus is on multiple dimensions of child development, aiming to help the schools reach the whole child. Comer emphasizes seven *pathways* to development: physical, cognitive-intellectual, social interaction, moral, psychoemotional, speech, and language.

Cumulatively, the structure, the principles, the operations, and the pathways are expected to improve four proximal outcomes: (1) the academic climate, (2) the social climate, (3) working relationships between the school and children's families, and (4) the extent to which staff reach out to students and their families, who take an increasingly active role in the school.

These four proximal changes, if achieved, then are predicted to influence student development and achievement. The implication is that if one first changes the academic and social climates and working relationships and outreach, then improved student development should follow. Student development in this model is also assumed to be influenced by past academic performance and poverty. The clear, explicit theory presents a valuable opportunity for testing empirically the conceptual structure of the model. (See also a videotape by Comer [1995] for his broad perspective on child development, children and schools at risk, and how to transform schools into "living communities of mutual support paying careful attention to individual child development.")

The Detroit Public Schools Initiative

The Skillman Foundation decided to invest millions of dollars in improving Detroit public schools. The Comer framework was selected as having a reasonable fit to Detroit's needs and a reasonable chance of success. In June 1993, a working group of all major players began a year's effort to develop a partnership agreement binding all parties and creating an operational structure for the Comer model in Detroit. The agreement was signed in April 1994 by the general superintendent, the president of the Board of Education, the president of the citywide school-community organization, the presidents of the teachers' and administrators' unions, the president of Eastern Michigan University, the president of the Skillman Foundation, and Dr. James Comer, director of the Yale Child Study Center.

Individual Detroit elementary schools (serving children in grades 1–5, from about age 6 to about age 12) submitted proposals to become Comer schools. The benefits of being selected included new on-site resources such as a full-time school facilitator, a half-time parent facilitator, a half-time study support team member, and about $15,000 in professional development and discretionary funds. Millsap et al. note, "For the first five years of the initiative, substantial resources were invested" (2000, chap. 1, p. 4).

The selection process for the winning schools aimed at maximizing success: a close match between the school's own objectives and the program, evidence the school was already working with vigor on school reform, and evidence of staff support for the initiative. The District Planning Team for the Comer initiative read proposals and visited the schools, eventually selecting six as Cycle I schools. In June 1995, another six schools—selected from among those who initially applied but were not as highly rated—became Comer Cycle 2 schools.

The Abt Evaluation

The basic evaluation design was a quasi experiment, involving matched Comer and non-Comer comparison schools. As a longitudinal study, the design permitted multiple repeated measures comparing the progress of individual students and schools as a whole for the matched Comer and comparison schools. The school (Comer or non-Comer) was the first unit of analysis; students within schools were the second, or nested, unit of analysis. As described by Millsap et al.:

> Each of the 12 Comer schools was carefully matched with two other schools in its area on the following school characteristics: average student enrollment; the percent of non-white students in the school; percent of students receiving free or reduced price lunch; and the percent of students scoring at or above grade on the California Achievement Test reading and mathematics achievement tests. These 24 matching schools became the comparison schools used in our evaluation. . . . the matching process resulted in two groups of schools with no statistically significant differences on the matching characteristics. (One school later dropped out.) (Millsap et al. 2000, chap. 1, p. 7)

> For the multiple regression analyses, school baseline characteristics included . . . enrollment, average prior achievement, percent of students receiving free lunch, percent minority students, average rate of absences, average number of times parents report moving in the past two years, average parent-reported education level, and percent of students new to the school in any one year. (Millsap et al. 2000, chap. 1, p. 11)

Because repeated measures were obtained, the evaluators could look developmentally at the value added of the Comer approach by the end of the evaluation. They could also test whether the program had an effect on *rate of change* over time on the key proximal outcomes (school climate, parent-school relationships) and the more distal outcome (student achievement).

The specific analytic models included ordinary least-squares (OLS) regression with baseline school covariates, analysis of covariance, second-level Hierarchical Linear Modeling (HLM) with school and student characteristics, and a fascinating instance of third-level HLM with time, school, and student characteristics (see Millsap et al. 2000, table 4). HLM, developed by Bryk and Raudenbush (1992), has received considerable attention in developmental studies because of its capacity concurrently to examine changes over time and nested complex variables such as community, neighborhood, school, familial, and individual-child characteristics.

Table 3.2 summarizes the evaluation questions, approach (design), and the measures used to answer each evaluation question.

The Findings

With regard to Comer *implementation,* the data suggest this is not an easy program to carry out. After four years of operation:

- Three schools were fully implementing Comer, four moderately, and four weakly implementing.
- On a global implementation measure, the average was 3.6 on a five-point scale.
- The highest rated school on a five-point scale scored 4.3; the lowest, 3.0., indicating considerable variability.
- Variation within schools was slight: if there was high rating by staff on one facet of Comer, then there were high ratings on most others.
- Implementation was start and stop, with some reversals. Only the most fully implementing Comer schools grew significantly and notably in implementation over the years.

Considering the matched comparison schools with regard to Comer-like structures:

- They looked a lot like the variations in Comer schools.
- The average was 3.4 on Comer-like structures; the highest rated school scored 4.3, and the lowest rated school scored 2.9 on implementation of Comer-like principles.
- However, overall, growth in implementation was relatively flat between 1996/97 and 1999 for the comparison schools.

Table 3.2. Evaluation Questions, Designs, and Measures

Question	Design	Measures
Implementation: How well has the Comer SDP been implemented? Is implementation variable? How many schools are fully implementing the SDP?	1a. Observation at school level.	1a. Periodic site visits, spring and fall each year. Interviews with school and parent facilitators, principals, chairs of the school improvement and student support teams, and others. In addition, interviews with district planning team, Comer coordinators, area superintendents, general superintendent.
	1b. Observation at district level.	1b. SIT and SST meetings were observed once a year at each school. Also directly observed were district planning team meetings and day-long retreats.
	1c. Self-report.	1c. Implementation surveys administered to all staff twice: spring in year 1 and in last year of study. Survey asked about SDP structures and activities.
	1d. Document analysis.	1d. Analysis of proposals, progress reports, SIT and SST meeting minutes, and internal memoranda.
Implementation: Have the matched comparison schools been implementing Comer-like structures and processes? To what extent are there differences in overall implementation between Comer and comparison schools?	2. Self-report. *Note:* No observations, interviews, or document analysis were done for the comparison schools.	2. The implementation survey asked the same questions as above, but they were framed as questions about the implementation of school reform. Administered to all staff in each comparison school at the same time.
Proximal: Given the status of implementation, what are the average effects of the Comer SDP?	Comparison of Comer schools and, for each, their matched comparison schools.	

(continued)

Table 3.2. continued

Question	Design	Measures
Proximal: Do fully implementing schools have better academic and social climates than matched comparison schools?	Self-report.	Two forms of a school climate survey were developed by Dr. Thomas Cook of Northwestern: one for school staff (Staff Climate Survey; taken by all staff in Comer and comparison schools in spring 1996, 1997, 1999) and one for fifth and sixth graders in Comer and comparison schools (Student Climate Survey).
Are parent-school relationships better in Comer schools?	Self-report.	Surveys of parents in grades 2 and 5, spring 1996 and spring 1999. Items about parent-school relationships and parent-child behaviors relevant to child's school performance.
Outcomes: Do students in fully implementing Comer schools have higher levels of achievement than students in low-implementing schools?	Within Comer schools only design: high-, moderate-, and low-implementing Comer schools.	Metropolitan Achievement Test Version 7 (MAT7) given annually by Detroit district schools. Scores in reading, mathematics, and science.
Impacts: What is the value added of Comer in high-implementing schools	Comer vs. matched comparison schools; high-implementing Comer vs. high-implementing Comer-like comparison schools.	In both comparisons, dependent variables are the MAT7 scores.
Theory: What is the relationship among implementation, social and academic climate, and student development?	Multiple regression.	All measures cited above.
Improvement: How can more fully implemented Comer schools be created?	Judgmental analysis.	All measures cited above.

If the evaluation had stopped here, one might conclude implementation was a failure. However, the evaluators appropriately drew on qualitative knowledge to interpret the results. It is crucial for evaluators to understand what else is happening in the program and policy space that could promote the same changes as the focal program or could thwart them. An important qualitative approach is constantly looking "outside the box," documenting what else is happening that could affect both proximal and distal variables.

Millsap et al. note:

> Since its inception in the late 1960s, the ideas central to the Comer SDP have become the common currency of school reform. Any school embarking independently on school reform would be expected to move close to what our surveys define as "implementing Comer." During the program implementation period, the Detroit public schools also began implementing features very similar to the Comer SDP in [all] schools, through the [Detroit] "Four Cornerstones." (2000, chap. 1, p. 13)

With regard to the *proximal variables,* the initial analyses suggested no evidence of effects on the changes expected from program theory to lead to improved child development:

- On average, there were no differences in staff ratings of social and academic climate between Comer and comparison schools.
- The average ratings of parent-school relationships did not differ.
- On average, with regard to student achievement and development, there were no detectable effects noted in the analyses.

Had the Abt evaluation stopped here, the conclusion would have been that the Comer approach was not detectably better than whatever else was happening in the schools. And here is where, through building the qualitative way of thinking into the architecture of the evaluation design—collecting and wisely applying qualitative data—the Abt study moves the evaluation field forward. The Abt evaluators had the data, and to investigate the effect on child development (change over time) of Comer principles when most fully implemented, they went beyond the nominal Comer versus non-Comer designations and used grouped analyses in addition to primarily regression-based analyses.

Did the program have effects in the Comer schools in which the model was most fully implemented? In 1999, yes, in science and mathematics, comparing the three fully implemented Comer schools with their five matched comparisons. In 1999, no, for reading.

With regard to the longitudinal analyses (i.e., the central question of improvement in child development over time that HLM permits), there were measurable benefits. As Millsap et al. report:

> For first grade students the scores are virtually indistinguishable, but the achievement scores begin to separate for each succeeding grade, so that for fifth graders, the students in Comer schools are outperforming their counterparts in the comparison schools in each subject matter area. In other words, when students are ready to start middle school (i.e., the sixth grade), students who attend Comer schools for at least three years have higher student achievement than students in comparison schools. (2000, chap. 1, p. 14)

Further, when high-implementing Comer Schools were compared with high-implementing comparison schools, benefits were found for the Comer approach. On the proximal variables of growth in implementing the Comer guiding principles, the high-implementing Comer schools grew and the high-implementing comparisons did not. The Comer initiative could take schools initially not implementing the principles and over the five-year period change the dynamics of these schools to look like other schools that, through whatever road, began looking like Comer schools. Also, for students who were studying in the high-implementing schools for at least three years, high-implementing Comer school students did better in reading than high-implementing comparison schools, but not in mathematics or science.

Thus, it appears that high levels of implementation of Comer principles can have a value added in promoting child development, over and above the strong influences of family risk/benefit variations and in neighborhoods where failure in school can be more frequent than success in school. This conclusion is opposite from the one that would have been reached had the evaluation *not* included the qualitative elements and analyses based on these.

The Exemplary Features of This Evaluation as an Instance of Mixing Qualitative and Quantitative Approaches

Two elements already have been highlighted in which, absent the qualitative way of looking at things, the conclusions would have been different.

Without the more qualitative approach, the study would have concluded that implementation was a failure and that there was no evidence that the Comer approach benefited children's development. With analyses based on qualitative methods, the conclusions were that Detroit itself had changed to Comer principles generally and that when the approach was well implemented, children's development improved.

A More Robust Basis for Recommendations

There is a third way in which the Abt study is exemplary in merging qualitative and quantitative approaches, shown in a chapter where the merger, methodologically, is most transparent. Chapter 5 in the Abt report, "Creating More Fully Implementing Comer Schools," takes program design elements as "givens" and looks at school, district, state, and technical support context factors and what could be done, practically, feasibly, to change them. Five school elements are discussed in depth: (1) energy and commitment of school staff to the program, (2) facilitative leadership by the principal and positive working relationships within the leadership team, (3) a welcoming environment for reform by school staff both at the outset and during the implementation process, (4) a shared vision of the Comer model and what it can accomplish in the school, and (5) school size (larger schools were much less able to implement Comer well).

At first glance, the elements seem confirmatory of much prior research and perhaps not worth five years and several million dollars to discover. As one reads the specifics, however, both the findings and advice seem unusually solidly grounded in evidence. For example, following a presentation on "a welcoming environment," Millsap et al. note:

> Creating a receptive working environment for reform also entails turning around cliques of indifferent staff and dealing with "naysayers," those teachers who find the Comer process antithetical to their personal beliefs or styles. Indifferent staff can be turned around through a supportive leadership team (as discussed above) and by building a critical mass of supporters from among veteran or new staff. Teachers who do not want to take part in the program could be given a "no-fault" transfer to schools with less emphasis on team-based management. Recalcitrant teachers consume energy that could be better spent elsewhere. (2000, chap. 5, p. 9)

One of the troubling issues in evaluation is the role of the evaluator and the extent to which evaluators should be involved in giving advice, making recommendations, and offering suggestions. The arguments against such a role include unjustified extrapolations from the data, evaluator preconceptions that may not be grounded in thorough policy analysis, and insensitivity to complex dynamics and contexts. There is much to be said for these arguments, yet it can seem to both evaluands and evaluators as if the effort has been lacking without a discussion of implications. The qualitative data provided a rich, authentic basis for the implications. This study thus exemplifies how qualitative and quantitative approaches, carefully carried out and sensitively interpreted, can support what seem like useful, sound recommendations.

Overall, what may be particularly intriguing about the Abt evaluation of the Comer schools is the relatively greater emphasis on qualitative, implementation data coupled with an important example of how to take into account what is happening in comparison schools and the elegant application of HLM. That is, here is a practical approach to *how* to make qualitative and quantitative approaches work together to improve our certainty in answering the evaluative questions.

Other examples may soon be available. A large-scale application of the HLM approach by Rauh, Lamb-Parker, and their colleagues (2000) is combining extensive data on a child's characteristics at birth (from the New York City Department of Health records), community/neighborhood and family data (census, New York City records), and in-depth child development data with information on the preschool and early school experiences (currently up to third grade), as part of a longitudinal evaluation of Project Head Start. Lamb-Parker reports that data collection includes qualitative case studies of individual children, families, and neighborhoods. How these will be integrated into the more quantitative analysis is not yet clear: whether they will be stand-alone examples illustrating and enriching the reports or more fully merged.

Already available is a compilation of two decades of World Bank experience merging qualitative and quantitative approaches in the context of community development. Chapter 1 of *Opportunities and Challenges for Integrating Quantitative and Qualitative Research* by Michael Bamberger (2000), for example, is of value for the practical, hands-on description of the working elements of an integrated, multidisciplinary approach. Bamberger notes, for example, that, the "research team should include primary researchers from different disciplines; that time must be allowed for the researchers to develop an understanding and respect for each other's disciplines and work; and that each should be familiar with the basic literature and current debates in the other field" (2000, chap. 1, p. 30).

This may seem a cliché, but it takes us valuable operational steps beyond the signpost "work together." As Trend (1978) noted years ago in a report of conflicts affecting a national evaluation of low-income housing programs, merging qualitative and quantitative methods can be difficult. In this instance, qualitative and quantitative approaches reached quite different conclusions, which required extensive further analyses to try to resolve. One needs guideposts such as Bamberger's to avoid unnecessary methodological conflicts.

The Importance of In-Depth Information
on Control/Comparison Group Experiences

The importance of the Abt study is underscored by a step backward nationally in understanding what methodologies are optimal for what evaluative questions in what contexts. Many evaluators have turned away from the benefits of randomization because of its sometime misuse in creating death-by-evaluation for ideas that may be worthwhile. Others have embraced randomization, believing that where biases need to be ruled out because strong attribution is needed *and when circumstances are appropriate,* randomized experiments are the best design.

At issue is the definition of when circumstances are appropriate. At one time, evaluators seemed to agree that randomized designs were well suited for reasonably well developed programs with a strong program logic framework and where there were reasonable populations that were nontreatment and likely to stay nontreatment. Absent such conditions, as evaluators such as Orwin, Cordray, and Huebner (1994) have indicated, there are other designs, including qualitative methods, that permit considerable confidence as to what is happening in a program, what changes are occurring, and the extent to which the program and its elements in its context are associated with these changes.

A U.S. General Accounting Office (GAO) report in 1997, however, stated that although there were longitudinal and quasi-experimental evaluations of Head Start, these were and would be inconclusive without randomization. GAO observed in 2000: "Most Head Start children have some school readiness skills, but because most of the studies did not use a control group to enable a comparison of Head Start outcomes with outcomes for non–Head Start participants, they did not provide conclusive evidence on whether children's having school readiness skills stemmed from being in Head Start" (2000, 7). The report highlighted a struggle between those who felt Head Start, as a preschool readiness program, should be administered through public schools only and those who felt Head Start is a comprehensive program best administered through Health and Human Services. Defining Head Start primarily as a preschool academic readiness program with a strong emphasis on literacy and reading skills, Congress mandated a randomized test of the effectiveness of Head Start. That is, local programs would overrecruit and children would be selected at random to participate or not participate in Head Start (GAO 2000).

From some perspectives, however, the context does not seem appropriate for such a design. To mention only one contextual factor, the welfare reform initiative requires widespread childcare so former welfare recipients can work full-time. By law, over 90 % of all Head Start children come from low-income families, precisely the families targeted in welfare reform. If families selected as controls are denied Head Start services and required to work, what will happen to the children? Some of these families may turn to friends and relations. Some may turn to custodial day care. Some may find other childcare, including preschools (Loewe and Weisner 2003). Many states are working to expand quality childcare to support welfare reform (Collins et al. 2000). According to early studies, some families find locating adequate childcare difficult, while others live in states with more adequate childcare (see, e.g., reports such as Kimmel 1998 and the series by the Urban Institute from the Assessing the New Federalism national study).

One can expect that the "control" group will not be a passive nontreatment condition, but proactive. This could likely mean that variability of experiences for the control children will be greater than for the Head Start "experimental" children of welfare reform. Without in-depth information on the quality of care experienced by these nominal controls and the comparisons, the cumulative and probably large variability in results for the control/comparison groups may be primarily assigned to "error variance." When error variance is high, opportunity for detecting true signals of program effects decreases, unless the error variance can be sensibly associated with theoretically meaningful constructs such as child development opportunities and then systematically tested. That is, labeling an experience "treatment," "comparison," and "control" is far from being enough. One needs hands-on, direct observational and similar qualitative data on the experiences the children are actually having.

The Abt design—with its attention to documenting what was happening in the comparison schools and its elegant sequence of (a) Comer versus matched comparisons, (b) high-implementing Comer versus matched comparisons, and (c) high-implementing Comer versus high-implementing comparisons—is one potentially powerful approach to avoiding death-by-control/comparison-groups in situations such as that facing Head Start and that experienced by Detroit.

Methodological Improvements

Some improvements could have been made in the way in which Abt used qualitative and quantitative data. These include:

- Looking at other aspects of middle-childhood development in addition to academic progress.
- Equal emphasis using qualitative and quantitative approaches to implementation for the treatment and nontreatment groups.
- More transparent analysis of qualitative data.

With regard to this concern, Millsap writes:

> It is interesting that when we did the technical appendices, I did not write up the qualitative methodology. We were very deliberate about what we did (e.g., racially diverse and highly experienced teams, three schools per team for some comparative purposes, some people visited the schools each time for continuity, training each fall and analytic meetings each spring, common question/answer reporting format for each school that was revised/added on to each year to test out hypotheses, site visitors reviewed survey data on each of their schools each year). We did summaries of the annual surveys for the individual schools that site visitors then discussed with school people, and we thought about where we needed depth (qualitative) and where we needed breadth (quantitative) in the implementation evaluation. (M. A. Millsap, pers. comm., September 8, 2000)

Millsap (pers. comm., September 8, 2000) also provided a discussion of the qualitative and quantitative evaluation design that greatly enriches our understanding of how Abt integrated the qualitative and quantitative methodologies. These points are presented in Table 3.3.

Another limitation was lack of connection in the report to previous studies of Comer's approach. It may be helpful to note here that an early review of the literature on Comer's program (Becker and Hedges 1992) concluded that overall, results could be interpreted as indicating support for Comer's model, both as a theory and in its results. In 1999, as part of a third-party evaluation of the Comer program in Prince George's County,

Table 3.3. How Abt Integrated Their Qualitative and Quantitative Methodologies

	Example
Questions addressed in site visits were elaborated and expanded on in surveys.	In surveys, all staff were asked about the effectiveness of the site-based management team. From site visits, we could provide examples of the topics the team addressed, how often they met, and how well they interacted with each other.
We expanded reporting formats to reflect new issues emerging from surveys and site visits.	We began in the third year to interview noninvolved staff to find out more about those who were more critical of the program. One reason we sought these staff out was to explore the range in responses we found in the initial surveys.
The implementation surveys were developed jointly.	The implementation survey was developed jointly by Tom Cook, the Yale Child Study Center, the Comer Schools and Families Initiative, and those of us who were conducting the qualitative implementation study. That is, both teams were involved in the design of the quantitative instruments.
Commingling staff: The director of the quantitative impact analysis was a senior member of a site visit team.	The director participated fully in one of the qualitative teams, visiting three Comer schools for five years. It was very important that the quantitative analysis be done by staff who were well acquainted with the schools. This also meant that both directors were methodologically multilingual and had firsthand reason to trust the meaningfulness of both types of data.
Commingling data: We reviewed the qualitative and quantitative data periodically (direct triangulation/verification).	In the data analysis for the final report, site visitors ranked their schools on the extent of implementation, and we reviewed the rankings derived from the implementation surveys. The rank ordering was the same.
Commingling reports: Annual reports to schools from the survey data were written by the qualitative site visit staff.	Annual school reports that presented staff and student survey data to schools were written by those doing the qualitative site visits. Sometimes, those doing fieldwork would debrief the principal or site-based management team on survey findings in the school report.
Annual and final report were authored by staff who conducted the fieldwork.	The senior author of the reports was the director of the fieldwork component even though the final report was largely quantitative.

Maryland, Cook et al. observed that a better description of the studies reviewed by Becker and Hedges would be "not proven," in part because almost all of these earlier studies were self-evaluations that used evaluation designs open to many sources of bias or that had other weaknesses, such as small samples. In their own study, which included analyses of implementation as well as results in the personal-social and academic areas, Cook et al. did not find evidence supporting the program model or establishing beneficial effects. They note that due to the relatively short time (two years) and other contextual variables, the Comer model may not have had a fair test. Cook, Murphy, and Hunt (2000) remedied the problems in a study of the Comer program in the Chicago public schools.

The Chicago study (Cook, Murphy, and Hunt 2000) focused on the most problematic schools serving the most difficult children and their families. Using an evaluation design similar to the Abt Detroit study, with about 10,000 students in elementary and middle schools, and a four-year period, Cook and his colleagues (2000) reported that Comer and non-Comer schools had many shared features, which they attributed to the district-wide intensive school reform movement, but Comer schools were, overall, more "Comer-like" at the end of four years. Interestingly, the same rankings for implementation were found using qualitative/ethnographic and quantitative approaches. Benefits for students were found, overall, for children and youth who had been in the program for several years. The effect sizes were larger than those that have been used to establish statewide policies. The effect sizes also were seen as important, given the Chicago context of overall school reform, efforts to serve the "hard-core" situations, and an "early out" program that increased the turnover rate for school principals about halfway through the study. With regard to the school climate and other variables seen as instrumental in the Comer theoretical model, changes were found but could not be linked reliably to student outcomes.

Cook et al. did not use the same analytic strategy as the Abt study. There are, however, some similar features in extensive use of qualitative data for interpretation of quantitative findings. Particularly noteworthy are insightful discussions of the evaluation implications of "commingling" two demonstration programs (Youth Guidance and Comer) and of the Chicago demonstration taking place as the national Comer model was being revised.

Millsap and Cook are preparing a joint paper on the Comer program in Detroit; cumulatively, the three studies (Detroit, Maryland, Chicago) should provide a reasonable estimate of the value of the Comer approach in the context of school reform efforts.

In Conclusion

Despite fairly widespread practical use of mixed methods, exemplary instances of national evaluations of human service programs are not numerous. Nonetheless, examples such as the Abt evaluation of the Detroit Comer school initiative show how insights from these good studies can be more widely applied to improve certainty, utility, and fairness of conclusions. In particular, the study demonstrates the returns from in-depth attention to what is happening in control and comparison instances and the application of this knowledge to transforming error variance into meaning for child development and organizational change.

References

Anson, A. R., T. D. Cook, F. Habib, M. K. Grady, N. Haynes, and J. P. Comer. 1991. "The Comer School Development Program: A Theoretical Analysis." *Urban Education* 26 (1): 56–82.

Bamberger, M., ed. 2000. *Opportunities and Challenges for Integrating Quantitative and Qualitative Research*. Directions in Development Series. Washington, DC: World Bank.

Becker, B. J., and L. V. Hedges. 1992. *A Review of the Literature on the Effectiveness of the Comer's School Development Program*. New York: Rockefeller Foundation.

Bryk, A. S., and S. W. Raudenbush. 1992. *Hierarchical Linear Models: Applications and Data Analysis Methods*. Newbury Park, CA: Sage Publications.

Collins, A. M., J. I. Layzer, J. L. Kreader, A. Werner, and F. B. Glantz. 2000. *National Study of Child Care for Low-Income Families*. Cambridge, MA: Abt Associates.

Comer, J. P. 1995. *Changing the American School*. Yale University Great Teachers Video Series. Florence, KY: Brenzel Publishing.

Comer, J. P., N. M. Haynes, E. T. Joyner, and M. Ben Avie. 1996. *Rallying the Whole Village: The Comer Process for Reforming Education*. New York: Teachers College Press.

Cook, T. D., F. N. Habib, R. A. Settersten, S. C. Shayle, and S. M. Degirmencioghu. 1999. "Comer's School Development Program in Prince George's County, Maryland: A Theory-Based Evaluation." *American Educational Research Journal* 36 (3): 543–597.

Cook, T., R. Murphy, and H. Hunt. 2000. "Comer's School Development Program in Chicago: A Theory-Based Evaluation." *American Educational Research Journal* 37 (2): 535–597.

Kimmel, J. 1998. "Child Care Costs as a Barrier to Employment for Single and Married Mothers." *Review of Economics and Statistics*, pp. 287–299.

Loewe, E., and T. S. Weisner. 2003. "'You have to push it—who's gonna raise your kids?' Situating Child Care in the Daily Routines of Low-Income Families." *Children and Youth Services Review* 25 (3): 225–261.

Millsap, M. A., A. Chase, D. Obeidallah, A. Perez-Smith, N. Brigham, and K. Johnston. 2000. *Evaluation of Detroit's Comer Schools and Families Initiative.* Cambridge, MA: Abt Associates.

Orwin, R., D. S. Cordray, and R. N. Huebner. 1994. "Judicious Application of Randomized Designs." In *Critically Evaluating the Role of Experiments,* ed. K. J. Conrad, 73–86. New Directions for Evaluation, vol. 63. San Francisco: Jossey-Bass.

Rauh, V., F. Lamb-Parker, H. Andrews, and R. Gonzales. 2000. "Community Influences on the Efficacy of Head Start." Paper presented at the Fifth National Head Start Research Conference, "Developmental and Contextual Transactions of Children and Families," Washington, DC, June 28–July 1.

Trend, M. G. 1978. "On the Reconciliation of Qualitative and Quantitative Analyses: A Case Study." *Human Organization* 37 (4): 345–354.

U.S. General Accounting Office. 1997. *Head Start: Research Provides Little Information on Impact of Current Programs.* GAO/HES 97-59. Washington, DC.

———. 2000. *Preschool Education: Federal Investment for Low-Income Children Significant but Effectiveness Unclear.* GAO/T-HEHS-00-83. Washington, DC.

Urban Institute. 1997. *Assessing the New Federalism.* Washington, DC: Urban Institute.

PART II

Ethnicity and the Development of Ethnic Identity in Childhood

4

The Ecology of Children's Racial Coping:
Family, School, and Community Influences

Deborah J. Johnson

The ability of children to cope with discrimination and prejudice in American society has largely been attributed to parental socialization patterns (e.g., Hughes and Chen 1999; Marshall 1995; Rumbaut 1994). In middle childhood these messages incorporate information about culture, contribute to ethnic identity formation, and increasingly begin to aid in the development of skills to manage experiences with discrimination (Hughes and Chen 1997, 1999). Parents' communications are affected by a variety of factors that include personality, region of the country (Thornton et al. 1990), their children's experiences with prejudice (Hughes and Johnson 2001), and their own adult experiences with prejudice (Johnson 2001; Hughes and Chen 1997). Despite the breadth of work on racial socialization, little attention has been given to the microprocesses that are involved as parents communicate their socialization goals for coping with discrimination to their children. In addition, current research in this area has typically focused on adolescence (Stevenson 1994, 1995; Phinney and Chavira 1995), with considerably less emphasis on earlier developmental periods. Moreover, few have explored influences

in the development of children's coping patterns beyond parental influences. For example, schools have been studied in terms of racial socialization and academic performance (Marshall 1995; Bowman and Howard
1985) but not in terms of school-based racial socialization influences. Although the exploration of parental socialization within contexts has been
addressed somewhat in the literature, the effect of the context on children's
coping has been left underexplored, especially in middle childhood.

The purpose of this chapter is to explore the multiple influences of racial
socialization on the racial-coping outcomes of African American children. I
accomplish this through a mixed-methods approach across three studies
centered on a single measure: the Racial Stories Task (RST). Other objectives of this chapter are to assess the extent to which the approach is successful and to describe the challenges of using the RST and conducting
work of this nature. I have divided the chapter into four major sections. The
first section centers on the conceptual and theoretical foundations of my
work on racial socialization. In the second section, I focus on the methodological strategies used. In this section, I argue for the utility and strength
of mixed methods in studying racial socialization as a relatively new area.
I present three studies that represent the levels of influence over children's
racial coping. Finally, in the last section, I summarize the merits and difficulties associated with the mixed-methods approach taken here and in the
area of research.

Conceptualizing Racial Socialization and Children's Racial Coping

Within the last few decades more attention has been focused on children of
color (Garcia Coll et al. 1996; Harrison et al. 1990; Johnson et al. 2003; Ogbu
1981). Social stratification factors (social position, racism/discrimination,
segregation) are *central,* not peripheral, issues in the development of African American children and their families. In the Garcia Coll et al. (1996)
model, social stratification factors operate as distal influences on children's
outcomes both directly and via the proximal influences of family context
and parental socialization processes. The influences of other adults and
contexts more distal than the home, for instance, the promoting or inhibiting contexts of schools and communities, contribute to the development of children's racial-coping skills. I will describe influences from these
factors briefly, and also touch upon the critical influence characteristics of
external familial contexts, such as homogeneity and heterogeneity of com-
munities/schools, can have on racial socialization processes. Finally, it will

be important to describe racial coping as a critical competency of African American children and to distinguish situational from global racial coping among children.

Racial Stress and Coping: Multiple Influences on the Child

Parental racial socialization is defined as intentional and unintentional messages, parent practices, child-rearing behaviors, and other interactions that communicate to the child how (s)he is to perceive, process, and respond to discrimination, prejudice, and other barriers based upon race (Johnson 2001). The protection of children's sense of self while simultaneously preparing them to cope with racial barriers and prejudice in the society is the core challenge and dilemma of African American parenthood and is steeped in a complex social history. Several studies have reported that 60–65% of African American families incorporate unique features into their child rearing because their children are black (Holiday 1992; Bowman and Howard 1985; Johnson 1988, 1994; Hughes and Chen 1997). Parents attempt to prepare children for the experiences of devalued status in the society while balancing and buffering the child's sense of self. Parents anticipate the events of discrimination and develop child-rearing strategies, messages, and goals to help their children combat them.

One dimension of parental preparation of children is to adjust their race-related messages to the child's developmental stage (Hughes and Chen 1997; Hughes and Johnson 2001). The developmental pattern of parental racial socialization is to emphasize messages that promote racial/cultural pride and ethnic history in early childhood and to delay messages about mistrusting whites until early adolescence.

Children's socialization is influenced in a multiplicity of contexts; race-related socialization is no exception. The major influences on children's race-related socialization occur in the home, school, and community contexts. Once children have reached school age, the educational institution is cast as a major socializing agent (Johnson 2001). Racial socialization has largely been studied in relation to what parents and family-based caregivers do, and it is important to address and assess race-related socialization experiences that occur outside those critical but narrow sets of experiences, particularly as children get older. Other adults, such as teachers and neighbors acting as facilitating agents, also socialize children with respect to coping with race.

Beyond individuals as socializing agents, characteristics of contexts external to the home can exert some influence over those who socialize (e.g., parents, teachers) and over the process of socialization. Racial composition as a characteristic of community and school context is an important influence of this type. Distal factors of social stratification leading to child competencies (e.g., racial-coping skills) are not limited to heterogeneous majority contexts (where conflict with Euro-Americans may be heightened). Homogeneous community and school settings also encourage the development of parental racial socialization strategies and the development of children's racial coping. African American children and families are typically embedded in larger ecological settings that impinge on parenting and children's coping even in homogeneous school and community settings; this is the common circumstance of numerical minorities. Parental socialization processes and children's race-related coping skills emerge from both contexts. Peters (1985) demonstrated that infants and toddlers were indirectly affected by the discrimination their parents experienced outside the home or within the workplace. In addition, children have experiences in schools where there are nonblack teachers, where there are no committed African American teachers (or "Dreamkeepers"; Ladson-Billings 1994), or where insensitive curriculum and school policies are in place (Tatum 1997). At home they experience the nightly news, children's shows, or other entertainment programming where positive images of racial groups may be limited or excluded. Additional community-based experiences are those, for example, of differential treatment in neighborhood stores or with law enforcement. Moreover, although the experience of prejudice likely differs between homogeneous and more racially heterogeneous community settings, it cuts across settings, both socially and economically.

Relationships among home, school, community, and the child exist in an ecology of what has been termed the ecology of "black stress" (McAdoo 1982) or "racial stress." The phenomenon has also been referred to as mundane extreme environmental stress (MEES), where both chronic (tangible but unpredictable racial stressors) and mundane (threat of chronic racial stressors) stressors work to debilitate parents and their children (Peters and Massey 1983; Pierce 1975). This ecology of racial stress is constantly impinging on these relations.

Children's Racial Coping

Garcia Coll et al. (1996) argue that racial-coping skills are critical competencies for African American children to develop. Although I have emphasized the role that external agents play in the development of racial-coping skills, children are not always merely acted upon. Children's individual personality characteristics and interpretations of their own unique experiences and contexts also contribute to the development of racial-coping skills. Children's racial coping, personal identities (self-esteem), and racial identities are thought to act as additional buffers between racialized events and children's ability to cope or the development of more global coping strategies. Global coping, ethnic identity, and cultural traditions provide a kind of protective armor against ongoing experiences with prejudice, discrimination, and contexts where the climate is racially charged and potentially volatile for children of color. Situational coping emphasizes responses to more chronic racial stressors, such as specific racial conflicts and acts of discrimination. Identity as a global coping mechanism stands outside specific events and is influenced by factors that play out over time, such as parental child-rearing behaviors and goals. Children's racial coping that is largely situational rather than global are of central interest here.

Racial Coping: Mixed Methods on a Single Construct

As utilization of mixed-methods approaches has increased, the "paradigm wars" (Datta 1994) have tapered off and these approaches have become more accepted. Mixed-methods approaches largely emphasize multiple methods within the same sample or within the same study. Many discussions of mixed methods focus on moving beyond the use of multiple measures of a single construct employing the same class of measures (e.g., questionnaires, surveys, and so on) (e.g., Reichardt and Rallis 1994; Greene and Caracelli 1997). These discussions seem to favor focusing on a single construct using a variety of methods that explore different facets of the same construct. These might include questionnaires, detailed coding of observations, and multiple analytic strategies applied to data produced by the same measure. The approach I take in this chapter is one of the more controversial applications of mixed methodologies (Datta 1997). That is, the focus is on a single construct, children's racial coping, as measured by a single instrument, the Racial Stories Task. Assessing this construct across three studies with three different samples of African American children challenges convention. Taken as a whole this represents a kind of component design or a design in which the complete story is generated from integrating findings from the various ecological and methodological vantage points (Greene and Caracelli 1997).

Three studies of children's racial coping are presented at three levels of influence: family, school, and community. In the first study, *parenting processes* and children's racial coping are addressed. In the second, *school influences,* defined as *school racial composition,* and children's racial coping are investigated. The focus of the last study is on *community influences* operationalized as *perceived violence* and its relation to children's racial coping.

The Racial Stories Task

The Racial Stories Task is used in each of the three studies presented (Johnson 1996). The Racial Stories Task II is composed of six closed-ended vignettes, each depicting an overt racial conflict involving another child. The stories are of two types (Appendix A). Between-group conflict characterizes four of the six vignettes (Jacob's story) and the remaining two are about within-group conflict (the busing story). Between-group conflict deals with explicit conflicts resulting from explicit instances of racial discrimination. Within-group conflict addresses issues of cultural authenticity and group affiliation.

Each story requires the child to make choices about what the character in the story should do. In the closed-ended version six options are given to the child, reflecting some variation in 6 of 9 coping domains within each item. (In Appendix B there are 11 conceptual coping domains represented that highlight all 23 racial-coping strategies. In subsequent analyses we determined reliability of 9 domains.) Only 8 domains are in continuous use; one was dropped for lack of use (Appendix C); that is, it was rare that children chose the domain or were coded into it. The coping domains were established in previous work where the vignettes were administered as open-ended items. Use of the multiyear Comer intervention data (Cook, Slaughter-Defoe, and Payne 1990; Johnson et al., forthcoming) provided an excellent opportunity to validate the measure with a large sample. The open-ended RST has four to six vignettes and is administered face-to-face with responses recorded verbatim. The open-ended responses of nearly 2,000 children were coded into 23 categories. One or two categories were dropped because they were rarely coded in the database; the remaining categories were collapsed into 12 groups of strategies, which were then subjected to factor analyses (see Appendix B for incidence of strategies grouped within domains presented across three waves of child data and Appendix C for the definitions of domains). In each analysis four or five factors accounted for 52–60% of the variance. Ultimately, 8 domains represented in the closed-ended version of the RST II are based on this work (Johnson 1996).

While the RST represents the same construct in each study, the data are used slightly differently. In the first study, individual strategies are important but not more so than the microprocesses around them. How parents respond to and encourage the generation of a strategy is central in that study. In the second study, children's individual racial-coping strategies as associated with racial composition in varying school contexts is another critical variation in the use of the RST. In the last study, the use of the RST shifts from the individual strategy to groups of strategies or coping domains in association with other key constructs.

Findings from three studies of children's racial coping explore contexts and processes influential to the development of these skills: individual factors (self-esteem), family socialization processes, external family socialization in schools, and the context of violence as a community factor. The data are derived from three different data sets and represent a broad range of methods employed to investigate burgeoning questions and issues. This approach allows for the understanding of the development of children's racial coping from a variety of ecological vantage points.

Racial Socialization and Parental Processes: Qualitative Evidence

In this qualitative study emphasis is placed on family socialization processes and child racial coping. A social interaction approach was applied that presumes that parent-child interaction provides opportunities for the parent to teach and the child to learn, practice, and develop new strategies for negotiating racial stress (Parke and Buriel 1998). Using observational methods to study racial socialization processes is rare, particularly in middle childhood. This study assesses microprocesses associated with parents' transmission of skills and values around coping with race that culminate in the specification of a strategy solution.

The RST was used in its open-ended form as a catalyst that would allow parents to express child-rearing behaviors and to act on racial socialization orientations. I was most interested in understanding how parenting processes influenced children's racial coping. In particular, the aspects of parent interaction related to competence building in children's coping and the effect of parents' use of race or racial themes on strategy usage by their children were central to the investigation.

Participants included 12 parent-child dyads, primarily mother-child dyads of fifth-grade children. The parent and child were left alone with the video camera running to work through the vignettes. Coding schemes for capturing aspects of the dyadic interactions were adapted from studies of parent-child interaction, communication, and play with black and nonblack children (Black 1992; Black and Logan 1995; McLoyd, Ray, and Etter-Lewis 1985). The dimensions coded included: (1) *negotiation strategies,* such as assigning a role to oneself or to the other (to read the story), extending the explanation of a strategy, or agreeing with or rejecting the strategy offered by the child; (2) *declaratives,* including threats, advice, permission, and positive reinforcement; (3) *imperatives* or *commands,* statements prohibiting or commanding; and (4) *questions,* including approval-seeking questions and information-, instruction-, or solution-seeking questions.

Previous work (Johnson 1988, 1994) indicated that some racial-coping strategies had greater long-term and cross-context potential and therefore should be utilized by children to a greater extent. It had also been established that a wide array of strategies is critical for a healthy balance of psychosocial competencies. Consistent with previous research, I found that on the whole parents were demonstrating parenting interactions that were directive and supportive. These parental approaches were paired with child strategies that were deferential to parents and respectful of their authority. Parents negotiated and prompted children for proactive responses to the open-ended vignettes. Children were actively engaged with their parents, negotiating through suggestions and questions to parents.

The open-ended questions and subsequent opportunity for dialogue provided a platform for parents and children to work through a racially themed scenario. Parents found the scenario compelling enough to push their children toward resolving the dilemma posed. This effort by parents and engagement by children provided the brief window from which to observe the crisp connection between parenting behaviors and coping outcomes of children. Children of parents who had the highest number of codable utterances and a greater tendency toward extending (adding complexity or lengthening the child's response) typically were more likely to use diverse racial-coping strategies that cut across the coping domains. For instance, parents who build onto or broaden children's coping responses and who spend a lot of time in dialogue with their children "hashing out" issues communicate enough information to expand the child's coping repertoire.

Weak parenting processes and behaviors were demonstrated in two instances. These problematic examples also illustrate the strong link between parenting behaviors and children's coping. In one parent-child dyad, the parent negotiation strategies were more negative (i.e., the strategies included more rejections of child solutions), and the child's coping included more negative internalizing strategies (inferiority, negating race). In another, more extreme case, the parent-child pattern was more child directed than in other parent-child dyads, and the child took on the task of assigning roles to the adult and performed adult roles of negotiation—agreeing with and extending the coping; in this case, the child's racial coping was almost entirely reactive or typically conflict confronting. Few racial-coping strategies were generated by this dyad.

Racial contextualization and decontextualization. Quantitative studies have shown a link between parents' racial socialization messages and children's racial coping (e.g., Bowman and Howard 1985; Stevenson 1994). The findings demonstrate that parental processes must also be paired with a philosophy and set of beliefs about racial socialization. Parental goals are supported through interactional structures that parents build over time through common child-rearing behaviors.

How parents handle race meaning in their interactions with their children is another aspect of parenting processes that is best observed and not elicited through direct questioning. With racial contextualization and decontextualization, one is either further developing race or racism as a theme in the problem being discussed or attempting to extricate race from a discussion of the problem at hand. In order to get at meaning, the analysis was shifted from microcoding to content analysis, a common approach in qualitative research.

While it was anticipated that racial contextualization or encouragement in the exploration of racial themes would expand the child's repertoire, it was not expected that decontextualization would yield the same result. In essence, however, this is what was found. Again, in both instances parents participated in a lot of extending and positive questioning of their children. Children are given seemingly endless opportunities to play out coping scenarios such that decontextualization of racial themes does not hinder the development or at least generation of racial-coping strategies. In the example below, the father is decontextualizing race. The father questions, gives advice, and is responsive to the child's view but also corrects and substitutes strategies, thereby demonstrating enormous complexity in parenting processes.

> Father: So you would say, "You're really white and really ugly" and that's
>   it? You'd let it go at that?
> Boy: I wouldn't go up to someone to tell them, "You're really white or
>   ugly." If they said it first, then I would.
> Father: My father told me . . . two wrongs don't make a right. He was
>   wrong to say that to Shirley, and you would be just as wrong to say

that back to him. N'kay, its hard to ignore something like this if said
to you . . .

Boy: What are you supposed to do then?

Father: Well, I usually put it to the authorities, report it to the teacher.

Overall, this approach to analyzing the data fostered an understanding
of what parents do that supports or undermines the acquisition of coping
competencies and how race meaning is potentially disentangled from the
strategy development process.

School Influences and Children's Racial Coping: Strategies and School Environment

Several studies suggest that the salience of race and racial self-
descriptors changes with racial composition in school (McGuire et al.
1978). Cross (1991) and Spencer (1985) referred to the critical interaction
between the child's knowledge of the evaluation of her racial-group membership communicated by others and the ability to reconcile that social understanding or cognition with what is known about the self and her affect
toward her own racial-group membership as a kind of transactional identity quagmire for the child. This dissonance is managed repeatedly by
African American children and represents a type of strategy for preserving
personal identity or self-esteem.

Recent studies (Richeson 2000; Sinclair, Hardin, and Lowery 2000) indicate that dissonance or other overt threats to positive group identity
change the behavior of African American college students in contexts where
other nonblack students are present. Younger children are no less sensitive
to differences in settings of varying racial composition. Tangible differences in the child's racial ecology lead to differing race stressors and the
need for an arsenal of strategies to accommodate these variations in ecologies. Variations across racial ecologies, in this case school racial composi-
tions, and accompanying stressors should create distinctions in racial coping by context.

The sample consisted of 1,797 third-grade African American children
from the Comer intervention project in Chicago (Cook, Slaughter-Defoe,
and Payne 1990). The focus was on racial composition as a school-level
variable influencing children's racial coping patterns (Kim 1999; Kim, Johnson, and Slaughter-Defoe 2002). The research questions and design required a count of the use of racial-coping strategies by individuals within
school types (several schools in each type). With respect to racial compo-

sition, children experience three types of settings: a *predominantly* (75% or more) African American school, a mixed-racial heterogeneous but *substantially* (25–75%) African American school, or a racially homogeneous (less than 25% African American) but non–African American context, the *extreme minority*.

Findings confirmed that school context does influence children's racial coping. In particular, we found that key strategies were more prevalent in some school settings than in others. In the predominantly black context, the strategy that was the least anticipatory of discrimination (persistence, e.g., expectation that raising your hand enough will result in the teacher recognizing you) emerged as most common among children. In the mixed-race school settings (substantial group), children were much more assertive (assert self), engaging (engage authority), and interested in fairness and cooperation (moral nonracial reasoning). In the extreme-minority setting, the use of the "strategic" strategy differed significantly from its prevalence in either of the other two school settings. Strategic planning is a strategy that evokes the need for an adult hierarchy of support and assistance (teachers, principals, parents). This strategy is typically more complex than others and suggests that children in extreme-minority settings are distinguished by the greater salience of race-based experiences and increased development of racial-coping mechanisms.

School context as defined by racial composition is a critical and important influence on children's racial coping. Although a variety of strategies were used across school settings, the preponderance or underusage of certain strategies by context does emphasize the disparity in racial stressors within these various settings. Moreover, the critical differences in racial composition that determined thresholds for the "minority" experience should be more thoroughly addressed. Methodologically, using the open-ended RST (coping strategies chosen from the universe of strategies) to compare differences in racial-coping strategy across different school environments is a strength of the measure and further demonstrates its versatility.

Children's Racial Coping and Community Influences: Modeling

Some research (e.g., Bradley 1995; Burton, Allison, and Obeidallah 1995; Garbarino 1992) links children's perceptions of the neighborhood to their development of social competence. Racial-coping skills are a unique type of social-problem-solving competence (Johnson et al., forthcoming). Perceived violence as a promoting or inhibiting environment (Garcia Coll et al. 1996) affects racial coping among African American children. As Garbarino, Kostelny, and Dubrow (1991) remind us, many urban children find themselves in dangerous settings, which have lasting effects on their psychological and adjustment outcomes. However, resilient children will use ecological resources and coping approaches to manage these more difficult contexts (Garbarino 1992).

In this study we focused on children's perception of violence and its effect on the relation of self-esteem to racial coping in children. The focal point in the study was the tension between the individual and the characteristics of the community environment. This study explored the role of perceived violence, as a community-level influence, on the racial coping of African American children. In addition, there is much to learn from the child's perspective. Methodologically, this meant that analysis domains, or coping orientations (Appendix C), were required rather than individual coping strategies (Appendix B). The data came from 95 African American middle school children (third to sixth graders) who were given the closed-ended version of the RST II (Johnson 1994).

The model developed predicted children's racial coping, by domain, from a characteristic of their personality, self-esteem (Bowman and Howard 1985). We expected that children with higher and lower levels of self-esteem might vary in their use of coping strategies and that children's perceptions of violence as victims and witnesses (Fox and Leavitt 1995) would moderate the relationship between self-esteem and racial coping.

Self-esteem was linked to particular racial-coping strategies, especially for older children (fifth to sixth graders), including Conflict Avoidance, Confronting, Forbearance, and Strategic. With respect to these four domains, perceived violence moderated the relation between self-esteem and racial coping. Specifically, context altered the use of conflict avoidance by children with low self-esteem. In the high-violence context these children used the conflict avoidance strategy more than high-self-esteem children did. Of the few children who used the confrontational strategy, most were found to be in the lower self-esteem groups under the condition of low risk. In high-risk environments a child might be more likely to endure bullying/victimization or to be more fearful of such events. Both high- and low-self-esteem children used the forbearance strategy at similar levels. However, the strategy was used more in high-risk environments. Children with low self-esteem in high-risk climates used the Strategic domain more often. Because this strategy/domain is more complex, it was a surprise that low-self-esteem children, who tend to have fewer coping resources, would use a strategy that incorporates a number of person-based resources.

In sum, several conclusions were drawn from these findings. High-self-esteem children appear to use the core strategies in both high- and low-violence contexts but the high-violence context seemed to intensify usage. Across strategies, children with low self-esteem in contexts where they perceive high violence appear to be the most vulnerable. And indeed, children with low self-esteem are particularly vulnerable. They rarely have the protections that higher self-esteem might provide (e.g., enhanced peer and teacher support), and often their racial-coping skills are less sophisticated. These challenges leave them open to stressors in their social ecologies. Finally, low-violence contexts appear to yield the greatest variety of coping among children with low self-esteem. It could be that the least risky environment produced the most opportunities to develop coping skills. High-risk environments for low-self-esteem children may truncate the development of coping skills.

At the community level, there was certainly a relation between violence and the child's coping orientation. In particular, children's perceptions of their social ecologies are most powerful for younger children, as the model was primarily not significant for the older group. More important, the child was an actor on his or her own behalf, and the child's perspective proved a powerful lens. What children see and process on a daily basis appears to influence their coping choices and how they perceive racial issues, and ultimately, their opportunities, attitudes, and skills shape their race-related coping development. Finally, the use of racial-coping domains increased the power of individual strategies and further crystallized children's racial coping.

Insights and Wisdoms: Measurement and Method

The Research Content: Learning from Mixed Methods

Because the study of racial socialization remains in its infancy, there are many roads from here. One of the more obvious pathways to be considered, at least from a research standpoint, is how to design projects that create linkages between the various levels and contexts of children's racial socialization. These contexts have been presented as separate entities that have singular effects on the development of racial-coping skills. However, in the life experiences of children these contexts overlap and may in some instances be mediated through other levels (e.g., institutions or persons). For example, children's racial coping can be influenced by parental participation in school events and their positive interactions with school personnel. From other research we know that community context affects parenting, parenting style, and even the goals of parenting. If these were accounted for simultaneously in a design, we might increase our understanding of the more complex nature of the parental racial socialization context. These are just some examples of the relations between contexts that may affect children's coping.

It is important to address the "so what?" question. Although the studies reviewed in this chapter are all interesting and add to the literature, "so what?" Maybe we were able to tell parents a few new things about parenting and their children's ecology and may have uncovered a few intriguing mechanics—again, "so what?" The added value of this research comes from its implications for systemic change and changes in policy (Danziger and Chih 2000). The power of the work is that it can inform schools about how they can better teach children social-problem-solving skills that include race as a focal point. However, in order for child training to be effective, the school and community climates must be considered. This may push the school beyond typical concerns. Some families have healthy goals for their children with respect to race issues, but their interactions undermine achievement of those goals. Concerning specific contexts and aspects of coping, parents could be helped to be more effective with their children. In terms of school policy and other policy initiatives, we can impress upon those who design programs for children and families and those who build communities or ignore their destruction that the nature of that community will in a significant way determine competencies of future generations. And certainly, these issues have critical salience for African Americans as well as other children and families of color.

Challenges in the Research

Employing a variety of methodological approaches has advantages and disadvantages. In this section I provide a couple examples of the strengths and weaknesses of mixed methods as the research questions were being addressed and as issues in data collection, measurement, and analytic strategies were being solved. The triangulation of various components from the three studies increases the strength of each study, and collectively certain threats to validity are easily nullified.

Mixed methods and the racial stories task II. In critiquing my own measure, I find the open-ended version of the measure to be superior for a number of reasons, including the broad range of children's responses and better assurance that their responses stem from their reactions to the story. On the downside, preparation of the data for analysis is time intensive and costly and the data collection requires an interviewer. An advantage of the closed-ended version is that it can be self-administered by children. Self-administration takes little time, and scoring is fast and easy. Its potential disadvantages are that children's responses must be chosen from what is provided rather than the universe of possibilities. Each version has a place if the researcher is interested in the construct. The ability to use the RST in these two forms offers flexibility to the researcher to choose given a specific research situation or setting.

Modes of data collection. When looking at research where mixed methods are employed, context responsivity and pragmatism play an enormous part, as has been indicated in the discussions of others (Datta 1997; Greene and Caracelli 1997). Using research components that require the participants to be involved in more than one venue over time creates some unevenness in data collection and reduces the number of children and families whose data could be used to illustrate triangulation of findings within the same study. For example, survey method phone calls may yield more participation than when families have to be taped in the lab or travel to another site for interviews. In the home privacy might be an issue, especially for poorer families. Families of color are often less willing to participate in videotaping than other modes of data collection. Parents were most likely to agree to the child's participation and be willing to complete and return a short demographic questionnaire if the form was simple and the return procedure uncomplicated. However, we lost 65% of African American families when we scheduled a parent-child videotaped observation in the local library. In this session the racial socialization task was videotaped and we also asked children and parents to complete additional measures. In a follow-up mailing of additional measures we recouped 40% of the targeted parents lost to the videotaped session.

While these were less-than-ideal circumstances under which to acquire data, the methods were developed to be sensitive to the needs of largely economically marginal families in an urban setting. Home visits from relative strangers might make many families uncomfortable. Since home visits are normally inexpensive, I had to generate an alternative that was cost effective. Local libraries were a good solution and considered to be familiar to the families, convenient, safe, and quiet places to conduct the research necessary, and they did not tax the budget because the spaces were free. This worked for many families; others were inclined to participate when face-to-face contact was not required. Some families did not appreciate the constraint of having to make an appointment to meet with the investigator. Having other options for these families worked well. Using a variety of methods can change participation across venues and methods. However, greater depth on some indices can be achieved through this multiplicity of measures and interview settings.

On Mixed Methods: New Directions

Looking at racial coping from ecological multilevel vantage points informs us about the development of children's racial coping skills (Garcia Coll et al. 1996). Each level contributes something different to our understanding of the developmental processes, sometimes emphasizing the nature of children's coping in racialized contexts and sometimes informing us about the nature and variation of coping in a context. The convergence of mixed methods on the question of how do children in middle childhood cope facilitated an investigation of the varying influences of micro- and macroprocesses upon their coping. The observational study allowed for a very intricate look at parental influences on children's coping but left questions about how the child's individuality and how other macrofactors, such as culture or characteristics of settings, might determine coping. However, in the settings where more contexts were assessed (school, community violence), there was no sense of daily microprocesses that contribute to the dynamics of the larger context. For instance, although school racial composition as a macroprocess was shown to influence children's coping, we know that it is not composition of itself that accounts for the findings. Rather, it is the thousands of daily interactions that children have in school with their peers, on the way to school on the bus, on the way home walking past the police station, or talking with the teacher during lunch, and the many transactions among those factors, that create the "actions and experiences" assessed in the "thing" measured as racial composition. The ability to address children's racial coping in more depth is made possible by this component approach and because each component or study had the RST in common.

The mixed-methods approach I used here infinitely complicates the work and made describing it more difficult. Furthermore, in spite of the complexity, gaps in our understanding remain. Nevertheless, what has been gained is a kind of mosaic puzzle with a few well-placed pieces forming a discernible picture. Its wholeness is attractive and some of the weaknesses of conducting research this way are tolerable. In the end, the studies converged to demonstrate that we cannot ignore any facet of the child's social world because they critically coalesce on the development of coping competencies and the child's use of those competencies for negotiating race in the world.

Appendix A: Two Sample Vignettes from the Racial Stories Task II

Between-Group Conflict Story

Jacob (Janice) is about your age. (S)He is very smart and his/her classmates really like him/her. Jacob (Janice) is the only Black person in his/her classroom; all of the other children and the teacher are White. Sometimes Jacob (Janice) raises his/her hand to answer the questions the teacher asks. Almost all the time the teacher chooses someone else to answer the question. Jacob (Janice) feels this is unfair because (s)he almost always knows the answer. What should Jacob (Janice) do about this problem?

Within-Group Conflict Story

Raymond (Raymona) is a boy (girl) about your age. Everyday Raymond (Raymona) takes a yellow school bus to a school outside his/her neighborhood where most of the children are White. Raymond's (Raymona's) Black friends in the neighborhood don't want to play with him/her anymore. They say (s)he likes his/her White friends better than his/her Black friends. What should Raymond (Raymona) do about this problem?

Appendix B: Racial Stories Task: Frequencies of RCS by Phase with Gender Differences

Domain	Phase I ($n = 545$)		Phase II ($n = 668$)		Phase III ($n = 698$)	
	n	%	n	%	n	%
Adult authority						
Defer to authority	445	(19.3)	534	(18.9)	263	(8.5)[d]
Proactive competence						
Authoritative directive	18	(0.8)	15	(0.5)	113	(3.7)[d]
Engage authority	50	(2.2)[d]	95	(3.4)[d]	58	(1.9)[d]
Assert selfhood	123	(5.3)	46	(8.7)[d]	307	(9.9)
Explore the problem	31	(1.3)[d]	28	(0.9)	86	(2.8)[c]
Project racial pride	26	(1.1)	23	(0.8)[e]	10	(0.3)[c]
Project superiority	18	(0.8)[e]	16	(0.6)	24	(0.8)
Moral						
Legal reasoning	3	(0.1)	2	(0.0)	63	(2.0)[c]
Moral reasoning ($n - r$)	115	(5.0)	192	(6.8)	167	(5.4)
Moral reasoning (r)	50	(2.2)[e]	98	(6.8)	129	(4.2)[d]
Conflict avoidance						
Avoid or withdraw	247	(10.7)[c]	237	(8.4)	211	(6.8)[d]
Accommodation						
Conform	234	(10.1)[d]	237	(8.4)[d]	81	(2.6)[d]
Forbearance						
Ignore or do nothing	181	(7.8)[c]	280	(9.9)[c]	187	(6.1)[e]
Competence						
Persist	97	(4.2)	85	(3.0)[e]	221	(7.2)[a]
Internalization						
Project inferiority	44	(1.9)	36	(1.2)	54	(1.7)[d]
Negate racial group	31	(1.3)	4	(0.1)	6	(0.1)[b]
Confronting						
Physical confrontation	47	(2.1)[b]	51	(1.8)[e]	18	(0.5)[c]
Verbal confrontation	95	(4.1)	41	(5.0)	69	(2.2)[d]
Support seeking						
Change environment	199	(8.6)[d]	205	(7.3)[d]	63	(2.0)[d]
Develop support systems	162	(7.0)[b]	166	(5.9)	51	(1.7)
Strategic						
Strategic plan	86	(3.7)[c]	128	(4.5)[b]	272	(8.8)[d]
Subvert	3	(0.1)[a]	8	(0.2)	28	(0.9)[c]
Total	2305	(100.0)	2827	(100.0)	3081	(100.0)
RCS						
No racial-coping strategy	277	(10.7)	273	(10.7)	140	(4.3)[d]
Total	2582	(100.0)	3100	(100.0)	3221	(100.0)

Note: Superscripts indicate significant T-tests performed on each variable by gender: [a] $p < .05$, [b] $p < .01$, [c] $p < .001$, [d] $p < .0001$, [e] $p < .10$.

Appendix C: Racial-Coping Domains: Definitions

Adult authority. This dimension is defined by the child's reliance on adult authority for problem solving. The child has in mind that the problem will be resolved or abated by adults working with children or with other adults. The complete confidence of the child in adult authority or power is typified by the child's unspecified conclusion to the event.

Proactive competence. Positive, self-promoting, and self-reflective actions and attitudes are included in this dimension. Central to its theme are the child's ability to think of him/herself as a competent individual in relation to adults and/or children and to provide coping behaviors and attitudes consistent with a self-assured perception of self.

Moral. Humanism, altruism, fairness, righteousness, and social convention are themes of this dimension. The moralistic considerations of children extend to racial and nonracial content and issues of prejudice and discrimination. These behaviors and attitudes also extend to religious doctrine, as well as to their understanding of the social rules and the law.

Conflict avoidance. To escape a difficult, stressful, painful, or otherwise challenging situation, a perhaps fearful child employs avoiding or evasive behaviors designed to avoid confronting others. The child exhibits no particular control over the situation and is more determined to "get away" from the problem.

Forbearance. The child's ability to "pick the fight" by ignoring or walking away from a situation suggests that the child may be exhibiting some competence in this more passive coping dimension. The control/restraint element in this coping dimension is critical in distinguishing it from conflict avoidance.

Support seeking. The strategies which make up this coping dimension reflect efforts to acquire support or to optimize support from specific individuals, especially peers (i.e., develop support systems), or from implied groups of people (i.e., change schools, change neighborhoods, change clubs). In particular, children want to extend or increase their contact with other African Americans.

Conflict confronting. The suggestions of verbally or physically assaultive behaviors as a way of concluding the offensive behaviors of others are indicators of this coping dimension. Verbal assaults typically take the form of quips or return name-calling. The child exhibits competence, but it is a reactive type of competence. Suggestions of physical assaults range from punching, hitting, and slapping to shooting, stabbing, and gang beatings.

Strategic planning. Thoughtful and complex plans are often described in this coping dimension. Children often demonstrate their understanding of adult chains of command to be used to resolve their problem. Others may describe complex plans that are more subversive in nature to accomplish the desired end.

Acknowledgments

National Institutes of Health Grant MH51339 supported part of the research presented in this chapter. My gratitude goes to Andrea G. Hunter for her close reading of the manuscript and to the many children and families who participated in the research described.

References

Black, B. 1992. "Negotiating Social Pretend Play: Communication Differences Related to Social Status and Sex." *Merrill-Palmer Quarterly* 38:212–232.

Black, B., and A. Logan. 1995. "Links between Communication Patterns in Mother-Child, Father-Child, and Child-Peer Interactions and Children's Social Status." *Child Development* 66:255–271.

Bowman, P. J., and C. Howard. 1985. "Race-Related Socialization, Motivation, and Academic Achievement: A Study of Black Youths in Three-Generation Families." *Journal of the American Academy of Child Psychiatry* 24:131–141.

Bradley, R. 1995. "Environment and Parenting." In *Handbook of Parenting: Biology and Ecology of Parenting,* vol. 2, ed. M. Bornstein, 235–262. Mahwah, NJ: Lawrence Erlbaum.

Burton, L. M., K. W. Allison, and D. Obeidallah. 1995. "Social Context and Adolescence: Perspectives on Development among Inner-City African-American Teens." In *Pathways through Adolescence: Individual Development in Relation to Social Contexts,* ed. L. J. Crockett and A. Crouter, 119–138. Penn State Series on Child and Adolescent Development. Hillsdale, NJ: Lawrence Erlbaum.

Cook, T., D. Slaughter-Defoe, and C. Payne. 1990. "Comer School Improvement Project." Evanston, IL: Center for Urban Affairs, Northwestern University.

Cross, W. E. 1991. *Shades of Black.* Philadelphia: Temple University Press.

Danziger, S., and A. Chih, eds. 2000. *Coping with Poverty.* Ann Arbor: University of Michigan Press.

Datta, L. 1994. "Paradigm Wars: A Basis for a Peaceful Coexistence and Beyond." In *The Qualitative-Quantitative Debate: New Perspectives,* ed. C. S. Reichardt and S. Rallis, 53–70. New Directions for Program Evaluation, vol. 61. San Francisco: Jossey-Bass.

———. 1997. "The Pragmatic Basis for Mixed Methods." In *Advances in Mixed Methods Evaluation: The Challenges and Benefits of Diverse Paradigms,* ed. J. Greene and V. J. Caracelli, 33–46. New Directions for Program Evaluation, vol. 74. San Francisco: Jossey-Bass.

Fox, N., and L. A. Leavitt. 1995. "Violence Exposure Index for Children Manual." Unpublished manuscript. University of Maryland, College Park.

Garbarino, J. 1992. *Children and Families in the Social Environment.* 2nd ed. New York: Aldine de Gruyter.

Garbarino, J., K. Kostelny, and N. Dubrow. 1991. *No Place to Be a Child: Growing Up in a War Zone.* Lexington, MA: Lexington Books.

Garcia Coll, C., K. Crnic, G. Lamberty, B. H. Wasik, R. Jenkins, H. V. Garcia, and H. P. McAdoo. 1996. "An Integrative Model for the Study of Developmental Competencies in Minority Children." *Child Development* 67:1891–1914.

Greene, J. C., and V. J. Caracelli, eds. 1997. *Advances in Mixed-Method Evaluation: The Challenges and Benefits of Integrating Diverse Paradigms.* New Directions for Evaluation, vol. 74. San Francisco: Jossey-Bass.

Harrison, A., M. Wilson, C. Pine, S. Chan, and R. Buriel. 1990. "Family Ecologies of Ethnic Minority Children." *Child Development: Special Issue* 61:347–362.

Holiday, B. 1992. *Black Maternal Beliefs.* Unpublished manuscript. Washington, DC.

Hughes, D., and L. Chen. 1997. "When and What Parents Tell Children about Race: An Examination of Race Related Socialization among African American Families." *Applied Developmental Science* 1:200–214.

———. 1999. "The Nature of Parents' Race Related Communications to Children: A Developmental Perspective." In *Child Psychology: A Handbook of Contemporary Issues,* ed. L. Balter and C. S. Tamis-Lemonda, 467–490. Philadelphia: Psychology Press.

Hughes, D., and D. J. Johnson. 2001. "Correlates of Race-Related Messages to Children." *Journal of Marriage and the Family* 63:981–995.

Johnson, D. J. 1988. "Parental Racial Socialization Strategies of Black Parents in Three Private Schools." In *Visible Now: Blacks in Private School,* ed. D. T. Slaughter and D. J. Johnson, 251–267. Westport, CT: Greenwood Press.

———. 1994. "Parental Racial Socialization and Racial Coping among Middle Class Black Children." In *Thirteenth Empirical Conference in Black Psychology,* ed. J. McAdoo, 17–38. East Lansing: Michigan State University.

———. 1996. "The Racial Stories Task: Situational Racial Coping of Black Children." Paper presented at the meeting of the International Society for the Study of Behavioral Development, Quebec City, Quebec, Canada, August.

———. 2001. "Parental Characteristics, Racial Stress and Racial Socialization Processes as Predictors of Racial Coping in Middle Childhood." In *Forging Links: Clinical/Developmental Perspective of African American Children,* ed. A. M. Neal-Barnett, J. Contreras, and K. Kerns, 57–74. Westport, CT: Greenwood Press.

Johnson, D. J., E. Jaeger, S. Randolph, A. Cauce, J. Ward, and NICHD Early Child Care Research Network. 2003. "Studying the Effects of Early Child Care Experiences on the Development of Children of Color in the U.S.: Towards a More Inclusive Agenda." *Child Development* 74:1558–1576.

Johnson, D. J., D. Slaughter-Defoe, L. Pallock, and E. Kim. Forthcoming. "Longitudinal Analysis of the Comer Intervention on Children's Race Related Social and Prosocial Problem Solving."

Kim, E. 1999. "Ethnic Minority Children's Racial Coping: Cultural Context, School Context, and Developmental Processes." Master's thesis, University of Wisconsin—Madison.

Kim, E., D. J. Johnson, and D. T. Slaughter-Defoe. 2002. "Developmental Processes and African American Children's Racial Coping." Unpublished manuscript. Michigan State University.

Ladson-Billings, G. 1994. *Dreamkeepers: Successful Teachers of African American Children.* San Francisco: Jossey-Bass.

Marshall, S. 1995. "Ethnic Socialization of African American Children: Implications for Parenting, Identity Development, and Academic Achievement." *Journal of Youth and Adolescence* 24 : 377–396.

McAdoo, H. P. 1982. "Levels of Stress and Family Support in Black Families." In *Family Stress, Coping, and Social Support,* ed. H. I. McCubbin, A. E. Cauble, and J. M. Patterson, 239–252. Springfield, IL: Thomas Books.

McGuire, W. J., C. V. McGuire, P. Child, and T. Fujimoto. 1978. "Salience of Ethnicity in the Spontaneous Self-Concept as a Function of One's Ethnic Distinctiveness in the Social Environment." *Journal of Personality and Social Psychology* 35 : 63–78.

McLoyd, V., A. Ray, and G. Etter-Lewis. 1985. "Being and Becoming: The Interface of Language and Family Role Knowledge Pretend Play of African American Girls." In *Play, Language, and Stories,* ed. L. Galda and A. Pellegrini, 29–43. New York: Ablex.

Ogbu, J. 1981. "Origins of Human Competence: A Cultural-Ecological Perspective." *Child Development* 52 : 413–429.

Parke, R., and R. Buriel. 1998. "Socialization in the Family: Ethnic and Ecological Perspectives." In *Handbook of Psychology: Social, Emotional, and Personality Development,* 5th ed., vol. 3, ed. W. Damon and N. Eisenburg, 463–552. New York: Wiley.

Peters, M. F. 1985. "Ethnic Socialization of Young Black Children." In *Black Children: Social, Educational, and Parental Environments,* ed. H. P. McAdoo and J. L. McAdoo, 159–173. Newbury Park, CA: Sage.

Peters, M. F., and G. C. Massey. 1983. "Mundane Extreme Environmental Stress in the Family: The Case of the Black Family in White America." In *Stress and the Family: Advances and Developments in Family Stress Theory and Research,* ed. H. I. McCubbin, M. B. Sussman, and J. Patterson, 199–218. New York: Haworth Press.

Phinney, J., and V. Chavira. 1995. "Parental Ethnic Socialization and Adolescent Coping with Problems Related to Ethnicity." *Journal of Research on Adolescence* 5 : 31–54.

Pierce, C. 1975. "The Mundane Extreme Environment and Its Effect on Learning." In *Learning Disabilities: Issues and Recommendations for Research,* ed. S. G. Brainard, 1–28. Washington, DC: National Institute of Education.

Reichardt, C. S., and S. Rallis, eds. 1994. *The Qualitative-Quantitative Debate: New Perspectives.* New Directions for Program Evaluation, vol. 61. San Francisco: Jossey-Bass.

Richeson, J. 2000. "On the Inside, Acting Out: Consequences of Exposure to Counter-Stereotypical Ingroup Member." Paper presented at the African American Scholars in Psychology Conference, University of Michigan, Ann Arbor, October 24–28.

Rumbaut, R. 1994. "The Crucible Within: Ethnic Identity, Self-Esteem, and Segmented Assimilation among Children of Immigrants." *International Migration Review* 28 (4): 748–794.

Sinclair, S., C. D. Hardin, and B. Lowery. 2000. "Self-Stereotyping in the Context of Multiple Social Identities." Paper presented at the African American Scholars in Psychology Conference, University of Michigan, Ann Arbor, October 24–28.

Spencer, M. B. 1985. "Cultural Cognition and Social Cognition as Identity Correlates of Black Children's Personal-Social Development." In *Beginnings: The Social and Affec-*

tive Development of Black Children, ed. M. B. Spencer, G. Brookins, and W. Allen, 215–230. Hillsdale, NJ: Lawrence Erlbaum.

Stevenson, H. C. 1994. "Validation of the Scale of Racial Socialization for African American Adolescents: Steps towards Multidimensionality." *Journal of Black Psychology* 20:445–468.

———. 1995. "Relationships of Adolescent Perceptions of Racial Socialization to Racial Identity." *Journal of Black Psychology* 21:49–70.

Tatum, B. D. 1997. *"Why Are All the Black Kids Sitting Together in the Cafeteria?" and Other Conversations about Race.* New York: Basic Books.

Thornton, M., L. Chatters, R. Taylor, and W. Allen. 1990. "Sociodemographic and Environmental Correlates of Racial Socialization by Black Parents." *Child Development* 61:401–409.

5

Sites of Belonging: Acculturation, Discrimination, and Ethnic Identity among Children of Immigrants

Rubén G. Rumbaut

We define our identity always in dialogue with, sometimes in struggle against, the things that significant others want to see in us. . . . The monological ideal seriously underestimates the place of the dialogical in human life.

Charles Taylor (1992, 33)

"Being American means that you feel like you're the norm," one of my friends tells me. . . . [But] in a splintered society, what does one assimilate to? . . . I want to figure out, more urgently than before, where I belong in this America that's made up of so many subAmericas. I want, somehow, to give up the condition of being a foreigner. . . . I have to make a shift in my innermost ways. I have to translate myself.

Eva Hoffman (1989, 202, 210–211)

My children, who were born in this country of Cuban parents and in whom I have tried to inculcate some sort of *cubanía,* are American through and through. They can be "saved" from their Americanness no more than my parents can be "saved" from their Cubanness. . . . Like other second-generation immigrants, they maintain a connection to their parents' homeland, but it is a bond forged by my experiences rather than their own. For my children Cuba is an enduring, perhaps an endearing, fiction. Cuba is for them as ethereal as the smoke and as persistent as the smell from their grandfather's cigars (which are not even Cuban but Dominican).

Gustavo Pérez Firmat (1994, 5)

My identity is hardly clear-cut. . . . To my parents, I am all American, and the sacrifices they made in leaving Korea . . . pale in comparison to the opportunities those sacrifices gave me. They do not see that I straddle two cultures, nor that I feel displaced in the only country I know. I identify with Americans, but Americans do not identify with me. I've never known what it's like to belong to a community. . . . I know more about Europe than the continent my ancestors unmistakably came from. . . . Though they raised me as an American, my parents expect me to marry someone Korean and give them grandchildren who look like them. . . . My parents didn't want their daughter to be Korean, but they don't want her fully American, either. Children of immigrants are living paradoxes. We are the first generation and the last. We are in this country for its opportunities, yet filial duty binds us. When my parents boarded the plane . . . I don't think they imagined the rocks in the path of their daughter who can't even pronounce her own name.

Carolyn Hwang (1998, 16)

What a difference half a century makes. Oscar Handlin's *The Uprooted,* a popular portrait of immigrant America by the leading immigration historian of his time, was published 50 years ago. From his vantage at midcentury, as he wrote in a postscript to the second edition two decades later, immigration was already "a dimly remote memory, generations away, which had influenced the past but appeared unlikely to count for much in the present or future," and ethnicity, not a common word in 1950, seemed then "a fading phenomenon, a quaint part of the national heritage, but one likely to diminish steadily in practical importance" (1973, 274–275). After all, the passage of restrictive national-origins laws in the 1920s, the Great Depression, and World War II had combined to reduce the flow of immigrants to the United States to its lowest point since the 1820s. But history is forever being ambushed by the unexpected. As it turned out, the so-called American century ended much as it had begun: the United States has again become a nation of immigrants, and it has again been transformed in the process. Today, the phenomena of immigration and ethnicity are anything but fading and decreasing in importance: there are now over 30 million immigrants residing in the United States, the largest total ever, and their U.S.-born children number around 30 million more, so that today more than 20% of Americans—and half of all Californians—are of "foreign stock." They hail overwhelmingly from Asia, Latin America, and the Caribbean this time, not from Europe. Never before has the United States received such diverse groups, immigrants who mirror in their origins and destinies the forces that forged a new world order in the second half of the 20th century, and who are, unevenly, engaged in the process of trying to figure out where they belong in this America that is made up of so many sub-Americas.

The increasing size and concentration of the foreign-born population, added to its extraordinarily diverse national and socioeconomic origins and modes of incorporation, have raised significant questions about the impact of immigration on American society and led to a burgeoning research literature. Less noticed in that literature, however, or in the public debates swirling about the topic, has been the fact that a new generation of Americans raised in immigrant families has been coming of age—transforming their adoptive society even as they themselves are being transformed into the newest Americans. Over time, its members will decisively shape the character of their ethnic communities, even as the larger society that receives them will decisively shape their own ethnic identities. The long-term effects of contemporary immigration will hinge more on the pathways and trajectories of these youths than on the fate of their parents.

Yet we know surprisingly little about them (it did not help that the critical question on parental nativity was dropped from the last three censuses, pulling the rug out from under the study of intergenerational mobility at the very moment that a new era of mass immigration was rapidly taking hold). Consider, for example, this handful of fundamental empirical questions: Among children of immigrants, what are their patterns of English- versus non-English-language use, preference, and proficiency? Is there any evidence of English-language assimilation over time among different national-origin groups? Is there a similar assimilative shift over time in their ethnic self-identities and sense of belonging? If so, what explains it? If not, how *do* they identify? Is ethnic identity mainly a function of filial-familial attachments, degree of acculturation, experiences of discrimination, or other factors?

Mixed Methods in the Contextualized Study of Ethnic Identity

In the Children of Immigrants Longitudinal Study (CILS), described in this chapter, I have extracted a great deal of analytical mileage on ethnic self-identity and the factors that shape it from a single open-ended question asked at two points in time, three years apart, in mostly structured surveys of a large representative sample of adolescent children of immigrants coming of age on both coasts of the United States. Those surveys were comprehensive in scope and supplemented by separate interviews with their parents, in which we were able to ask some similarly worded questions for comparative analysis, including items on racial self-identification. Moreover, the sampling frame on which the study is based allows us to generalize our findings to the population universes from which the samples were drawn, enhancing the utility of our results. Nonetheless, I remain keenly aware of the limitations involved in this analysis—both substantively and methodologically—and of the value added by the use of mixed methods in the contextualized study of ethnic identity.

Ethnic self-identities can be understood as "definitions of the situation of the self." For children of immigrants, they emerge from the interplay of racial and ethnic labels and categories imposed by the external society and the original identifications and ancestral attachments asserted by the newcomers. They are contextually malleable and may be hypothesized to vary across different social situations, across different developmental stages throughout the life course, and across different historical contexts. Our survey instruments could not examine the situational contexts in which ethnic self-identities may be differentially deployed; yet, in theory, the way an ethnic identity may be expressed in one's presentation of self—indeed, of multiple selves—can differ depending on one's audience. For instance, it is possible in principle to identify as "Chicano" with one's peers, as "Mexican American" in varying secondary relations, as "Hispanic" in filling out official forms, as "Mexican" with one's parents at home . . . and ironically as "American" not in the United States but when making a visit to Mexico to see relatives who might focus on the poor Spanish or other insignia of "Americanization" that make the U.S.-based visitor suddenly conscious of cultural differences vis-à-vis his or her Mexican counterparts. These kinds of contextual influences on the definition and presentation of the self suggest that mixed-methods work on ethnic identity should be an essential part of a comprehensive view. At the conclusion of this chapter, I discuss some of our current research that involves such mixed-methods work.

Furthermore, we surveyed our respondents from their mid- to their late teens. But adolescence is, among other things, a developmental period of "identity crisis" and identity formation; the results reported here are thus limited to that period of the life course and may not apply to samples of, say, middle-aged adults with children of their own, in whom they may be trying to inculcate a sense of ethnic attachment (an issue echoed by the quotations from Pérez Firmat and Hwang above). And as seen especially among Mexican-origin respondents with respect to reactive self-identifications expressed in the aftermath of the Proposition 187 campaign in California (discussed in what follows), the larger sociopolitical and historical context matters. But our surveys were limited to the same locales (in California and Florida) in the mid-1990s.

Methodologically, the quantified coded responses given by thousands of individuals from dozens of diverse national origins in our surveys revealed a handful of distinct patterns that advance our explanation of complex processes of self-identification. But they do not tell us much about the (likely varying) *subjective meanings* that particular ethnic or racial labels may have had for individual respondents. Ethnicity is likely to some degree to be racialized in the respondents' own notions of these modes of group identity (as noted in William Cross's Commentary in this volume). For that matter, there is a strong possibility that the same label (e.g., "Latino") may take on different meanings for the same individual at a later time (e.g., in young adulthood) or in different circumstances (e.g., in college) (see chapters 1 and 11 in this volume). Such considerations underscore the need to both broaden and deepen our research by incorporating mixed methods as appropriate to get at those dimensions of varying subjectivity and situationality and to facilitate a more thoroughly contextualized study of ethnic identity and social belonging. In particular, mixed-methods considerations suggest the need to extend our study longitudinally into adulthood and to complement the survey methods we have employed in CILS — and the representative sample on which the study is based — with in-depth qualitative interviews, oral histories, and targeted ethnographies. In the following sections of the chapter, I lay out my research design and key findings on ethnic identity. In a final section I return to further work using mixed methods grounded in the survey studies.

The CILS Study and Sample Characteristics

The Children of Immigrants Longitudinal Study (CILS) has followed the progress of a large sample of youths representing 77 nationalities in two main areas of immigrant settlement in the United States: Southern California (San Diego) and South Florida (the Miami and Fort Lauderdale metropolitan area). The initial survey, conducted in spring 1992 ("T1"), interviewed 5,262 students enrolled in the eighth and ninth grades in schools of the San Diego Unified School District ($n = 2,420$) and of the Dade and Broward County Unified School Districts ($n = 2,635$, with another 207 enrolled in private bilingual schools in the Miami area). The sample was drawn from the junior high grades, when dropping out of school is rare, to avoid the potential bias of differential dropout rates between ethnic groups at the senior high school level. Students were eligible to enter the sample if they had been born in the United States but had at least one immigrant (foreign-born) parent or if they themselves were foreign born and had come to the United States at an early age (before age 10). The resulting sample is evenly balanced between males and females and between foreign-born (the 1.5 generation) and U.S.-born children of immigrants (the second generation) (for details see Rumbaut 1994).

Three to four years later, in 1995–1996, a second survey ("T2") of the same panel of children of immigrants was conducted—this time supplemented by in-depth interviews with a stratified sample of their parents. The purpose of this follow-up effort, which succeeded in re-interviewing 82% of the baseline sample, was to ascertain changes over time in their family situation, school achievement, educational and occupational aspirations, language use and preferences, ethnic identities, experiences and expectations of discrimination, and psychosocial adjustment. By this time the youths, who were originally interviewed in junior high when most were 14 years old, had reached the final year of senior high school (or had dropped out of school); most were 17–18 years old at the time of the T2 survey. (The study, still ongoing, returned to the field in 2001–2003 ["T3"], a decade after the baseline survey, with the respondents now in their midtwenties and in many cases located across the country; while results were not available at this writing, preliminary findings—this time adding indepth, open-ended oral histories to survey methods of data collection—will be noted toward the end of the chapter.)

As shown in table 5.1, the principal nationalities represented in the San Diego CILS sample are Mexican, Filipino, Vietnamese, Laotian, Cambodian, and smaller groups of other children of immigrants from Asia (mostly Chinese, Japanese, Korean, and Indian) and Latin America. In the South Florida CILS sample, the principal national-origin groups consist of Cubans, Haitians, Jamaicans, Nicaraguans, Colombians, Dominicans, and others from Latin America and the Caribbean. The modest family origins of many of these children, the highly educated backgrounds of the parents of others, and their varying patterns of employment and homeownership are all reflected in the sample. For example, only a small proportion of Mexican and Indochinese fathers and mothers had college degrees, well below the

Table 5.1. Size, Location, and Family Socioeconomic Status by National Origin
of Respondents

		Location of CILS sample		
National origin	Size of sample (n)	Miami/Fort Lauderdale, FL (n)	San Diego, CA (n)	SES Ranking[a]
Latin America:				
Mexico	755	28	727	0.269
Cuba (private school)	182	182	0	0.612
Cuba (public school)	1,044	1,042	2	0.455
Nicaragua	344	340	4	0.443
Colombia	227	223	4	0.451
Dominican Republic	104	100	4	0.416
Other Latin America	366	311	55	0.474
Haiti and West Indies:				
Haiti	178	177	1	0.382
Jamaica, West Indies	272	253	19	0.484
Asia:				
Philippines	819	11	808	0.516
Vietnam	370	8	362	0.342
Laos (Lao)	155	1	154	0.233
Laos (Hmong)	53	0	53	0.103
Cambodia	95	1	94	0.172
Chinese	72	23	49	0.501
Other Asia	100	22	78	0.551
All other countries[b]	126	120	6	0.559
Total	5,262	2,842	2,420	0.424

Source: Children of Immigrants Longitudinal Study.
[a]Composite index (0 to 1) of father's and mother's education, occupational prestige, and homeownership.
[b]Of these 126 respondents, 88 are of European or Canadian origin, and 38 hail from the Middle East or Africa.

1990 U.S. norm of 20% for adults 25 and over. By contrast, 41% of Filipino mothers had college degrees, well above national norms. The contrast is made even sharper by the proportion of parents with less than a high school education—that is, less than what their children have now already achieved. Most of the more recently arrived foreign-born children from Mexico, Haiti, Vietnam, Laos, and Cambodia had fathers and mothers who never completed secondary-level schooling. Rates of labor force participation varied widely by nationality for both fathers and mothers: the Indochinese had very low rates of labor force participation, indicative of their eligibility for and use of public assistance, whereas most of the other groups had labor force participation rates that exceed national norms. And there was a huge gap between ethnic groups in their proportion of home-owners, ranging in 1995 from a low of 4% among Hmong families from Laos and 8% among Cambodians to over 80% among Filipinos.

Table 5.1 provides a socioeconomic status (SES) ranking of the major ethnic groups in the CILS sample, as measured in 1992 by a standardized composite index of father's and mother's education, occupational prestige, and homeownership. These standardized scores are transformed to a scale of 0 to 1, with higher scores indicating higher parental SES. As these rank-ings show, most advantaged were Cuban-origin students attending private schools in Miami (with a score of 0.612), followed by groups from Europe, Canada, the Middle East, and Africa (0.559), "other Asia" (0.551), the Fil-ipinos (0.516) and the Chinese (0.501). In the middle, with SES scores hov-ering around the sample average of 0.424, were the Jamaicans and other West Indians and all other Latin American groups except Mexico. At the bottom were the Haitians (0.382) and Mexicans (0.269) and all of the Southeast Asian refugee groups: the Vietnamese (0.342), Lao (0.233), Cam-bodian (0.172), and Hmong (0.103).

Immigrant Families and Forms of Parent-Child Acculturation

Among these groups, there are also significant differences in family struc-ture and in the character of parent-child relationships. Growing up in im-migrant families is often marked by *dissonant acculturation,* when linguis-tic and other acculturative gaps develop between parents and children that can exacerbate intergenerational conflicts, cause the children to feel em-barrassed rather than proud of their parents as they try to fit in with native peers, or lead to role reversals, as children assume adult roles prematurely by dint of circumstance. There are other types of intergenerational adap-tation; for example, we have also identified and distinguished between *consonant* and *selective acculturation* (Portes and Rumbaut 1996, 2001). But all immigrant families must contend not only with the "generation gaps" and the "storm and stress" of adolescence but with acculturation to a new society as well.

Table 5.2 shows several key objective and subjective indices of family structure and parent-child relations, broken down by national origin and the children's level of acculturation and language ability. "Intact Fam-ily" in table 5.2 refers to those cases in which both biological parents were present at both the 1992 and 1995–1996 surveys (61%). Table 5.2 also

Table 5.2.   Family Structure and Perceptions of Family Relationships, 1995–1996, by National Origin and Children's Acculturation and Language Ability

	Intact family[a] (%)	Family cohesion[b] (% high)	Parent-child conflict[c] (% high)	Embarrassed by parents[d] (%)	Familism[e] (% high)
National origin:					
Cuba (private school)	69.5	41.1	35.6	26.7	24.0
Cuba (public school)	55.1	35.8	38.3	28.9	24.3
Dominican Republic	46.1	38.5	35.9	14.1	24.4
Mexico	55.4	38.6	32.2	14.2	31.2
Nicaragua	58.4	42.0	31.7	21.7	25.6
Colombia	57.3	37.3	35.1	23.2	28.6
Other Latin America	59.3	40.4	33.9	28.9	24.3
Haiti	42.2	22.2	57.0	41.5	31.1
Jamaica	39.0	28.8	39.8	22.0	24.6
Other West Indies	42.2	30.1	41.0	38.6	20.5
Vietnam	71.3	27.7	49.4	38.1	43.9
Laos (Lao)	70.8	32.6	42.4	30.6	50.0
Laos (Hmong)	56.0	30.0	66.0	48.0	46.0
Cambodia	60.7	24.7	55.1	43.8	33.7
Philippines	76.9	28.6	46.7	33.7	24.3
Chinese, other Asia	77.4	34.2	37.4	52.3	21.9
Europe, Canada	59.6	28.1	26.3	35.1	21.0
$p =$	<.001	<.001	<.001	<.001	<.001
Acculturation index:[f]					
Low (<0.33)	60.4	42.2	34.5	18.1	37.3
Middle (0.50)	61.4	35.7	37.2	24.7	28.3
High (>0.66)	61.9	29.6	43.9	36.9	24.4
$p =$	N.S.	<.001	<.001	<.001	<.001
Language dominance:[g]					
Fluent bilingual	58.8	47.0	30.6	21.3	23.0
English dominant	64.5	27.9	43.1	36.1	23.5
Foreign language dominant	54.2	42.7	33.3	17.4	42.1
Limited bilingual	61.9	26.3	48.6	31.3	37.8
$p =$	<.001	<.001	<.001	<.001	<.001
Total	61.4	34.0	39.9	29.3	28.2

Source: CILS (longitudinal sample, $n = 4,288$).

Note: N.S. = not significant.

[a] Both biological parents present in the home at both surveys.

[b] High score (>4.0) in three-item family cohesion index; items measured from 1 to 5.

[c] High score (>2.0) in four-item parent-child conflict index; items measured from 1 to 4.

[d] Embarrassed or ambivalent over parents' ways.

[e] High score (>2.0) in three-item familial obligations index; items measured from 1 to 4.

[f] Score on composite index of child's preferences for English language and American ways reported at both surveys.

[g] Based on scores in English proficiency and foreign-language proficiency indices, 1995–1996.

provides information on four subjective dimensions of the parent-child relationship: family cohesion, parent-child conflict, embarrassment over parents' ways, and attitudes of familial obligation (for details on these scales, see Rumbaut 1994). As noted above, immigrant families and groups can be located along a continuum ranging from situations where parental authority is fully preserved to those where it is thoroughly undermined by generational gaps in acculturation—particularly in English knowledge and the extent to which second-generation youth retain their parents' language. In operational terms these patterns should be reflected in the degree of intergenerational cohesion or conflict between immigrant parents and their children and the extent to which these youths report being embarrassed by their parents or attached to them by filial duty.

The results in table 5.2 show that Asian-origin families are comparatively more likely to remain intact (the low-SES Hmong and Cambodian refugees are the main exceptions among Asian groups in this regard, in part as a result of a greater proportion of widowed mothers than other groups). The Dominicans are the only Latin American nationality to exhibit the pattern of high family structural instability seen among the Haitians and West Indians. As table 5.2 shows, there is no significant association between family structure and the youths' level of acculturation. But a different picture emerges when we examine the various subjective indices of family integration. Without exception, the Latin American nationalities exhibit the most cohesive families as well as the lowest levels of parent-child conflict. Most of the Latin groups also exhibit lower proportions of youths who report being embarrassed by their parents, with the lowest (14%) found among two groups of modest SES, the Mexicans and the Dominicans. Indeed, a Spanish-language background was the strongest predictor of fluent bilingualism in our sample, indicative not only of the significant advantage of Spanish speakers relative to other languages in this sample but also of its association with consonant or selective forms of acculturation among parents and children of Latin American origin. By contrast, all of the Asian, European/Canadian, and black Caribbean groups fell below the sample average in their percentage of high-cohesion families; and nearly all of the Asian and black Caribbean groups scored above the sample average for high-conflict families. Overall, those families were more strongly associated with patterns of dissonant acculturation. However, the same rank order was not seen with the remaining index of familism. The youths who most strongly adhered to attitudes granting primacy to familial obligations were the Southeast Asians (especially the Laotians and the Vietnamese) and the Mexicans. The least familistic (i.e., those more oriented to individualistic, rather than collectivistic, outlooks) were the Europeans and Canadians, most of the Latin Americans and the West Indians, and the Filipinos, Chinese/other Asians.

But as table 5.2 underscores, all of the four subjective family indices were strongly associated with the youth's level of acculturation and language dominance. The acculturation index is a composite measure of the child's preferences for the English language and for American ways as reported at both surveys (a score of 0 indicates that no preference for either was reported at either survey, while a maximum score of 1 indicates that a preference for both was reported at both surveys). The typology of language dominance is based on the youths' varying levels of proficiency in both English and the parental language. The data show that as the youth's level of acculturation increases — and, by implication, as acculturative gaps widen and the degree of intergenerational dissonance increases — the level of parent-child conflict and of embarrassment over parents' ways increases, while that of family cohesion and of familistic attitudes decreases. Conversely, greater family cohesion and familism are associated with lesser acculturative preferences for English and American ways — and, by implication, with consonant acculturation in intergenerational relations.

These patterns are clearly graphed in figure 5.1 and are reinforced by the data on language dominance. Youths classified as English dominant and limited bilinguals (i.e., who are not fluent in the parental language) exhibit much higher parental conflict and embarrassment profiles and much lower family cohesion than do youths classified as fluent bilinguals and

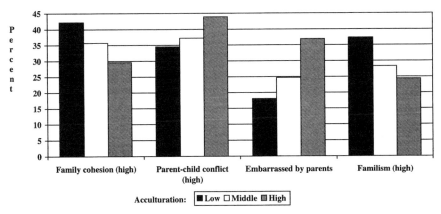

Figure 5.1. Family indices and level of acculturation, 1995–1996. Probability of differences being due to chance is less than 1 in 1,000 for all associations shown. Level of acculturation is measured from a composite index of child's preferences for the English language and American ways reported at both surveys. See text for details of family indices.

foreign-language dominants (i.e., who are fluent in the parental language). Significantly, the familism pattern diverges here. The fluent bilinguals and English dominants (those who are fluent in English and most acculturated) are the least familistic, while the limited bilinguals and foreign-language dominants (those who are neither fluent in English nor highly acculturated) are much more likely to adhere to familistic attitudes.

Language Maintenance and Language Shift

Over 90 % of these children of immigrants reported speaking a language other than English at home, mostly with their parents. But at the T1 survey in 1992 already 73 % of the total sample preferred to speak English instead of their parents' native tongue, including 64 % of the foreign-born youth and 81 % of the U.S.-born youth. By the T2 survey three to four years later, the proportion who preferred English had swelled to 88 %, including 83 % of the foreign born and 93 % of the U.S. born. Even among the Mexican-origin youth living in San Diego—a city on the Mexican border with a large Spanish-speaking immigrant population and a wide range of Spanish-language radio and TV stations—the force of linguistic assimilation was incontrovertible: while at T1 only a third (32 %) of the Mexico-born children preferred English, by T2 that preference had doubled to 61 %; and while just over half (53 %) of the U.S.-born Mexican-Americans in San Diego preferred English at T1, that proportion had jumped to four-fifths (79 %) three years later. More decisively still, among Cuban-origin youth in Miami, 95 % of both the foreign born and the native born preferred English by T2.

A main reason for this rapid shift in language use and preference has to do with the youths' increasing fluency in English (both spoken and written) relative to their level of fluency in the mother tongue. Respondents were asked to evaluate their ability to speak, understand, read, and write in both English and the non-English mother tongue; the response format (identical to the item used in the U.S. census) ranged from "not at all" and "not well" to "well" and "very well." Over three-fourths of the total sample at both T1 and T2 reported speaking English "very well," compared to only about a third who reported an equivalent level of spoken fluency in the non-English language. Even among the foreign born, the percentage of those who spoke English very well (69 %) surpassed those who spoke the foreign language just as well (41 %). And the differences in reading fluency were greater still: those who could read English "very well" tripled the proportion of those who could read a non-English language very well (78 % vs. 24 %).

As a consequence, the bilingualism of these children of immigrants becomes increasingly uneven and unstable. The CILS data underscore the rapidity with which English triumphs and foreign languages atrophy in the United States, as the second generation not only comes to speak, read, and write it fluently but overwhelmingly prefers it to their parents' native tongue. It bears adding that these results have occurred while the youths were still residing as dependents in their parents' home, where the non-English mother tongue retains primacy; once they leave the parental fold to lead independent lives of their own, the degree of English-language dominance and non-English-language atrophy is almost certain to accelerate, all the more among those living outside dense immigrant enclaves.

But what about their sense of identity, of belonging and ethnic loyalty? Does it too shift rapidly, like language, in straight-line fashion toward dominant American models as these youths seek to fit in with their new social settings? In the jargon of sociology, what is their "definition of the situation"? Perhaps the best way to begin this analysis is with a story.

The Question of Identity

In Los Angeles a few years ago, a well-acculturated Southern California native and high school senior, Stephanie Bernal, thought of herself as a "mixed chocolate swirl." Half Latin and half Anglo by her reckoning, she had not had more than a fleeting connection with Mexico, her mother's homeland, until Proposition 187 exacerbated ethnic tensions in California in the fall of 1994. The measure aimed to "Save Our State" by denying social and nonemergency health care services—and access to public schools—to undocumented immigrants and their children. It also required school districts to verify the legal status of students' parents or guardians and to report to state officials any persons suspected of being in the United States unlawfully so that they could be detained and deported. Stephanie reacted by joining with friends who were organizing her school's anti-187 movement and by affirming, even reveling in, the identity of her maternal ancestry: "When we get together to talk about it, we speak Spanish and just feel good about being Mexican" (Pyle and Romero 1994).

The week before, more than 70,000 people had marched in protest through downtown Los Angeles—the largest such march in memory, which was heavily covered on television and by the news media—spawning subsequent marches and student walkouts on local campuses. To the marchers, who included many second-generation youths from area high schools,

Proposition 187 was an affront to their parents, friends, and neighbors, according to local news accounts of the events at the time (McDonnell 1994; Navarrette 1994; Pyle and Romero 1994). Parents too joined in some of the marches or encouraged their children's participation, making the initiative an issue through which the budding teenage activists could bridge the generational divide and express themselves in solidarity with their parents.

Proposition 187 was attacked by activists as a measure which would invite if not incite pejorative stereotyping and discrimination against anyone fitting a "brown" racial profile. The initiative was being advanced in a context of rising anxiety about the changing racial-ethnic composition of California, which, it was regularly noted, was expected to become the nation's first "majority minority" state shortly after the year 2000. Referring to "that commercial," a frequently repeated ad on television which showed people running across the California-Mexico border, sophomore Jorge Higareda complained that "they show Mexicans, but they don't show Asians coming over in boats or anybody else. It's like we're the only ones coming here. And then they call us illegal." Students at another high school insisted that "this is mostly a Latino school and everyone's proud of their heritage—they want to defend it." In yet another over 200 students walked out of school in protest; and, as in the huge march that had preceded it, the teenagers carried banners saying "No on 187" and waved Mexican flags (Pyle and Romero 1994).

The red, white, and green flags were meant as a spontaneous show of pride and self-validation by people who felt that their Mexican heritage was under siege; but to non-Latino voters the flags were seen as symbols of anti-American defiance and of suspicious allegiance to a foreign country. A former Marine, watching the high school marchers, reacted with anger: "You see these kids walking down the street with a Mexican flag and demanding that this country give them a free education. It aggravates people." But a 15-year-old sophomore, Mariela Flores, shot back: "Why should we carry American flags when this country wants to kick my friends out of school and send them back to Mexico? We carry Mexican flags because they give us pride in where we come from" (Banks 1994).

Proposition 187 won in a landslide, getting 59% of the statewide vote; in populous San Diego and Orange Counties, south of Los Angeles, the measure passed with 67% of the votes cast. But Stephanie's Mexican ethnic self-identity was "thickened" in the process, a sense of belonging made more salient than ever as she came to define who she was and where she came from in opposition to who and what she was not. The divisive campaign had the unintended consequences of accentuating group differences, heightening group consciousness of those differences, hardening ethnic identity boundaries between "us" and "them," and promoting ethnic-group solidarity and political mobilization.

Modes of Ethnic Identity Formation

This process of forging a *reactive ethnicity* in the face of perceived threats, persecution, discrimination, and exclusion is not uncommon. On the contrary, it is one mode of ethnic identity formation, highlighting the role of a hostile context of reception in accounting for the rise rather than the erosion of ethnicity (see Aleinikoff and Rumbaut 1998; Portes and Rumbaut 1996). A few years earlier, for example, second-generation Korean-Americans saw over 2,300 Korean-owned stores in Los Angeles' Koreatown targeted by African Americans and burned during the rioting that followed a "not guilty" verdict in the 1992 trial of four white police officers charged with the brutal beating of a black motorist. The event caused many young Koreans born or raised in the United States to become self-conscious about their common fate and distinctiveness as Koreans. They reacted by participating in multi-generational solidarity rallies and by moving to organize politically to protect the interests of the parent generation and the image of the group in the larger society (Min 1995; Bozorgmehr, Sabagh, and Light 1996).

In contrast, conventional accounts of ethnic identity shifts among the descendants of European immigrants, conceived as part of a larger, linear process of assimilation, have pointed to the "thinning" of their ethnic self-identities in the United States. For them, one outcome of widespread acculturation, social mobility, and intermarriage with the native population is that ethnic identity became an optional, leisure-time form of "symbolic" ethnicity (Alba 1990; Gans 1979; Waters 1990). As the boundaries of those identities become fuzzier and less salient, less relevant to everyday social life, the sense of belonging and connection to an ancestral past faded "into the twilight of ethnicity" (Alba 1985).

This mode of ethnic identity formation, however, was never solely a simple linear function of SES and the degree of acculturation—that is, of the development of linguistic and other cultural similarities with the dominant group—but hinged also on the context of reception and the degree of discrimination experienced by the subordinate group. Gordon, in his seven-stage portrayal of assimilation in American life, saw "identificational assimilation"—a self-definition as an "unhyphenated" American—as the culmination of a complex sequence made possible only if and when it was accompanied by an absence of prejudice and discrimination in the core society (Gordon 1964; Warner and Srole 1945). Whether ethnicity will become similarly optional—a matter of individual choice—for the descendants of immigrants who are today variously classified as nonwhite, or whether they will be collectively channeled into enduring, engulfing, racially marked subordinate statuses and forge oppositional identities, remain open empirical questions.

Drawing on the European experience and on the eve of the new immigration from Asia and Latin America, the prevailing view of the matter was framed succinctly by Nahirny and Fishman: "the erosion of ethnicity and ethnic identity experienced by most (but not all) American ethnic groups takes place in the course of three generations . . . ethnic heritage, including the ethnic mother tongue, usually ceases to play any viable role in the life of the third generation" (Nahirny and Fishman 1996, 266). However, compared to language loyalty and language shift, generational shifts in ethnic self-identification are far more conflictual and complex. To those authors the "murky concept of ethnic identification" did not lend itself to intergenerational analysis along a unidimensional attitudinal continuum, since "fathers, sons, and grandsons may differ among themselves not only in the *degree* but also in the *nature* of their identification with ethnicity" (Nahirny and Fishman 1996, 267).

Thus, paradoxically, despite rapid acculturation, as reflected in the abandonment of the parental language and other ethnic patterns of behavior, the second generation were *more* conscious of their ethnic identity than were their immigrant parents. The parents' ethnic identity was "so much taken for granted and accepted implicitly" that they were scarcely explicitly aware of it, but the marginality of their children made them acutely self-conscious and sensitive to their ethnicity, "especially when passing through adolescence." Moreover, at least under reigning conditions of dissonant acculturation, "the generational discontinuity between the formative experiences and dominant environments of most immigrant fathers and sons rendered the family ineffective as an agency for the transmission of traditional ethnicity. So pronounced was this generational gap that by the time the sons reached adolescence the immigrant family had become transformed into two linguistic sub-groups segregated along generational lines." Finally, by the third generation "the grandsons became literally outsiders to their ancestral heritage," and their ethnic past was an object of symbolic curiosity more than anything else. "There was no doubt about the national identity of the grandsons—they were simply Americans of one particular (if not mixed) ethnic ancestry. Neither was there any trace left of the 'wounded identity' of the sons, for in contrast with the sons, the grandsons had never experienced the full brunt of marginality" (Nahirny and Fishman 1996, 277–278).

Complex Allegiances and Contrasting Identities

Indeed, as is the case with respect to language maintenance and language shift, the decisive turning point for change in ethnic and national self-identities can be expected to take place in the second, not in the first, generation. For the children, the process of "becoming American" today has itself taken a new turn and may now include the adoption or rejection of such officially constructed pan-ethnic categories as "Hispanic" and "Asian / Pacific Islander," which lump together scores of nationalities into one-size-fits-all minority-group labels. Relative to the first generation, the process of ethnic self-identification of foreign-born immigrant children and U.S.-born children of immigrants is more complex and often entails the juggling of competing allegiances and attachments. Situated within two cultural worlds, they must define themselves in relation to multiple reference groups (sometimes in two countries and in two languages) and to the classifications into which they are placed by their native peers, the schools, the ethnic community, and the larger society.

Pressure from peers and from parents can tauten the tug-of-war of ethnic and national loyalties, contributing unwittingly to a sense of marginality. This state of affairs can be further complicated when identities are racialized, group boundaries are sharpened by a visible color line, and the metaphorical definition of who one is on the "inside" conflicts with the definition of who one is on the "outside," raising questions about the "authenticity" of either identity and doubts about fully belonging to any group. Thus, for example, a young Korean woman feels the sting of being called a "twinkie" ("yellow on the outside, white on the inside") by coethnics during her freshman year in college "just because I grew up in a white suburb and was a cheerleader," while her mother does not let her forget that she has to marry a Korean (she had a dream in English that she was "dating a non-Korean guy and my dad showed up speaking Korean"). More complicated is the identity juggling act of 17-year-old José Mendoza, a U.S.-born, Spanish-speaking Dominican who is not black enough for many African Americans, not light enough for most Hispanics, and advised by parents to "marry light." The way he figures it, "From the inside we're Dominicans;

from the outside we're black." And while with his friends he talks mostly in "black Spanglish"—a mix of Spanish and hip-hop English—he feels that "I'm still part Dominican. That's my nationality. If you become African American you give your nationality away. That's like saying you're betraying your country" (Escobar 1999).

To their parents, who came of age before they came to America, such concerns are almost entirely irrelevant. Immigrants who arrive as adults seldom lose their original linguistic allegiances or accents, even while learning English; neither, for that matter, do they readily shed their homeland memories and self-images, even after becoming naturalized American citizens. On the contrary, they come with preexisting and fully formed identities, along with their hopes for the future. Their experience of migration, nostalgia for the homeland, desire to instill in their children a sense of pride in their cultural heritage, and anxiety over their children's rapid Americanization may all actually deepen the parents' own sense of identification with "home," perhaps most poignantly among exiles and sojourners who migrate reluctantly and sustain ritually affirmed hopes of an eventual return. The central theoretical and empirical question is rather what happens to their children and, specifically, how they come to define their ethnic identities and sites of belonging, particularly during their passages to adulthood—the youthful years of "identity crisis" and heightened self-consciousness when the self-concept is most malleable (Erikson 1968; Rosenberg 1965; Phinney 1990). That developmental process can be complicated for U.S.-reared children of immigrants by experiences of intense acculturative and generational conflicts as they strive to adapt in American contexts that may be racially and culturally dissonant, and in family contexts where the differential acculturation of parents and children may take a variety of forms.

Youths see and compare themselves in relation to those around them, based on their social similarity or dissimilarity with the reference groups that most directly affect their experiences—especially with regard to such socially visible and categorized markers as gender, phenotype, accent, language, name, and nationality (Tajfel 1981). Their social identities, forged in terms of those contrasts with others, represent the way they self-consciously define the situation in which they find themselves and construct an ongoing account of who "we"—and "they"—are. Ethnic identification begins with the application of a label to oneself in a cognitive process of self-categorization, involving not only a claim to membership in a group or category but also a contrast of one's group or category with other groups or categories. Such self-definitions also carry affective meaning, implying a psychological bond with others that tends to serve psychologically protective functions—indeed, they may be adopted in part because they protect the individual's self-esteem, whereas negative self-esteem can precipitate an alteration of identification (Deaux 1996). Ethnic self-awareness is heightened or blurred, respectively, depending on the degree of dissonance or consonance of the social contexts which are basic to identity formation. For majority-group youths in an ethnically consonant context, ethnic self-identity tends to be taken for granted and is not salient; but contextual dissonance heightens the salience of ethnicity and of ethnic-group boundaries (Rosenberg 1979). People whose ethnic, racial, or other social markers place them in a minority status in their group or community are more likely to be self-conscious of those characteristics. Youths may cope with the psychological pressure produced by such dissonance by seeking to reduce conflict and to assimilate within the relevant social context—the modal response of the children of European immigrants in the American experience. An alternative reaction may lead in an opposite direction to the rise and reaffirmation of ethnic solidarity and self-consciousness, as exemplified by Stephanie Bernal in the vignette sketched earlier. For Stephanie, the newfound sense of belonging she experienced in joining the movement against Proposition 187 helped dissolve the marginality and ambiguity of a "mixed chocolate swirl" identity.

In what follows, I examine various factors shaping ethnic self-identification in our sample of immigrant-origin youths in late adolescence. The way that these youths define themselves is significant, revealing much about their social attachments (and detachments), as well as how and where they perceive themselves to "fit" in the society of which they are its newest members. Self-identities and ethnic loyalties can often influence long-term patterns of behavior and outlook as well as intergroup relations, with potential long-term political implications. Accordingly, I hypothesize that the process of language learning and acculturation, as well as experiences of racial-ethnic discrimination, among other factors, will be accompanied by changes in the character and salience of ethnicity—ranging from "linear" to "reactive" forms, from "thick" to "thin" identities—and hence by divergent modes of ethnic self-identification. In particular, I address these questions: What are their ethnic (or pan-ethnic) self-identities? How salient or important are they to these youths, and how have they shifted over time? What characteristics distinguish the different types of ethnic (or pan-ethnic) identities from each other? And among those characteristics, which are the main predictors of different types of ethnic (and pan-ethnic) identities?

Forms of Ethnic Self-Identification

In both the 1992 and 1995–1996 surveys, an open-ended question was asked to ascertain the respondent's ethnic self-identity. No closed categories or checklists were provided, which required the respondents to write their answers in their own words and in their own hands. Those written self-designations were then coded and quantified, and they established the main outcomes that I seek here to describe and explain. From the variety of responses given, four mutually exclusive types of ethnic self-identities became apparent, which accounted for over 95% of the answers given in both surveys. These four types were classified as follows: (1) a foreign national identity (e.g., Mexican, Vietnamese); (2) a hyphenated-American identity, explicitly recognizing a single foreign national origin (e.g., Cuban-American, Filipino-American); (3) a plain American national identity; and (4) a pan-ethnic minority-group identity (e.g., Hispanic, Latino, Chicano, black, Asian). The first two of these identify with the immigrant experience and original homeland, if at different degrees of closeness, whereas the last two types are exclusively identities "made in the U.S.A." The first three involve chiefly national identifications (past or present or a bridging of both); the fourth reflects a denationalized identification with racial-ethnic minorities in the United States and self-conscious differences in relation to the white Anglo majority population.

Ethnic Identity Shifts

Figure 5.2 presents the frequency distribution of the results from both surveys for the longitudinal sample as a whole. In the 1992 survey, when these youths were in the eighth and ninth grades, just over a quarter (27%) identified by the foreign national origin; a plurality (41%) chose a hyphenated-American identification; 13% identified as American; and 16% selected pan-ethnic or racialized self-identifications. By the 1995–1996 survey, as they were finishing high school, over a third (35%) of the same respondents now identified by national or ethnic origin; less than a third (31%) chose a hyphenated-American identification; only 4% identified as American; and over a quarter (27%) selected pan-ethnic self-identifications. Figure 5.3 breaks down the results for the specific types of

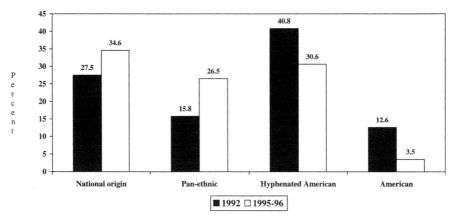

Figure 5.2. Ethnic self-identity shifts among children of immigrants, 1992 to 1995–1996. See text for description of ethnic self-identity types. Not shown are mixed identities, chosen by about 4% of the respondents in both surveys. Source: CILS (longitudinal sample, $N = 4{,}288$).

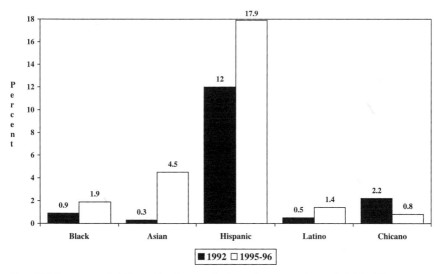

Figure 5.3. Percentage of children of immigrants selecting various types of pan-ethnic identities, 1992 and 1995–1996. See text for description of pan-ethnic self-identity types. Source: CILS (longitudinal sample, $N = 4{,}288$).

pan-ethnic identities reported at both surveys; each type except "Chicano" (which decreased from 2.2% to 0.8%) reflected increases during this period. "Hispanic" was reported by 12% of the sample in the first survey and by 18% in the follow-up; a "Latino" self-designation was selected by a much smaller number of youths of Latin American origin, but it increased more rapidly, from 0.5% to 1.4%. While very few youths had identified as "Asian" or "Asian American" in the first survey (0.3%), that category grew noticeably to 4.5% in the second survey. "Black" self-identities doubled from 0.9% to 1.9%.

These results show substantial change over time, underscoring the malleable character of ethnicity. The magnitude of the change, however, is moderate: nearly half (44%) of the youths reported exactly the same ethnic self-identity in their written responses to the open-ended question in the follow-up survey. This degree of stability takes on added significance when it one considers that several years had passed between surveys, spanning a relatively volatile developmental period from middle to late adolescence in changing cultural contexts. If ethnic identity does not emerge here as a "fixed" characteristic, then neither is it so "fluid" as to fit what E. L. Doctorow's character Billy Bathgate called his "license-plate theory of identification," the idea that "maybe all identification is temporary because you went through a life of changing situations" (quoted in Deaux 1996, 792). Still, the fact that over half of the respondents reported a change in their ethnic self-definitions in the span between surveys underscores the need not to take such identities as givens but to track their evolution across the life course.

Moreover, the direction of the shift was unexpected. If their rapid language shift to English documented previously were to have been accompanied by a similar acculturative shift in ethnic identity, then we should have seen an increase over time in the proportion of youths identifying as American, with or without a hyphen, and a decrease in the proportion retaining an attachment to a foreign national identity. But as shown in figure 5.2, the results of the 1995 survey (conducted in the months after the passage of Proposition 187 in California) pointed in exactly the opposite direction. In 1992, over 53% identified as American or hyphenated-American, but only 34% did so several years later—a net *loss* of nearly 20 percentage points. Meanwhile, both the foreign national origin and pan-ethnic identifications combined for a net *gain* of almost 20 percentage points. The shift, therefore, has been not toward mainstream identities but toward a reaffirmation of the immigrant identity for some groups (notably Mexicans and Filipinos in California, Haitians and Nicaraguans in Florida) and toward pan-ethnic minority-group identities for most others, who become increasingly aware of and adopt the ethnoracial markers in which they are persistently classified by the schools and other American institutions. How and why this occurred is a complex story. Part of it has to do with the stability and salience of different types of ethnic self-identities, and I turn first to that issue.

Stability and Salience

Table 5.3 presents a detailed cross-tabulation of these results. For each of the identity types chosen in 1992, the table shows the proportions of re-spondents who reported exactly the same identity in 1995–1996 (a measure of the *stability* of that identity), as well as the proportions who shifted to a different type of ethnic self-identification. As table 5.3 shows, 58% of the youths who identified by their own or their parents' foreign national origin in 1992 did so again three years later (the most stable and "fixed" type of self-identification), compared to 47% of those choosing pan-ethnic identities, 45% of those reporting a hyphenated-American identity, and a mere 15% of those who had identified as plain Americans (by far the most

Table 5.3. Continuity and Change in the Ethnic Self-Identities of Children of Immigrants, 1992 and 1995–1996

| Ethnic self-identity reported in 1992 | Ethnic self-identity reported in 1995–96 | | | | | Total: n in 1992 (%) |
	National origin	Pan-ethnic	Hyphenated American	American	Mixed, other	
National origin	57.7	20.2	17.4	1.2	3.6	1,181 (27.5)
Pan-ethnic	32.5	46.5	16.8	0.6	3.5	677 (15.8)
Hyphenated American	28.1	20.6	44.6	2.7	4.0	1,748 (40.8)
American	10.7	33.8	32.8	14.8	7.9	542 (12.6)
Mixed, other	22.9	27.9	26.4	3.6	19.3	140 (3.3)
Total:						
n in 1995–1996	1,482	1,135	1,314	150	207	4,288
(%)	(34.6)	(26.5)	(30.6)	(3.5)	(4.8)	(100.0)

Source: CILS (longitudinal sample, n = 4,288).

Note: Figures are row percentages, indicating the proportion of respondents who reported in the 1995–1996 survey the same or a different type of ethnic identity as that given in 1992. Overall, 44% of the respondents reported the same identity in the follow-up survey, while 56% reported a different type. See text for a description of ethnic identity types.

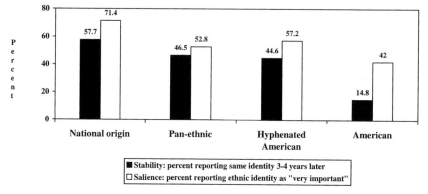

Figure 5.4. Stability and salience of ethnic self-identities, 1995–1996. Source: CILS (longitudinal sample, N = 4,288).

unstable and "fluid" type of self-identification). Of those shifting to other identities, table 5.3 suggests the patterning of the shifts: they either added a hyphen or dropped the hyphen in favor of a pan-ethnic or a foreign nationality identity. Very few shifted to a plain American identity by the second survey (overall it plummeted from 13% to 3.5%); among those who had initially identified as American only, a third shifted to a hyphenated-American identity, while another third adopted a pan-ethnic type.

In the follow-up survey, the youths were asked how important their reported ethnic self-identity was to them. The responses, on a three-point scale from "very important" to "not important," provide a measure of the *salience* of the different identity types. Figure 5.4 compares the different identity types by their degree of stability (the percentage reporting the same identity years later) and salience (the percentage reporting their identity as "very important"). Once again foreign national-origin identities command the strongest level of allegiance and attachment: over 71% of the youths so identifying considered that identity to be "very important" to them, followed by 57% of the hyphenates, 53% of the pan-ethnics, and only 42% of those identifying as plain American. The latter emerges as the "thinnest" identity, with the lowest stability and salience scores—fitting theoretical expectations for a highly acculturated, majority-group self-image in socially consonant contexts. The foreign national identity, in contrast, emerges as the "thickest" identity, with the highest stability and salience scores—fitting theoretical expectations for a less-acculturated, more acutely self-conscious image in socially dissonant contexts. In the salience-stability hierarchy of ethnic identities, the pan-ethnic and hyphenated-American types fall between those two poles.

Multivariate logistic regressions (not shown) were carried out to identify the factors most likely to predict ethnic identity and salience. A large
array of possible predictors was examined—but only a handful of variables
emerged as significant determinants of stability and salience. Identities
tended to be most stable among less-acculturated respondents (i.e., those
who reported lesser preferences for English and American ways of doing
things) and those high in perceptions of discrimination (i.e., those who reported experiences and expectations of unfair treatment because of one's
ethnicity or race). Identities were also more stable among those youths
whose parents were both born in the same country, and who spoke the
parental language at home. Females were also more likely than males to
have retained the same ethnic identity over time. Those same predictors
also determined salience, except that gender had no significant effect on
salience whereas our measure of family cohesion did—that is, net of other
factors, the more cohesive the family, the more likely were the youths
to consider their ethnicity as being very important to them. Put another
way, "thicker" (stable and salient) ethnic self-identities were least likely to
be found among second-generation youth who experienced little discrimination, had become more acculturated, and spoke English in homes with
low family cohesion—a recipe for dissonant acculturation and ancestral
dis-identification.

Ethnic Self-Identities by National Origin

How did these patterns of ethnic self-identification vary among the major nationalities in the study? Table 5.4 provides a breakdown by national
origin, showing both the percentages selecting the four main ethnic identity types in the most recent survey, as well as the percentage change (+/−)
in each identity since the initial survey. In addition, "internal ethnicity" (see
Bozorgmehr 1997) is specifically considered in this table by separating the
Vietnamese and the ethnic Chinese from Vietnam, and the Lao and the
Hmong from Laos—the ethnic Chinese and the Hmong were segregated
and disparaged minority groups in their countries of origin, and as such
their identity choices and homeland attachments bear closer comparative
scrutiny. A number of points merit highlighting.

First, a glance at table 5.4 reveals that the patterns discussed so far do
not apply equally to every nationality, and that in fact there are very large
discrepancies in some cases. For example, I found that 35% of the total
sample identified by a foreign national origin in the latest survey, a gain of
7% from the first survey. But that figure is an average that ranges from a

Table 5.4. Ethnic Self-Identities of Children of Immigrants, by National-Origin Groups, 1995–1996

| | Type of ethnic self-identity | | | | | | | |
| National-origin groups | National origin | | Pan-ethnic identities | | Hyphenated American | | American identity | |
	% in 1995–96	(% change since 1992)	% in 1995–96	(% change since 1992)	% in 1995–96	(% change since 1992)	% in 1995–96	(% change since 1992)
Latin America:								
Cuba (private school)	6.2	(+2.7)	19.2	(+15.1)	70.5	(+13.0)	2.1	(−32.9)
Cuba (public school)	16.5	(−0.4)	31.5	(+23.2)	42.0	(−11.1)	6.1	(−14.6)
Dominican Republic	5.1	(−20.5)	71.8	(+44.9)	10.3	(−15.4)	2.6	(−16.7)
Mexico	41.2	(+23.5)	25.0	(−21.0)	28.9	(−2.0)	1.2	(−1.8)
Nicaragua	54.1	(+19.6)	25.6	(−13.2)	17.4	(+2.1)	0.4	(−8.2)
Colombia	15.7	(−7.6)	62.7	(+36.8)	13.0	(−17.3)	3.2	(−15.7)
Other Latin America	16.7	(−10.0)	43.3	(+53.2)	23.3	(−7.1)	13.3	(−16.7)
Haiti and West Indies:								
Haiti	37.8	(+6.7)	4.4	(−7.4)	43.7	(+5.2)	0	(−14.1)
Jamaica	39.0	(−13.6)	15.3	(+10.2)	29.7	(+2.5)	2.5	(−10.2)
Trinidad, other West Indies	14.5	(−13.3)	55.4	(+47.0)	16.9	(−10.8)	2.4	(−24.1)
Asia:								
Vietnam (Vietnamese)	57.9	(+13.1)	11.9	(+11.5)	29.4	(−18.3)	0	(−4.0)
Vietnam (ethnic Chinese)	25.9	(−1.7)	29.3	(+29.3)	39.7	(−10.3)	1.7	(−1.7)
Laos (Lao)	66.7	(+4.9)	11.8	(+9.0)	19.4	(−9.7)	0.7	(+0.0)
Laos (Hmong)	48.0	(−14.0)	38.0	(+36.0)	12.0	(−14.0)	0	(−4.0)
Cambodia	48.3	(+7.9)	21.3	(+19.1)	30.3	(−15.7)	0	(−3.4)
Philippines	55.1	(+24.0)	1.9	(+1.2)	37.0	(−22.8)	1.7	(−3.6)
Chinese, other Asia	19.4	(−12.9)	43.9	(+42.6)	23.2	(−24.5)	5.8	(−8.4)
Europe, Canada	8.8	(−14.0)	7.0	(−3.5)	10.5	(−10.5)	57.9	(+15.8)
Total	34.6	(+7.0)	26.5	(+10.7)	30.6	(−10.1)	3.5	(−9.2)

Source: CILS (longitudinal sample, n = 4,288).

Note: See text for description of ethnic self-identity types. Not shown is a residual category of mixed identities chosen by 4.8% of the respondents in the 1995–1996 survey. Figures are row percentages.

high of 67% among the Lao (compared to 48% of the Hmong), 58% of the Vietnamese (compared to 26% of the ethnic-Chinese Vietnamese), and over 50% of the Filipinos and Nicaraguans, to a low of only 5% of the Dominicans and 6% of the Cubans in private schools. The Mexicans and Filipinos—in California—registered the strongest gains in foreign national-origin identities from the baseline survey (each increasing by 24%), vividly documenting (especially in the Mexican case) the Proposition 187–induced process of reaction formation sketched in my earlier vignette. Most of the Mexican shift came from youths who had identified as Chicano, Latino, or Hispanic in the 1992 survey.

Other groups registered significant losses in national-origin identification, especially Dominicans, West Indians, and the Hmong, Chinese, and smaller Asian-origin groups. All of these smaller groups instead posted very large increases in pan-ethnic identities, with 72% of the Dominicans choosing "Hispanic" or "Latino" self-identities, as did 63% of the Colombians. The Hmong and the Chinese, virtually none of whom had identified pan-ethnically as "Asian" in 1992, had made large inroads into this type of self-identification by 1995. This result is clearly not explained by socio-economic factors, since the Hmong had the lowest family SES of all the groups in this study (and the highest poverty rate in the United States, for that matter), whereas the Chinese in this sample mostly came from professional families. By contrast, virtually none of the Filipinos identified in pan-ethnic terms (less than 2%), as did only 4% of the Haitians. The Filipinos and Haitians stand out from all other groups in that they almost entirely identified either by national origin or as hyphenated-Americans, maintaining an explicit symbolic attachment to their parents' homeland.

Every group, with one exception, posted losses in the plain American identity by the latest survey. Even upper-middle-class private-school Cubans, over a third of whom had identified as American in 1992, had abandoned that identity almost entirely by 1995–1996 (a loss of 33%). The sole—and telling—exception involves the Europeans and Canadians: not only were they the only groups who increased (by 16%) their proportion identifying as plain American, but by the last survey over half (58%) had adopted that majoritarian, mainstream identity as their own. All other groups were in the low single digits, marking a sharp segmentation of identities. SES alone would not explain this divergence; as noted, the high-status private-school Cubans dropped that identity, and another relatively high status group—the Filipinos—consistently posted minuscule numbers identifying as unhyphenated Americans. Neither would acculturation to American ways by itself explain it; again the Filipinos, easily the most highly acculturated Asian-origin group, serves as a counterexample. In the following I attempt to disentangle this puzzle.

Nativity, Family, and Identity

Ethnic identity is, in part, a way of answering the question "where do I come from?" The answers given are often expressed in a metaphorical language of kinship (e.g., "homeland," "fatherland," "mother tongue," "blood ties") with reference to a "birth connection" (see Cornell and Hartmann 1998, 54; Horowitz 1985) to nation and family—to an imagined common origin or ancestry. Even the "thinnest" ethnicities tend to be rooted in such kinship metaphors. Thus, while ethnic identities may be socially and politically constructed, they are experienced and expressed as "natural." In this regard, nativity variables (where one was born, to whom one was born, where one's parents were born) are clearly important to ethnic and national self-definitions. For children of immigrants, they are also variables that can significantly complicate a clear-cut answer to basic questions of ethnic self-definition, particularly when the parents' country of birth differs from that of the child and (in cases of interethnic marriage) from each other. The extent of such differences in the nativity patterns of our respondents and their parents is depicted in table 5.5, broken down by national-origin groups.

Half of the children of immigrants in the CILS sample were born in the United States (the second generation), while the other half were foreign born (the 1.5 generation). However, as table 5.5 shows, there are wide differences by national origin. Well over 90% of the Laotians, Cambodians, and Nicaraguans were foreign born, as were 84% of the Vietnamese. By contrast, over 90% of the Cubans in private school were born in the United States, as were 86% of the Europeans and Canadians and well over half of the Mexicans, Filipinos, and other Asians and West Indians. Note that only three-fourths of the children in the sample had parents who were both born in the same country—and hence who could transmit to their children a common national origin. These rates of homogamy vary widely by nationality, with the highest proportions of endogamous conational parents (between 85% and 95%) found among the Laotians, Vietnamese, Haitians, Nicaraguans, and Cubans in private school, while fewer than one-fourth (23%) of the Europeans and Canadians had conational parents—indicative of high levels of interethnic marriage.

How do these nativity patterns affect ethnic self-identification? That

Table 5.5. Nativity Patterns of Children of Immigrants and of Their Parents

National-origin groups	Nativity of children		Nativity of father and mother		
	foreign born (1.5 generation) (%)	U.S. born (2nd generation) (%)	Both born in same country (%)	In different countries (%)	One parent born in U.S. (%)
Latin America:					
Cuba (private school)	8.9	91.1	85.6	9.6	4.8
Cuba (public school)	32.2	67.8	74.8	14.1	11.1
Dominican Republic	32.1	67.9	79.5	1.3	19.2
Mexico	38.2	61.8	73.0	9.5	17.5
Nicaragua	92.9	7.1	85.8	13.2	1.1
Colombia	48.1	51.9	64.9	25.9	9.2
Other Latin America	53.9	46.1	74.3	7.1	18.6
Haiti and West Indies:					
Haiti	54.8	45.2	85.9	9.6	4.4
Jamaica	63.6	36.4	78.0	11.9	10.2
Trinidad, other West Indies	32.5	67.5	50.6	24.1	25.3
Asia:					
Vietnamese	84.2	15.8	89.0	8.1	2.9
Laos (Lao)	98.6	1.4	95.1	4.9	0
Laos (Hmong)	94.0	6.0	90.0	10.0	0
Cambodia	96.6	3.4	80.9	19.1	0
Philippines	42.5	57.5	79.1	3.9	17.0
Other Asia	43.9	56.1	64.5	7.1	28.4
Europe, Canada	14.0	86.0	22.8	3.5	73.7
Total	49.9	50.1	76.8	10.4	12.9

Source: CILS (longitudinal sample, $n = 4,288$).
Note: Figures are row percentages.

question is vividly answered in figure 5.5, which graphs each of the main types of ethnic self-identity by the place of birth of the child and his or her parents. Among those who reported a foreign national-origin identity, 75% were foreign born, compared to 31% of those who reported a hyphenated-American identity and a minuscule 8% of those identifying as plain American. Fewer than half (47%) of those identifying by pan-ethnic categories were foreign born. In families where both parents came from the same country of birth, their offspring were much more likely to incorporate that national origin as part of their own identity (either wholly or as a hyphenated-American identity). In families where both parents were foreign born but came from different countries of birth, their offspring were

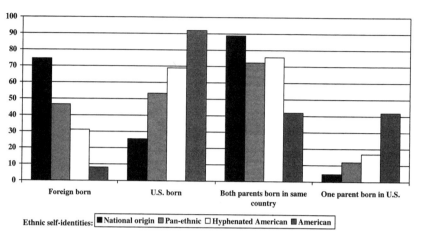

Figure 5.5. Ethnic self-identities, 1995–1996, by native origin of self and parents. Probability of differences being due to chance is less than 1 in 1,000 for all associations shown.

more likely to simplify the complexity of mixed origins by adopting either a pan-ethnic (minority) or plain American (majority) identity, thus resolving the conflict of identifying with one parent rather than the other. For example, asked how she identified, Rosa, the 15-year-old U.S.-born bilingual daughter of a Cuban-born father and a Salvadoran-born mother told me, "If I said I'm Cuban, that'd make my mom mad; and if I said I'm Salvadoran, my dad would get all upset, so I think I'm . . . Hispanic!" The pan-ethnic identity label "made sense" for her as a simplified category that focused on shared traits (and was popular with her Spanish-speaking school friends as well) while avoiding the dilemma of privileging one or the other parental "birth connection"—to have done so would have been tantamount, to this offspring of a hybrid marriage, to an act of ethnic disloyalty to one or the other parent.

Language, Acculturation, and Identity

Of course, even when the nativity patterns of the youths and of their parents are held constant, many other factors are likely to impinge independently on the process of ethnic self-identification. Table 5.6 lists a variety of factors related to patterns of acculturation of both parents and children (measured in the 1992 survey) that are strongly predictive of the children's identity outcomes (measured three to four years later in the 1995–1996 survey). A glance at the data in this table makes clear that each identity

Table 5.6. Selected 1992 Predictors of Ethnic Self-Identities Reported by Children of Immigrants in 1995–1996

	Ethnic self-identity in 1995–1996				
Predictor variables, 1992[a]	National origin (%)	Pan-ethnic (%)	Hyphenated American (%)	American (%)	Total sample (%)
Child's nativity:					
Foreign born	74.5	46.6	31.1	8.0	49.9
U.S. born	25.5	53.4	68.9	92.0	50.1
Parents' nativity:					
Both born in same country	88.9	72.3	75.7	42.0	76.7
Born in different countries	6.5	15.8	7.5	16.0	10.4
One parent born in U.S.	4.6	11.9	16.8	42.0	12.9
If both parents foreign born, year of immigration to U.S.:					
Before 1970	4.5	14.2	20.9	40.2	13.0
In 1970s	15.8	26.8	35.4	37.9	25.8
In 1980s	79.7	59.0	43.7	21.8	61.2
Socioeconomic status:					
Family owns home	48.7	52.8	66.4	73.3	56.6
Parent is a professional	20.6	24.3	26.2	40.0	24.3
Education: 12 or more (mother)	53.3	58.9	64.6	76.7	59.7
Language and acculturation:					
Speaks foreign language "very well"	37.9	38.5	26.9	14.0	33.0
Speaks English "very well"	66.6	79.1	84.6	95.3	77.4
Parent speaks English "very well"	22.3	26.9	38.5	59.4	30.3
Speaks English with parents	32.7	32.0	48.7	70.0	40.2
Speaks English with friends	30.3	27.7	34.4	62.0	32.8
Prefers English	64.4	71.9	79.8	91.3	72.9
Prefers "American ways"	34.8	39.9	46.4	74.7	41.9
Parents prefer "American ways"	19.8	23.5	28.1	60.1	25.6
Attitudes toward parents/family:					
Embarrassed by parents, 1992	22.9	23.4	27.1	30.0	24.6
Embarrassed by parents, 1995–96	26.5	28.3	31.2	42.0	29.3
Believe that only relatives can help with serious problems, 1992	19.6	16.4	12.2	7.3	15.5
Believe that living close to family is "very important," 1995–96	46.8	42.7	39.7	24.8	42.0

Source: CILS (longitudinal sample, $n = 4{,}288$).
Note: Figures are column percentages. The probability that the differences by type of identity are due to chance is less than 1 in 1,000 for all variables in the table. The ethnic self-identities are those reported in the follow-up survey of 1995–1996. For simplicity of presentation, a small residual category of mixed identities is not included.
[a] Predictor variables were measured in the baseline survey of 1992, unless otherwise noted; parents' English ability was measured at the time of the separate parental interviews in 1995–1996.

type has a distinct social profile that differs significantly from each of the others. For example, the parents' length of residence in the United States provides an indicator of their own level of acculturation. As table 5.6 shows, the longer the parents had resided in the United States, the more likely their children were to assimilate their identities along the continuum from foreign national to pan-ethnic to hyphenated-American to plain American. That same linear progression is evident for each of the different indicators of parental SES shown (homeownership, occupation, and education), for foreign- and English-language proficiency and use, and for preference for "American ways" reported separately by both the youths and their parents. Language, in particular, is closely connected to the formation and maintenance of ethnic identity. The shift to English is associated with a shift in self-definition and seems to entail abandoning not only a mother tongue but also a personal identity. Those youths most loyal to the mother tongue were also most loyal to a national-origin identity; conversely, those youths who preferred English and spoke only English with their parents and close friends were much more likely to identify as a plain American.

Finally, table 5.6 presents selected indicators pertaining to the youths' attitudes toward and attachment to their parents and family, and the effect of those on ethnic self-identifications. One item asked at both surveys—measuring the youths' response to a question about feeling embarrassed about their parents' ignorance of American ways—provides an empirical indicator of dissonant acculturation within the family. As table 5.6 shows, again the same linear relationship obtains as with the other measures of acculturation: least embarrassed were youths who identified by national origin, and most embarrassed were those who identified as plain American (with the proportion widening over time). A different set of items tapped attitudes expressing felt collective obligations toward the family; two of them are shown in table 5.6 (believes that only relatives can help with serious problems and that living close to family is very important). The higher the level of agreement on these items, the more likely the youth identified by national origin; the less the agreement, the more likely the youth identified as plain American, with the other two identity types falling in between.

But perhaps most revealing of the effect of parental ethnic socialization and of the strength of parent-child bonds on the children's ethnic self-definitions were two open-ended questions (asked in the 1992 survey) asking the respondents to write down what they perceived to be the self-identities of their mothers and fathers. Those responses were coded, quantified, and correlated with the children's own ethnic self-identities re-

Table 5.7. Patterns of Ethnic Socialization within the Family: Correlations of Children's Perceptions of Their Parents' Ethnic Identities in 1992 with Their Own Ethnic Self-Identities in 1992 and 1995–1996

Children's ethnic self-identities	Time of survey	Parents' identity as perceived by child in 1992				
		National origin	Hyphenated American	American	Pan-ethnic	Mixed identity
National origin	1992	.373***	−.229***	−.202***	−.058***	−.024
	1995–96	.206***	−.085***	−.167***	−.032*	.020
Hyphenated	1992	−.192***	.280***	.005	−.066***	−.045**
	1995–96	−.120***	.131***	.059***	−.043**	−.053***
American	1992	−.201***	.015	.251***	−.028	−.023
	1995–96	−.089***	−.002	.128***	−.031*	−.016
Pan-ethnic	1992	.015	−.088***	−.019	.186***	.050**
	1995–96	−.029	−.034*	.030*	.083***	.022
Mixed identity	1992	−.063***	−.045**	.063***	.002	.123***
	1995–96	−.063***	−.021	.072***	.020	.039**

Source: CILS (longitudinal sample, $n = 4{,}288$).
*** Probability of correlation being due to chance is less than 1 in 1,000.
** Probability of correlation being due to chance is less than 1 in 100.
* Probability of correlation being due to chance is less than 5 in 100.

ported in the 1992 and 1995–1996 surveys. Table 5.7 presents the correlations for the main identity types over time, which effectively provide a measure of the degree of *consonant or dissonant identification* of the youths with their parents. It is remarkable to see that even after the passage of several years, and despite the attenuation of the correlation coefficients over this time, the way the children had perceived their parents' ethnic identities remained significantly associated with their own modes of self-identification, mirroring them as if they were reflections in an ethnic looking glass. The strongest consonant identification (i.e., the strongest correlation) involved national-origin identities, which, as seen above, were also the most stable and salient identity type.

Clearly, the family plays a central role in the process of ethnic socialization. It is the crucible of the child's first notions of belonging and of "home," and it is within the family that the child first learns about and forms ethnic attachments and self-concepts. Even in the sometimes bumpy passage through adolescence and under varying degrees of differential acculturation, how these youths think and feel about themselves continues to be affected by the parents' modes of ethnic socialization and by the strength of the attachment that the child feels to the parents.

Discrimination, Reactive Ethnicity, and Identity

The story of the forging of an ethnic self-identity in the second generation, however, plays out on a much larger stage than that of the family. I began by focusing attention on social forces outside the family that shape the creation both of racial-ethnic categories and of ethnic self-definitions, particularly those involving discrimination and the politics of reactive ethnicity and not only those involving acculturation and the psychology of linear ethnicity. I now return to those concerns.

Regional location (in Southern California or South Florida) and the type of school these youths attended (inner-city or suburban, public or private schools) are two such extrafamilial contextual factors. They delimit the youths' exposure to different social worlds, shape differential associations with peers in those contexts, and influence attendant modes of ethnic socialization and self-definition. As table 5.8 shows, slightly over half of the sample (52%) was located in South Florida, and slightly less than half (48%) in the San Diego area. But two-thirds (67%) of those identifying by a foreign national origin were in San Diego, while about four-fifths (79%) of those identifying as plain Americans were in South Florida. The distribution of the main types of pan-ethnic identities—as specified in table 5.8—is even more skewed by location, reflecting the varieties of groups that have settled in those areas. The location of the junior high school attended—which is in part a function of family SES—remains associated with the self-identities reported by the youths several years later. Those identifying as plain Americans were most likely to have attended suburban schools (73%), followed by those identifying as hyphenated-Americans (70%); by comparison, the youths identifying by each of the different varieties of pan-ethnic labels were more likely to have attended inner-city schools with peers who tend to be primarily native racial and ethnic minorities. Although only a third (35%) of the sample attended schools in the inner city, half of those identifying as black did so (49%), as did 43% of the Asians, and 38% of the Hispanics or Latinos.

The process of growing ethnic awareness among the children of immigrants in the CILS sample is especially evident in their perceptions, experiences, and expectations of racial and ethnic discrimination. As table 5.8 shows, reports of actually being discriminated against increased from 54% to 62% of the sample in the last survey. Virtually every group reported more such experiences of rejection or unfair treatment as they grew older, with the highest proportions found among the children of Afro-Caribbean and Asian-origin immigrants, followed by Mexicans and other Latin Americans, and the lowest proportions among Cuban youth in Miami.

Table 5.8. Location, Experiences of Discrimination, Perceptions of the United States, and Self-Reported Race, by Main Types of Ethnic Self-Identities Reported by Children of Immigrants in 1995–1996

| Predictor variables | Ethnonational self-identity in 1995–96 | | | Pan-ethnic self-identity in 1995–96 | | | |
	National origin (%)	Hyphen-ated American (%)	Ameri-can (%)	His-panic, Latino[a] (%)	Asian (%)	Black (%)	Total Sample (%)
Location:							
Southern California	67.3	47.6	21.3	19.8	75.1	16.3	48.1
South Florida	32.7	52.4	78.7	80.2	24.9	83.7	51.9
School attended in 1992:							
Inner-city school	37.4	30.4	26.7	38.4	43.0	48.8	35.4
Suburban school	62.6	69.6	73.3	61.6	57.0	51.2	64.6
Experienced discrimination:							
Reported in 1992	60.3	53.5	44.0	44.7	57.0	68.8	54.5
Reported in 1995–96	66.4	62.0	52.7	51.4	66.8	80.0	62.2
Expects discrimination:							
Reported in 1992	36.6	33.0	22.7	21.7	33.2	61.3	32.0
Reported in 1995–96	39.7	35.3	27.3	25.4	34.2	62.5	35.1
Agrees that "The U.S. is the best country to live in":							
Reported in 1992	57.7	65.9	73.3	58.3	66.8	47.5	60.8
Reported in 1995–96	67.9	76.0	78.0	72.2	72.0	54.4	71.3
Child's self-reported "race":							
White	6.0	17.4	58.7	20.8	—	—	14.3
Black	5.7	6.7	2.7	0.8	—	85.0	6.6
Asian	40.4	23.1	3.3	—	92.2	—	25.8
Multiracial	5.1	15.0	16.0	11.5	6.2	13.8	11.4
Hispanic, Latino	16.4	17.2	10.0	57.8	—	—	23.5
Nationality	23.3	18.0	2.7	4.8	0.5	—	14.9
Other response	3.2	2.7	6.7	4.4	1.0	1.3	3.6
Parent's self-reported "race":							
White	16.8	32.9	63.8	60.8	0.9	4.7	30.2
Black	6.2	7.4	1.4	1.4	0.9	81.4	7.4
Asian	39.7	29.9	13.0	0.7	76.9	2.3	29.2
Multiracial	8.9	8.6	10.1	15.6	0.9	2.3	9.6
Hispanic, Latino	2.6	2.4	1.4	6.7	—	—	3.2
Nationality	20.1	13.0	2.9	6.3	18.8	—	14.2
Other response	5.7	5.9	7.2	8.4	1.7	9.3	6.3

Source: CILS (longitudinal sample, n = 4,288).
Note: Figures are column percentages. The probability that the differences by type of identity are due to chance is less than 1 in 1,000 for all variables in the table. The types of self-identities are those reported in the 1995–96 survey. For simplicity of presentation, a small residual category of mixed identities is not included.
[a] Reported self-identity as "Hispanic," "Latino," or "Chicano."

As seen in table 5.8, there are significant associations between experiences and expectations of discrimination reported at both surveys and the types of ethnic and pan-ethnic self-identities expressed in the later survey. Indeed, discrimination sharpens ethnic-racial identity boundaries and increases the salience of the category on the basis of which persons experience unfair treatment. Among the three main types of ethnonational identities, the highest proportions of experienced and of expected discrimination were reported by those who identified by national origin, and the lowest by those who identified as American, with hyphenates in between. Among the three main types of pan-ethnic identities, by far the highest proportions were seen among "black"-identified respondents and the lowest among "Hispanic"-identified youth, with "Asian"-identified pan-ethnics in the middle. This latter result was most clearly seen among Latin American–origin youth in South Florida, where they constitute a numerical majority in dense ethnic enclaves that buffer them from external discrimination.

Still, it is important as well to underscore the fact that despite their growing awareness of racial and ethnic inequalities, most of the youth in the sample (almost two-thirds) continued to affirm a confident belief in the promise of equal opportunity through educational achievement. Even more tellingly, as table 5.8 shows, 61 % of these youths agreed in the 1992 survey that "there is no better country to live in than the United States," and that endorsement grew to 71 % several years later — despite a growing anti-immigrant mood in the country and especially in California during that period. Again there were significant differences by ethnic identity types, and even wider differences by national-origin groups. Tellingly, the groups *most* likely to endorse that view were the children of political exiles who found a favorable context of reception in the United States: the Cubans and the Vietnamese. The groups *least* likely to agree with that statement were those who had most felt the weight of racial discrimination: the children of immigrants from Haiti, Jamaica, and the West Indies. In reacting to their contexts of reception and in learning how they are viewed and treated within them, the youths form and inform their own attitudes toward the society that receives them — and their own identities as well.

Race and Identity

Near the end of the follow-up survey, the respondents were asked to answer a semistructured question about their "race." They were given the option to check one of five categories: "white," "black," "Asian," "multiracial," or "other"; if the latter was checked, they had to write in their own words what that "other race" was. The results (also presented in table 5.8) are revealing.

Fewer than half of the total sample checked the conventional categories of white, black, or Asian; 11 % reported being multiracial; and over 40 % checked "other." When those "other" self-reports were coded, it turned out that nearly a quarter of the sample (24 %) wrote down "Hispanic" or "Latino" as their "race," and another 15 % gave their nationality as their "race." Among those youths adopting pan-ethnic identities, as table 5.8 indicates, there is an obvious conflation of race and ethnicity in the way they define their identities: 92 % of those who identify as "Asian" give that as their race, as do 85 % of those who identify as "black," while 58 % of those who identify as "Hispanic" or "Latino" extend racial meaning to that label as well. Among those youths identifying by the other ethnonational types, racial self-definition as "white" makes a decisive difference: 59 % of the plain American youths said they were white, compared to 17 % of the hyphenated-Americans and only 6 % of those identifying by a foreign national origin.

The explicit racialization of the "Hispanic-Latino" category, and the substantial proportion of youths who conceived of their nationality of origin as a fixed racial category, are noteworthy both for their potential long-term implications in hardening group boundaries and for their illustration of the arbitrariness of racial constructions. The latter point is made particularly salient by directly comparing the youths' notions of their "race" with that reported by their own parents (the same "race" item was used in the parental interviews of 1995–1996). Those results are cross-tabulated in table 5.9, by national origin.

The closest match in racial self-perceptions between parents and children is evident among the Haitians, Jamaicans, and other West Indians (most of whom self-report as black), among the Europeans and Canadians (most of whom label themselves white), and among most of the Asian-origin groups except for the Filipinos. The widest mismatches by far occur among the Latin American–origin groups. For example, 93 % of Cuban parents identify as white, compared to only 41 % of their children; 68 % of Nicaraguan parents see themselves as white, but only 19 % of their children agree, as is the case among all other Latin-origin groups except Mexicans. The children of Cuban parents largely adopt "Hispanic" or "Latino" as a racial label (36 %), whereas scarcely any of their parents do so (1 %). Among the Mexicans, whose pattern differs from all of the others, the children preponderantly racialize the national label, whereas Mexican parents are more likely to use "other" (mestizo) and "multiracial" as descriptors.

Table 5.9. Self-Reported "Race" of Children of Immigrants and Their Parents, by National-Origin Groups, 1995–1996

National-origin groups	Respondent (child/ parent)	White (%)	Black (%)	Asian (%)	Multi-racial (%)	His-panic, Latino (%)	Nation-ality (%)	Other (%)
Latin America:								
Cuba	Child	41.2	0.8	—	11.5	36.0	5.5	4.9
	Parent	93.1	1.1	0.3	2.5	1.1	0.5	1.4
Mexico	Child	1.5	0.3	—	12.0	25.5	56.2	4.5
	Parent	5.7	—	2.1	21.6	15.9	26.1	28.5
Nicaragua	Child	19.4	—	—	9.7	61.8	2.7	6.5
	Parent	67.7	0.5	1.6	22.0	5.4	0.5	2.2
Other Latin America	Child	22.8	1.9	—	14.7	52.9	4.6	3.1
	Parent	69.5	4.6	0.8	17.8	2.3	1.9	3.1
Haiti and West Indies:								
Haiti	Child	—	75.9	—	8.4	—	9.6	6.0
	Parent	—	85.5	1.2	—	—	6.0	7.2
Jamaica, West Indies	Child	3.4	66.4	7.6	15.1	—	—	—
	Parent	8.4	65.5	5.0	8.4	—	6.7	5.9
Asia:								
Philippines	Child	1.1	—	61.6	13.2	—	23.0	1.1
	Parent	0.3	0.5	44.1	11.1	—	41.4	2.7
Vietnam	Child	—	—	89.8	1.6	—	7.0	1.6
	Parent	—	—	99.6	—	—	—	0.4
Laos, Cambodia	Child	0.4	—	87.8	3.4	—	7.2	1.1
	Parent	—	—	74.9	—	—	23.6	1.5
Other Asia	Child	1.5	—	82.4	13.2	—	2.9	—
	Parent	2.9	1.5	76.5	1.5	—	8.8	8.8
Europe, Canada	Child	76.0	—	—	8.0	12.0	—	4.0
	Parent	84.0	—	—	8.0	4.0	—	4.0
Total	Child	12.1	6.5	32.1	10.3	20.3	15.5	3.2
	Parent	30.2	7.4	29.2	9.6	3.2	14.2	6.3

Source: CILS (longitudinal sample, $n = 4,288$).
Note: Figures are row percentages.

These remarkable results point to the force of the acculturation process and its impact on children's self-identities. Fully exposed to American culture and its racial definitions, children learn to see themselves more and more in these terms and even to racialize their national origins. We turn now to a multivariate analysis of these self-perceptions and their determinants.

Determinants of Ethnic Self-Identities

Thus far I have examined a number of variables that were theoretically and empirically linked to specific patterns of ethnic self-identification. Among these factors are parental socioeconomic resources, nativity and national origin, parent-child relations within the family, acculturation and language, discrimination and race. Which of these predictors have the strongest independent effects on the various ethnic and pan-ethnic identity outcomes? A series of multivariate logistic regressions (not shown) examined the effects of the same set of predictor variables on each identity type. To establish unambiguously the temporal ordering of effects, the predictors were measured in 1992, while the outcome variables were measured in 1995–1996. Some of the main results are briefly summarized below.

The relationship of a few of these predictor variables to the identity outcome variables are sketched in figures 5.6–5.8. Figure 5.6 shows the clearly linear patterns of the relationship between SES, acculturation, and discrimination in the continuum from a national-origin self-identity to hyphenated-American to plain American. Figure 5.7 sketches the relationship of the

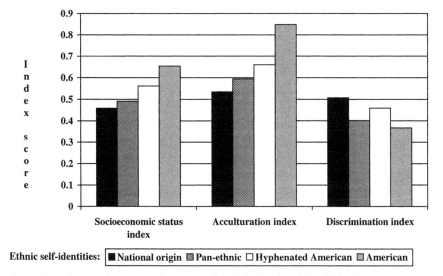

Figure 5.6. Socioeconomic status, acculturation, and discrimination, by ethnic self-identities, 1995–1996. The SES index is a standardized composite index (0 to 1) of parents' education, occupational status, and homeownership. The acculturation index is a composite index (0 to 1) of preferences for the English language and American ways reported at both surveys. The discrimination index is a composite index (0 to 1) of experiences and expectations of discrimination reported at both surveys. Probability of differences being due to chance is less than 1 in 1,000 for all indices.

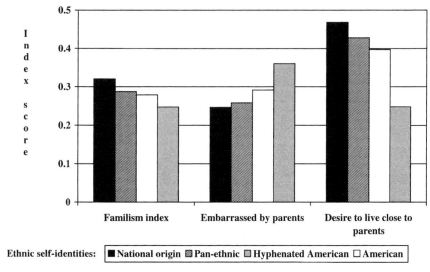

Figure 5.7. Indices of family attachment, by ethnic self-identities, 1995–1996. The indices of attitudinal familism and being embarrassed by parents are composite indices (0 to 1) of attitudes reported at both surveys. See text for description of items. The third index is the proportion who ranked living close to parents as "very important" in 1995–1996. Probability of differences being due to chance is less than 1 in 1,000 for all indices.

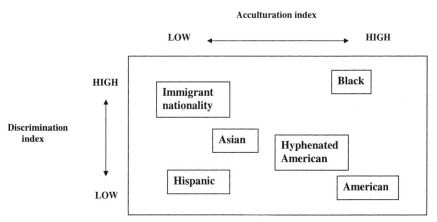

Figure 5.8. Patterns of ethnic self-identification among children of immigrants, by levels of acculturation and discrimination. The acculturation index is a composite measure (0 to 1) of preferences for the English language and American ways reported at both surveys. The discrimination index is a composite measure (0 to 1) of experiences and expectations of discrimination reported at both surveys.

different identities to indices of the youths' attitudes toward their parents and family. And figure 5.8 depicts the manner in which identities are forged in a social field shaped by the interaction of two powerful social forces, *acculturation* and *discrimination,* each pulling and pushing in different directions in the process of ethnic self-definition. The main types of ethnic and pan-ethnic identities have been mapped onto the space formed by the intersection of the two axes of acculturation and discrimination, based on their respective mean scores in the acculturation and discrimination indices. As figure 5.8 shows, the national-origin identity occupies the high-discrimination, low-acculturation top-left quadrant of the social field, while at the opposite end is found the plain American identity, occupying the low-discrimination, high-acculturation bottom-right quadrant. The hyphenated-American identity is located along the diagonal between these two, although closer to the American than to the national-origin location. In the low-discrimination, low-acculturation lower-left quadrant is found the "Hispanic" pan-ethnic identity (and its variants). This identity was adopted preponderantly by youth in the Miami metropolitan area, where Latin American–origin groups form a majority of the population— and where an institutionally complete community has emerged that may serve both as a buffer against external discrimination and as a brake to rapid acculturation. Finally, in the high-discrimination, high-acculturation upper-right quadrant are found second-generation youth who define themselves as "black." Their adoption of a pan-ethnic identity has little to do with a lack of acculturation—they clearly prefer the English language and American ways—and much to do with persistent high levels of racial discrimination and the inexorable sense of otherness that accompanies it.

The patterns that emerge from the multivariate analyses confirm a continuum of determination from national-origin to hyphenated-American to plain American self-definitions (the three main ethnonational identities), as well as distinct profiles for the three main pan-ethnic identities (Asian, black, Hispanic). First, nativity variables remain powerfully linked to self-identity. Being born in the United States was the strongest predictor of identifying as a hyphenated-American and was a significant predictor of selecting a plain American identity; it was also by far the strongest *negative* predictor of identifying by the parental national origin. Among pan-ethnic identities, being born in the United States was also predictive of identifying as Hispanic or black (both of which are made-in-the-U.S.A. identities). Similarly, becoming a naturalized U.S. citizen positively predicts American self-definitions, with or without a hyphen, and negatively predicts a foreign-nationality identity—but it is not associated with pan-ethnicity. Citizenship influences national self-definitions, over and above nativity, but it seems to be irrelevant for the adoption of racially bounded minority identities. The acquisition of citizenship may be interpreted as signaling a stake in the society as a full-fledged member, legally as well as subjectively, with an accompanying shift in one's frame of reference. These two variables—nativity and citizenship—had much stronger effects on ethnic self-identification than our measure of years in the United States. Thus, it is not so much the length of residence in the receiving country but rather the nature of one's sociopolitical membership status in it that appears to be more determinative of the psychology of ethnic identity.

The parents' own nativity in turn exerts a strong independent influence on the ethnic socialization of the child. Having both parents born in the same nation strongly boosted the odds that the child would identify with the parents' nationality, or at least keep part of it by identifying binationally as a hyphenated-American. When the parents were not conationals, having one parent born in the United States also strongly increased the probability of adopting a hyphenated-American identity. Conversely, children whose parents were born in different (typically Latin American) foreign countries were more likely to identify pan-ethnically as Hispanic or Latino, showing again the impact of parental intermarriage on the lack of continuity of ancestral identities. As illustrated earlier in the case of Rosa, the native-born daughter of a Cuban father and a Salvadoran mother, interethnic marriage blurs the boundaries of ethnicity for the children and clearly complicates and may derail the transmission of an ancestral identity.

Second, among the set of predictors involving the children's perceptions of their parents and family, three such variables retained significant effects on ethnic identification: early perceptions of the parents' own subjective ethnic identity and the embarrassment and familism indices. Indeed, respondents who reported feeling embarrassed by—and hence not proud of—their parents were less likely to identify by national origin and more likely to identify as a hyphenated-American. This index was also the strongest determinant of choosing an "Asian" self-identity: the more embarrassed by their parents, the more likely they were to adopt that pan-ethnic identity. By contrast, those high on the attitudinal familism index were more likely to identify by national origin. These results point to the varying effects on ethnic self-identity of the loosening of family ties and of the maintenance of family attachments. In general, these variables involving various aspects of the parent-child relationship underscore the fundamental influence of the family as a crucible of ethnic socialization in this diverse population of children of immigrants.

Third, parental SES washed out in most of these regressions, suggesting that its effect on modes of self-identification is indirect and more likely to be mediated through other variables. However, the two cases where direct effects are observable are noteworthy. Immigrant parents who are higher-status professionals were *more* likely to influence their children's selection of a foreign national identity. Conversely, a Hispanic minority identity was associated with *lower*-status parents, suggesting that, with other predictors held constant, more vulnerable low-SES youths were also more susceptible to that pan-ethnic mode of self-definition. In more resourceful, upper-middle-class immigrant families children may have more reason to associate social honor with and to feel pride in the national identity of the parents—and to affirm it for themselves. Indeed, as Rosenberg has observed, the child's sense of self-worth is in part contingent on the prestige of the elements of social identity (1979, 13). This finding is in accord with theoretical expectations that identity shifts tend to be from lower- to higher-status groups and not vice versa, all other things being equal.

Fourth, acculturation and language use, preference, and proficiency remain significantly but only moderately linked to most of the forms of ethnic self-identification. Youths who did not prefer the English language or American ways (low acculturation scores) and who were not proficient in English (as measured in the 1992 survey) were somewhat more likely to identify by a foreign national origin in the later survey. Those who identified as Hispanic, by contrast, were youths who also did not prefer English or American ways (low acculturation) yet were proficient in English while also regularly speaking Spanish at home. Highly acculturated respondents who preferred and were proficient in English but who also used the foreign language frequently at home were most likely to identify binationally as hyphenated-Americans. If they were equally acculturated but spoke only English at home, they were more likely to drop the hyphen and identify as plain American. Yet the strongest effect on the probability of identifying as "black" or "black American" was the frequency of speaking only English at home (an identity selected primarily by native-English-speaking West Indians but not by Haitians, whose mother tongue is not English). In sum, these identity choices reflect not only varying levels of linguistic fluency but also the nuances of how and which languages are used with significant others in varying social contexts. As noted earlier, the switch to English is part of a larger acculturation process bound to entail the abandonment not only of an ancestral language but also of an ancestral identity. What the switch to English per se does not predict is the form that alternative self-identity will take.

Finally, discrimination and racialization also influence ethnic self-identification. Youths who scored high on the discrimination index were significantly *less* likely to identify as "American" and more disposed to identify with a foreign national origin, without any "American" qualifier attached. Such experiences and perceptions of exclusion and rejection on ascribed racial-ethnic grounds clearly undercut the prospect of identificational assimilation into the mainstream. Moreover, when a "white" racial self-conception was entered into the equation, that variable had by far the strongest effect on the determination of plain American identities. An "American" ethnic identity and a "white" racial identity emerge as nearly synonymous in these results. What is more, when national-origin groups were entered in the models (as dummy variables), the *only* ones who retained strong and positive net effects on the odds of selecting a plain American identity were Europeans and Canadians. Without exception, none of the Latin American, Caribbean, or Asian groups in the sample had a significant positive association with that particular identity outcome.

Among the various pan-ethnic identity types, high scores on the discrimination index were significantly associated only with the selection of a black self-identity. But discrimination had a strong *negative* effect on the selection of a Hispanic identity, underscoring the observation made earlier about the comparatively protective aspects of the Miami enclave as a buffer against experiences and expectations of discrimination among Latin-origin youths. In this regard, a contextual variable — the type and location of the school (and, by inference, of the neighborhood and the proximal peer groups) in which these youths were placed — made an additional difference in the process of self-definition. With all other predictor variables held constant, having attended inner-city junior high schools where most students were racial-ethnic minorities significantly increased the likelihood of developing a racial or pan-ethnic identity (particularly for youths reporting a black or Hispanic-Latino self-identity), while decreasing the probability of identifying ancestrally by national origin. These results provide empirical support for a segmented assimilation perspective, here applied to the process of ethnic (and racial) self-definition.

Did any particular nationalities continue to affect the types of ethnic self-identification once the other predictors were taken into account? In many cases they did not; that is, despite the wide range of differences between them, many nationalities (entered as dummy variables into the regression equations) retained no significant effects in the models tested. In some cases, however, they did—suggesting that there is more about those national-origin groups and their contexts of reception that is not explained by the set of predictors included in the model. For example, I already noted the strong independent effect of European and Canadian national origins on the selection of a plain American identity. More than any other nationality, Cubans stood out for their strong attachment to a hyphenated-American identity—a "life on the hyphen" (Pérez Firmat 1994)—and they were followed closely in this propensity by the Vietnamese, net of all other factors. Two other important cases involve the Mexicans and Filipinos, both of whom retained strong positive effects on the likelihood of adopting a foreign national identity.

As shown earlier (in table 5.4), those two California-based nationalities shifted to the foreign national identity by greater percentages than any other group on either coast. And in the case of the Mexicans in particular, anecdotal evidence was provided to illustrate how the California sociopolitical context in which the divisive Proposition 187 campaign was conducted had heightened the salience of ethnic and racial boundaries and accompanying processes of reaction formation. As a test of this effect, I entered into the regression a dummy variable for regional location. When this contextual factor was accounted for, the Mexican nationality effect completely washed out of the equation—but the Filipino effect, although reduced in magnitude, remained strong. The results suggest that the propensity of the Mexican-origin youths to identify by national origin at the time of the 1995–1996 survey was accounted for by the effect of the California context. However, the similar propensity of Filipino youths was not explained by any of the predictor variables in the model, raising intriguing theoretical and empirical questions as to why this is so. Perhaps the history of U.S. colonialism in the Philippines and the valence of that colonial past in Filipino collective consciousness may have more to do with the identity choices of Filipino youth as forms of ethnicity that react as much against that past as to their present circumstances. Indeed, the larger theoretical significance of national-origin groups as proxies for their contexts of reception in the United States—and as proxies for the histories of the relations of those countries with the United States—further underscores the complexity of the factors that may impinge on the determination of ethnic self-identities in the second generation.

Expanding the CILS Study: Current Mixed-Methods Research

As noted earlier, with support from the Russell Sage Foundation, we returned to the field in 2001–2003 to locate and contact as many of our respondents as possible (from the baseline sample drawn a decade ago in fall 1991, when most were 14 or 15 years old)—something made much more feasible now with new technologies and Internet companies that have vastly enhanced the success rate of computerized searches on the basis of a few key items of information. We succeeded in locating most of the original respondents, even though many of them (who were now 24 or 25 years old) were no longer living with their parents in the San Diego and Miami metropolitan areas and some, in fact, had moved to many different states across the country. The new (T3) survey focused on the social, cultural, and economic trajectories of this diverse sample of young adults over the previous six years since the last follow-up of 1995–1996. It also included a checklist inventory of major experiences and life events (including contact with the criminal justice system) over the same time period. During these critical years, our respondents have been making their transitions to adulthood: completing their education, leaving the parental home and establishing independent households, securing stable employment, marrying or cohabiting, forming a family and becoming a parent, and some becoming civically involved or even maintaining transnational ties.

Although the results of this latest phase of the study are not yet available, preliminary findings show the wide range and ethnic segmentation of their fates to date: from dropouts to medical school graduates, from county jail to ivy league schools, from aimless drifting in junior colleges and the labor market to well-paying full-time jobs in mainstream careers. The majority remain single and without children to date, but some already have as many as four or five children, whether married, cohabiting, or single-parenting, and substantial proportions are involved in interracial and interethnic relationships. For the men, arrest and imprisonment are the life events most likely to derail them from the educational and occupational paths they had earlier aspired to, while having children early is especially likely to derail the women from their own youthful ambitions. They move back and forth rather than in a linear fashion from one status to the next, depending on a variety of factors, contexts, and turning points. We aim to map in detail the sequence and patterning of these trajectories in early adulthood and analyze their general direction and determinants; trace the degree to which ethnic differences in achievement, acculturation, and experiences of discrimination in adolescence are maintained, widened, or reduced in young adulthood; and probe their implications for social mobility, intermarriage, and ethnic self-identity.

As so many of our findings show, both subjectivity and situationality are essential to understanding the meaning of and changes in ethnic self-definitions among these young new members of American society. Contextualization both helps us account for differences in survey data and requires further study using nonsurvey methods such as in-depth interviews, oral histories, and ethnography. Accordingly, with support from the John D. and Catherine T. MacArthur Foundation Research Network on Transitions to Adulthood and Public Policy, we began a series of in-depth, open-ended, qualitative interviews with a stratified sample of up to 150 of our original San Diego respondents. Through these intensive interviews and oral histories (which are taped, transcribed, and coded via specialized computer software for qualitative analysis) we aim to explore and probe in much greater detail and nuance the kinds of issues that survey instruments and methods constrained us from delving into. Among the themes we have identified for detailed exploration is that of ethnic self-identity, including issues of situational ethnicity, change in ethnic self-identity over time and in different social contexts, the subjective meanings of ethnic and racial labels and identities to the respondents, and—with respect to the effect on ethnonational self-definitions of major historical events—their perceptions of and reactions to the terrorist attacks of September 11, 2001, in the United States, and the concerns which these have provoked about national membership, belonging, and loyalty in a time of war. Given the time-consuming and labor-intensive nature of these qualitative interviews, their transcription, coding, and qualitative analysis will extend well into 2004, and then the results will be merged with the quantitative survey data, which will by that time have been collected, coded, and processed.

Still, early results from these transcribed interviews are already providing a wealth of information about the dynamic processes and contexts that shape ethnicity. For instance, two Mexican-American men in their mid-twenties focused on very different facets of their modes of ethnic self-definition. One focused on the importance of asserting a Mexican identity to others: "It's important for me to say that I'm Mexican. I cross out, like when they give me something on an application to fill in what I am, and Mexican's not there, I put 'other' and I put 'Mexican.'" For the other, poignantly, such an assertion was hard to maintain with his own family: "We were all *pachucos* . . . considered not Mexican because we were born in the U.S., and because we were Mexican and didn't know Spanish. We were looked down on by our own family members because we weren't born in Mexico and weren't speaking Spanish." A young man from Ecuador, by contrast, eagerly identified the United States as his homeland, a conviction cemented during a trip to Ecuador when he was a senior in high school. He went with his family for a two-week vacation, but "after three days, I was soooo ready to go home!" He hated the experience: lack of water for showers, limited electricity, no streets—"just dirt with a bunch of rocks." Yet he strongly identifies as "Ecuadoran-American," he said, because most people in California think that he is Mexican or "Latino" and he wants them to know that he was born in Ecuador and his roots are there. He does not want to forget where he came from.

Contexts shape the meanings of identity assignments and assertions. A young woman identified strongly as Mexican because it is "her blood roots." Even though she went to a predominantly white high school, she said, she never wanted to be white. But she noted that when she went to Mexico, she did identify as American because her cousins imposed this ethnicity on her, whereas when she is in the United States, others tend to impose the Mexican identity on her, not "American." A 25-year-old Vietnamese man put it this way: "I'm from Vietnam but I live in America . . . kind of a hybrid. I . . . identify more with one part or the other when I'm in the opposite setting, you know? So, if I'm in a very non-Vietnamese setting, I'll feel different and I'll identify more as Vietnamese. But when I was in Vietnam, I felt very American in some ways. When I felt tired of speaking only in Vietnamese, I could kind of hang out with these other foreign students and be kind of a tourist. And when you're a tourist in Vietnam, like in a lot of other countries, then the cultural rules don't really apply. So it gave me a lot of freedom, 'cause I could kind of switch."

Identities change and evolve over time and lived experience as well as social space. When he was growing up, a Vietnam-born young man told us that he considered himself American, did not want to associate with other Vietnamese, and hated the Vietnamese Saturday language school that his parents sent him to. In high school most of his friends were "Anglos" and he had no Vietnamese friends. It was only when he attended the University of California that he was "exposed to a lot of cool Asians, Vietnamese, Chinese . . . and my friends were Asians." This was when he started identifying himself as Vietnamese American and became more aware about his origins. A different case is Joseph, who currently identifies as "Asian American." He chooses the label because it is a "broader category," although this identity is not important to him at all. "American" to him means being part of the United States. When he was younger, he identified as Chinese because "we spoke Cantonese at home." When he found out that he was born in Vietnam, he identified as Vietnamese. When he grew up more, he identified as Chinese Vietnamese. Now, he identifies as Asian American because his primary language is English. And still another case is that of a young woman who while in high school considered herself Vietnamese as a way to explain her differences with the broader society. It was in college that she began to consider herself "Vietnamese American: ethnically Vietnamese, culturally American," adding that she has had the most conflict when dating Vietnamese males because she is expected to behave in accordance with female Vietnamese norms. She has adopted the American ideal of gender equality rather than the "traditional foundation" provided by Vietnamese norms. If she has children, she says, she will raise them to identify as American.

The meaning of an asserted identity is not self-evident. For instance, a young woman told us that she identifies as "Filipino American." Although she does not know much about the culture, she is proud to be Filipino and to be living in the United States. She prefers this identity to a pan-Asian label because she would like others to appreciate individual cultural differences, not lump them all together. Before entering college, she used to identify only as "Filipino" because of "the pride thing," she said, but since college, she includes "American" as part of her ethnicity "because 'American' means anyone living in the U.S., not just whites." In sharp contrast, a young Cambodian woman insisted on defining "American" in racial terms, saying emphatically: "How could I be American? I black skin, black eyes, black hair . . . my English not good enough and my skin color black." In further contrast, a 26-year-old man identifies as "Filipino African American." He notes that it is very important because "it says everything about me," who he is. He is proud that he has two different ethnic backgrounds because it gives him a different outlook on how he sees life and other people. He identifies more as black because of his skin color but was raised surrounded by Filipino food, language, and traditions and remembers how his mother would compare everything here to how it was in the Philippines, a frame of reference he still applies. And for yet another respondent, who considers herself Chinese, the distinction between Chinese and Chinese American depends on one's birthplace as well as one's knowledge of Chinese language and culture. While growing up in the United States (she came when she was eight), she watched only Chinese movies until she discovered during her 1996 visit back home, much to her chagrin, that people in China listen to American music. Despite that "betrayal," it was then that she began to accept American English. It is important that her significant other be able to communicate with her parents; therefore, she will date and marry only a Chinese or a Chinese-speaking Chinese American. She notes that some of her friends only look Chinese, but they are Chinese Americans who cannot talk to her parents.

As these brief examples illustrate, the study of ethnic identity is multi-layered and can gain a great deal from mixed methods in comparative research. By combining quantitative and qualitative approaches, and by extending our longitudinal study to encompass a full decade across a critical transitional period of the life span, we will significantly enhance and contextualize our understanding of identity formation processes. Although the final results of these new efforts will not become available for some time, one lesson we have learned through our research to date is plain: namely, the importance of employing mixed methods in order to be able to extend and deepen the analysis of complex issues such as those addressed in this chapter and in this book.

Conclusion

Ethnic identities are not inevitable outcomes but complex products of people's ongoing efforts to interpret, understand, and respond to the social structural, cultural, and historical situations in which they find themselves, within their sets of resources and vulnerabilities. In the present era of civil rights, affirmative action, and ethnic revivals (and in contrast to the way immigrants were treated during the heyday of hegemonic Americanization in the early 20th century), today's newcomers are recategorized in broad racialized pan-ethnic clusters that the host society deems appropriate for those sharing (or imagined to share) a particular language or phenotype—and that convey the symbolic message, with its attendant stereotypes, that they belong to a subordinate status in the national hierarchy. Although the state, the school system, the mass media, and the society at large insist on redefining these immigrants and their children into one-size-fits-all pan-ethnic labels such as "Hispanics" and "Asians," the children themselves are quite plural in their ethnic self-definitions. Challenged to incorporate what is "out there" into what is "in here" and to crystallize a sense of who they are, they "translate themselves" and construct a variety of self-identities. Some cling tenaciously to their parents' national loyalties and retain their parents' national identities, with or without a hyphen. Others shift to an unhyphenated American self-image and identify symbolically with the mainstream, banking on their unaccented English and consonant phenotypic traits. Still others internalize the racial and pan-ethnic categories into which they are constantly classified and identify symbolically with national minorities.

As we have seen, the paths to those different forms of ethnic self-definition are shaped by a variety of social and psychological forces. The results of our surveys show major differences in patterns of self-identification among teenage children of immigrants from scores of sending countries growing up in two distinct corners of the United States. They suggest some of the complex, conflictive, often incongruous and unexpected ways in which race and class, discrimination and acculturation, family relationships, and personal dreams can complicate teenagers' sense of who they are. And they suggest that identities are neither fixed nor irreversible but always a function of relational processes, whose meaning is embedded in concrete social and historical contexts.

Indeed—to return to the four epigraphs with which I began this chapter (by Taylor, Hoffman, Pérez Firmat, and Hwang)—in this dialogical process of "translating themselves," some gain in translation, while others may be lost in it. In *Life on the Hyphen,* Gustavo Pérez Firmat wrote of the 1.5 generation of Cuban-Americans: "One-and-a-halfers are translation artists. Tradition bound but translation bent, they are sufficiently immersed in each culture to give both ends of the hyphen their due. . . . One-and-a-halfers gain in translation" (1994, 7). But in the absence of perceived discrimination and reaction formation (which remain open empirical questions, as suggested by the unexpected responses reported among young Cuban-Americans in Miami during the recent Elián González saga [see Santiago and Dorschner 2000]), the straight-line process of acculturation may well "thin" a Cuban ethnicity and take its inevitable generational toll on Pérez Firmat's U.S.-born, Miami-raised children, if without interfering with their sanguine sense of belonging, as vividly portrayed in the epigraph. Yet in another context, the experience of self-translation and the quandaries of identity can take on a "thickened" and quite different meaning, as expressed by Caroline Hwang, the daughter of Korean immigrants, whose reflections on race and marginality serve as a countervailing epigraph. If for some the search for identity may with time and acceptance blur and fade into the twilight of ethnicity, for others it may with sharpened salience lead into the high noon of ethnicity—and for still others something in the wide range between those poles. But the underlying process is one in which all children of immigrants are inescapably engaged and of which they are acutely aware: making sense of who they are and finding a meaningful place in their adoptive society.

Acknowledgments

I gratefully acknowledge the support provided by the William and Flora Hewlett Foundation for a fellowship year in residence at the Center for Advanced Study in the Behavioral Sciences, Stanford, during 2000–2001; by the John D. and Catherine T. MacArthur Foundation Research Network on Transitions to Adulthood and Public Policy; and by research grants from the Russell Sage, Andrew W. Mellon, Spencer, and National Science Foundations to Alejandro Portes and Rubén G. Rumbaut, Principal Investigators, for the Children of Immigrants Longitudinal Study (CILS), 1991–2003.

References

Alba, R. D. 1985. *Italian Americans: Into the Twilight of Ethnicity.* Englewood Cliffs, NJ: Prentice-Hall.

———. 1990. *Ethnic Identity: The Transformation of White America.* New Haven: Yale University Press.

Aleinikoff, T. A., and R. G. Rumbaut. 1998. "Terms of Belonging: Are Models of Membership Self-Fulfilling Prophecies?" *Georgetown Immigration Law Journal* 13 (1): 1–24.

Banks, S. 1994. "Unflagging Controversy." *Los Angeles Times,* November 10.

Bozorgmehr, M. 1997. "Internal Ethnicity: Iranians in Los Angeles." *Sociological Perspectives* 40 (3): 387–408.

Bozorgmehr, M., G. Sabagh, and I. Light. 1996. "Los Angeles: Explosive Diversity." In *Origins and Destinies: Immigration, Race, and Ethnicity in America,* ed. S. Pedraza and R. G. Rumbaut, 346–359. Belmont, CA: Wadsworth.

Cornell, S., and D. Hartmann. 1998. *Ethnicity and Race: Making Identities in a Changing World.* Thousand Oaks, CA: Pine Forge.

Deaux, K. 1996. "Social Identification." In *Social Psychology: Handbook of Basic Principles,* ed. E. T. Higgins and A. W. Kruglanski, 777–798. New York: Guildford Press.

Erikson, E. H. 1968. *Identity: Youth and Crisis.* New York: W. W. Norton.

Escobar, G. 1999. "Dominicans Face Assimilation in Black and White." *Washington Post,* May 14.

Gans, H. J. 1979. "Symbolic Ethnicity: The Future of Ethnic Groups and Cultures in America." *Ethnic and Racial Studies* 2 (1): 1–20.

Gordon, M. M. 1964. *Assimilation in American Life: The Role of Race, Religion, and National Origins.* New York: Oxford University Press.

Handlin, O. 1973 [1951]. *The Uprooted.* 2nd ed. Boston: Little, Brown.

Hoffman, E. 1989. *Lost in Translation: A Life in a New Language.* New York: Penguin Books.

Horowitz, D. L. 1985. *Ethnic Groups in Conflict.* Berkeley and Los Angeles: University of California Press.

Hwang, C. 1998. "The Good Daughter." *Newsweek,* September 21.

McDonnell, P. J. 1994. "Complex Family Ties Tangle Simple Premise of Prop. 187." *Los Angeles Times,* November 20.

Min, P. G. 1995. "Korean Americans." In *Asian Americans: Contemporary Trends and Issues,* ed. P. G. Min, 199–231. Thousand Oaks, CA: Sage.

Nahirny, V. C., and J. A. Fishman. 1996 [1965]. "American Immigrant Groups: Ethnic Identification and the Problem of Generations." In *Theories of Ethnicity: A Classical Reader,* ed. W. Sollors, 266–281. New York: New York University Press.

Navarrette, R., Jr. 1994. "At the Birth of a New—and Younger—Latino Activism." *Los Angeles Times,* November 13.

Pérez Firmat, G. 1994. *Life on the Hyphen: The Cuban-American Way.* Austin: University of Texas Press.

Phinney, J. S. 1990. "Ethnic Identity in Adolescents and Adults: Review of Research." *Psychological Bulletin* 108 (3): 499–514.

Portes, A., and R. G. Rumbaut. 1996. *Immigrant America: A Portrait.* 2nd ed. Berkeley and Los Angeles: University of California Press.

———. 2001. *Legacies: The Story of the Immigrant Second Generation.* Berkeley and Los Angeles: University of California Press; New York: Russell Sage Foundation.

Pyle, A., and S. Romero. 1994. "Prop. 187 Fuels a New Campus Activism." *Los Angeles Times,* October 25.

Rosenberg, M. 1965. *Society and the Adolescent Self-Image.* Princeton, NJ: Princeton University Press.

———. 1979. *Conceiving the Self.* New York: Basic Books.

Rumbaut, R. G. 1994. "The Crucible Within: Ethnic Identity, Self-Esteem, and Segmented Assimilation among Children of Immigrants." *International Migration Review* 28 (4): 748–794.

Santiago, F., and J. Dorschner. 2000. "Outside Image Bewilders Exiles." *Miami Herald,* April 23.

Tajfel, H. 1981. *Human Groups and Social Categories.* London: Cambridge University Press.

Taylor, C. 1992. "The Politics of Recognition." In *Multiculturalism and "The Politics of Recognition,"* ed. A. Guttman, 33. Princeton, NJ: Princeton University Press.

Tilly, C. 1996. "Citizenship, Identity, and Social History." In *Citizenship, Identity, and Social History,* ed. C. Tilly, 1–17. Cambridge: Cambridge University Press.

Veerasarn, O. 1999. "The Faces of Asian America." *Common Quest* 4 (1): 46–55.

Warner, W. L., and L. Srole. 1945. *The Social Systems of American Ethnic Groups.* New Haven, CT: Yale University Press.

Waters, M. C. 1990. *Ethnic Options: Choosing Identities in America.* Berkeley and Los Angeles: University of California Press.

Commentary

Toward Varied and Complementary Methodologies in the Study of Ethnic Identity in Childhood

Diane Scott-Jones

In part 2 of this volume, we have two interesting and important chapters on the role of ethnicity in children's lives. In chapter 4, Johnson offers us a fascinating view of her work on the strategies African American children use to cope with discrimination in the years of middle childhood. She demonstrates how she has used the measure she developed to assess children's coping strategies in relation to parents' interactions, to the "racial" composition of schools, and to the perception of violence in communities. In chapter 5, Rumbaut describes longitudinal data aimed at understanding stability and change in the ethnic labels adolescents use for themselves. He examines in detail the correlates of these ethnic labels and is able to build a plausible and intriguing story about the adaptation of adolescents in various immigrant groups on opposite sides of the United States.

The findings reported in these two chapters are important in themselves, and indeed, the general lines of research both Johnson and Rumbaut are pursuing are yielding important insights. These comments are focused on the methodological approaches Johnson and Rumbaut have used, as much as on their findings.

The importance of this volume, it seems, is not simply to foster the use of mixed methods in a routine or formulaic manner. Instead, the critical value of this volume is its encouragement of openness regarding what is required and what is acceptable in scientific inquiry. This collection of essays will contribute to the ongoing shift toward creative approaches and away from rigid adherence to particular methodologies. The creativity that is encouraged extends not only to methods of data collection but also to the presentation and interpretation of data. This shift is especially important in research on children from immigrant families in the new wave of immigration and on children of color with a long-standing history in the United States. Children from these groups have been understudied and inappropriately studied. Their inclusion in research requires careful attention to the adequacy of methodology as well as to the conceptual frames guiding the work.

Both Johnson and Rumbaut illustrate the importance of considering the historical context in interpreting data. Identity development is dependent upon the historical period in which children live as well as the particular child's development over time. Rumbaut's 1995–1996 survey followed closely California's passage of Proposition 187. This critical political event is associated with a decline in adolescents' identification as "American" or "hyphenated-American" and an increase in their foreign national and pan-ethnic identifications. Developmental shifts in the adolescents Rumbaut studied, from age 14–15 to age 17–18 years, were confounded with historical shifts from 1992 to 1996. The increase in the percentage of adolescents giving a foreign national identity was greatest for Mexicans and Filipinos (24% each), compared to all other groups. Although both Mexicans and Filipinos lived in Southern California, Rumbaut concluded that the region of the country and the divisiveness of the Proposition 187 campaign explained Mexican, but not Filipino, adolescents' increasing use of their national origin as their self-identity. None of the predictor variables in Rumbaut's model explained the increase in national-origin identity among Filipino adolescents. Without attention to historical context, the difference between the Mexican and Filipino adolescents and the difference between these two and the other groups might have been misinterpreted.

Johnson also acknowledges the importance of the historical context, not through a specific political action as Rumbaut did, but through the general social climate characterizing a historical period. She framed her conceptualization of African American parents' socialization of their children in terms of the parents' experiences of discrimination. Given their own experiences, Johnson reasoned, parents anticipate discrimination toward their children and socialize them accordingly.

Both Johnson and Rumbaut show an important recognition of the social context outside the family. For example, Rumbaut considered the schools' role in adolescents' forging their ethnic identities. He found that adolescents giving "American" as their identity were more likely to have attended suburban schools; in contrast, adolescents who gave pan-ethnic labels were more likely to have attended inner-city schools with adolescents who were American-born ethnic minorities.

Johnson examined schools as contexts varying in percentage of African American students. She found that in schools where African Americans are the majority, children's strategies for coping with discrimination were the least confrontational and children were least likely to anticipate discrimination. This finding is similar to Rumbaut's conclusion that Cubans in Miami are buffered by the large ethnic enclave. Johnson also found that in ethnically heterogeneous schools, children were more assertive and chose strategies that excluded adults but were also fair and aimed to bridge groups of children. In schools in which African American children were a small minority, children used a complex, strategic hierarchy of adults — teachers, principals, parents — to cope with discrimination.

Rumbaut, in figure 5.8, illustrates what he calls the push and pull of acculturation and discrimination on ethnic self-identification. This figure maps various identity groups onto the four quadrants created by crossing acculturation and discrimination. This figure reflects the complexity and differences among groups of adolescents' adaptation to the United States. Rumbaut's depiction of these results is a fine example of the creative use of graphics to illustrate a finding. A recent *American Psychologist* article (Smith et al. 2000) pointed out that early psychologists in the 19th century, before inferential statistics, used a rich array of techniques, such as graphs and tables, to present data, and that many of these techniques are underutilized in current research. Smith et al. recommend that researchers consider ways to present data meaningfully, as Rumbaut has, instead of opting for the uniformity of most current statistical presentations.

A difficult issue in using mixed methods is the movement from open-ended measures to more structured measures that are quick and easy to administer to large groups. In Johnson's measure, the Racial Stories Task, she developed vignettes with an open-ended response format. From the open-ended version, she then developed a version with closed-ended response options. This movement from open-ended to structured measures is one way to develop measures that are grounded in the experiences of participants. Yet Johnson is convinced that the open-ended version of the Racial Stories Task is superior to the structured version she subsequently developed. In the structured version, Johnson notes, children may choose responses from the array presented and may not express their own thoughts if those thoughts are not clearly reflected in the response options.

Johnson also developed a procedure in which the open-ended version of the Racial Stories Task is used as a measure of parent-child interaction. In this procedure, parent-child dyads are videotaped while working together on the Racial Stories Task. Johnson then developed a series of codes for the parent-child interactions. The videotaping and coding were labor intensive and also cost Johnson some participants. Some parents who were willing to participate simply did not follow through with the videotape sessions although they completed other measures. Johnson emphasizes the importance of being practical and tailoring methods to the circumstances and preferences of the participants. She also discusses trade-offs in research using mixed methodologies. Her fear—that rigor might be sacrificed in mixed methodologies—is allayed by her belief in the triangulation of findings and in disciplined procedures for collecting and coding data.

Both Johnson's and Rumbaut's work includes areas in which more descriptive data might have bolstered the findings. Johnson acknowledges that a variable such as her "school racial composition" is merely a proxy for the everyday interactions of children, teachers, and others in different schools. A more detailed description of these interactions would be a great contribution to our understanding of children's coping with discrimination.

Similarly, Rumbaut's study is of self-reported labels and not of the complex construction of ethnic identity in adolescents' lives. Rumbaut has masterfully gleaned many conclusions from survey data but still needed is research that assesses the dependent variable, ethnic identity, in a more complex manner. The meaning of ethnic identity in an adolescent's life could have changed even though the reported label remained the same. In addition, research of this type might benefit from more recognition of and description of the developmental changes that occur for 14- to 18-year-olds generally and in the transition from middle school to high school.

Clearly, methodological change is occurring in the social and behavioral sciences. For example, researchers continue to ponder the usefulness of statistical significance tests (e.g., Mittag and Thompson 2000). Further, researchers continue to call for a range of methodological approaches in the study of ethnic groups and improvement in both the quantity and quality of such work (Sue 1999). One of the most provocative titles in the recent methodological discussions is Tom Weisner's "Why Ethnography Should

Be the Most Important Method in the Study of Human Development" (Weisner 1996). Although his own title might appear to suffer from what Tom calls "methodocentrism," in this article he admonishes researchers to be wary of false dichotomies such as "qualitative/quantitative" and to seek the complementary benefits of a variety of methods. Let us hope that both methodocentrism and ethnocentrism are on the decline and that studies of children of color and children of immigrant families will proceed with conceptual and methodological freedom. Johnson's and Rumbaut's chapters are excellent efforts in that direction.

References

Mittag, K. C., and B. Thompson. 2000. "A National Survey of AERA Members' Perceptions of Statistical Tests and Other Statistical Issues." *Educational Researcher* 29:14–21.

Smith, L. D., L. A. Best, V. A. Cylke, and D. A. Stubbs. 2000. "Psychology without *P* Values: Data Analysis at the Turn of the Century." *American Psychologist* 55: 260–263.

Sue, S. 1999. "Science, Ethnicity, and Bias: Where Have We Gone Wrong?" *American Psychologist* 54:1070–1077.

Weisner, T. S. 1996. "Why Ethnography Should Be the Most Important Method in the Study of Human Development." In *Ethnography and Human Development: Context and Meaning in Social Inquiry,* ed. R. Jessor, A. Colby, and R. A. Shweder, 305–324. Chicago: University of Chicago Press.

Ethnicity, Race, and Identity

William E. Cross, Jr.

The two chapters in part 2 of this volume are at radically different stages of development. Johnson's work (chapter 4) can be considered exploratory, tentative, and somewhat daring, while Rumbaut's piece (chapter 5) is a polished product that conjures notions of the "state of the art." It is that good.

The Three Studies by Johnson

Deborah Johnson's chapter presents three studies conducted at the family, school, and community levels and reflecting her interest in the human ecology of racial coping. From Johnson's perspective, children born to socially stigmatized groups must develop social competencies for negotiating everyday encounters with stigma. Her first study examined the role played by parents in teaching and modeling stigma management. Parent-child dyads were observed while they read and then tried to think of ways to resolve racial conflicts depicted in a handful of written stories (Racial Stories

Task). The child's behavior was coded for the number of utterances made and the number of strategies she/he created to resolve the conflicts. During the child-parent interactions, some parents were observed to contextualize racial cues and racial themes (race accorded high salience), while others decontextualized racial cues (race accorded low significance).

Contrary to what Johnson predicted, parents who decontextualized racial cues embedded in the stories were as effective as parents who contextualized racial cues. This suggests that a race-conscious approach may be no more efficacious than an assimilationist approach in helping children cope with stigma. One might conclude that assimilationist-oriented parents strive to help their children see beyond race in the face of what appear to be racially loaded situations, and that their frame of reference has the potential to draw from their children a rich array of strategies and utterances. On the other hand, the results showed that parents who made race salient (contextualized race) were also very effective in stimulating their children, even though their thrust diverged from the assimilationist approach. Most black parents contextualize race and stigma, and Johnson's work is but a beginning in trying to isolate *modal* patterns of how black parents transfer their race-sensitive perspectives to their children.

In the second experiment Johnson found that the repertoire of coping strategies evidenced by black children changed with variations in the racial-cultural demographics of schools. If nothing else, such findings reject a one-size-fits-all concept of coping and reinforce the conclusion that children modify coping strategies in accordance with the realities of their school environments.

In the final and third study, the racial-coping themes of third to sixth graders were found to be correlated with self-esteem scores; level of perceived community violence (perception of degree of violence in one's community) was treated as a possible moderator. The results for this study are not easy to interpret, because the model tested is inconsistent with the themes from the first two studies. The first two studies showed that parents help their children develop various racial-coping skills, and the second study suggested that the child's environment, such as the type of school attended, may influence which coping strategies will be triggered and which will be employed less frequently. I think it makes more sense to explore how racial-coping skills and perceived violence are associated, with self-esteem inserted as the possible moderator. In the model actually tested, self-esteem is accorded the status of a "racial-coping factor" when in fact it is an individual-difference variable.

In the early part of her paper Johnson argues that a single measure of racial coping (the Racial Stories Task), used with three separate samples and involving three distinct studies, should be included as an alternative "model" in the mixed-methods discourse. To be frank, I think she has failed to muster support for this argument. At the core of the mixed-methods strategy is the administration of multiple measures collected through divergent procedures and involving the same sample. Although Johnson's experiments are interesting, we cannot link the three, because the samples differ from one study to the next.

The Study by Rumbaut

In the counseling psychology literature, there is considerable debate about the possible distinction to be made between ethnic versus racial identity. Phinney (1996) as well as Helms and Cook (1999) are comfortable with the differentiation, constructing their definitions of ethnicity on historical-cultural terms, whereas concepts of race are derived from the physical-visual characteristics of a person's exterior features. This observer (Cross and Vandiver 2001) has argued that in the case of African Americans, no such distinction can be made because black identity can refer to race or culture. Neither Phinney nor Helms and Cook have offered convincing evidence of the separation of the two domains, but in Rubén Rumbaut's magnificent study, we have perhaps the best statement to date that ethnicity and race are not necessarily the same. He also offers rather telling evidence that with regard to both white identity and black identity, there is an inseparable fusion of race and ethnicity.

Using mixed methods (survey data and personal interviews) and a developmental design, identity information was gathered from children and their parents. The two data waves were collected when the target children were enrolled in the eighth and ninth grades and then three to four years later, when the subjects were about to finish high school or were transitioning into early adulthood. The parent perceptions and target-subject interviews were collected at time 2 (T2). The Children of Immigrants Longitudinal Study (CILS) data set incorporates 77 nationalities, including Canadian and white ethnic subsamples. Rumbaut's results show how, early on, both the parents and their children overwhelmingly use nationalist, ethnic, or cultural categories to frame their social identities. In effect, ethnic and bicultural categories dominate the analysis, but a fair number of subjects self-identified as "American"—plain and simple. The use of these categories varied from one ethnic group to the next, and the category of choice was influenced by such factors as social class.

By T2, acculturation had taken hold across all the groups, the most dramatic indicator being a shift in language skills and preferences toward English. From several angles, at least, there is the appearance that almost all of the groups are moving in the direction of Americanization and cultural deracination. However, in an intellectual tour de force, Rumbaut strips away veil after veil to show that with regard to the labels the youth use to categorize themselves at T2, they seem, at first, to be becoming *more* ethnic and bicultural than assimilated! This thickening of ethnicity seems, on the surface, to be just the opposite of what transpired with white ethnic groups at the turn of the 20th century, although I will have more to say about this shortly. In a careful and meticulous analysis, Rumbaut shows the reader that at T2 the various ethnicities have been transformed into *ethno-racial* categories. As the youth immerse themselves in the new culture, their self-labels become racialized independent of whether they speak or prefer English or show signs of an attraction to being American. The racial part of the identity is often forged by experiences with discrimination, while the rapprochement with ethnicity is, in part, a reaction to being labeled as racially different. Again, this trend carries across the various groups, but Rumbaut highlights group differences. At a key point in Rumbaut's story, it becomes clear that the "transformed" ethnicities for these groups have been *racialized.*

For two groups, white ethnics and blacks from the Caribbean, the interlacing of race and ethnicity has reached the point of inseparability. White ethnics become simply "American" with a near invisible hyphen: [white]-American. Likewise, for all the pride they have in their points of origin, blacks from the West Indies and Caribbean selected the label "black" as a category of choice, so much so that the term "black" has two meanings. First, black can be a racial category, and second, black can be a pan-ethnic category that addresses one's interior cultural sense of self. In effect, Rumbaut shows how ethnicity and race can be differentiated for many ethnic groups, but with regard to [ethnic] whites and [ethnic] blacks, the two constructs are nearly impossible to disentangle.

Rumbaut's analysis leaves little room for critique; however, I do take issue with his interpretation of the literature from the early 1920s that focused on white ethnic identity development. He interprets this literature as suggesting that ethnic whites moved from a thick ethnicity to gradual assimilation, resulting in the embracing of a final identity category: "American." But in point in fact, Rumbaut's own data stand as a corrective. Recent cultural studies of Eastern European Jews, the Irish, and other white ethnic groups show that at the turn of the century they, too, went through a *racialization* process (Brodkin 1998; Ignatiev 1995). They moved from ethnic identities to white identities, in which only whites could be labeled as "American." As it turns out, this is what Rumbaut recorded in his current analysis of the Canadian and white ethnic subsamples. Rumbaut's empirical analysis shows in detail how the racialization of white ethnicity is happening among white immigrant groups today, and his findings give more than a hint of how racialization likely operated in the past. Thus, rather than show people of color moving in a different direction than was true for white ethnics at the turn of the century, Rumbaut's analysis demonstrates that racialization is an ongoing process in the psychological socialization of new immigrants, period. *Deculturalization* and *racialization* are opposite sides of the *same* coin with regard to America's socialization and categorization of its newest immigrants.

Methodological Issues and the Study of Black Identity

In addition to reviewing various conference papers, each reviewer has been asked to reflect on the pros and cons of the mixed-methods approach to the study of certain topics, which, in my case, is the study of ethnic identity development. Given my research interests, I will narrow the focus to the study of black identity.

From the late 1930s (Horowitz 1939) and early 1940s (Clark and Clark 1947) and continuing up to the present (Cross and Vandiver 2001; Gordon 1980; Sellers et al. 1998; Spencer 2001), the theoretical orientation guiding the study of black identity has remained amazingly consistent. Researchers depict the black self-concept (BSC) as having two subordinate domains: the general personality (GP) component and the reference group orientation, or, more straightforwardly, the group identity (GI) domain. The GP domain addresses psychological functioning, psychological well-being, "mental health," and universal personality tendencies (psychological propensities found in all human beings). On the other hand, the GI dimension encompasses those group or groups to which the person makes reference in the construction, maintenance, modification, or conversion of his or her orientation toward life, at the practical, secular, spiritual, and existential levels.

To address the *totality* of a black person's self-concept, information must be collected on each domain (BSC = GI data + GP data). A broad

range of personality variables have been employed in the operationaliza-
tion of GP (e.g., self-worth; self-confidence; interpersonal competence;
ego-identity-status; introversion-extraversion, neuroticism; levels of rage,
anger, or hopefulness-hopelessness, etc.), but in the study of black identity
an inordinate emphasis has been accorded self-esteem. Typically, researchers collect GP information from black subjects in order to say something about black psychological well-being or self-hatred and level of psychological functioning or dysfunctionality. Switching the focus to GI, we
note that it is also multidimensional and has been tapped with measures
of racial identity, group identity, race awareness, race ideology, race evaluation, race centrality, race esteem, race image, race self-categorization,
racial miseducation, racial self-hatred, etc. These various measures of GI
are designed to isolate the affective, cognitive, and behavioral sectors of
one's social sense of self.

The history of the study of black identity reveals *a search for the personality and psychodynamic characteristics (GP characteristics) thought to be
associated with certain types of black identity attitudes, ideologies, and beliefs.* There is a broad range of black orientations but researchers have
tended to highlight any one or combination of the following black identity
categories: marginal, assimilationist, bicultural, biracial, nationalistic, immigrant, male-female, gay-lesbian, and racial-self-hating.

From the late 1940s to the mid-1960s, research on black identity "stag-
nated" for both political and methodological reasons. The political issues
are not of concern here and can be reviewed elsewhere (Cross 1991; Scott
1997). Although black identity research has been driven by the BSC = GI
+ GP model described above, it went through two long phases of *unidimensional* emphasis wherein data would be collected on one variable, for
example, GI, and then the results of the study would be discussed and interpreted as if information had been collected on both factors. This was
true because researchers of the time did not think it necessary to collect information on two variables presumed to be so highly correlated and thus in-
terchangeable. The exaggerated role accorded black self-hatred stemmed
from studies that never directly measured black self-esteem. Very little information about black psychological functioning was collected during this
period, resulting in intellectual stagnation and stereotypic thinking about
the black psyche and identity development (Cross 1991; Scott 1997; Gordon 1980).

One of the first mixed-methods studies ever conducted on black identity was completed right in the middle of this period of stagnation. Goodman
(1952) orchestrated an intensive study of black and white nursery school

children; data were collected using child behavior ratings by trained observers, interviews with teachers, social workers, and parents, and a series of projective tests. Although her findings provided some support for the black self-hatred syndrome, Goodman also found evidence of black strengths and psychological resilience, but those data, for whatever reason, were relegated to an appendix and were "downplayed" in the main analysis. Parts of her analysis also called into question some of the negative stereotypes about the black family, for she did not find the degree of single-parent households commonly associated with working-class blacks, a key group represented in her study. By gathering data from multiple sources and engaging multiple methods, Goodman's study produced one of the most three-dimensional pictures of black child development, black youth identity dynamics, and black family functionality ever constructed between 1940 and 1960. However, her study is seldom referenced because it was quickly overshadowed by two book-length studies, one published a year before and the other a few years after the publication of her text. These two works, one a literature review of unidimensional empirical studies (Clark 1955) and the other an original study based on individual administration of a single projective test to a small number of black adults (Kardiner and Ovesey 1951), highlighted what were thought to be racial-self-hatred tendencies.

Ironically, an important possible link between these studies on self-hatred and Goodman's results was never considered. Each of the self-hatred studies conducted by Clark and Clark (1939, 1940, 1947) employed a cross-sectional design, making it possible to compare the identity patterns for one age cohort with another. The out-group racial preference pattern shown by black children aged three to four was "reversed" in the older cohorts, who showed an increasingly in-group orientation. These findings showed evidence of "change" and/or that self-hatred did not automatically gain a firm psychological foothold in many of the children as they grew older. Such an interpretation fits well with Goodman's findings. With one of her measures, she recorded modest support for the self-hatred thesis, but based on observation ratings and interview data from a variety of significant others in the target children's lives, the resulting picture was one of black children who reflect resilience and functionality. Be that as it may, Goodman's study is typically not referenced in any important way in the history of the discourse on black psychological functioning.

Goodman's study aside, the first major breakthrough in black identity research occurred in the early 1970s when researchers finally decided to measure each component of the black self-concept within the same study.

Scores of direct measures of self-esteem were compared to scores of direct measures of group identity. McAdoo (1970, 1985) was one of the first to conduct such a study, and with her longitudinal and multidimensional design, she found that racial preference (GI) is a very poor predictor of children's self-esteem (GP) during both the preschool and the early school years. That is, she discovered many children with high self-esteem but an out-group perspective and others with high self-esteem and an in-group orientation. McAdoo had a difficult time finding an outlet for her study because not only did she show that racial preference was a poor predictor of black children's mental health, but she also demonstrated that black children, on average, have average to high self-esteem, findings which mainstream psychologists found nearly impossible to comprehend, given the popularity of the black self-hatred thesis.

A similar study that did make it to a top-tier research journal was conducted by Spencer (1982), who showed that at a very early age, black children, as a group, may evidence a preference for white, independent of their average level of self-esteem. However, with age, very few black children record both low self-esteem and an out-group orientation. She wondered if any study using preschool black children would find a preference for white that is more a marker of a Western color preference and not self-denigration. Because the early racial preference studies that established the self-hatred thesis relied on preschool samples, Spencer speculated that the self-hatred thesis was an experimental artifact of the age of the sample. As happened in the early Clark and Clark (1947) studies, Spencer found that black children "outgrew" the out-group preference pattern. Spencer was also able to isolate a small number of children who were, in fact, self-hating in that they scored low on self-esteem and held strong out-group perceptions. The percentage of children was very small and their scores were atypical for the sample as a whole. Spencer's work, along with that of dozens of others, redefined the discourse on black personality and black identity development for black children from the preschool to early adolescence stages (Cross 1991). From my vantage point, Spencer and McAdoo showed that short of a mixed-methods design, the discourse on black identity development in young children can move forward only if the black self-concept is understood to have no fewer than two key components (GI and GP) that each must be measured with separate, independent measures.

As the weight of the Civil Rights and Black Power Movements crushed discrimination barriers that once impeded the aspirations of black adults, the focus of most black identity studies shifted from children to adolescent and college-age samples. The spotlight on young adults has produced fewer

rather than more mixed-methods studies, although practically every identity study conducted with black adults has been decidedly multidimensional. Typically, the researcher will develop hypotheses about a myriad of
GP and GI variables, each variable is then operationalized by a unique paper-pencil measure, and all of the separate measures are combined in a
"packet" and administered to adult subjects (usually college students).

As previously discussed, the construct "personality" (e.g., GP) is multidimensional and there are scores of paper-pencil measures, each focusing
on a separate personality trait, that researchers can use in the construction
of survey packets. More problematic has been the GI construct, but in recent years several researchers have worked to show that it, too, is multidimensional. The MEIM (Multi-ethnic Identity Measure; Phinney 1992), CSE
(Collective Self-Esteem; Luhtanen and Crocker 1992), MIBI (Multidimensional Inventory of Black Identity; Sellers et al. 1998), and CRIS (Cross-Racial
Identity Scale; Vandiver et al. 2001) are all paper-pencil scales which, with
the exception of the CRIS, measure GI in the form of both a "total score"
(e.g., overall sense of GI) and component scores (e.g., specific subdimen-
sions of the overall sense of GI). Ironically, these multidimensional GI scales
are producing results that seem to be at odds with the current trend in identity studies conducted with children, as discussed above. That is, while the
studies with children suggest a very complicated relationship between GI
and GP, studies with adults and adolescents point to a straightforward, positive linear relationship between GI and GP. That is, total scores and/or
some component scores for the MEIM, MIBI, or CSE have been associated
with high self-esteem. However, factor analysis of each of these scales reveals that the different levels of the MEIM, MIBI, and CSE are overlapping,
and thus it is not clear whether the subcomponents for each scale are truly
independent, and without proof of psychometric independence, it is not
clear that the scales are actually measuring multiple dimensions of the GI
construct.

Furthermore, given that all the information is being collected through
one methodology, self-report paper-pencil procedures, this too may lead to
simplistic results no matter how multidimensional the scale in question.
Perhaps only a mixed-methods research agenda can reliably uncover the
more stable relationships between GI and GP in the psychodynamics of
black people. It should be pointed out that in the case of the CRIS, the scale
development process put a premium on the nonoverlap of the subcomponents being tapped by the scale (Vandiver et al. 2001). With this in mind it
is interesting to note that contrary to the findings that have been reported
when researchers have employed the CSE, MEIM, or MIBI, which show a

straightforward, positive linear relationship between GI and GP, results from studies using the CRIS reveal complex patterns of identity development. Thus, while the more frequent use of mixed-methods studies of black identity may help override problems of multidimensional identity scales that are not really, in any factor analytic sense, multidimensional, the CRIS shows that it is possible to operationalize multiple GI levels in a single-method study.

As shown in the study by Rumbaut, mixed-methods research may hold the most potential for moving the discourse on black identity and ethnic identity to a higher level of analysis. Recently, Spencer (2001) conducted a study of black adolescents involving interview data, school records and grades, parent perceptions, ecological ratings of the neighborhoods, and self-perception data. Her findings have made it possible to contest the myth associated with the so-called black oppositional stance reportedly found in black adolescents (Fordham and Ogbu 1986). Black oppositionality suggests that high scores on black identity will often be associated with low achievement motivation, poor school performance, and negative parental attitudes which reinforce this negativity. Spencer's findings explode such simplistic thinking. Based on identity data and school records, she identified students with high black identity scores and good school performance as well as those with high identity but low achievement patterns, suggesting the absence of a *simple* relationship between identity and school achievement. In trying to isolate why identity can be linked to divergent achievement patterns, she turned to her other data points. The parental information provided few insights because, for the sample as a whole, black parents showed positive attitudes toward achievement. In fact, she even found that those black students who were hostile toward school retained a clear understanding that school achievement was important to everyone's success in the long run. It was only when she began to juxtapose identity, school, and neighborhood information that Spencer was able to isolate how some black students begin with a positive attitude toward school and life in general, and others become cynics before their time. Spencer's empirical works have long been guided by a theoretical variant of Brofenbrenner's (1989) ecological theory of human development, and just as has been suggested by Burton, Dilwort-Anderson, and Merriwether-deVries (1995), Spencer argues that *ecologically valid empirical studies of human development practically require a mixed-methods research perspective.*

Collecting observational data on neighborhoods, reviewing census records, isolating key school files, conducting interviews with parents, teachers, and the target children, and capturing self-perceptions on both

GI and GP paper-pencil scales are time-consuming and expensive. However, Spencer and her associates were able to (1) rehumanize black kids, who are often turned into monsters in the popular press; (2) challenge myths about the achievement attitudes of working-class and poor black parents; (3) record that identity in and of itself is a poor predictor of school success; and (4) isolate what it is about a black child's overall environment that can trigger reactionary versus proactive coping strategies. If well-developed, multidimensional paper-pencil measures, with nonoverlapping subcomponents, can help us better comprehend the multiple layers of the self, mixed-methods studies have the potential of mapping the person's identity cognitions, feelings, and behavior across multiple contexts, across interactions with different significant others, and, in the case of longitudinal designs, such as Rumbaut's research, across different points in the life span.

References

Brodkin, K. 1998. *How Jews Became White Folks and What That Says about Race in America.* New Brunswick, NJ: Rutgers University Press.

Bronfenbrenner, U. 1989. "Ecological Systems Theory." In *Annals of Child Development,* ed. R. Vasta, 187–248. Greenwich, CT: JAI Press.

Burton, L. M., O. Dilwort-Anderson, and C. Merriwether-deVries. 1995. "Context and Surrogate Parenting among Contemporary Grandparents." *Marriage and Family Review* 20 (3/4): 349–366.

Clark, K. B. 1955. *Prejudice and Your Child.* Boston: Beacon Press.

Clark, K. B., and M. P. Clark. 1939. "Segregation as a Factor in the Racial Identification of Negro Pre-school Children: A Preliminary Report." *Journal of Experimental Education* 8 (2): 161–163.

———. 1940. "Skin Color as a Factor in the Racial Identification of Negro Pre-school Children." *Journal of Social Psychology* 11 : 159–169.

———. 1947. "Racial Identification and Preference in Negro Children." In *Readings in Social Psychology,* ed. T. M. Newcomb and E. L. Hartley, 169–178. New York: Holt.

Cross, W. E., Jr. 1991. *Shades of Black.* Philadelphia: Temple University Press.

Cross, W. E., Jr., and B. Vandiver. 2001. "Nigrescence Theory and Measurement." In *Handbook of Multicultural Counseling,* 2nd ed., ed. J. G. Ponterotto, J. M. Casas, L. A. Suzuki, and C. M. Alexander, 331–393. Thousand Oaks, CA: Sage.

Fordham, S., and J. Ogbu. 1986. "Black Students' School Success: Coping with the 'Burden of Acting White.'" *Urban Review* 18 (3): 176–206.

Goodman, M. E. 1952. *Race Awareness in Young Children.* Cambridge: Addison-Wesley.

Gordon, V. V. 1980. *The Self-Concept of Black Americans.* Washington, DC: University Press.

Helms, J. E., and D. A. Cook. 1999. *Using Race and Culture in Counseling and Psychotherapy: Theory and Process.* Needham Heights, MA: Allyn and Bacon.

Horowitz, R. 1939. "Racial Aspects of Self-identification in Nursery School Children."
    Journal of Psychology 7:301–338.

Ignatiev, N. 1995. *How the Irish Became White.* New York: Routledge.

Kardiner, A., and L. Ovesey. 1951. *Mark of Oppression.* New York: W. W. Norton.

Luhtanen, R., and J. Crocker. 1992. "A Collective Self-Esteem Scale: Self-Evaluation of
    One's Social Identity." *Personality and Social Psychology Bulletin* 18:302–318.

McAdoo, H. P. 1970. "Racial Attitudes and the Self-Concepts of Black Preschool Chil-
    dren." PhD diss., University of Michigan. Abstract in *Dissertation Abstracts Interna-
    tional* 22 (11): 4114.

———. 1985. "Racial Attitude and Self-Concept of Young Black Children over Time."
    In *Black Children,* ed. H. P. McAdoo and J. L. McAdoo, 213–242. Beverly Hills, CA:
    Sage.

Phinney, J. 1992. "The Multigroup Ethnic Identity Measure: A New Scale for Use with
    Diverse Groups." *Journal of Adolescence* 7:156–176.

———. 1996. "When We Talk about American Ethnic Groups, What Do We Mean?"
    American Psychologist 51:918–927.

Scott, D. M. 1997. *Contempt and Pity.* Chapel Hill: University of North Carolina Press.

Sellers, R. M., N. Shelton, D. Cooke, T. Chavous, S. J. Rowley, and M. Smith. 1998. "A
    Multidimensional Model of Racial Identity: Assumptions, Findings, and Future
    Directions." In *African American Identity Development,* ed. R. L. Jones, 275–302.
    Hampton, VA: Cobbs and Henry.

Spencer, M. B. 1982. "Personal Identity and Group Identity of Black Children." *Genetic
    Psychology Monographs* 106:59–84.

———. 2001. "Racial Identity and School Adjustment: Questioning the 'Acting White'
    Assumption." Paper presented at SRCD symposium "Achievement and Affective
    Correlates of Race-Linked Stereotypes: Developmental Implications," Minneapolis,
    MN, April 2.

Vandiver, B. J., P. E. Fhagen-Smith, K. Cokley, W. E. Cross, Jr., and F. C. Worrell. 2001.
    "Cross's Nigrescence Model: From Theory to Scale to Theory." *Journal of Multicul-
    tural Counseling and Development* 29:174–200.

PART III

Culture and Developmental Pathways

6

Taking Culture Seriously:
Making the Social Survey Ethnographic

Tom Fricke

Building on earlier knowledge of the village, living smack in the research site (like any good anthropologist), and keeping the population to a manageable size is paying off with excitement and the riches of detail not possible in Sangila. And look! The return to a village pays off in quantum in the kind of information that can be gotten—I feel like a real live anthropologist again, strolling the village in search of stories, pulling out forms completed by interviewers to tell them that this or that fact needs checking because I *know* the person involved. . . . I am exploding with enthusiasm at being back here. I had hoped that some of the disappointment of the Sangila site (re: coming up with the real mix of anthropology and the survey) would be cleansed here. And so it is. I am a practicing anthropologist here and I'm running a survey at the same time. And I'm having a ball. . . . [Y]ou will be interested to know that the interviewers have been coming back with the censuses and genealogies . . . and have been saying, "Hey, these questions really work here. I see now why you made them that way!" . . . I feel vindicated in constructing some of those questions the way we did.

Nepal field letter, November 16, 1987

Not so long ago, driving an empty grain truck down a scoria graveled road, hauling my trail of red dust west into the blue sky, following the other grain truck driven by [my friend], listening to the recently returned meadowlarks, and taking in the sweep of all this purity of space I woke up to myself and started laughing. I am enjoying this work too much to call it that! It feels so good to try getting these gears to shift up or down in the ancient truck, grinding away and finally slipping in with that sweet click of accomplishment. Feels good, too, to smell dust and oil and the near ferment of old grain in the bins. And to have grease and dirt worked into the cracks on your knuckles so that you can't quite get it all out by washing your hands. Grass-stained, oil-stained, grainstained jeans. Cow shit on the boots. With these occasional epiphanies, I break from thinking about all this as data, just long enough to savor the clear stream of my joy at what I do.

North Dakota field letter, April 29, 2000

That famous Bostonian Willie Sutton, when asked why he robbed banks, replied, "Because that's where the money is." In a similar spirit, I would like to suggest that the short answer to why a social scientist would want to conduct field research is because that's where the people are. Although it is not often stated quite so straightforwardly, this seems to me to be the main attraction for the cross-disciplinary appeal of combining social surveys with other forms of data collection that bring researchers closer to the people they study.

Of course, one common way of thinking about mixed methods is to place the use of social surveys against the foil of something called ethnography. The advantages of ethnography and mixed-methods approaches to social research have been repeated in so many publications that it begins to become an issue as to whether anything new can be said. Well-done ethnographies, we are told, give attention to meaning; they are able to do so by requiring observation and immersion in the lived realities of the everyday world (Van Maanen 1988; Shweder 1996; Weisner 1996). In combination with the social survey, ethnography contributes all manner of advantage to the survey alone. Mixed-methods survey-ethnographies, we are told, reduce errors of nonobservation and measurement; they allow relevant new variables to be added to surveys during data collection itself; and they provide insight into the meaning of variables (Axinn, Fricke, and Thornton 1991; Caldwell, Reddy, and Caldwell 1988; Caldwell, Hill, and Hull 1988).

Putting it like this seems to close the book on the topic very much like the way responses to a closed-ended survey question are hoped to exhaust the range of relevant possibilities. But I believe there is more to be said. The problem with putting this in terms of "advantages" is that it leaves intact a number of assumptions about the relationship between ethnography and the social survey. To speak of advantage is to imply a standard of evaluation. Opposing the social survey to ethnography seems to mask an underlying argument that can never be satisfactorily answered outside the disposition of a particular researcher.

Thus, survey and ethnography in the received view stand in some kind of fundamental opposition that roughly tracks such other oppositions as quantitative and qualitative or science and humanities. In addition to establishing a misleading parity of level that suggests that something called the survey is properly compared to something called ethnography, oppositions like these miss more fundamental issues and confuse discussions. On the one hand, "ethnography" seems to be a synonym for "participant observation." On the other, it appears to include any qualitative method where people are allowed relatively unconstrained talk. The former is discouraging for researchers who lack the time or inclination to spend substantial chunks of a research calendar in the field. The latter leads us to weirdly conflate a variety of methods, such as focus groups and long interviews, as doing essentially the same thing (Fricke 1997a, 1997c). Finally, those researchers who use surveys as a key component of their ethnographic work get categorized as odd hybrids doing neither one thing nor the other. To avoid this, it makes sense to clarify that "ethnography" is not a method in the same way that the social survey is clearly a method for collecting a specific kind of information.

Willie Sutton's answer to his interlocutor entices us by all that it says with so few words. It assumes a whole structure of relationships and a social universe that makes this thing called money workable and desirable to obtain (Searle 1998, 126–128): the cultural agreements, the political economy of banks, and all the rest. Although I cannot compete with Sutton's elegance in my "going where the people are," I imply a good deal with that phrase and would like to use this essay to place it in context and illustrate the value of this activity for specific research questions. This requires a discussion of ethnography, of useful theories of culture that can guide mixed-methods research, and of examples from my own field research. It requires that we rethink our consideration of ethnography as a method and revisit the values of particular data collection activities to our analytical goals.

I want to argue that going to where the people are, that is, having primary researchers actually spend time with the subjects being studied in their "natural" settings, confers special data collection and analytic possibilities of great use to certain kinds of questions for which survey instruments are also a data collection tool. The issue of the researcher's location with respect to data collection seems to me to be behind many discussions of ethnography's advantage. As Basso puts it, place is the thing that is taken for granted until "as sometimes happens, we are deprived of these attachments and find ourselves adrift, literally *dislocated*" (1996, xiii). The dislocation that researchers feel with respect to reliance on social surveys is relative to their analytic desires. And the place the researcher needs to be is similarly relative.

All this is to say that, without quite realizing it, the contemporary interest in bringing ethnography into conversation with surveys may be a way of smuggling the notion of place back into social research. Thus, in discussing the role of ethnography in human development research, Weisner (1996) was explicit about the centrality of something he called a "cultural place" to any human's well-being and, because of that, to any research pretending to be concerned with human beings. "Ethnography," he writes, "gets us out there in the midst of some cultural place and in the midst of cultural practices and it gets at the meanings and experiences and moral significances of those cultural activities to the participants themselves" (1996, 309). Becker spends a substantial part of his book *Tricks of the Trade* discussing the importance of place: "Everything has to be someplace" (1998, 50–57). Being someplace, however, depends on where you draw the boundaries. One can be different degrees of distance from the people being studied and still share a cultural space. Weisner's attention to behavior or practices points to a location in everyday life. The bounds of shared meaning systems can also extend beyond this local community of face-to-face encounters.

For many, it must seem a contrived kind of housekeeping to make the distinction between ethnography and the researcher's location. After all, most ethnographers are precisely among the people they are studying during their data collection. But the issue arises because several disciplinary traditions highly reliant on survey modes of investigation have recently turned to a concern with meaning and culture (Kertzer and Fricke 1997; King, Keohane, and Verba 1994; Jessor, Colby, and Shweder 1996). Nearly any cultural anthropologist would argue that culture is always important, at the very least by constituting a background horizon against which any individually measured variable achieves its meaning. Still, a good deal of sound research gets done by keeping that meaning in the background. The turn toward an interest in meaning is a novel enterprise for many who have been wedded to the social survey as a primary method. They have appropriately turned to anthropology, the discipline most associated with a concern for culture, for help in pursuing this new interest. The paradox in that turn is that anthropologists, already doing everything within an ethnographic context and with a notorious, if not universal, distrust of method (Shweder 1996, 15–16), were often ill-prepared to offer what these other practitioners needed. A situation like this cries out for a return to fundamentals on all sides (Fricke 1997a, 248–250; MacIntyre 1988, 355).

Ethnography as Taking Culture Seriously

One way to begin considering what ethnographically informed social research might look like, as opposed to social research that could not care less about ethnography, is to look at the relevance of culture to the specific questions being asked. Shweder suggests that the product of anthropological investigations, also called ethnography, "is about something called culture" (1996, 19). This seems the essential criterion for defining ethnography as an approach in a way that avoids the logical mistakes that come from thinking of ethnography as a discrete method.

We know that outstanding ethnographic accounts have been written in the absence of participant observation. Martin's *The Woman in the Body: A Cultural Analysis of Reproduction* is an example of how a solid ethnography can be written using a sample of women, a team of research assistant interviewers, and a healthy reliance on the long qualitative interview as a primary method (1987, 3–14).[1] We can also think of accounts that are based on some form of participant observation but that are not centrally "about something called culture," or perhaps no more centrally than much survey-based social science. George Orwell's *Road to Wigan Pier* and James Agee and Walker Evans's *Let Us Now Praise Famous Men* are both powerfully detailed documentaries but are generally felt to lie outside the canon for ethnography.[2]

Some of my own work shows how data collected in the social survey can be used to answer ethnographic questions. One such question about meaning and behavior, for example, is whether people grouped into an undifferentiated kinship category such as cross-cousin are treated differently by virtue of whether they are first cousins or a more distant degree of cousin. Some anthropologists might argue that they are not if there is no term to make them different. My own information from a social survey in Nepal suggests that they are treated quite differently in spite of sharing a common kin designation (Fricke 1995, 211). Are the data that allow me to look at this question any less ethnographic for being from a survey?

I define doing ethnography for my students as using a suite of methods to gather information within an overall orientation and set of research questions that are directed toward cultural understanding. Ethnography is research that takes culture seriously. The methods are various and the specific ones chosen are directed toward gathering data that will open up aspects of culture. The suite includes participant observation, the long un-structured interview, genealogical reconstruction, content and other textual analyses, social surveys designed for later quantitative analyses, and more. The anthropologist Roy Rappaport, when speaking to the classes that we taught together at the University of Michigan, defined anthropology as no more than "the study of the human condition." To the extent that culture is a key element of the human condition for living people, then any method that unlocks a portion of that culture can be thought of as ethnographic.

The Cultural Framework

This raises the issue of what, exactly, culture is. If interdisciplinary bor-rowing of methods has occasioned its share of mystery, the uses of culture outside anthropology have been at least as confusing and the source of even greater frustration. Hammel comments on one element of that frustration:

> Without putting too fine a point on it, the use of "culture" in demography seems mired in structural-functional concepts that are about 40 years old, hardening rapidly, and showing every sign of fossilization. . . . Over the last 40 years, anthropological theory has moved away from the institu-tional, structural-functionalist approach it has long presented to its sister social sciences, toward the elucidation of local, culture-specific rationali-ties, in the building of which actors are important perceiving, interpreting, and constructing agents. (1990, 456)

The example of demography's engagement with the concept is a par-ticular instance of a more general condition in the nonanthropological so-cial sciences. But it is also true that within anthropology itself the urge to be current gives some anthropologists pause when I argue that Geertz's now aging definition of culture, with some modification, may be adequate for contemporary uses (Fricke 1997a, 1997b). The frustration for non-anthropologists comes from this moving-target quality.[3] There seems to be little in the way of a stable definition for this concept across the history of the very discipline to which it is most central.

The concept's tenacity, however, is testimony to its usefulness. Moreover, most theories of culture since the shift from the structural-functionalist models of the past bear a strong enough similarity to inspire confidence. The title of Hammel's essay, "A Theory of Culture for Demography," implies that beyond the agreed-upon similarities among definitions, the main criterion for favoring one over the other has something to do with its usefulness to the problem at hand.

Geertz's now classic definition of culture as "an historically transmitted pattern of meanings embodied in symbols, a system of inherited conceptions expressed in symbolic forms by means of which men [and women] communicate, perpetuate, and develop their knowledge about and attitudes toward life" (1973, 89), and his further notion that culture constitutes both models *of* and models *for* reality are still serviceable in spite of their age. More recent theoretical statements recycle some version of them (Alexander 1988, 1990), and the crucial mechanisms for bringing Geertz's emphasis on shared meanings and the relative autonomy of culture into individual variation have been usefully developed (Strauss and Quinn 1997; D'Andrade and Strauss 1992).[4]

The important element of Geertz's distinction between culture as a model of and a model for reality is that it distinguishes between culture as worldview (the perceived worlds of human actors that should define the significance of behaviors and institutions for the analyst) and culture as motivation (or the moral worlds of human actors). These two elements find their parallels in another, more recent definition of culture that also highlights the elements of community and construction so important to contemporary thinking:

> I have been telling my own students that a culture is "a reality lit up by
> a morally enforceable conceptual scheme composed of values (desirable
> goals) and causal beliefs (including ideas about means-ends connections)
> that is exemplified or instantiated in practice." Members of a culture are
> members of a moral community who work to construct a shared reality
> and who act as though they were parties to an agreement to behave ra-
> tionally within the terms of the realities they share. (Shweder 1996, 20)

These models of and models for quality of culture suggest something about location. If culture can be taken as a metaphorical place, as Weisner has it, then it is a place that is under construction within a community of existing commitments. Categorical models for reality may exist at different levels of generality beyond the local group. Given the "ethnographizing" of virtually all human cultural groups, researchers have access to many of these without necessarily experiencing them on the ground. But models for reality, the moral universe in practice, are instantiated in behavior by and among people in concrete communities. Research that means to explore this aspect of culture in action is obviously enjoined to go to where the people are.

Making Culture Usable

These concepts are useless if they imply no procedures for getting at them in the field. Fortunately, Shweder's point that these models or schemes are "exemplified or instantiated in practice" offers an entry into the world of meaning beyond the self-reflection of respondents who might be asked, "What does this mean?" Philosophical literature and anthropological lore both make the case that the relationship between behavior and implied moral goods need not be conscious to the cultural actor (Flanagan 1991, 21; MacIntyre 1992, 16–17). For the analyst, people share a frustrating lack of concern about their culture-based motivations or the details of their underpinning. My own field questions as a doctoral student in Nepal usually elicited the "because that's how it's done" response. But "we do it because that's how we've always done it" is a quite reasonable answer given the process by which cultural notions of the good are internalized (MacIntyre 1992; Blum 1994). This process is largely an unconscious building of habitual orientations and practices. The unconscious quality means that all access to cultural models requires analysis. Both Weisner's and Shweder's mention of behavior ties one possible avenue for entry into cultural analysis to tangible, observable information available to any researcher. This suggestion that such cultural indices exist outside a person's head echoes those other cultural theorists who emphasize that cultural analysis should not deter the empirically minded (Wuthnow 1987; Ortner 1973).

To speak of behavior is to talk about culturally meaningful action. Making analytic sense of that meaning involves interpretation, itself an imaginative act. This is the crux of nervousness for researchers concerned with replicability; it ups the ante for those who are used to accepting their data at face value. It helps, of course, that interpretations are subject to evaluation; they are judged more or less good, or plausible, against the standard of coherence: "Ultimately, a good explanation is one which makes sense of the behavior; but then to appreciate a good explanation, one has to agree on what makes good sense; what makes good sense is a function of one's readings; and these in turn are based on the kind of sense one understands" (Taylor 1985, 24).

In agreement with nervous empiricists, Shweder acknowledges that we cannot get inside other people's heads. But he insists that it is possible to make interpretations of meaning through a similar process of "mind reading" or looking for pattern and coherence among disparate actions or other indices of cultural meaning:

> Whichever interpretation we settle upon, a true ethnography is a mind read in which we rely on our mental state concepts to interpret the discourse and praxis of members of some moral community. Whatever interpretation we settle upon, we do not treat what people tell us in an interview as an incorrigible representation of their inner life but rather as one more piece of information to be made use of, as we construct a model of the mental state concepts exhibited in their behavior. (1996, 28–29)

Both Taylor and Shweder are here concerned with the subjective meaning of action for an individual. But the materials, the unstated frame or background horizon, conferring much of that meaning come from the cultural context in which behaviors occur. That being so, any analysis seems to require a prior interpretive act involving discovery and characterization of key themes, symbols, or scenarios for a given culture. Most anthropologists would argue for a limited number of such key, or recurrent, themes (Ortner 1973, 1989; Shweder 1996). Ortner suggests that among the indications that the analyst has stumbled onto a key symbol are the following: being told it is so by an informant, noticing that people react positively or negatively to it, noticing that an element or theme appears across different domains, noticing an unusual elaboration around a theme or symbol, and noticing a higher level of sanctions and rules around a particular theme (1973, 1339).

Such themes could be of the level of generality as the popular notion of American individualism (Bellah et al. 1996) or the characterization of the leitmotif of reciprocity and exchange in other societies (Fricke, Axinn, and Thornton 1993). They may be highly localized, too, bringing the operation of these more general themes into specific settings where details of local history and face-to-face interactions are relevant (Fricke 1990, 1995; Ortner 1989).

Shweder illustrates the process of imaginatively reconstructing experience in another culture in an ethnographically oriented research program. "Mind reading," he writes, "begins with conceptual analysis" (1996, 27). He suggests we start with the local concept of person and that we work out from there to local conceptions of the world and the possibilities for action in that world (see also Fricke 1997b, 196–200).

Going to Where the People Are

The nature of the social survey is that it emphasizes information about individuals. The individual is the case (Ragin and Becker 1992). Although it is certainly possible to gather some information on context[5] in the social survey, the overwhelming advantage of this method is its ability to gather standardized information on individual characteristics, behaviors, and attitudes from the point of view of the interviewee. The most suitable analyses for this kind of information are examinations of variation across individuals on specific measures and the patterns of variation between multiple measures across individuals. Because of costs in time and money, the survey by itself imposes severe restrictions on the kinds of information that can be gathered for both individuals and contexts, although that range has been dramatically expanded in some recent experiments (Axinn, Barber, and Ghimire 1997; Axinn, Pearce, and Ghimire 1999).

Although the social survey emphasizes information about individuals, the respondents are meant to reflect the experience of people within some large or small unit. National- or regional-level surveys involving random samples most clearly dislocate information for individual people from the concreteness of their local context but are nevertheless intended to refer to a kind of imagined context for the sampled population. Surveys within communities or neighborhoods most obviously lend themselves to analyses that make use of information from the localized moral community in which the surveyed people live.

While it is always true that culture is implicated in any human activity, the direct relevance of cultural understanding to any particular research varies with the questions being asked. It is possible to imagine a continuum in which, at the one end, a narrow set of individual-level causal questions allows the researcher to more or less ignore questions of constructed meaning and, at the other, a deep concern with meaning makes culture a central theme. Thinking of culture as either a place or a moral community suggests that it is a context in which individual behavior becomes meaningful. The more important concrete and local context is to the research problem at hand, the more valuable it is for the researcher to know about it firsthand. The more important the concern with moral enactment, or models for reality, the more important the local context.

In my own work, I have analyzed survey data sets representing the full range from national, through regional, to highly localized community surveys. All of the studies I have been involved with have concerned issues relating to family life, individual life course transitions, and intergenerational relationships. The survey data for these studies include nationally representative samples from Taiwan (Thornton and Lin 1994), a regional sample from the Pakistani Punjab (Fricke, Syed, and Smith 1986), and ethnographically oriented community surveys in Nepal (Fricke et al. 1991). I am more recently involved in data collection for a rural community on the Northern Plains in the United States. Although this work varies in the extent to which survey and other methods are combined in the actual data collection process, all of it has been concerned with cultural meanings and themes.

My location as a researcher across these projects has been at varying removes from the people being studied. The Taiwan research involved an island-wide representative sample in an entirely unfamiliar culture region with which I became familiar only through reading existing ethnographies. The Pakistan work also used a representative survey data set but was located within a general South Asian context which I knew from my own research and training. My Nepal work most closely represented the mix of bringing the researcher to the people in combination with social survey since it took place in two communities in which I lived during various data collection phases. And the North Dakota work, still ongoing, brings me closest of all to the people I study, both because of the participant observation that is primary and because of the cultural assumptions I share with people in my study community.

In the remainder of this essay, I want to use the experience of three different projects to illustrate the uses of ethnography and mixed methods in social research with reference to different levels of integration between the survey and going to where the people are.

Culture at a Distance: Making Existing Survey Data Ethnographic

While it is true that all concern with meaning involves an imaginative act, the specificity of the analyst's required mind reading varies. Even without going to the field, ethnographic knowledge can be used with the social survey. This is good news for researchers lacking the time to actually engage in fieldwork; it also means that existing survey data sets can use ethnographic materials, although it places limitations on the range of methodological integration. Bringing ethnographic materials to bear on existing survey data is a useful way to more precisely define the meaning of variables.

Even the addition of meaning as models of reality can leave results open to dramatically altered interpretations. The simple example below comes from an analysis of a survey conducted in a single region in rural Pakistan and involves an analysis of age at marriage (Fricke, Syed, and Smith 1986). The survey benefited from an international collaboration in which variables for local marriage practices were incorporated into the data set. In this example, however, I want to look at a measure that is less obviously thought of as a "cultural" matter.[6]

One of the classic "modernization" variables in the demographic analysis of age at marriage is education. Across the world there are few relationships more consistent than the positive one between these two measures: any schooling at all seems to be related to later ages at marriage; and the higher the schooling levels, the greater the age at marriage. Nevertheless, our understanding of this relationship is deeply interpretive. Older demographic transition theory took education to be an indicator of modernization and argued that it was correlated with secularization, increased rationality, and heightened individual autonomy. Even the successors to this theory seldom question the common meaning of education across settings. Their interpretations of its impact on other variables may differ, as for example when they suggest that parental desires to educate their children keep them out of the marriage market longer. The explanations for a positive relationship between age at marriage and educational attainment have two basic forms in these different approaches. One focuses on the autonomy education confers on individual children (modernization theory), and the other allows for parental controls over the marriage timing of children but suggests a fairly mechanical relationship between the incompatibility of schooling and marriage.

But neither of these explanations is concerned with the specific meaning of education in context, and this might vary considerably across settings. In our analysis of survey data gathered in rural Punjabi villages, my colleagues and I noted that women's education had the usual positive relationship with age at marriage even when controls for numerous other individual characteristics were accounted for in multivariate models. Table 6.1 displays the relationships.

Knowing nothing about the setting, the analyst might be tempted to interpret these results in terms of a modernization framework: education leads to greater autonomy, which leads to more control over one's destiny and results in higher ages at marriage. But the results also show that the substantial fraction of women who attended school only briefly, without

Table 6.1. Education and Age at Marriage among Rural Punjabi Women in Pakistan

Woman's education	A	B	C	(n)
No schooling	16.1	16.3	16.4	(72)
Attended, 0 attainment	17.7	17.3	17.5	(74)
1–12 years completed	19.3	19.1	18.5	(19)

Source: Fricke, Syed, and Smith 1986, 501.
Note: A = zero-order mean. B = controlling for birth cohort, father's occupation, and woman's work before marriage.
C = controlling for variables in B plus the following: relationship between families before marriage, age at menarche, engagement status, type of dowry, payments to husband's family, marriage type, and wealth flows at marriage.

completing a year, marry at later ages than those who have never attended school at all.

Neither the demographic transition theory explanation nor the incompatibility explanation works for these relationships. My coauthors and I argued that the relationship could not be understood without reference to highly specific features of the local context. We argued that education had become part of a larger world of symbolic indicators of status and that any schooling at all conferred a standing on the natal family of a woman and allowed them to wait longer to marry off their daughter since this status counterbalanced the loss of a woman's value in marriage as a result of increasing age.

We noted that the relationship between education and employment was hardly relevant here. Women were not likely in this setting to be serious supporters of their families in monetary work, certainly not in monetary work requiring education. We also noted that all marriages in this setting were arranged marriages. The failure of standard explanations that ignored context caused us to turn to the ethnographic literature on Punjabi marriages. We focused on literature that discussed marriage within the context of wider relationships organized by family and kinship, including material on the symbolic significance of women, the relation between person and group, the social organization of marriage, prestige systems, and cultural theories of personhood and gender. Our reading of education as a marker of quality, influencing the desirability of marriage connections, placed the experience of schooling within a wider array of prestige markers that operate in marriage negotiation. The actual educational content, and the implications for autonomy in a setting where no woman chooses her own spouse, were secondary to our thinking.

Our examination of schooling converted the measure from a story about education to a culturally meaningful symbol that made a statement about a woman's family. In so doing, we drastically altered the possible interpretation of an empirical relationship. In the same way any researcher is concerned with plausibility (Becker 1996), our interpretation trumped received models devoid of cultural content because it more coherently accounted for what was anomalous in these other models. It did so, moreover, using a framework that established a consistent culture-based story for all other variables in the analysis.[7]

While attention to existing ethnographic materials can, in a sense, reconstitute the social survey toward ethnography by modifying our understanding of variables, the use of materials from data collections separated by time and space make our interpretation plausible but less conclusive than if we were able to provide testimony from the surveyed sites themselves. Our analytic process in this reconstitution parallels Shweder's injunction that we begin, like the survey, with the individual and locate her within ever widening contextual circles or fields of meaning. Because of the separation between ethnography and the survey, however, these fields are imagined and confined to general cultural models. They do not include the concrete locations of the actual study participants, pay little attention to the details of physical place, and are more inferential in drawing the connection between shared models and individual behavior than if survey and fieldwork were simultaneous. Our confidence was based on the coherence of our interpretation in its ability to bring empirical relationships revealed by survey data into conformity with ethnographies removed from the actual sites in time and space.

Culture Up Close: Social Survey and Participant Observation

> The paper is disappointing. The research was conducted in small villages of Nepal and as such belongs to the new, emerging field of microdemography. The analysis, however, could have been done with a much larger data set. It neither has the advantage of anthropological small-scale, indepth studies, nor of a large-scale sample survey. (Reviewer's comments on the manuscript that became Fricke and Teachman 1993)

> Fricke's chapter is one of those *Mad Magazine* anthropological articles where you have to memorize the names of districts and clans in order to follow the argument. (Reviewer's comments on the manuscript that became Fricke 1995)

If existing representative sample surveys can make use of ethnographic materials to inform analysis, the possibilities for integrating cultural models and quantitative analysis are immeasurably enhanced by more intensive mixed-methods strategies. Part of this expansion of possibility in the combination of survey with the simultaneous ethnography of everyday life has to do with the sheer variety of data types that can be gathered from the same people. Connections only imagined in the reinterpretation of existing surveys can be made concrete. The concerns about the plausibility of interpretation in the Pakistan example can be addressed with correspondingly closer reference to the actual study participants; hypotheses can be generated with a much deeper specificity, and more information can be brought to bear in their testing; actual mechanisms by which a shared culture becomes personal are observed; the element of discovery is enhanced. Many of these characteristics have been accounted for in the already cited literature on ethnography.

The model of such research for most people is a study that simultaneously combines social survey and residence by the primary investigator in the setting of interest. Even here, there is a good deal of variation in how well the researcher knows her community or individual people in it. My own research of this type has been most developed in ethnographic survey and participant observation research in Nepal with the Tamang Family Research Project (TFRP), an effort to gather data on and understand transformations in family relationships and demographic outcomes in two rapidly changing communities called Timling and Sangila. Although sharing a general cultural orientation and ethnic identity, the two communities were chosen because they differed in their proximity to the large urban area of Kathmandu. The more remote of the two communities, Timling, had been the site of my earlier participant observation research in 1981. Sangila was added as a research site during the combined survey and participant observation phase of research in 1987. In that second research phase, survey instruments were administered to all 1,520 residents of the two communities aged 12 and older (Axinn, Fricke, and Thornton 1991; Fricke et al. 1991).[8]

Data collection by both trained interviewers and primary researchers included lengthy residence in both communities. My earlier fieldwork in Timling allowed an intensification of local knowledge that was not possible in Sangila, where the simultaneous supervision of the survey and involvement in more participant observation types of data collection created a tension between the two activities. As the first field letter excerpt at the head of this chapter shows, local knowledge gained previously at the remote site allowed the design of a questionnaire well suited to that setting and the use of community knowledge that enhanced my ability to check the accuracy of questionnaires, and perhaps most important, it allowed a mutual familiarity and trust between researcher and study community that created a much more welcoming environment for data collection. Nevertheless, the multilevel analytic possibilities that grow out of this intensive mixed-methods ethnography are well illustrated by the overall project.

The theories of culture that are most useful to researchers who wish to use social surveys are those that allow hypotheses to be developed in terms of local frames of meaning and motivation. In the Pakistani example, we can see that the specific meaning of a common variable can be quite different across contexts. But the contexts include cultural frameworks for motivation that may have profound implications for developing the analytic stories we want to test with our quantitative data. The above discussion of culture as model of and for reality suggests that these frameworks may be made available to the researcher through the experience of everyday life in the community of interest. Shweder's suggestion that we begin with concepts of the person is in line with an interest in those models of reality. Other morally charged themes get at those models for reality that are a part of the motivational contexts for behavior.

Several statistical analyses from the TFRP data make direct use of such models. When primary researchers go where the people are, they have the luxury of both discovering these and identifying their operation in daily life while they are still in the data collection phases of their work. An important characteristic of these models is that they may seem far removed from the research problem motivating the data collection itself. At the same time, the cultural argument is that they are more or less shared frameworks and their variation from person to person will be restricted. Thus, while their exploration may not warrant the allocation of precious space and time on questionnaires, living in the study community allows for both discovery and deeper investigation.

For the Tamang, as for any people, the cultural construction of personhood is a central concept for understanding why people do what they do or how they see themselves in relationship to others. It makes a difference if, as for the Tamang, a person's physical substance is thought to be inherited in highly specific ways from each parent.[9] In Tamang reproductive models, mothers contribute the ephemeral flesh and blood of the body while fathers contribute the enduring bony parts. To an analyst concerned with, for example, explaining changes in age at marriage, this may seem sufficiently removed from the research problem at hand as to be an item of cultural trivia. But this cultural idea powerfully undergirds the structure of relationships between kin related through the two parents. Coupled with key cultural themes that emphasize reciprocity and exchange, an understanding of these cultural elements informs any analysis that involves relationships between people. As an ethnographer looking for resonances across domains, I might note that the quality of flesh and blood is that it decays when not renewed through reproduction. I might further note that the alliances that are orchestrated through a woman's marriage create relationships that will also decay if they are not renewed through further marriages in subsequent generations. In a contrast that parallels that between flesh and bone, membership in and relationships organized among people sharing patrilineal clan names endure across time and generation. I have used these themes to develop statistical analyses of such demographically important topics as the timing of first birth (Fricke and Teachman 1993), age at first marriage (Dahal, Fricke, and Thornton 1993), and the local politics of marriage (Fricke 1990, 1995).

Discovering basic categories requires an iteration of direct questioning and observation. Specific notions of personal substance can obviously be had by asking. More general cultural themes such as reciprocity require observation in everyday life to gauge their resonance. Ortner's argument that a clue to a theme's cultural centrality lies in its appearance across many different domains (1973) suggests how one might discover them. In the case of reciprocity, its salience emerged as a consequence of its appearance in myth, in the layout of fields, in the everyday behaviors associated with hospitality, and in the request for explicit elaborations of what informants meant when they talked about a "good" wife or a "good" husband (Fricke 1990, 1997b).

For any society, behavior is loaded with meaning in light of such repetitive themes. Nearly any action can take on a symbolic load that conveys a message to those who share a set of cultural assumptions. Often, that message is conveyed in the failure to perform an action. For the Tamang, for example, the theme of reciprocity is played out in the necessity of sharing. Sharing implies an increase in value, not diminution, through the conversion of material items such as food into socially binding relationships. A widespread myth recounts the failure of a young man to report his capture of a tiny bird to his father-in-law when they were hunting together. When the father-in-law discovers the subterfuge, he rebukes the young man, who then gives him the bird. It immediately grows to such a size that the two of them have to carry it on a pole suspended between them as they return to the village. The story is a charter for relationships between in-laws as much as for the general notion of giving as a moral virtue.

Local Knowledge in Questionnaire Design

If behavior is construed meaningfully as symbolic of wider cultural themes, knowledge of key symbols allows the survey to include measures for meaning in addition to those on attitudes and preferences that already form a part of the survey armament. The Pakistani example above showed how a standard measure might change its meaning in a given context. In the Nepal data collection, my prior fieldwork as principal investigator allowed the research team to include discrete measures of behaviors linked to exchange and reciprocity themes. The TFRP questionnaires included an elaboration of questions on events surrounding the marriage process because of the known importance of marriage to Tamang social organization and kinship relations. Many of these focused on exchanges of labor and goods. Others focused on precise accounts of the existing kinship links between husbands and wives before their marriages. The case of labor exchanges in which new husbands provide help to their in-laws is a good example of a variable that could be interpreted as purely economic or in terms of its meaningfulness within a cultural framework where such behavior is found in mythic themes.

Including such variables on surveys, easily measured because they are behavioral, can open up the possibilities for a dynamic ethnography. Confinement to cross-sectional slices of time is one of the common characteristics of ethnographic investigations, apart from those that involve longitudinal data collections (and even these rarely extend beyond the life of the principal investigator). The inclusion of measures with culturally loaded content allows investigators to talk about change with more empirical precision in spite of their actual presence in the field for single periods. Thus, those questions about the life course transition of marriage and exchanges linked to the ethos of reciprocity can be arrayed by cohort as in table 6.2. The case is discussed in greater detail elsewhere (Fricke 1997b) but serves here to make the point that the behavioral and symbolic buttresses to the ethic of reciprocity are changing across time. The practices of pong (flasks of alcohol) exchange, first-cousin marriage, indirect dowry (goods given by a husband's family and ultimately going to the wife at marriage), and bride service (labor service from a new husband to his wife's family) are all in decline. Such declines in individual practice across time are suggestive of the

Table 6.2. Percentage of First Marriages including Selected Practices by Marriage Cohort in Nepal

	Marriage cohort			
	<1960 (n = 61) (%)	1961–74 (n – 44) (%)	1975–87 (n = 80) (%)	Total (n = 185) (%)
Spouse choice				
Senior	49	41	31	40
Jointly	26	18	33	30
Respondent	14	41	36	30
Pong exchange	66	50	46	54
First-cousin marriage	31	25	24	26
Indirect dowry	61	39	41	47
Bride service	80	73	59	69

Source: Fricke 1997b, 201.

world into which succeeding cohorts of children are socialized and lead to ethnographic questions about cultural change in this community. By themselves, they are only suggestive, but coupled with the change away from arranged marriages and knowledge of community practices, such as the declining participation in ritual events that ratify clan solidarity, the investigator is better able to avoid oversimple and static portrayals of the moral community.

Redirecting Analysis in the Discovery of Meaning

Placing researchers in local contexts has implications that go beyond more sensitively nuanced questionnaires. Measures included in survey instruments for one kind of analysis may be discovered through the experience of everyday life among the subjects of study to have entirely new analytic uses that take advantage of newly discovered meaning. An example from the TFRP involves the inclusion of a question on whether or not a woman returned to her natal home for a period of a week or longer after relocating to her spouse's residence after marriage.

The question had originally been included as a control variable for an analysis of first-birth timing. In the course of combined data collection, I noticed the repeated clusters of recently married women working in the yards of their natal homes with their mothers and sisters. The pattern was inescapable enough that I began to ask about it in casual conversations, the answers to which motivated me to tape some of the responses. One 34-year-old woman's response to the question of why a young wife would want to return to her natal family home was typical:

> Who knows? It's just something she likes. In her married house, it's a little like she doesn't know the people there. "What sort of work should she do there?" This is in her mind. She has to be small maybe, and where will the food come from? And what work will she do maybe? She's a little unfamiliar [with the new surroundings]. And her own parents' place where she has lived up to then is a little . . . Uhh . . . whenever they see you, it's "Oh daughter, here you must eat this and here's the old familiar work you must do. Here's how much work is left and how much work is finished." And this is what is in her own mind and her heart says, "Go, go [to her natal home]." Even after you've married, when you return home they treat you so special! [But in your marital home] they say, "Do this work! You have to work here!" They don't understand what comes from the heart. Oh yes, she [a daughter-in-law] has to do much work. (Quoted in Fricke, Axinn, and Thornton 1993, 399)

Comments like this sensitized me to the subjective feelings that motivated the action of returning to the natal home: the predictability of its pace, the contrast with the imperious demands of in-laws, and the comforts of residing with people who were well known. But other comments, especially from men, alerted me to other emotions implicated in these visits:

> Oh yes, there's definitely worry—if she stays for longer than a week, one's heart is touched by worry. "Has she gone with another?" or "Why isn't she coming?" This is the kind of thinking one does. . . . But you might hear that she has gone off with another and if this thing happens, you think, "Aho, so that's it." She's done a very bad thing. . . . Yes. If things become so very bad then the husband himself may decide to split, too. Some people, even though they are married, live in separate houses and eventually end the marriage. (Quoted in Fricke, Axinn, and Thornton 1993, 400)

Recognizing the larger context in which these subjective statements played out (the structure and meaning of Tamang marriage as an alliance experienced across generations between families and patrilines), I interviewed other relevant people—in-laws and parents—for their views on these natal visits. The existence of a survey measure for making these visits, even though it had been included for an entirely different purpose, allowed my colleagues and I to address the issue of how these visits were related to a woman's social security after marriage and how the likelihood of making such visits increased with experiences of autonomy in work and travel before marriage (Fricke et al. 1993).

These findings were extended in a subsequent analysis that showed how such visits affected the timing of a woman's first birth (Fricke and Teachman 1993). We found that socially secure women were most likely to make natal home visits in the first year of marriage and also began their marital childbearing more rapidly than women who did not make these visits. Neither of these analyses would have been undertaken without the unplanned encounters and initial casual conversations in the process of simultaneous survey and participant observation.

How Local Do You Want to Get?

An intrinsic feature of going to where the people are is that the researcher is exposed to a bewildering mass of information, a huge part of it having potential as data. By itself, the simple act of being there is not enough to decide what is relevant. In many respects, the survey mode of investigation has it easy because of its constraints. If information is not recorded in the finite space allotted, then it can be fairly ignored. When the survey is coupled with information available through participant observation and deep community knowledge, analytic possibilities are magnified, and their presentation requires judgment and forbearance for those reviewers unused to such detail.

All interpretation is, at some level, inferential. And all results, even the most quantitative, require interpretation. Ultimately, our acceptance of a particular interpretation rather than another relies on its plausibility. When the investigator goes to a field site, speaks to respondents outside the context of a survey instrument, and gathers reinforcing kinds of information at both individual and other levels, her plausibility arguments go beyond the internal statistical relationships among variables gathered on the survey. There is an "I was there" quality to any argument from experience that cannot be entirely discounted, however maddening it can be for the empirically minded.

But that act of being there also opens up new kinds of investigation, especially those having to do with the discovery of moral communities. Shweder (1996, 34) writes that a moral community is that group of people who "take an interest in sanctioning and regulating each other's behavior" and who are "usually conscious of themselves, and of their honor, prestige, and well-being as a moral community." One way to think of them is as a kind of "natural grouping" in the sense that their identity and membership are largely determined internally. They can be as small as members of a household, larger extended kinship groups, neighborhoods, and communities. Such groups are precisely those that random samples of individuals will likely miss since their bounds are unlikely to be known in the detail that will allow for sampling. Everybody is, of course, a member of many such communities, and even a sample of individuals will allow access to some of their features as they relate to individuals. But their dynamics as communities require a comprehensive investigation. These dynamics are inherently interesting for a number of cultural questions revolving around such issues as the force of family traditions, historical relations between moral communities organized at the same level, and relative power among groups organized at the same level. Their specificity confers exactly the *Mad Magazine* quality that puts off some reviewers of anthropological manuscripts.

The combination of survey, participant observation, and genealogy offer an ideal opportunity for the researcher to investigate dynamic relationships within locally constituted moral communities. My mixed-methods ethnographic work in Nepal, for example, uses historical relationships among clans and patrilines to show that extended family groupings in Timling have different morally charged traditions. These traditions, moreover, have implications for a whole range of behavior (Fricke 1995), from age at marriage to age at first birth, even when other variables are controlled for in multivariate models. When a variable such as "family membership" (a quick and dirty way to talk about patriline) retains its effects in a multivariate model, the temptation is to say that there is some unmeasured other variable that is causing the relationship. But why shouldn't family identity, or membership in a moral community, be a bona fide "thing" since it clearly can be for the people themselves?

Table 6.3 gives just a taste of how things can vary by this level of moral community. The complexity of the original analysis has been stripped down to just three patriline clusters to illustrate how the distribution of culturally interesting measures plays out against membership in a group. In the table, we can see that Gangle women are more likely than the other two groups to have their marriages arranged by seniors, more likely to have cloth exchanged at their marriages, and much more likely to marry first cousins of a particularly highly charged relationship.[10] Indeed, these Gangle report

Table 6.3. Clan Groupings and Selected Characteristics of Married Women
         in Timling, Nepal

| | Patriline clusters | | | |
	Tamang (%)	Chetgle (%)	Gangle (%)	Total (%)
Spouse choice				
Senior	39.3	33.3	59.0	42.1
Jointly	31.0	33.3	25.0	30.3
Respondent	29.8	33.3	16.0	27.6
Cloth exchange	45.2	41.7	62.5	48.0
Marriage and kinship link				
No relation	32.1	30.6	21.9	29.6
FZD/categorical	38.1	13.9	18.8	28.3
FZD/first cousin	16.7	16.7	18.8	17.1
MBD/categorical	9.5	30.6	18.8	16.5
MBD/first cousin	3.6	8.3	21.9	8.6

Source: Fricke 1995, 211.
Note: FZD = father's sister's daughter. MBD = mother's brother's daughter.

that, although things have gone downhill in terms of the power and wealth they once held in Timling, they must still honor their traditions because of who they are.

Insider Culture: The Anthropologist as Native

Earlier, I had asked [my friend] why he stays in farming. He said because he doesn't have a boss, he can pretty much do what he wants. He said because he gets to work with his family. He said, "because I get to be out in this," gesturing to the land in front of us. To the north the land rose up beyond the alkaline and canted toward the sky, white clouds just over us and darker moisture bearing stuff on the far horizon; to the south the long hollow and then the abrupt rise to West River. [My friend] said he couldn't think of any other job that would let him wake up and stand in this. He can't imagine having to get into a car and drive to a place with four walls. (North Dakota field letter, April 13, 2000)

In a dry country so much depends on rain. It's all the difference in the world for a farmer. He rises or he falls on the pinpoint splash of water on furrowed ground. Diamond hard truths of this order encourage most of us to more tightly link our futures to the present. We know what the payoff is for an hour's employment; we know how the money comes. For the farmer though, all the weeks of planning and all the work of putting seed into the ground are more obviously acts of faith, gestures toward an incalculable future. I can't think of another kind of life where so much is unknowable. And this kind of uncertainty makes for a general reluctance to speak in definites. You don't want to jinx things. Nor do you want the gaudy reputation earned by reckless hubris. No one here would taunt the skies by demanding their due; better to assume the postures of reverence. A good season invites gratitude for unearned grace. (North Dakota field letter, June 21, 2000)

This section proceeds in a dicier fashion than the previous discussions. It rests on work that is still ongoing for one thing. So it lacks the finished quality, the ability to refer the reader to the full published discussion, of the earlier examples. It is also work that up to now has not included a survey of the closed-ended, formal-instrument type that most people have in mind when they hear the word.[11] Most distinctively, I am a near native of the place I am studying—a near native because I was raised just 80 miles east of the field site but native enough in that the topic of my study has to do with the transformation of family relationships that results when children leave their home place as I and my brothers have done.

Since the summer of 1999 I have been doing ethnography in the world of farms, ranches, and small towns centered on a place I call West River. I went there interested in how the culture of work and family gets shaped by a place and its history. And I was interested, too, in how changes in work and career choices might affect relations between those who stay and those who leave. Life course theories tell us that events and contexts will have much to do with how people see the world. My work concentrates on how enculturation in a rural world, with all its implications for how family and work are defined, will structure the responses of people to contemporary American work and family changes.

Studying West River is one project of many conducted through the Center for the Ethnography of Everyday Life. The town is my case study, a single instance of all those places in rural America, especially in the Great Plains, founded on scuttled dreams of robust growth. West River is one of many that advertised its "excellent farming and grazing lands all around, healthy climate, congenial people, fresh air, and sunshine" in an effort to attract immigrants in the early 1900s. People came, mostly German

Catholics, and settled the land in 160- and 320-acre chunks. The town grew, but never much.

West River's history is mostly a history of leaving. By 1970, it began its steady loss of young people and population decline after edging up to its census peak of 799. I looked at the graduating classes of 1973–1975, people in their mid-forties, and found that of the 100 (out of 116) people for whom I could find addresses only a quarter still lived in West River or on its neighboring farms. When the high school principal assigned an essay to the graduating seniors of the class of 2000, only 3 out of 25 thought they would be living in the area five years from now.

For this phase of research, the numbers were scaffolding for the real focus of my data collection. Working as a cultural anthropologist, I was concerned more with the key cultural categories and symbols that local people used to structure their world. Out here, those symbols turned on the relations of work and character, family and place. My efforts to understand West River had me collecting data of many kinds. I spent hours in the community's Benedictine Abbey archives ferreting through a hundred years of historical documents. I collected genealogies from selected families to discover the movements of people from home communities in Europe to the Northern Plains and the later spread of families out of the area. I pored over microfilmed newspapers from the early years of the town, looking for stories from the current residents' ancestors. I lived and worked with a farm family to open up the intimacies of their world in the most direct way possible.

Sharing lives may be the most classic of ethnographic methods. In my case, it meant sleeping in a farm family's spare room and rising at 5:00 A.M. to start the day with them. It meant driving tractor and combine, breaking machinery, and helping with repairs. It meant walking fence line and being bitten by deerflies in a high hot wind. It meant pulling calves when cows needed help with a birth: learning how to tie chains around those delicate hooves, attach them to a pulley, and avoid the pour of afterbirth when the newborn calf yanks free, and learning who calls whom in an emergency. And it meant staying in the fields until the red sun crossed the western buttes at 10:00 and we could all go home to eat dinner.

This project brings me up against one of the paradoxes of doing ethnography: when working with cultures with which we are least familiar, we try to find a means to enter that cultural place or to read the minds of others, but when we work closest to home, we look for distance. Worried about objectivity, we get skittish at the edge of subjectivity in our research.[12] In this chapter, I have structured these examples along a scaffold of increasing engagement with a local community. The closer we can be, I have argued, the greater our opportunities to make use of materials that link individuals directly to their cultural models. By seeing as much as possible, we enhance the plausibility of our analytic stories.

I have argued, following Shweder's point that we cannot get inside people's heads, that ethnography involves imaginative reconstructions of the categorical and moral worlds of the people we study. The clues we look for are public — in behaviors and stories and the way people talk about the lay of the land. My return to North Dakota and the experience of familiarity after a 20-year absence were also recognitions of the striking difference between that place and where I now live. My sense of homecoming at the return to a cultural place is, to some extent, true for any of us doing ethnography in the United States. The question is whether we can uncover cultural clues that are more subtle than the public symbols and behaviors that we rely on in more unfamiliar settings.

The joke in international demography is that to get a native perspective on international survey research one often relies on a local collaborator who went to the United States to have the culture trained out of him or her in the course of getting a Ph.D. Natives learn to distrust what they already know, in part because that knowledge is part of an unconscious background horizon against which action achieves its meaning (Taylor 1985). Coming back to my cultural place after a long absence brought some of that dilemma to the foreground for me. The question was, could I trust my knowledge? Was it merely subjective? Was I giving up mind reading for self-analysis?

When the farmer whose family I lived with, and with whom I worked when I was not running around conducting interviews or digging through the Benedictine Abbey archives in West River, said, "because I get to be out in this" in the excerpt from the field letter heading this section, I thought I knew exactly what he meant. It was not long after that letter that I wrote another one with a story about learning to drive the tractor while trailing a grain tank, a seeder, and a fertilizer tank:

> [My friend's] tractor is a Versatile with eight wheels steered by a pivot
> joint in its center. A finger touch on the wheel is enough to move the rear
> wheels to either side and turn. It pulls the air tank that holds the seed, the
> air seeder with its shanks, and knives, and coils of pipe that place the
> seed into the ground, and the tank of anhydrous ammonia that serves as

fertilizer for the grains — altogether 97 feet of linked machinery, a third
of a football field coiling along the earth. The effect is of mass and mo-
tion. [My friend's] fully loaded assemblage is 37 tons of machine, grain,
and liquid making its way across the ground at the speed where a fast
walk elides into a jog, between 4.6 and 5 miles per hour. A 160 acre
field amounts to something like a 40 mile drive on a tractor. (Field letter,
April 29, 2000)

The story became one of those classic accounts of anthropological inepti-
tude and ended with me breaking the machinery. I thought it was funny
and innocuous and showed it to my farmer friend and informant.[13] He
liked it, and, because I number the letters when I write them, pointed out
that this one was number eight and asked to see the other seven. And so
began an experiment in which I tested my subjective states and my trial interpretations of the world around me against a native's view of things.

After five months of living with this family, the letters included stories
about work, about children leaving home for school and coming back to get
married, about the uncertainties of farming, shared work with neighbors,
angry disputes over inheritance, and trial shots at the key symbols of
Northern Plains living. My informant's response to all this was, "You put
this stuff into words that I feel, but I can't say it this way."

Discovering the Salience of Key Symbols

As with my Tamang informants in Nepal, many of the key symbols that
organize West River culture play below the consciousness of cultural actors
in everyday life. Even when a suspicion exists that a theme or symbol is
relevant in a setting, its salience may emerge only from the serendipitous
encounters that are a feature of participant observation and follow-up. My
discovery of one such symbol, the inside/outside distinction, and its structuring of intergenerational tensions illustrates how being where the people
are might generate greater analytic possibilities for understanding how culture and individuals are connected. As Ortner writes, clues to the existence
of such symbols are found in their appearance across different domains of
cultural expression and in the heightened reaction of people to them. For
West River, clues to the existence of the inside/outside distinction as a cultural category can be found in a reasonably sensitive reading of existing
materials, but its relevance to interpersonal relations might be more elu-
sive if this were the only source of information. Although the following

sketch is not a complete analysis, it draws attention to the value of increasingly close engagement with the people we study.[14]

The idea of local distinctiveness relative to the outside world is a widespread feature of Great Plains identity. James Shortridge documents the distinctive self-image that Great Plains residents have of themselves. Within the core region of the Northern Plains, 93 % of his respondents mentioned characteristics related to the Jeffersonian ideal of yeoman farmers when asked to list features of Midwestern identity. These traits included any mention of words such as "friendly," "easygoing," "naïve," "thoughtful," "honest," "moral," and "modest" (1989, 79), and their mention in this region is at a much higher level than for respondents from elsewhere in the Midwest or beyond. The self-image he documents is consistent with the casual reports I heard in my own conversations with West River residents (see also Shortridge 1997).

Although Shortridge was not concerned with comparative reflections on the character of outsiders in other regions, contemporary sentiment rests on a history of tense relationships that have emphasized differences in character and power. North Dakotans are painfully reminded of their current status as residents of "fly-over country." In an especially well-known incident, they were even excluded from one edition of the *Rand McNally Road Atlas* because the major highways cutting through the state were already evident from the national map. Such casual disrespect from the outside takes its toll and even finds itself ratified in official representations of their history:

> Striving for equality of status permeated North Dakota life. There was, of course, nothing unusual about either the feelings of inferiority or the compensations for them. . . . But universality made such feelings no less real and significant in the history of North Dakota. They were solidly based upon North Dakota's status as a rural, sparsely settled, semiarid plains and prairie state, *a colonial hinterland exploited by and dependent upon outside centers of trade, manufacturing, and culture.* (Robinson 1966, 551–552, my emphasis)

Robinson's account points to the ambivalence that North Dakotans feel about their status, the hint of inferiority and the resentment that might translate into defensiveness. These are the complex reactions that emerged in long, taped interviews with West River residents. On the one hand, the outside is viewed as a world where local virtues are unappreciated or difficult to live out, as the following two excerpts illustrate:

[B]ut, you hear stories and you read things and it just seems like, people in this area it's just like we all grew up in the same type of background with the same type of values. You know, we saw it here three years ago with the flooding situation, people helping out. Our own situation in June when we had flooding problems we had four neighbors in our basement all night with their wives helping us keep the water out of our basement, all we had to do was give them a call. People are just so willing to help and it's just the type of values that it seems like everybody has, to help out. And it doesn't appear that it's like that in other larger metropolitan areas. (Interview with JM, a 45-year-old man, July 27, 2000)

I think family does mean more [here]. Because it does seem like you talk to other people in bigger cities and . . . their kids are scattered all over creation. And they don't get together with them and they don't seem like they have the closeness. . . . But yeah, I don't know, yeah, I think they just do [treat family differently]. (Interview with SZ, a 44-year-old woman, August 4, 2000)

At the same time, the outside world is viewed as a source of potential threat to the distinctiveness and soundness of local character:

I think there's a lot of factors contributing to [a distinctive local character]. . . . Maybe being from a small town had something to do with it. Maybe being from a large family where there were responsibilities of taking care of the younger ones had something to do with it. . . . Do you know when I was ten years old we lived fifty-five miles from Glendive following the road and seventy-five miles from Dickinson following the road? That's not very far away and yet if I was in Dickinson and Glendive combined four times a year that would have probably been a lot. So we were isolated. Now, kids will jump in a car in Beach and go to a movie in Dickinson. So, the world is coming in and the morality, [because of things] presented to children through television or through the magazines or in the newspapers or on billboards, has eroded. Everyone is becoming homogenized. (Interview with KK, a 64-year-old man, August 18, 1999)

Methodologically, this incremental movement from existing sources to lengthy interviews corresponds to an increasingly close association with the subjects of study themselves. My research is, however, concerned with the implications for family processes, including intergenerational relationships, of movement away from West River by young people in pursuit of their careers. It took a closer step into everyday life, in this case working a fence line with a farmer a few days before his daughter's wedding, to bring this cultural symbol of inside/outside to life in the emotional world of a cultural actor.

On a hot June morning, that farmer and I drove and walked along the fence line on his southeast pasture looking for slack wire and talking about whatever came to mind, his father's steady move to real retirement, neighbors' farming practices, his son wanting to farm for a living. The truck jarred along the line in rising heat and high wind and we hopped in and out of the pickup to staple line to 100-year-old cedar posts. My friend's mind was on his daughter's impending wedding and we eased into that topic. He talked about how tough it was to have his daughter away at college in Minneapolis and the consequent need to wedge all the unsaid things into the short space of her visit. The rhythms were wrong, not like it would be if she lived in West River, where you could build to a conversation, where the minor irritations of family got diffused every day and solved themselves.

"It's her attitude since she's been back," he said between the twists and clipping of barbed wire. "I need to talk with her." But he could never quite find the time. With the wedding was just two days away, his daughter slept late when he needed to move early. She'd be off when he wanted her around. It hurt when she and her fiancé crunched those pickup tires out of the yard without stopping in the shop to say where they were headed. His daughter's leaving was bad enough, but this fast and this abrupt change just made it harder. Part of it was the quick change from shaper to bystander, but there seemed to be more to it than that. The clues to what else began to emerge in that pasture itself and in subsequent conversations that tied it to the tensions of her leaving home for the outside.

As we moved along the wire, I noticed that to the west were three lines strung between a quarter section's worth of posts. Up ahead to the south, at the boundary with another farmer's land, there were four lines. Asked why some rows have three lines and some four, my friend looked and said, "Well, maybe it's when the next field is our own and when it's somebody else's. . . . I don't know, we just follow what was there before." Later, he decided that the inside/outside boundary explained it. It's a lot more trouble if the cows get into a neighbor's field. My friend saw that his daughter was crossing a kind of line by marrying and he was trying to figure out if this was a three-wire or a four-wire boundary. I followed up with questions in longer taped interviews. The first comment suggests a sense of rejection:

TF: [Your daughter] never got interested in [the farming life]?

JJ: No. Never. And it's getting worse.

TF: This upsets you?

JJ: Yeah. Her attitudes about North Dakota and what we do here, it, and if
it's not for her that's fine, but I wish she would quit shoving it at us.
That's, if she doesn't like what we do, fine. . . . I mean, as she grows
and matures she's more vocal about how she feels about it. When she
was a kid and you'd take her out she was willing to do things but now
it's completely off the other end and she's vocal about it. (Interview,
September 12, 2000)

In elaborating, he draws in some of the contrasts brought about by context:

JJ: And I think that's a part of being in the city and among their friends.
You know, they need to have the new cars, they need to have a nice
place to live, they need to put on a show. And when they come home
[my son-in-law] talks a lot about how good this job is and how much
money he's making and, we don't need to hear that, just tell us you're
doing okay. But he has a, and I think they both have, a need to put
an outward show on that they're successful. I have no pride. Look
at the pickups I drive and the vehicles around here. (Interview, September 12, 2000)

The emotional relevance of this cultural category, inside/outside, begins
to emerge with the increasing localization of available data. My explorations in general interviews were motivated by understandings available
to any researcher who takes time to read the existing literature. It took the
concrete case of a farmer's interactions with a daughter planning to marry
and already certain that she would live elsewhere to demonstrate how the
cultural category is dynamically integrated into an emotional world that
turns on intergenerational relations, movement, and sense of self. My en-
countering the case was serendipitous, but its concreteness allowed me to
anchor my opening research questions to a case study.

My argument about how this cultural category operates in everyday life
is independent of survey data. In the complete analysis I suggest that the
sense of historically constituted local identity finds its way into people's
sense of self. In this context, coupled with the ambivalence of images of
West River and its relationship to the outside, the common American oc-
currence of young family members seeking careers can take on heightened
emotional meanings that color intergenerational relations.

This insight has the potential to inspire new kinds of questions in survey instruments. As in any culture, rural North Dakotans have their share of key symbols and motivations that are local elaborations of the larger culture of individualism that they share with other Americans (Bellah et al. 1996; Shweder 1996). Some of those key symbols have to do with the grid of township and range that shapes their physical environment and the recurrent theme of insider and outsider that marks the kinds of fences that get put up along section lines, the attitudes marking town and country relations (Williams 1973), and the way local people view the world of cities and jobs that siphon their children away from the Northern Plains and threaten to intrude on their world.

Family as moral community, inside and outside, the importance of place in socialization—these are among the things that need to find their way onto measures in an eventual survey. And the lessons of this ongoing work for ethnography and mixed methods are that we find ways to make the most local kind of knowledge respectable in social research.

Some Final Remarks

I opened this chapter with two suggestions: first, that the recent attraction of mixed-methods approaches is motivated by a sense that we need to get closer to the people we study; second, that we are better off defining ethnography in terms of an orientation to cultural questions rather than as a coherent method unto itself. The first of these suggestions frames my strategy of providing examples that move progressively closer to bringing the researcher together with his or her subjects. The second is intentionally provocative. It asks us to more directly consider as researchers the links between what we do and why we do it. If there are cultural questions that can be answered with survey data, then what are the questions that urge us into everyday life?

Approaching this question requires some usable notion of culture for the survey researcher. Because the definition of culture is a rolling stone that shifts with the disciplinary questions and orientations of the moment, there is no point in searching for that stable angle of repose where all anthropologists can rest in final agreement. Given that, I argue that the general agreement on the contours of the Geertzian framework, with some suitable modifications to address the question of how public models of and for reality can get into the heads of people, suggests a viable working model with application to survey research. Most social scientists who use survey modes of investigation direct their inquiry to questions other than the mechanisms of cultural dynamics that concern cultural theorists. For these outside interests, the choice of a cultural framework is largely a practical matter.

Culture as worldview is a useful framework because it directs the researcher's attention to the logic of human action within a setting. Going further to look for the symbolic content of behaviors allows researchers to develop behavioral hypotheses that take account of the perceptual world of human actors. As I have illustrated with examples from three field settings, the cultural categories that people employ may be available in many cases from existing literature. At the same time, new categories and the symbolic content of behaviors may emerge from closer contact with people. Long interviews, more or less standardized, with a range of people can reveal clues to the symbolic content of behaviors. More intensive relationships with informants carry the connection between these categories and individual circumstances even further by allowing an exploration of the links between public meanings and private actions.

Finally, throughout this chapter, I have excerpted letters written in the process of my own fieldwork in various settings. My purpose was partly to illustrate the extraordinary concreteness of the fieldwork enterprise. The details from such close, experiential encounters with the people of study are the sources of plausibility for all subsequent arguments. I also wanted to convey the well-kept secret that going where the people are is often fun and always transforming.

Acknowledgments

My thanks to Dilli R. Dahal, Sallie Han, Rebecca Upton, and Tom Weisner for helpful comments. Support for writing this chapter was provided by the University of Michigan's Alfred P. Sloan Foundation–funded Center for the Ethnography of Everyday Life.

Notes

1. I recognize that Martin could be said to be very much "in the field" by virtue of living as a woman in the broadly defined culture system characteristic of the United States. Nevertheless, her discussion of methods makes it clear that her approach involved important methodological differences from her earlier work in Taiwan in its sampling and decision to forgo a more standard community-based fieldwork.

2. This is not to say that they should be excluded from bibliographies of ethnographic interest. See Coles 1997 for other examples of this method of participant observation used for written works that are, at most, ambiguously ethnographic.

3. I remember the exasperation of a demographer colleague when I pointed out in a seminar that the definition of culture she was using was exactly of the fossilized character immortalized by Gene Hammel. "Anthropologists are *always* changing the definition!" she said. And so they are.

4. See Fricke 1997a, 252–256, and 1997b, 189–190, for additional discussion of why these models are useful for mixed-methods research involving ethnographically oriented survey research.

5. We are all familiar with the practice of requiring the interviewer to indicate features of the setting on questionnaires.

6. The original survey and the article from which this example comes include attention to kinship relations and other locally relevant variables that were incorporated into the analysis. Notably, our interpretation of these variables often involved a reconstruction that differed from the purpose behind their original inclusion in the survey.

7. These other variables included a range of more obviously "cultural" measures such as kinship links between families and locally relevant marriage exchanges.

8. There were actually 1,521 eligible respondents in that age range. We missed 1 person.

9. It makes a difference, too, if physical inheritance is conceived of as being equally possible from either parent as in the general American culture of reproduction. This is irrespective of whether the American model is biologically closer to the facts. Still, even in America, biology and cultural models do not completely overlap, as with the curious theories that are widespread concerning inheritance of male pattern baldness and some notions prevalent on the Northern Plains that mental instability is a sex-linked characteristic inherited through females.

10. For those who just can't get enough of this sort of thing, the marriages they are more likely to contract are with their matrilateral cross-cousins, a marriage that connotes a particularly high status in this community and that is tied to a long-standing tradition in this family group that they are the "kings" of Timling (Fricke 1995).

11. It does, however, include an open-ended, long qualitative interview component in its data collection. These interviews are being conducted with a random sample of high school graduates over a three-year period.

12. The anthropologist Rosaldo examines the issue of objectivity in a collection of essays (1993). Ortner, another anthropologist working in the United States as a native, touches very briefly on some of these concerns (1993). Chodorow addresses these concerns most directly in a work that also poses important modifications to the Geertzian framework that I use as a starting place (1999).

13. This is the same letter as the excerpt at the start of this essay.

14. The more complete analysis is taken up in a work in progress (Fricke, forthcoming).

References

Agee, J., and W. Evans. 1989. *Let Us Now Praise Famous Men.* New ed. New York: Houghton Mifflin.

Alexander, J. C. 1988. *Action and Its Environments: Toward a New Synthesis.* New York: Columbia University Press.

———. 1990. Analytic Debates: "Understanding the Relative Autonomy of Culture." In *Culture and Society: Contemporary Debates,* ed. J. C. Alexander and S. Seidman, 1–27. New York: Cambridge University Press.

Axinn, W. G., J. S. Barber, and D. J. Ghimire. 1997. "The Neighborhood History Calendar: A Data Collection Method Designed for Dynamic Multilevel Modeling." *Sociological Methodology* 27:355–392.

Axinn, W. G., T. Fricke, and A. Thornton. 1991. "The Microdemographic Community Study Approach: Improving Survey Data by Integrating the Ethnographic Method." *Sociological Methods and Research* 20 (1): 187–217.

Axinn, W. G., L. D. Pearce, and D. J. Ghimire. 1999. "Innovations in Life History Calendar Applications." *Social Science Research* 28:243–264.

Basso, K. 1996. *Wisdom Sits in Places: Landscape and Language among the Western Apache.* Albuquerque: University of New Mexico Press.

Becker, H. 1996. "The Epistemology of Qualitative Research." In *Ethnography and Human Development: Context and Meaning in Social Inquiry,* ed. R. Jessor, A. Colby, and R. A. Shweder, 53–71. Chicago: University of Chicago Press.

———. 1998. *Tricks of the Trade.* Chicago: University of Chicago Press.

Bellah, R. N., R. Madsen, W. M. Sullivan, A. Swidler, and S. M. Tipton. 1996. *Habits of the Heart: Individualism and Commitment in American Life.* Updated ed. Berkeley and Los Angeles: University of California Press.

Blum, L. A. 1994. *Moral Perception and Particularity.* New York: Cambridge University Press.

Caldwell, J. C., A. G. Hill, and V. J. Hull, eds. 1988. *Micro-approaches to Demographic Research.* London: Kegan Paul International.

Caldwell, J. C., P. H. Reddy, and P. Caldwell. 1988. *The Causes of Demographic Change: Experimental Research in South India.* Madison: University of Wisconsin Press.

Chodorow, N. J. 1999. *The Power of Feelings: Personal Meaning in Psychoanalysis, Gender, and Culture.* New Haven: Yale University Press.

Coles, R. 1997. *Doing Documentary Work.* New York: Oxford University Press.

Dahal, D. R., T. Fricke, and A. Thornton. 1993. "The Family Contexts of Marriage Timing in Nepal." *Ethnology* 32 (4): 305–323.

D'Andrade, R. G., and C. Strauss, eds. 1992. *Human Motives and Cultural Models.* Cambridge: Cambridge University Press.

Flanagan, O. J. 1991. *Varieties of Moral Personality: Ethics and Psychological Realism.* Cambridge: Harvard University Press.

Fricke, T. 1990. "Elementary Structures in the Nepal Himalaya: Reciprocity and the Politics of Hierarchy in Ghale-Tamang Marriage." *Ethnology* 29 (2): 135–158.

———. 1995. "History, Marriage, Politics, and Demographic Events in the Central Himalaya." In *Situating Fertility: Anthropology and Demographic Inquiry,* ed. S. Greenhalgh, 202–224. Cambridge: Cambridge University Press.

———. 1997a. "Culture Theory and Population Process: Toward a Thicker Demography." In *Anthropological Demography: Toward a New Synthesis,* ed. D. I. Kertzer and T. Fricke, 248–277. Chicago: University of Chicago Press.

———. 1997b. "Marriage Change as Moral Change: Culture, Virtue, and Demographic Transition." In *The Continuing Demographic Transition,* ed. G. W. Jones, R. M. Douglas, J. C. Caldwell, and R. M. D'Souza, 183–212. Oxford: Oxford University Press.

———. 1997c. "The Uses of Culture in Demographic Research: A Continuing Place for Community Studies." *Population and Development Review* 23 (4): 825–832.

———. Forthcoming. "The Geography of Moral Sentiment: Placing Work and Family in Western North Dakota."

Fricke, T., W. G. Axinn, and A. Thornton. 1993. "Marriage, Social Inequality, and Women's Contact with Their Natal Families in Alliance Societies: Two Tamang Examples." *American Anthropologist* 95 (2): 395–419.

Fricke, T., D. R. Dahal, A. Thornton, W. G. Axinn, and K. P. Rimal. 1991. *Tamang Family Research Project: Summary Report on Ethnographic and Survey Research Conducted March 1987–January 1988.* Kathmandu: Center for Nepal and Asian Studies, Tribhuvan University.

Fricke, T., S. Syed, and P. Smith. 1986. "Rural Punjabi Social Organization and Marriage Timing Strategies in Pakistan." *Demography* 23 (4): 489–508.

Fricke, T., and J. D. Teachman. 1993. "Writing the Names: Marriage Style, Living Arrangements, and Family Building in a Nepali Society." *Demography* 30 (2): 175–188.

Geertz, C. 1973. *The Interpretation of Cultures.* New York: Basic Books.

Hammel, E. 1990. "A Theory of Culture for Demography." *Population and Development Review* 16 (3): 455–485.

Jessor, R., A. Colby, and R. A. Shweder, eds. 1996. *Ethnography and Human Development: Context and Meaning in Social Inquiry.* Chicago: University of Chicago Press.

Kertzer, D. I., and T. Fricke. 1997. "Toward an Anthropological Demography." In *Anthropological Demography: Toward a New Synthesis,* ed. D. I. Kertzer and T. Fricke, 1–35. Chicago: University of Chicago Press.

King, G., R. O. Keohane, and S. Verba. 1994. *Designing Social Inquiry: Scientific Inference in Qualitative Research.* Princeton: Princeton University Press.

MacIntyre, A. 1988. *Whose Justice? Which Rationality?* Notre Dame: University of Notre Dame Press.

———. 1992. "Plain Persons and Moral Philosophy: Rules, Virtues, and Goods." *American Catholic Philosophical Quarterly* 56 (1): 3–19.

Martin, E. 1987. *The Woman in the Body: A Cultural Analysis of Reproduction.* Boston: Beacon Press.

Ortner, S. B. 1973. "On Key Symbols." *American Anthropologist* 75 (4): 1338–1346.

———. 1989. *High Religion: A Cultural and Political History of Sherpa Buddhism.* Princeton: Princeton University Press.

———. 1993. "Ethnography among the Newark: The Class of '58 of Weequahic High School." *Michigan Quarterly Review* 32 (3): 410–429.

Orwell, George. 1937. *The Road to Wigan Pier.* London: Victor Gollancz.

Ragin, C. C., and H. S. Becker. 1992. *What Is a Case? Exploring the Foundations of Social Inquiry.* New York: Cambridge University Press.

Robinson, E. 1966. *History of North Dakota.* Lincoln: University of Nebraska Press.

Rosaldo, R. 1993. *Culture and Truth: The Remaking of Social Analysis.* Boston: Beacon Press.

Searle, J. R. 1998. *Mind, Language, and Society: Philosophy in the Real World.* New York: Basic Books.

Shortridge, J. 1989. *The Middle West: Its Meaning in American Culture.* Lawrence: University Press of Kansas.

———. 1997. "The Expectations of Others: Struggles toward a Sense of Place in the Northern Plains." In *Many Wests: Place, Culture, and Regional Identity,* ed. D. Wroebel and M. Steiner, 114–135. Lawrence: University Press of Kansas.

Shweder, R. A. 1996. "True Ethnography: The Lore, the Law, and the Lure." In *Ethnography and Human Development: Context and Meaning in Social Inquiry,* ed. R. Jessor, A. Colby, and R. A. Shweder, 15–52. Chicago: University of Chicago Press.

Strauss, C., and N. Quinn. 1997. *A Cognitive Theory of Cultural Meaning.* New York: Cambridge University Press.

Taylor, C. 1985. "Interpretation and the Sciences of Man." In *Philosophy and the Human Sciences,* 15–57. Cambridge: Cambridge University Press.

Thornton, A., and H. Lin. 1994. *Social Change and the Family in Taiwan.* Chicago: University of Chicago Press.

Van Maanen, J. 1988. *Tales of the Field: On Ethnographic Writing.* Chicago: University of Chicago Press.

Weisner, T. S. 1996. "Why Ethnography Should Be the Most Important Method in the Study of Human Development." In *Ethnography and Human Development: Context and Meaning in Social Inquiry,* ed. R. Jessor, A. Colby, and R. A. Shweder, 306–324. Chicago: University of Chicago Press.

Williams, R. 1973. *The Country and the City.* New York: Oxford University Press.

Wuthnow, R. 1987. *Meaning and Moral Order: Explorations in Cultural Analysis.* Berkeley and Los Angeles: University of California Press.

7

Combining Ethnography and GIS Technology to Examine Constructions of Developmental Opportunities in Contexts of Poverty and Disability

Debra Skinner, Stephen Matthews, and Linda Burton

We have two main aims in this chapter. One is to demonstrate the use of ethnographic methods and Geographic Information Systems/Analysis (GIS/GIA) technologies to examine how low-income families construct developmental opportunities for their young children with disabilities. Another aim is to discuss how the combination of these two methods contributes to sociocultural and ecological understandings of development, helps situate families' actions and experiences in time and space, and enhances data analysis and interpretation.

The data reported here were collected for the Three-City Study, carried out in Boston, Chicago, and San Antonio. This study comprised three interrelated components: (1) a longitudinal in-person survey of approximately 2,400 families with children 0–4 years of age and 10–14 years of age in low-income neighborhoods, about 40% of whom were receiving case welfare payments when they were first interviewed in 1999; (2) an embedded developmental study of a subset of about 630 children aged 2–4 years and their caregivers; and (3) an ethnographic study of 256 families. Of these

256 families, 45 were recruited specifically because they had a child aged birth to 8 years with a moderate or severe disability. In all three components and in all three cities, African American, Hispanic, and non-Hispanic white families were represented. A detailed description of the Three-City Study and a series of reports are available at www.jhu.edu/~welfare.

In the ethnographic component, fieldworkers employed participant observation and in-depth interviews to assess how children and families were faring in contexts of economic hardship and reforms in public assistance programs. Ethnographers followed a method of "structured discovery," by which they employed interview and observation protocols that focused on specific topics of interest but allowed for flexibility to capture unexpected findings and relationships (Burton et al. 2001; Winston et al. 1999). In the intensive data collection period (12–18 months), which began in 1999, ethnographers met once or twice a month with families, examining through interviews and observations the family's work and welfare experiences, daily routines, health and health care access, child-rearing practices and beliefs, childcare arrangements, home and neighborhood environments, family economics and resources, and the interrelations of these domains. After this intensive period of fieldwork, ethnographers continued to meet with families every 4–6 months to collect more data on the domains of interest and any changes in these domains.

For this chapter, we have analyzed the ethnographic data collected through February 2001 on 42 families of young children with disabilities, specifically for the ways in which these families constructed developmental opportunities for their children with disabilities. Guiding our analysis are anthropological and sociocultural perspectives on child development that provide models for conceptualizing and documenting the influence of sociocultural contexts and activities on child outcomes.

There is a long history of anthropologists examining child socialization and development within cultural contexts (Super and Harkness 1980; Whiting and Edwards 1988; Whiting and Whiting 1975), and there is a more recent movement among some developmental psychologists to examine the influence of culture on child development (Cole and Cole 1996; Rogoff 1990; Valsiner 2000; Winegar and Valsiner 1992). Whether the emphasis is on developmental niches (Super and Harkness 1980), ecocultural niches (Weisner 1984), ecological contexts (Bronfenbrenner 1979), activity settings (Farver 1999; Rogoff 1990; Tharp and Gallimore 1988), cultural places (Weisner 1996), or cultural worlds (Holland et al. 1998), the fundamental premise shared by these studies is that children develop within settings and daily activities that are coconstructed and inhabited by cultural and social others, imbued with meanings, and shaped to some degree by larger sociocultural, economic, and political conditions. Specific settings and activities, such as the family's daily routines, caregiving practices, and educational and therapeutic services, organize children's experiences and place individual children on particular developmental trajectories (Harkness and Super 1996).

Another related premise guiding our analysis is the understanding of development as a process that takes place on and among different levels: the individual, interpersonal, community, national, and even global. As Rogoff and colleagues state: "Development is a process of participating in sociocultural activities. We regard individual development as inseparable from interpersonal and community processes" (1995, 45). Viewed from this approach, when parents of children with disabilities work with professionals to plan the therapeutic and educational interventions their children may need, they are involved in a culturally organized activity, one shaped and mutually constituted by the parents themselves, professionals, formal institutions, programs, and policies. The activity has implications not only for the child's development but also for the development of other individuals and systems.

Our analysis is also informed by ecological approaches as developed and expanded by studies on families of children with disabilities, the adaptations they make, and the ecological and systems factors that influence adaptations and outcomes (Gallimore et al. 1996; Guralnick 1997; Sameroff and Fiese 2000; Trivette, Dunst, and Deal 1997; Weisner, Matheson, and Bernheimer 1996). It is from this literature that we borrow the notion of developmental opportunities.

Garbarino and Ganzel, in a chapter entitled "The Human Ecology of Early Risk," defined "opportunities for development" as "relationships in which children find material, emotional, and social encouragement compatible with their needs and capacities as they exist at a specific point in their developing lives" (2000, 77). Employing an ecological systems approach, they see both developmental risks and opportunities for the child constructed in the interaction of biological, psychological, social, and cultural forces. For children at risk or with disabilities, developmental opportunities and risks exist in the home; in community institutions such as hospitals, day care, early-intervention services, and schools; and in state and federal programs and policies that provide services and financial assistance (e.g., Medicaid, SSI, IDEA, TANF). Creating developmental opportunities for children with disabilities takes caregivers beyond the confines of the home to interactions with a number of individuals, agencies, and policies.

Families' ability to garner resources, navigate a path through bureaucracies, link agencies and information, fight for their child's services and rights, and access sources of support in these endeavors may significantly affect their child's developmental trajectory.

Although important ethnographies of persons with disabilities and families of children with disabilities exist (Angrosino 1998; Edgerton 1967, 1984; Estroff 1981; Langness and Levine 1986; Weisner, Beizer, and Stolze 1991), ethnographic studies have not focused specifically on the intersection of poverty, childhood disability, and child development. Little is known of low-income families' experiences with childhood disability and the impact of disability and limited economic resources on a child's development. We address this question in part by examining our ethnographic data for the ways in which low-income families organize and construct developmental opportunities for their children with disabilities within the larger community context.

The Study

The data reported here are from observations and interviews with 42 families that, at the time of recruitment into the study, had a child 8 years or younger with a moderate to severe disability. We purposely included families whose children represented a broad range of disabilities and needs and, thus, presented different issues for families (e.g., children with autism [high-impact behavioral issues], Down syndrome [cognitive delays and possible health problems], spina bifida [high-impact medical], and cerebral palsy [physical and perhaps cognitive delays]). Diagnoses of the children include cerebral palsy, Down syndrome, seizure disorder, severe attention deficit/hyperactivity disorder (ADHD), significant developmental delays, visual and hearing impairments, spina bifida, Pervasive Developmental Disorder, autism, chondrodysplasia punctata, various syndromes (e.g., Kartagener syndrome, Angelman syndrome, and Cri-du-chat syndrome), severe asthma, and other involved medical conditions. Of the 42 children, 26 (62%) received supplemental security income (SSI) at the time of recruitment, and 3 more were approved for SSI benefits during the course of the study. The average age of focal children at the time of recruitment was 52 months. Ten children were 6 years of age or older. The average age of the main caregiver was 33 years. In 34 of the 42 families, biological mothers were the main caregivers. In 4 families, grandmothers were the guardians or foster mothers of the child, and in 2 families, aunts served as adoptive mothers or guardians. There was one family where a widowed father was the main caregiver and another where the adoptive mother was not a relative of the child. One-fourth of the caregivers worked, though mostly at part-time jobs with low wages and few benefits, and over one-fourth of the primary caregivers had some kind of disability or functional limitation themselves. Twenty-four percent ($n = 10$) of the households had another member with a disability in addition to the focal child and caregiver. This incidence of disability resulted in 77 % of the households receiving SSI payments for at least one member. At the time of recruitment, half of the 42 families were receiving cash assistance from Temporary Assistance for Needy Families (TANF). The other families were below 200 % of the poverty line. Forty-four percent of all households received both SSI and TANF support.

Ethnographic Findings

For many of the families, because the needs of the child with a disability were profoundly evident, the child's development was not a taken-for-granted experience. The families in our sample had a heightened sensitivity of having to work harder to facilitate their children's health and development. There was often an immediacy and an emotional and moral urgency to caring for the child on an hour-to-hour basis, standing by as needed for emergencies, and procuring the services and resources that they perceived their child as needing. For most of the families, having a child with a disability necessitated routines built around the child and piecing together and navigating a network of therapeutic, educational, and social services.

The majority of families in this study viewed fostering their children's health and development as encompassing a range of activities. When asked how they promoted their children's development, they talked about trying to provide a safe and clean environment, good nutrition, and a variety of learning opportunities. They sought out inexpensive toys, games, books, and recreational and educational experiences for their children and worked to include the child with disabilities in these and other family activities. Salient also to their notions of development was the provision of appropriate health and medical care and therapeutic treatments. It was not unusual for a child to have a host of therapists, doctors, and teachers, and for caregivers to have numerous appointments every week with these and other specialists.

Rosa, a Mexican American mother living in San Antonio, recounted to the interviewer how she promoted her daughter's development. At age three, her daughter Maria had severe visual impairment and seizure disorder. Rosa was concerned especially with Maria's physical and language development. She had sought out a number of service providers for Maria since her birth, including speech, physical, and occupational therapists, pediatricians, a vision impairment teacher, a nutritionist, and a special-education teacher. When she was three, Maria received all her services in a school-based program, but Rosa also worked with her at home. Rosa constantly exercised Maria's arms and legs. She used musical toys to help Maria learn to discriminate different sounds and hum different tunes; she gave her stuffed animals and other objects so that Maria could palpitate them and feel their texture, size, and shape. During activities with Maria (e.g., mealtime, bedtime, bathing time), Rosa talked to her, telling her what she was going to do. She worked to promote her self-help skills, but this was more difficult since Maria did not yet have the physical capacity to feed or dress herself. For this reason, Rosa searched for a physical therapist who could work with Maria at home on her motor skills. Previously, when the early interventionists came to her house, Rosa watched what they were doing with Maria and learned from them techniques and therapies she continued to carry out with her. Rosa saw this work as crucial to developing the skills Maria would need to succeed in school, and this work included not only her own activities with Maria in the home but finding the specialists she needed.

Most of the families were involved in enlisting a wider community to support their children's health and development. They expended a great deal of effort seeking out and piecing together a variety of services. They had constructed, sometimes on their own and sometimes with the aid of other persons and agencies, a community of resources focused on the child with disabilities: early-intervention or special-education services; specialized medical care and treatments; social services and public assistance programs that helped provide necessities for the child and family (e.g., SSI, TANF, food stamps, Medicaid, transportation, specialized equipment); and other family supports (counseling, parent education, and advocacy and legal efforts). Some caregivers became increasingly involved in monitoring the child's services, volunteering in the child's classroom, becoming active participants in deciding therapies, and sometimes fighting with the schools for appropriate services. Caregivers also learned therapies from the child's service providers or teachers, which they then administered at home.

Leticia, a mother in Boston, whose seven-year-old son had been diagnosed with Pervasive Developmental Disorder, provides an example of these kinds of activities. Her son, Roberto, was in a special program at school where he received some services. Leticia told the interviewer, "Roberto is a very, very difficult child." She sought out special training on how to care for him in the home, and she attended a mothers' support group which provided information and emotional support on issues involving her children. Leticia told the interviewer, "So many people work together for me," and named the therapists, counselors, teachers, physicians, pediatrician, psychiatrist, nutritionist, and social worker who worked with Roberto. She also talked about SSI, food stamps, and Medicaid as providing crucial resources. Managing all the appointments and paperwork put stress on her and other family members. Leticia said she sometimes felt depressed and wanted to run away, but she continued her efforts to help Roberto.

Families viewed this community of services as providing developmental opportunities for their children and supports that helped them in sustaining daily routines and basic needs that promoted family well-being (see also Gallimore, Bernheimer, and Weisner 1999). From a sociocultural and ecological perspective, these systems and activities in part shaped parents' notions of disability and what their children needed. As caregivers enter cultural worlds, such as the world of early intervention, and become coparticipants with professionals in managing services for the child, they may adopt the language or discourse of early intervention, disability, development, services, and advocacy. They may become agents and advocates for the child, and their identities as mother or advocate may form in particular ways (see Skinner et al. 1999). Many caregivers devote much of their time to optimizing developmental opportunities for their children by caring for them, procuring services and therapies, and garnering the resources necessary to make ends meet. As they construct these developmental opportunities, they engage in worlds and activities that foster certain identities and transformations in themselves. As caregivers increasingly participate in their children's services, there is potentially a codevelopment of child, caregiver, and systems, and historically, parents' activities have brought about changes in service systems, professional practices, and policies.

Geographic Information Systems and Geospatial Data

Geographic Information Systems (GIS) technology or Geographic Information Analysis (GIA) provides another way to look at the time-consuming nature and intensity of effort many families put forth to piece together a community of services. GIS is a computer-based system for the manipulation and analysis of spatial information in which there is an automated link between data sets and their spatial locations (Burrough and McDonnell

1998; Huxhold 1991; Longley et al. 1998; Martin 1996). Using the concept of geographic overlay, data from different sources can be linked to common geographic coordinates or areas (e.g., street block and cross-street locations or census tracts and zip-code areas). GIS can pinpoint circumscribed areas and particular locations as well as depict events and movements. GIS technologies allow researchers to take space into account and thereby enable an assessment of when, how, why, and where location is relevant. They allow the user to visualize and analyze data in ways not necessarily accessible through numerical or textual analysis alone. While GIS and related technologies are often perceived as a tool for drawing "pretty" maps, these technologies are increasingly used to go beyond basic mapping and description to inform exploratory and confirmatory spatial analyses that may identify important spatial dimensions of social structure and process (Martin 1996). In this study, we used ethnographic field notes, geographic coordinates, and GIS technology to link data and create visual displays of the spatial and temporal aspects of how caregivers of children with disabilities navigate and link services.

By integrating ethnographic data on families and neighborhoods within a GIS in the three cities of the Three-City Study, we have tried to extend the work on child well-being both conceptually and methodologically. Our goals have been to think creatively about how GIS can be used in research related to child well-being and also how to expand the technology and revise the methodologies we currently use. Our application of GIS focuses on retrofitting data on contexts or "neighborhoods" (necessitating a reconceptualization of context) and integrating ethnographic data on low-income families of children with disabilities. The aim of combining these methods is to better understand families' mobility, access to, and utilization of services and the contextual factors that enable or constrain their efforts. Combining ethnographic data and GIS methods helps researchers see both "context" and "content" in a spatial dimension. This alternative way of representing data may identify issues that would not be apparent otherwise. In brief, we use existing data sets, augment them with new and refined measures of spatial context and structure, integrate these geographic data sets with an array of ethnographic data products (i.e., field notes, recoded notes, family profiles, photographs, etc.), and then analyze the result with data visualization/mapping techniques and spatial statistical analysis.[1]

Here we present case studies of two families' routines built around meeting their children's health and development needs. These cases highlight the daily, weekly, and monthly routines of families as they navigate a

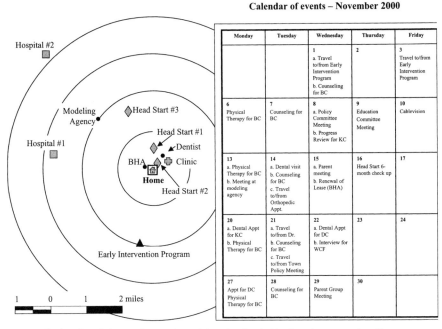

Calendar of events – November 2000

	Monday	Tuesday	Wednesday	Thursday	Friday
			1 a. Travel to/from Early Intervention Program b. Counseling for BC	2	3 Travel to/from Early Intervention Program
	6 Physical Therapy for BC	7 Counseling for BC	8 a. Policy Committee Meeting b. Progress Review for KC	9 Education Committee Meeting	10 Cablevision
	13 a. Physical Therapy for BC b. Meeting at modeling agency	14 a. Dental visit b. Counseling for BC c. Travel to/from Orthopedic Appt.	15 a. Parent meeting b. Renewal of Lease (BHA)	16 Head Start 6-month check up	17
	20 a. Dental Appt for KC b. Physical Therapy for BC	21 a. Travel to/from Dr. b. Counseling for BC c. Travel to/from Town Policy Meeting	22 a. Dental Appt for DC b. Interview for WCF	23	24
	27 Appt for DC Physical Therapy for BC	28 Counseling for BC	29 Parent Group Meeting	30	

Map 7.1. The location of the meetings and appointments attended by the primary caregiver (November 2000). GIS is used to organize and map the data points. (Map produced by Stephen A. Matthews, December 2000.)

world of services for their children with disabilities — services they view as promoting their children's health and development. Maps 7.1–7.3 are geographic representations of selected field notes on two families from Boston. These maps include geocoded information derived from the field notes and geospatial data from secondary sources.

The first family is European American. The mother, Delores, was 30 years old and had seizure disorder and partial paralysis due to a stroke when she was 5 years old. She was the main caretaker of John, her 2-year-old son with gastrointestinal problems, seizures, and allergies; a 3-year-old daughter who required leg braces; and an 11-year-old son. The father of the two youngest children sometimes resided in the household. We have extensive field notes on 17 interviews and observations over a 12-month period on this family, including Delores's records for November 2000 of her activities related to her children's medical, educational, and therapeutic services. During November, Delores met 20 times with her children's therapeutic specialists, educators, doctors, and dentists. Of these meetings, 10

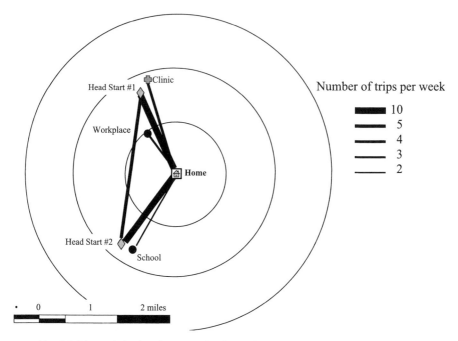

Map 7.2. Trips made by the primary caregiver (November 2000). (Map produced by Stephen A. Matthews, April 2001.)

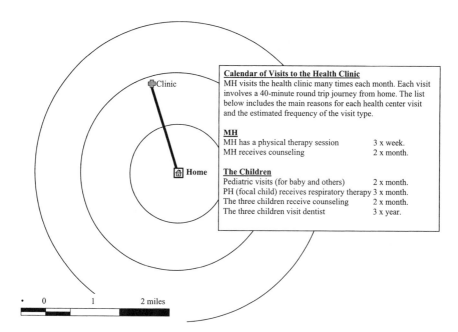

Map 7.3. Visits to the health center by the primary caregiver up to four times per week (November 2000), including link to field notes. (Map produced by Stephen A. Matthews, April 2001.)

were in the home, where early interventionists came to provide counseling and physical therapy for John. The remaining 10 appointments were at seven locations in the city: two Head Start programs, two hospitals, one early-intervention center, one health clinic, and one dentist's office. Delores met with Head Start teachers to review her children's progress and revise their education plans, attended parent meetings, and obtained medical and therapeutic services her children required. In addition to these activities, Delores also traveled to a modeling agency for a possible job for her daughter, to the Boston Housing Authority to renew her lease, and to three Head Start centers as part of her volunteer work to inform parents about options and services. She did this work because she felt it was important to foster relations between parents and service providers, the outcome being better services for children.

The field notes include a description of the events and meetings Delores attended, but another way of representing the data is to integrate the ethnographic data within a GIS. Using a GIS, we are able to create maps that show the locations of the places to which Delores had to travel for services and their distance from her home (see map 7.1). With hot-link tools, each map or location on a map can be linked to original field note files or other pertinent data so that contextual information is readily available for analysis purposes. Integrating ethnographic data within a GIS, we obtain a picture of how families access and link services. These maps provide a depiction of a family's "community of development"—those agencies that provide services geared to enhancing the development and well-being of children and their families.

Another GIS example depicts both the spatial network of services and the intensity of time and effort in constructing developmental opportunities for children in community settings. This case involves an African American family. Marjorie was the main caregiver and mother of four children. She received SSI for her own disability, and three of her children received special health, counseling, or education services. On any given day, Marjorie drove four hours to take her children to school or Head Start and to medical and health centers where they received services. Map 7.2 depicts not only the locations where Marjorie's children received services but the intensity of time and effort of the visits per week. Map 7.3 shows the link to field notes that record the reasons Marjorie traveled to the health center two to four times per week (e.g., for therapies, counseling sessions, dental and medical treatments). Using GIS mapping, we gain a visual portrayal of the community resources that figured into Marjorie's routines constructed around her children's health and development.

Discussion

Ethnography and GIS, alone and in combination, have much to offer to the study of children's developmental pathways in community contexts and cultural places. Weisner (1996) contends, and we agree, that the ethnographic method is the most important method in the study of human development because it ensures the description and understanding of those places, practices, and activities in and by which children and families develop and the factors that constrain or enable their efforts. It allows us to examine the complex relationships among contexts and activities that sociocultural and ecological approaches to development require. The value of the ethnographic approach for our study was the prolonged contact with families and the resulting rich descriptive data that provide us with in-depth and nuanced understandings of what it is like to be low-income, minority, and disabled within a particular time in U.S. society and within a political climate of welfare reform. Ethnography provides a breadth and depth of information on the day-to-day lives of families of children with disabilities, the processes and contexts of their development, and the larger cultural, economic, and political worlds that influence children's developmental trajectories. It provides evidence not only of the constraints that poverty and disability place on children's development and families' abilities to respond to disability but also on the ways that caregivers creatively adapt and work to construct opportunities for their children in the midst of constraints.

When GIS was first posed to members of the ethnographic team as a methodology to use in tandem with ethnographic analysis, there was reluctance on the part of some researchers, including the first author. Some of us were not convinced that the time spent collecting the necessary geographic information was worth whatever additional analysis GIS could add. We were not convinced that GIS would contribute significantly to interpretations that could be made from textual data alone or that GIS would offer a better portrayal of families' lives than a coherent ethnographic narrative. There was concern that complex stories would be simplified and flattened out in two-dimensional models and that, taken out of the context, these models could distort the analysis or be easily misread.

Any methodology has its limitations and any genre of representation has potential for misrepresentation, and there are limitations and dangers with GIS. Curry (1998), in his critique of this technology, argues that there are substantial limits to its ability to enhance the objects, relationships, people, and places it is meant to represent. Burrough (1986) and Matthews

(1990) point out other potential sources of error in spatial representations, data input, and analysis. As we began to explore ways of combining GIS with ethnographic data, we tried to stay aware of the limitations and sources of error in both methods. We checked and rechecked locations and family routines, and the geographic data sets on which these were mapped. When necessary, ethnographers returned to families and neighborhoods to verify data points and families' explanations of their routines and experiences.

Through this exercise of combining methods to examine caregivers' constructions of developmental opportunities, we have come to see the advantages of GIS. First, GIS proved to be an effective tool to depict, in a single image, the intense effort it takes for families to create and maintain a network of services aimed at promoting their children's health, well-being, and development—an effort that might surprise some policy makers. The ethnographic description of a family's efforts and experiences is still crucial, but for some audiences, a GIS image may have an immediate impact and provide a more powerful statement than a narrative account. GIS provides a visual representation of a point one mother wanted us to make to our readers: "You tell them that I don't just sit on my butt all day watching TV. I'm out there working for my children."

Second, beyond this more political use, GIS is also an effective tool in analysis. Maps can suggest interpretations that we might otherwise overlook. For our study, GIS can quickly identify families who are more isolated, have fewer supports, and fewer outside resources and services. GIS can show how far afield families have to go for different types of services. We can borrow concepts from geographers to talk about an individual's activity space, or the sum of movements taken by individuals to and from various locations (Jakle, Brunn, and Roseman 1976), and look for differences in caregivers' activity spaces. By depicting differences in neighborhood and community resources, GIS can suggest possible reasons why discrepancies exist and lead us to conclusions about the relationship of community resources to a family's ability to garner services and establish a community of developmental opportunities. Maps of families' navigations may foster comparisons not easily perceived through reading text alone, for example, how families' constructions of developmental opportunities may differ within and between sites, ethnic groups, and groups of different socioeconomic status. GIS can also help us plot any significant changes in families' constructions or routines over time. For example, Gallimore et al. (1996) found that the intensity of families' functional accommodations made to sustain daily routines for a child with disabilities decreased for children aged 7 to 11. GIS could be used to identify changes in intensity and range of families' accommodations around community services and activities over time. Another use of GIS to determine change relates to an issue of concern to professionals who provide services to children with disabilities. Some fear that if caregivers of children with disabilities are moved from welfare to work, they will have less time to devote to locating and managing services their children need, resulting in their children receiving fewer services and interventions. Without these services, children may develop additional or secondary disorders and lose mobility and cognitive gains (Sameroff and Fiese 2000). Development would be less than optimal. GIS mapping of changes in service utilization after leaving the welfare rolls could help document whether this constricting of service use is in fact happening.

In spite of these advantages of employing GIS technology, we caution that GIS and the resulting maps are not enough by themselves. We need ethnographic data to understand the child and family factors, the cultural meanings and places, as well as the political and sociocultural influences, that account for differential access to resources and different configurations (or nonexistence) of communities of development.

The integration of GIS and ethnographic methodologies in this analysis has provided an example of the multiple sites where development takes place and the impact of child disability on family routines as depicted in time and space. We have found GIS methodology to be highly compatible with sociocultural and ecological perspectives on development, increasing awareness and providing spatial displays of contextual features that may impact child outcomes. The combination of ethnographic data and GIS plotting has expanded our thinking about developmental opportunities to include a world of services and programs that are part of the sociocultural context of a child's development and has increased our ability to visualize developmental pathways as including actual sociospatial pathways that connect services, children, and families.

Note

1. Stephen Matthews and his team at Pennsylvania State University are developing a GIS database, or "virtual ethnography prototype," for the Three-City Study. This prototype can be used by analysts to pull up an array of neighborhood profile data on "context" (e.g., demographics, socioeconomic characteristics, crime events/patterns) and "content" (e.g., ethnographic field notes and project-specific data). As Penn State is the coordinating site and GIS analysts are based there and are not in the individual cities, this virtual ethnography allows them to gain a better understanding of each city and the time-space constraints faced by the study families.

References

Angrosino, M. V. 1998. *Opportunity House: Ethnographic Stories of Mental Retardation.* Walnut Creek, CA: AltaMira Press.

Bronfenbrenner, U. 1979. *The Ecology of Human Development.* Cambridge: Harvard University Press.

Burrough, P. A. 1986. *Principles of Geographical Information Systems for Land Resource Assessment.* Monograph on Soil and Resource Survey no. 12. Oxford: Clarendon Press.

Burrough, P. A., and R. A. McDonnell. 1998. *Principles of Geographic Information Systems.* Oxford: Oxford University Press.

Burton, L. M., R. Jarrett, L. Lein, S. Matthews, J. Quane, D. Skinner, C. Williams, and W. J. Wilson. 2001. "Structured Discovery: Ethnography, Welfare Reform, and the Assessment of Neighborhoods, Families, and Children." Paper presented at the biennial meeting of the Society for Research in Child Development, Minneapolis, MN, April.

Cole, M., and S. R. Cole. 1996. *The Development of Children.* New York: W. H. Freeman and Company.

Curry, M. R. 1998. *Digital Places: Living with Geographic Technologies.* New York: Routledge.

Edgerton, R. B. 1967. *The Cloak of Competence: Stigma in the Lives of the Mentally Retarded.* Berkeley and Los Angeles: University of California Press.

———, ed. 1984. *Lives in Process: Mildly Mentally Retarded Adults in a Large City.* Washington, DC: American Association on Mental Deficiency.

Estroff, S. E. 1981. *Making It Crazy: An Ethnography of Psychiatric Clients in an American Community.* Berkeley and Los Angeles: University of California Press.

Farver, J. 1999. "Activity Setting Analysis: A Model for Examining the Role of Culture in Development." In *Children's Engagement in the World: Sociocultural Perspectives,* ed. A. Göncü, 99–127. Cambridge: Cambridge University Press.

Gallimore, R., L. P. Bernheimer, and T. S. Weisner. 1999. "Family Life Is More than Managing Crisis: Broadening the Agenda of Research on Families Adapting to Childhood Disability." In *Developmental Perspectives on Children with High Incidence Disabilities,* ed. R. Gallimore, L. P. Bernheimer, D. L. MacMillan, D. L. Speece, and S. Vaughn, 55–80. Mahwah, NJ: Lawrence Erlbaum Associates.

Gallimore, R., J. Coots, T. S. Weisner, H. Garnier, and D. Guthrie. 1996. "Family Responses to Children with Early Developmental Delays, II: Accommodation Intensity and Activity in Early and Middle Childhood." *American Journal on Mental Retardation* 101:215–232.

Garbarino, J., and B. Ganzel. 2000. "The Human Ecology of Early Risk." In *Handbook of Early Childhood Intervention,* 2nd ed., ed. J. P. Shonkoff and S. Meisels, 76–93. Cambridge: Cambridge University Press.

Guralnick, M. J. 1997. "Second Generation Research in the Field of Early Intervention." In *The Effectiveness of Early Intervention,* ed. M. J. Guralnick, 3–20. Baltimore: Paul H. Brookes.

Harkness, S., and C. Super, eds. 1996. *Parents' Cultural Belief Systems.* New York: Guilford Press.

Holland, D., W. Lachicotte, D. Skinner, and C. Cain. 1998. *Identity and Agency in Cultural Worlds.* Cambridge: Harvard University Press.

Huxhold, W. E. 1991. *An Introduction to Urban Geographic Information Systems.* New York: Oxford University Press.

Jakle, J. A., S. Brunn, and C. C. Roseman. 1976. *Human Spatial Behavior: A Social Geography.* North Scituate, MA: Duxbury Press.

Langness, L. L., and H. G. Levine. 1986. *Culture and Retardation.* Dordrecht, Netherlands: D. Reidel.

Longley, P. A., M. F. Goodchild, D. J. Maguire, and D. W. Rhind. 1998. *Geographical Information Systems: Principles, Techniques, Management, and Applications.* Vols. 1 and 2. New York: John Wiley.

Martin, D. 1996. *Geographic Information Systems: Socioeconomic Applications.* 2nd ed. Routledge: London.

Matthews, S. A. 1990. "Epidemiology Using a GIS: A Need for Caution." *Computers, Environment, and Urban Systems* 14:213–221.

Rogoff, B. 1990. *Apprenticeship in Thinking.* New York: Oxford University Press.

Rogoff, B., J. Baker-Sennett, P. Lacasa, and D. Goldsmith. 1995. "Development through Participation in Sociocultural Activity." In *Cultural Practices as Contexts for Development,* ed. J. Goodnow, P. J. Miller, and F. Kessel, 45–65. San Francisco: Jossey-Bass.

Sameroff, A. J., and B. H. Fiese. 2000. "Transactional Regulation: The Developmental Ecology of Early Intervention." In *Handbook of Early Childhood Intervention,* 2nd ed., ed. J. P. Shonkoff and S. Meisels, 135–159. Cambridge: Cambridge University Press.

Skinner, D., D. Bailey, V. Correa, and P. Rodriguez. 1999. "Narrating Self and Disability: Latino Mothers' Construction of Meanings vis-à-vis Their Child with Special Needs." *Exceptional Children* 65:481–495.

Super, C., and S. Harkness, eds. 1980. *Anthropological Perspectives on Child Development.* San Francisco: Jossey-Bass.

Tharp, R., and R. Gallimore. 1988. *Rousing Minds to Life: Teaching, Learning, and Schooling in Social Context.* Cambridge: Cambridge University Press.

Trivette, C. M., C. J. Dunst, and A. G. Deal. 1997. "Resource-Based Approach to Early Intervention." In *Contexts of Early Intervention: Systems and Settings,* ed. S. K. Thurman, J. R. Cornwell, and S. R. Gottwald, 73–92. Baltimore: Paul H. Brookes.

Valsiner, J. 2000. *Culture and Human Development: An Introduction.* London: Sage.

Weisner, T. S. 1984. "Ecocultural Niches of Middle Childhood: A Cross-Cultural Perspective." In *Development during Middle Childhood: The Years from Six to Twelve,* ed. W. A. Collins, 335–369. Washington, DC: National Academy of Sciences Press.

———. 1996. "Why Ethnography Should Be the Most Important Method in the Study of Human Development." In *Ethnography and Human Development,* ed. R. Jessor, A. Colby, and R. A. Shweder, 305–324. Chicago: University of Chicago Press.

Weisner, T. S., L. Beizer, and L. Stolze. 1991. "Religion and Families of Children with Developmental Delays." *American Journal on Mental Retardation* 95:647–662.

Weisner, T. S., C. Matheson, and L. P. Bernheimer. 1996. "American Cultural Models of Early Influence and Parent Recognition of Developmental Delays: Is Earlier Always Better than Later?" In *Parents' Cultural Belief Systems: Their Origins, Expressions, and Consequences,* ed. S. Harkness and C. M. Super, 496–531. New York: Guilford Press.

Whiting, B., and C. Edwards. 1988. *Children of Different Worlds: The Formation of Social Behavior.* Cambridge: Harvard University Press.

Whiting, J., and B. Whiting. 1975. *Children of Six Cultures: A Psychocultural Analysis.* Cambridge: Harvard University Press.

Winegar, L. T., and J. Valsiner. 1992. *Children's Development within Social Context.* Vol. 2, *Research and Methodology.* Hillsdale, NJ: Lawrence Erlbaum Associates.

Winston, P., R. J. Angel, L. M. Burton, P. L. Chase-Lansdale, A. J. Cherlin, R. A. Moffitt, and W. J. Wilson. 1999. "Welfare, Children, and Families: Overview and Design." Johns Hopkins University.

PART IV

Using Mixed Methods in Social Experiments to Understand Impacts on Children's Pathways

8

Bullets Don't Got No Name:
Consequences of Fear in the Ghetto

Jeffrey R. Kling, Jeffrey B. Liebman, and Lawrence F. Katz

Since 1995 we have been studying the Boston site of a federal demonstration program known as Moving to Opportunity (MTO). MTO provides families living in high-poverty public housing projects with rent subsidy vouchers to help them move into private-market apartments, often in substantially better neighborhoods. Studying families participating in housing mobility programs such as MTO offers the opportunity to evaluate how a marked change in neighborhood circumstances affects low-income families. In general, however, it is difficult to identify the impact of residential neighborhoods on families, because families choose where they live. Thus, families living in different neighborhoods typically differ in unmeasurable ways, and it is impossible to isolate the impacts of neighborhoods from the impacts of these unmeasurable family characteristics. MTO addresses this concern directly because its subsidies are administered through a random lottery in which a limited number of housing vouchers are offered to some families and not to others. The resulting random differences in residential location among otherwise similar families can be used analyze the causal effect of residential location on subsequent outcomes of participating family members by comparing the outcomes of those offered vouchers through the lottery with those in the lottery who are not offered vouchers.

As part of our research on MTO, we conducted both qualitative and quantitative analyses. Our qualitative work included direct observation of the operation of the MTO program in Boston and in-depth interviews with program participants. Our main quantitative work consisted of the design and analysis of a survey of MTO-Boston families (administered both to families in the treatment groups, who had been offered vouchers through the lottery, and to those in the control group, who had not been offered vouchers), which was implemented about two years after program enrollment, and of analyses of administrative data on employment and welfare receipt.

Our qualitative fieldwork had a profound impact on our MTO research. First, it caused us to refocus our quantitative data collection strategy on a substantially different set of outcomes. In particular, our original research design concentrated on the outcomes most familiar to labor economists: the earnings and job-training patterns of MTO parents and the school experiences of MTO children. Our qualitative interviews led us to believe that MTO was producing substantial utility gains for treatment group families, but primarily in domains such as safety and health that were not included in our original data collection plan. In our subsequent quantitative work (see Katz, Kling, and Liebman 2001), we found the largest program effects in the domains suggested by the qualitative interviews; MTO appears to have had important impacts on safety, child behavior, and health, but no effects on adult earnings or welfare usage.

Second, our qualitative fieldwork led us to develop an overall conceptual framework for thinking about the mechanisms through which changes in outcomes due to moves out of high-poverty areas might occur. Our conversations with MTO mothers were dominated by their powerful descriptions of their fear that their children would become the victims of violence if they remained in the high-poverty housing projects. For the most part, MTO mothers did not conceive of crime in the ghetto as directed purposefully at them, as with the theft of a purse at knifepoint. Rather, they were bystanders to the fray, terrified that a stray bullet might find their child. This fear appeared to be having a significant impact on the overall sense of well-being of these mothers, and it was so deep-seated that their entire daily routine was focused on keeping their children safe. They appear to be experiencing an extreme form of the neighborhood poverty that has been associated with the distinct family protection and child-monitoring strategies studied in other research that focuses on inner-city families, such as that reviewed by Jarrett (1997) and Furstenburg and colleagues (1999). We hypothesized that the need to live life on the watch may have broad implications for the future prospects of these families—including potential impacts on children's development and also on the education and employment of their mothers.

Third, our fieldwork has given us a deep understanding of the institutional details of the MTO program. This understanding has helped us to make judgments regarding the external validity of our MTO findings, particularly regarding the relevance of our results to the regular Section 8 program. In addition, this understanding has prevented us from making some significant errors in interpreting our quantitative results.

Fourth, by listening to MTO families talk about their lives, we learned a series of lessons that have important implications for housing policy. For many of the things we learned, it is hard to imagine any other data collection strategy that would have led us to these insights.

This chapter is structured so as to illustrate each of the four contributions of our qualitative fieldwork to our overall research program. We begin by providing background on the MTO program and then discuss our qualitative and quantitative research methods. In the next section we describe our main findings from our qualitative work. Then we summarize previously reported quantitative findings that were motivated by this work as well as by new quantitative results that are relevant for evaluating our hypotheses regarding the mechanisms through which ghetto violence impacts families. In the next section we illustrate the ways in which the knowledge of institutional details of the program obtained from our fieldwork has affected our interpretation of our quantitative results. Then we describe other lessons we learned from listening to MTO families. We conclude by discussing some implications of our findings as well as some general lessons regarding the integration of qualitative and quantitative methods that we have drawn from this research experience.

Background

In the MTO program, families are chosen by lottery from a waiting list of eligible families who applied for the program. Families are eligible for participation if they have children and currently reside in public housing or project-based Section 8 assisted housing in a neighborhood with a high concentration of poverty (i.e., a census tract in which more than 40% of families had incomes below the poverty line in 1990). Five cities are included in the demonstration: Baltimore, Boston, Chicago, Los Angeles, and New York.

In 1994, interested eligible families responded to local outreach efforts and placed their names on a waiting list. Between October 1994 and July 1998, each site began to draw names from its waiting list. On average about 20 families per month were enrolled in the MTO program at each site. After verification of program eligibility and completion of a Baseline Survey, each family was randomly assigned to one of three program groups: the Experimental group, the Section 8 Comparison group, and the Control group. Families in the Experimental group received a Section 8 certificate or voucher that could be used only in a census tract where the 1990 poverty rate was less than 10%. These families also received some counseling assistance from a local nonprofit organization to help them find a new apartment and to help them adjust to the new neighborhood. Families in the Section 8 Comparison group received a geographically unrestricted Section 8 certificate or voucher and no counseling assistance. Families in the Control group did not receive a Section 8 certificate or voucher, although they continued to receive their project-based assistance. MTO enrolled 4,600 families across the five sites from 1994 to 1998. Families in the Experimental and Section 8 Comparison groups were given four to six months (depending on the site) to submit an approval request for an apartment that they would like to lease. Forty-eight percent of families in the Experimental group signed a lease for a new unit, while 62% of those in the Section 8 Comparison group eventually leased a new apartment through MTO.

As shown in table 8.1, the majority of MTO families are headed by a single mother who is a member of a racial or ethnic minority. In Boston, 37% of MTO families are black, 46% are Hispanic, and the remainder are largely white or Asian. These mothers are typically not working and are receiving public assistance. Families generally have between one and three children, and more than half have at least one child who is less than six years of age.

Before beginning our MTO research, we were aware of the experiences of similar families involved in the oldest and most well known housing mobility demonstration, the Gautreaux program in Chicago, which began helping families move in 1976. The first comprehensive report on the program was completed in 1979 (Peroff, Davis, and Jones 1979). More than one-third of Gautreaux families reported that the most important reason for wanting to move was to be near better schools. Roughly a quarter of families cited desire for better-quality housing, and slightly fewer wanted to live in an area with less crime. Researchers from Northwestern Univer-

Table 8.1. MTO Baseline Survey Descriptive Statistics of Households in Five Cities

	Baltimore	Boston	Chicago	Los Angeles	New York	All
If female household head	0.98	0.92	0.96	0.81	0.93	0.91
If black	0.97	0.37	0.99	0.52	0.50	0.64
If Hispanic	0.02	0.46	0.01	0.45	0.49	0.32
Main reason to move:						
Drugs, gangs	0.55	0.54	0.51	0.60	0.48	0.53
Better apartment	0.26	0.29	0.18	0.13	0.26	0.22
Better schools	0.12	0.09	0.24	0.23	0.19	0.18
In the past 6 months a householder has been:						
Beaten or assaulted	0.25	0.17	0.25	0.27	0.26	0.24
Stabbed or shot	0.12	0.08	0.12	0.13	0.12	0.11
Sample size	637	961	895	1,034	1,081	4,608

Note: Authors' calculations using the October 1999 extract of the MTO Data System, containing data on all program enrollments (October 1994–July 1998).

sity have since presented evidence suggesting that parents and children who moved to suburban areas had significantly improved employment and educational outcomes than similar families who remained in distressed central-city neighborhoods (Rosenbaum 1995), though the small sample sizes and high rates of attrition in these studies have led some to question the validity of the findings.

As we began to study MTO, we quickly realized that the priorities of public housing residents in high-poverty areas had changed by the mid-1990s; fear of crime is now at the top of the list. Each MTO family's head of household filled out a questionnaire upon enrolling in the program. Selected results from the Baseline Survey are reported in table 8.1. About half of MTO families (including those in Baltimore, Chicago, Los Angeles, and New York) reported that the most important reason they want to move is "to get away from drugs and gangs," and another 25% cited this crime category as the second most important reason to move. Only 18% now report that their most important motivation for moving is to send their children to better schools. The shift in motivation is not totally surprising, given the rise in urban crime through the early 1990s, especially among minority youth.[1] Particularly alarming, is the shocking number of episodes of reported physical harm inflicted on family members through criminal activity. One-quarter of household heads responded that someone who lives with them had been assaulted, beaten, stabbed, or shot within the past six months. An additional 25% reported that someone had tried to break into their home, or that someone who lives with them had been threatened with a knife or a gun or had her purse or jewelry snatched in the past six months. These victimization rates are about four times higher than those computed from a recent national survey of public housing households in family developments.[2] Even if the victimization rates reported by MTO families are somewhat overstated, it is clear from our MTO fieldwork that fear of crime is ubiquitous.[3]

Methods

Our use of qualitative and quantitative research methods has been sequential and iterative.[4] We began by analyzing the Baseline Survey data of all enrollees of the MTO program, examining their reasons for wanting to move, their connections to their neighborhoods, their current employment, and related issues. We then undertook qualitative fieldwork with three goals in mind. First, we wanted to understand the institutional details of the intervention, both in order to document the key elements of the program that would need to be implemented in order to replicate MTO in other places and to aid us in interpreting our quantitative results. Second, we hoped to further explore issues, such as the importance of drugs and gangs, highlighted in the Baseline Survey and previous literature (e.g., Canada 1995). Third, we wanted to listen carefully to the stories of MTO families in order to develop new themes for our research that we had not anticipated in advance.

Qualitative Methods

We have conducted our observation of the MTO site in Boston since September 1995. During that first year, we observed the function of the program—attending briefing sessions, survey administrations, and resource room workshops. We talked at length with Experimental group counselors and accompanied them on visits to participants' homes.

In this chapter, we focus largely on qualitative data from twelve 90-minute interviews with participants from both the Experimental and Section 8 Comparison groups.[5] The respondents were recruited from a random sample—stratified on race and ethnicity (Hispanic vs. non-Hispanic black) and on whether they had successfully used their voucher to move through the MTO program.[6] Each family completed one interview during the second half of 1996. We had proposed expanding the qualitative component of our study to a larger sample of families to be interviewed multiple times over a three-year period. This proposal was not accepted by the Department of Housing and Urban Development (HUD), apparently due to concern that these respondents would "burn out" and be less willing to participate in the fifth- and tenth-year evaluations, which were HUD's highest priority.

Our interview technique, heavily influenced by Weiss (1994), was to ask open-ended questions that allowed the families to tell us their stories with as little intervention from us as possible. Our goal was to let the respondents steer the discussion to the topics that were most important to them. We used a prepared interview outline as a checklist to make sure that all of our key areas of interest were covered in each interview but did not ask a fixed set of questions to each respondent or cover the topics in any particular order (we always began by asking the respondent to describe her family's move and to explain the family's experience with the MTO program, pretending that we did not know anything about how the program worked).

These interviews were taped, transcribed, and analyzed by the authors according to their relevance to various themes. Respondents were paid $20 in appreciation for their time and effort. Our methodology for analyzing the qualitative data was to identify themes from reading the complete set of transcripts and then to examine everything that any respondent had said about that theme. Some themes were specified prior to coding, such as neighborhood violence, housing quality and search, and contrasts between old and new neighborhoods. Other themes emerged during coding, such as safety of play areas and parental monitoring behavior. The quotations presented below are chosen as the most representative of the complete set of statements on each topic. During each interview discussed below, the participants chose aliases for themselves; to preserve confidentiality, we have used no actual names and some incidental details have been altered.

Quantitative Methods

After completing our qualitative interviews, we developed a 45-minute survey instrument which was the basis for our quantitative analysis. Beginning in June 1997, we interviewed household heads from the first 540 families randomly assigned to the MTO program in Boston, completing interviews with 520 household heads (for a response rate of 96%). These data are described further and have been analyzed extensively in Katz, Kling, and Liebman (2001).

In general, a central issue in the study of the impact of residential location on individual outcomes is the selection problem arising from the likely systematic sorting of individuals among neighborhoods on the basis of important (unobserved) determinants of socioeconomic outcomes. The key to our analysis is that the offer of the subsidy is randomly assigned by lottery. Thus, the Control group is used to identify the average outcomes corresponding to the counterfactual state that would have occurred for individuals in the treatment group had they not been offered a rental subsidy through the lottery.

The econometric methods we use to analyze the survey data are straightforward and are expressed below in a regression framework. Let Z be an indicator variable for being eligible for an MTO program voucher, or treatment group assignment. The coefficient π estimates a difference in outcomes between the treatment and control group that is known as the "Intent-To-Treat" (ITT) effect and is an average of the causal effects including both those treatment group members who take up the treatment and those who do not. This causal effect is captured by the ordinary least-squares estimate of the coefficient π in a regression of the outcome (Y) as in the following equation, including controls for other characteristics (X) to improve the precision of the estimates:[7]

$$Y_i = Z_i\pi + X_i\beta + \varepsilon_i$$

The ITT estimate tells us the impact of being offered the opportunity to move with an MTO voucher. We computed separate estimates for the Experimental versus Control group difference and the Section 8 Comparison group versus Control group difference. For a policy design that would offer a similar voucher to a similar population, this parameter is directly of interest.

In interpreting the results in this study, it is worth emphasizing that they reflect the overall impact of the program on the entire Experimental and Section 8 treatment groups, including those who did not move through the program. Under the plausible assumption that the program had little or no impact on those not moving with program subsidies, the impact on the program *movers* within the Experimental and Section 8 Comparison groups is substantially larger than the average differences between groups reported here. In this case, the simple mean differences in outcomes for the Experimental and Control groups should by inflated by a factor of 2.1 to produce the impact on program movers in the Experimental group (known as the impact of treatment on the treated). The reported estimates should analogously be inflated by 1.6 for the Section 8 Comparison group.[8]

Qualitative Evidence

This section focuses on the evidence from our qualitative interviews that led us to refocus our quantitative work and to develop our conceptual framework for thinking about how MTO moves are likely to affect various outcomes. We met with families just starting to look for new apartments as part of our program observation process and then conducted extended interviews with families who had already moved and families who had tried to find a new apartment but did not succeed. Talking with these families allowed us to learn about daily life in their original neighborhoods—some of the poorest in Boston—as well as to hear about their experiences in their new neighborhoods.

These interviews confirmed the finding from the Baseline Survey that fears about safety for children were the families' top motivation for wanting to leave their original neighborhoods and further suggested that these fears may have important influences on adult behavior as well as on child outcomes. Families that moved out of public housing through the MTO program indicated that their fears and anxiety were substantially reduced, and that they experienced various benefits, such as safer places for their children to play outside and increased involvement in the community.

Sources of Fear in Public Housing

In our interview with a black woman named Mary Jones, the overriding importance of fear induced by her residence in public housing was immediately obvious. Ms. Jones had lived in a housing project for many years before moving to a subsidized unit outside the project in 1992 and later to an apartment in the suburbs through MTO. At the beginning of our interview, we first asked how she had found out about the MTO program.

> The first time I heard about this program, it said Boston Housing. But I
> already had lived in Boston Housing before. It had got so bad with the

crime scene, you know. Every time I looked out my window, there was dead bodies. So I didn't want my kids to grow up in that atmosphere. Plus, it was overcrowded up there too. I had my boy and my girl, and only two bedrooms (my baby wasn't born yet). And I signed up for Section 8, but they said it would take, like, four years for me to be eligible for it. Anyway, so I walked the pavement, and I find another place. First it was kind of nice. A nice park up there. Walkin' kids to the park and stuff.

Then I don't know what happened. A little boy got shot in the store. I took the kids to the park, and a girl said, "That boy said he gonna be back in five minutes." I say, "They say they're coming back, we got to go." And when we got back in the house, she came back and said they had shot the boy. We were standing right there where the boy had got shot at. So then, one night they had a drive-by shooting. The kids had to jump on the floor. Even the baby, she was under two year old. And then my son was coming home from school the next day—and because they didn't hit their target, they wanted to come back. I hear pow-pow-pow. My baby was laying on the bed sleepin'. It was like a quarter to two. And I knew my son was comin' round the corner. And I went outside and I didn't see him. But the boy, he had got shot and he ran over to the store. They told me to call the police. I went in the hallway, and you could smell all the smoke and stuff. I thought the bullet had came through the window. I lived on the first floor, so you know I was really freakin' out, right? And so then, my son, instead of him comin' down the street his usual way, he came down the street where the person who was shootin' went up the street. And he like clashes between 'em. And I said, "Oh my god, I got to move out of here." And this wasn't no better. You see, I thought the housing would be better if it wasn't no Boston Housing, because Boston Housing is usually with the projects.

Our interpretation of her response is that the images of crime and distress in her previous neighborhoods were so strong that she felt the need to tell us about them immediately, when we asked our first general question about the MTO program. In her first sentence, she began to tell us that she had initially thought MTO was a program for families who wanted to move into the projects. But after bringing up "Boston Housing," she began to immediately tell us the story that was most important in her mind—her horrifying experiences while living in the projects and then in a publicly subsidized building under private management—and the images just poured out.[9] We interpret her description as imagery that remained salient in her mind, and not literally as seeing death "every time" she looked out the window. Ms. Jones went on to tell us more about her children's experiences. "They would see the dead bodies. And if they didn't die on the scene, they would see the blood. It was the older kids doing the shootin': 17–21 years old." Her kids never were victimized. "I always keep them with me. I could always tell when somethin' bad was going to happen."

Other families also described their frequent encounters with violence. A Hispanic woman named Maria Diaz told us, "In this entryway, a woman was raped. People have been robbed, beaten, and stabbed right here." At another interview, both the mother, Bianca Rodriguez, and one of her teenage sons were present. Her son described how the front door of their building was always propped open. "This was a problem because people would come in and sit on the steps, be in the way, smoke cigarettes, and whatever. On the rooftops there were empty crack vials everywhere. It was pretty violent. Gunshots, fights every day. I saw someone die over there. Some guy was shot in the neck." Ms. Rodriguez expressed concern that something would happen to her children on their way home from school or from work.

The random nature of these violent acts greatly distressed the mothers living in these areas, because they never knew when a fight would break out or when gunfire would erupt and endanger their children. Brenda Hernandez described her neighborhood as very loud—full of youngsters hanging out, listening to loud music, and drinking in public. She felt there was a lack of respect among these youth; they would not care who was around when they spoke foul language. There were also gangs that would fight in the park near her home. In Spanish, she said, "There were gunshots all the time. My kids saw a friend get shot in the leg. I was always worried for my children. Worried that they may be shot like that child was. Or that somebody would do something to them." Making the sign of the cross, she said, "Thank God nothing happened to my children."

Omnipresent violence was associated with a deep-seated fear among families. After telling us about a friend of her daughter who had been beaten up, a Hispanic woman, Amparo Quinonez, went on to tell us in Spanish about her family's experience.

> No one in our family had a problem like this, but such events don't give one much confidence in the place. At midnight you would hear loud music at full volume. You would hear people screaming and fighting—people who had drunk too much. On weekends in my building, the husband on

the first floor drank a lot, and the wife would lock the door to keep him out. He would shout, "Open the door! I'm going to . . . " Nothing happened to us. We just saw things. But it made me scared.

She did not really communicate with anyone in her building, other than saying hello and goodbye.

Social Isolation and Intensive Monitoring of Children Resulting from Fear

This atmosphere of fear appears to have led many mothers to avoid potential dangers by socially isolating themselves, as well as restricting the activity of their children. Rosa Lopez is a Hispanic woman who had lived in the projects for over 20 years. She did not have any close friends in the projects herself; she told us that she does not like having close friends that she would see all the time. She knew her children's friends. "Where there is evil, boys will be involved," she said. One or two would come over occasionally, but not too often because she did not want them to. In Spanish, we were told that her kids would often see drug dealers, syringes, and broken pieces of crack vials. "I would clean up my space, and then all the drug users would come and leave all their trash." She would pick up syringes so that her children would not play with them. "I would clean the place so that my child wouldn't get sick. When they were very young, I would not let them play outside at all. We knew not to touch that stuff." If they did venture outside, she and the mothers of other small children would sit outside and watch them while they played.

The fear and mistrust induced by these surroundings motivated mothers to ensure that their children were under a watchful eye at all times. Diane Gonzalez had lived in various housing projects with her young children during the past seven years. She told us that neither she nor anyone in her family was ever threatened or attacked. Once, she did give her keys to an elderly neighbor to watch her apartment when she went on a vacation and came back to find that her microwave and her son's video games had been "borrowed," and only the microwave was returned when she asked about them. She believes that someone else actually took the video games, and not the old woman herself, but she said, "You can't trust nobody there." Ms. Gonzalez described a typical day for us. She would get her nine-year-old son ready for school and wait with him at the bus stop on the corner. Then she would take her daughter to stay with her son's grandmother, after which she took a train and a bus to GED (general equivalency diploma) class half an hour away. Her son would get home around 2 P.M..

He spent from 2 to 7 P.M. each day with a 55-year-old male nurse's aide whom Ms. Gonzalez had found through the local hospital and who was meant to serve as a "father figure" in her son's life, since he was always getting into fights with children in the neighborhood.

We came to realize during our interviews that these mothers were more than simply concerned for their children. They had organized their entire lives around protecting their sons and daughters from the genuine dangers of ghetto life. These children had witnessed gunshots in their parks, drive-by shootings, bloodstained bodies, domestic violence, frequent fights, and play areas littered with broken drug paraphernalia. In response, their mothers tended to isolate themselves, communicating with few others and developing feelings of mistrust. These mothers became intensely focused on their children—always taking them along on errands, waiting with them at the bus stop, and keeping them inside or watching them play from a window or a seat on the stoop.

We believe this organizing principle has ramifications for these families that extend well beyond physical safety. Younger children in particular were seldom allowed outside the apartment, and never beyond the mother's watchful gaze. Mistrust of others extended to children's playmates, who were typically not invited to come over to the apartment and play. The enormous amount of energy channeled into monitoring the activities of children also left scant opportunity for personal development of the mothers themselves. Watching the children always took precedence over attending English as a Second Language classes, GED instruction, job training, or job search. For many women with little education and work experience to access these types of outside and professionally enhancing activities, such activities not only must be close enough so that mothers can reach them efficiently using public transportation but must also be scheduled during hours while children are in school. If there are young children in the household too young to attend school, however, then there is no time left at all for the personal development of low-income mothers.

Why not have someone else watch the children? In addition to financial constraints, we found that most mothers have a profound distrust of others who might provide childcare, including their own sisters in many cases; with the exception of grandmothers or perhaps aunts, mothers do not feel that their children will be adequately looked after by others. These are, of course, generalizations and there are likely to be many individual exceptions. Nonetheless, we believe they accurately characterize the situations facing many MTO families.

Qualitative Impacts of Moving Out of Public Housing

To illustrate the impact on a mother and her children of living in the ghetto and then getting the chance to move out, we relate the full details described to us by Shelly Brown. Ms. Brown is a middle-aged black woman who had lived in public housing for 25 years prior to enrolling in MTO in 1994. She said that she had often thought about moving but did not know how she could afford it since she does not make much money and she has children. Her two oldest children now live on their own, but her two teenage daughters live with her. The children's father is deceased, so the family receives some Supplemental Security Income, which Ms. Brown augments by working part-time.

She said she wanted to move because there was so much crime. "I would come from work and find police wagons filling up my street. It got so bad that I was telling myself that 1994 would be my last summer. That was the worst summer that I had experienced in twenty-five years," she said. "The shooting, it was ridiculous. I had to see my kids yelling and screaming, hiding under cars, and trying to get into our house. I come home from church and had bullets flying through my hallway window." She said it was not the drugs that she was afraid of in her neighborhood. It was the shooting. Drug dealers did not approach her or her kids.

> Those people know who I am. I preach "Thy kingdom come and thy will be done." That's the kind of woman I am. I will preach the word to them. I don't care who you are. So they knew where I was coming from, and they knew where my kids were comin' from. And the same with some of my friends there also. So with them, it was more like, "Hi, Ms. So-and-so." So they know who my kids are. It's not really the kids in the neighborhood, but the people driving through. You don't know where they hang at. You know, they do their drugs on the corner, next to the park. You gotta pass by them and they say, "Hey, you want some?" They was bold day and night. They would do their stuff inside, or sit outside and smoke their reef. . . .
>
> And like I said, the main shooting and stuff was coming in from outside of the neighborhood. We would be sitting outside and see them drive by and shoot at each other. My kids had to duck underneath cars. One Sunday I happened to leave my kids home. I came back and the cops was everywhere. I couldn't jump the van fast enough to see if my kids were OK. They had my car taped out and everything. They had a shootout next

door. What happened was, the people whose car was next to mine was all shot up. The bullets didn't hit my car, but they had to tape mine down because it was in that area. I said to my kids, "You're not staying home by yourselves no more. That's it." . . .

You wouldn't want to raise your kids in that. Being around seeing that. Kids pick up in different kinds of ways. If I were the type of mother that let my kids go-go-go and they could have visited anybody's house, then you never know what could have happened. . . . I'm the type of mother who doesn't let her kids go loose. I'm very self-conscious about my kids, so I sat with them or I sat at the window and watched them. If I'm gonna go someplace, they're gonna go with me. My kids are not used to violence. They're not used to fussing and fighting. It gets them upset. So they'd rather not go outside. Or if we were outside and they saw a complication, they'd come over and sit with me.

In addition to the high levels of exposure to violence in front of her home and the deep sense of fear and entrapment associated with it, Ms. Brown's children did not have a safe place to play in the neighborhood at large. In the projects, for instance, the park in which they played was built on cement. "The place was not safe for the children to play. They had swings on concrete. Everything was on concrete. And that's where most of the accidents happened." A couple of times her daughter fell off the swing and hit her head; once she was hurt seriously enough to be taken to the emergency room at the hospital. Eventually, they had to stop playing in the park because shooting began to take place there as well. "In the last five or six years, it has just gone down. People were coming from other areas." She said that gangs from two nearby areas were not getting along, so there was a war zone.

So that's why all the war's going back and forth. Boom-boom-boom. That lady got killed one day, driving her car. There was crossfire. She got blown away. When you walk in there, you've got to really pray.

What scared my kids was the drugs and the shooting. They were never the type of kids that were on the loose, because from day one since they were born, they were headed to church. They really never had a chance to get out into that world and see what it was like, so when it started coming around them, that's when the fear came around. They kept saying, "Mama, we're gonna move. Mama, we're gonna move. We're gonna move out of here." And I'd say, "Mark my words, this is gonna be my last year."

Shortly thereafter, Ms. Brown was offered a subsidy through the MTO program to help pay the rent if she moved her family out to a private-market apartment. With the help of her MTO counselor, she found an apartment in a demographically older and more racially mixed part of Boston. But when asked where she would have moved if she had not enrolled in MTO, she said that she would still be living the projects. "I'm not gonna lie to you. It takes money to save up. I'd have been still there." After enrolling in MTO, however, "the doors opened on my behalf."

In describing her new neighborhood, Ms. Brown said, "It's so beautiful. So nice. The neighbors are very friendly. . . . I like the peace and quiet. . . . I have peace of mind. I'm closer to the stores, and the transportation, too." Comparing the old and new neighborhoods, she said that her children do not have as many children to play with, but they have peace of mind and they love the area. "Here, we go outside and the kids ride their bikes." She says that the new landlord was very nice and knew that there were not a lot of kids to play with, so she put up a basketball hoop in the backyard. They know many other children from school and from church, but Ms. Brown still prefers to keep home life separate from school and church—so her daughters rarely have friends come over to play.

The children never get into fights at school. She has a time for her children to leave the house and a time for them to be back, so they do not have time to get into trouble on the way to and from school. "They know I'm gonna be there, or if I'm not there then they're gonna know where I am so they can call me." Ms. Brown is very involved in her children's schools. "You see, I take my kids to school every day. Their teachers, they know me."

She feels that the teachers in the new schools are a bit more attentive to the individual needs of each child. She also says that she feels more comfortable letting her children get involved in school activities, because the school is in a good neighborhood and there is less crime. The school is also "a good mixture, with different races." In the project, everyone was the same race. Ms. Brown prefers a mixed racial environment for her children, like the one in which she grew up elsewhere in Boston—where she had more white friends than black friends. She says that her children do not see their friends from the old neighborhood. "When we left, we left everything behind." In the old neighborhood, there were so many sirens and police at night, "it was like sitting and watching the movies. It's sad to say that, but it's true. Now I sit here and I don't see nothing walk past by here after seven o'clock. . . . But there's no runnin' and no yellin' here. I have no problem walking out here at nighttime." When asked what she likes the most about the new neighborhood, she said, "What more could I ask for? My kids, they're happy. That's the most important thing."

When Ms. Brown was living in the projects, her daughters were terrified of the gunfire. Her response was to make sure that she was always watching them, and she took them with her everywhere. They desperately wanted to move out. Since her family has moved, she clearly feels that they have all achieved some "peace of mind." Our interpretation is that their fear dissipated quickly, which has slowly begun to manifest itself in behavior changes.

Regarding employment, for instance, Ms. Brown works part-time so that she can be at home when her children come home from school. She has worked in the schools in her old neighborhood for the past seven years, starting out as a volunteer when her youngest child entered kindergarten ("so I could keep an eye on them in school, too") and then applying when a paid position opened up. "I'm very particular about them staying home by themselves, and about babysitters. When my youngest one gets into the ninth grade, I'll feel more comfortable getting a full-time job." Recall that in the old neighborhood's atmosphere of sirens and flying bullets, Ms. Brown had vowed that her children would not be home alone—including her older daughter, who was in the eighth grade at the time—so considering full-time work appears to represent an incremental change.

She also anticipates that her daughters will be granted more and more independence. As a first step, she now waits after school for her daughter on the next block rather than in the schoolyard. Of the younger one (who has just turned thirteen) she says, "I'm not gonna let her come home and let herself into the house. I don't care where I live at, that's just me. My older girl, she's in the tenth grade. I'll go out shopping knowing that she's here. My baby, I won't do that with her. She's got another year to go." Ms. Brown remains reluctant to allow outsiders into her home but has allowed her daughters to become more involved in after-school activities like basketball, track, dance, cheerleading, and Junior ROTC than she would have in her former neighborhood.

Other families have also related to us their impressions of how their new neighborhoods differ from the projects. Ms. Rodriguez's son told us that he has seen minor things after moving, such as people smoking pot, but unlike in the projects there are no crackheads. He says that in his new neighborhood everyone carries weapons too, but in the projects people would pull them for any reason. "Here, I see fistfights, and no one pulls their weapons. Over there, people pull out their guns." Ms. Garcia told us,

"I was always a little anxious when I walked in my old neighborhood, because you never knew what was going to happen to you. Now, in my new neighborhood, I don't worry at all."

Ms. Jones has since moved through MTO to an apartment in the suburbs and seldom goes back to the projects. She said, as for "visiting my friends—they come down and visit me. Because it would still be the same. I still might get shot by just coming to visit, you know. I remember when my sister used to come and visit my mother. We used to run to get in the car to leave out the place." When she has returned to her old neighborhood with her four-year-old daughter, Ms. Jones says, "Even now, we can't drive up the street. My baby, she so scared that she start cryin'. 'No-no-no.' She don't even want to go near there. It's amazing how little kids remember that stuff," especially since she was not yet two years old at the time. Ms. Jones says that she is glad she had the opportunity to move.

> As long as the kids is safe, that what my main concern was. . . . They can't grow up normally in an atmosphere of fear. They can't play games and stuff. So I had to do it. And that was the best chance when they said we had to move in the suburbs. Living in the same area, that's not good. Even the elderly people, they living in fear, captive in their own homes. My mother lives like that. It's terrible. . . . In the 'hood—my kids, they had friends. But I wouldn't let them go out, because I was afraid. Bullets don't got no name.

When living in the projects, MTO families seem to feel that they are not the targets of crime but the witnesses. Our fieldwork with residents of Boston housing projects bears out the national statistics on crime, which tell us that most incidents are perpetrated by young men upon young men. However, these families fear being caught up in the crossfire. Fear has led mothers to constantly monitor their children's activities, leaving little time for personal development. Children are often kept indoors, and their social activity is limited and always under a watchful eye. All the families we met that have moved seem much more at ease in their new neighborhoods. Housing programs such as MTO that help families move out of housing projects into areas of less concentrated poverty appear to be quite successful in reducing this apprehension and hold promise for releasing families from the captivity of the defensive behavior patterns they have adopted.

Quantitative Evidence

The qualitative evidence described in the previous section led us to focus our quantitative data collection on measuring the impacts of MTO on safety and health. It also led us to develop an overall conceptual framework and hypotheses about the mechanisms through which MTO moves would lead to changes in adult and child outcomes. In this section, we begin by summarizing our results that have been published elsewhere on the impacts of MTO on safety and health. Then we present new quantitative results from questions in our survey that were designed to explore a specific hypothesis about the mechanisms through which MTO moves might affect outcomes. Based on our fieldwork, we hypothesized that offers of housing vouchers leading to residence in safer neighborhoods would reduce the level of parental monitoring of children. Further, we speculated that this reduced monitoring might lead to more freedom for adults to pursue activities that could lead to greater economic self-sufficiency.

Summary of Results on Safety and Health

Since safety was such an important factor for the public housing residents in our qualitative interviews, one of the first tasks of our survey research was to quantify the magnitude of changes induced by moves to new neighborhoods for our entire sample. We found very significant declines in measures such as the frequency of gunfire and presence of drug dealers among both groups receiving housing vouchers. Based on our qualitative research combined with our reading of prior studies, improvements in safety were also hypothesized to lead directly to fewer victimization incidents involving children, to fewer injuries (say, from broken glass or needles), to decreased asthma from reduced stress (Wright 1998), to fewer behavior problems among children brought on by exposure to violence (Groves et al. 1993), and to improved adult mental health from a reduction in anxiety about safety. These hypotheses about the positive impact of lower-poverty neighborhoods on various child outcomes were tested using our survey data.

Some of the key results on health and safety outcomes from Katz, Kling, and Liebman (2001) are summarized in table 8.2, where we display the Control group mean in column 1, the regression-adjusted difference between the Experimental and Control groups in column 2, and the regression-adjusted difference between the Section 8 Comparison and Control groups in column 3. We found that families offered housing vouchers through the

Table 8.2. Summary of Health and Safety Outcomes from the MTO-Boston Follow-up Survey

	Control mean (1)	Intent-to-treat difference	
		Exp. − Control (2)	Sec. 8 − Control (3)
Family			
Seen drugs in neighborhood	0.205	−0.122**	−0.098**
		(0.037)	(0.045)
Heard gunfire in neighborhood	0.359	−0.196**	−0.125**
		(0.045)	(0.054)
Children			
If attacked, robbed, threatened	0.127	−0.059*	−0.030
		(0.031)	(0.040)
If injury requiring medical attention	0.105	−0.059**	−0.037
		(0.027)	(0.033)
If asthma attack requiring attention	0.098	−0.051*	−0.004
		(0.029)	(0.037)
Behavior problems index (boys)	0.326	−0.090**	−0.113**
		(0.041)	(0.053)
Behavior problems index (girls)	0.193	−0.023	−0.050~
		(0.030)	(0.034)
Adults			
Overall health good or better	0.578	0.115**	0.162**
		(0.048)	(0.056)
Calm and peaceful "a good bit of the time or more often"	0.465	0.107**	0.138**
		(0.050)	(0.063)
"Most people can be trusted"	0.078	0.052~	0.017
		(0.033)	(0.037)

Note: Standard errors are reported in parentheses, adjusted for household level clustering; ~ = p-value < .15; * = p-value < .1; ** = p-value < .05. Results are from Katz, Kling, and Liebman 2001, which contains a complete discussion of specifications and sample sizes.

MTO program had significant improvements in neighborhood safety; fewer injuries and asthma attacks (mainly in the Experimental group); reductions in child behavior problems, particularly for boys; and better adult mental health. In addition, we found marginally significant evidence of increased social trust in the Experimental group (p-value = .11)—consistent with some of our qualitative observations—that may be related to such outcomes as child behavior problems and adult mental health.

By focusing special attention in our survey on outcomes such as safety and health that the families in our qualitative interviews indicated were important to them, we accurately predicted many areas of inquiry where there were interesting effects of moves out of high-poverty neighborhoods. Moreover, the systematic data collection in our survey gave us a fuller understanding of these issues than we had obtained from our small number of qualitative interviews. Within our survey research itself, we also included open-ended questions to obtain contextual details about victimization incidents and injuries. These open-ended responses allowed us to later develop a coding system that fit the respondents' experiences, instead of pre-specifying closed-ended response categories.

Quantitative Assessment of Hypotheses on Parental Monitoring

To assess the extent to which safety concerns were influencing parental monitoring behavior, we asked several direct questions in our survey:

- When [CHILD] is outdoors on a weekday afternoon, do you need to closely monitor (his/her) activities—for example, by sitting at the window?
- On a typical weekday, did there need to be someone keeping a constant eye on [CHILD] after school because of safety concerns?
- [if yes]: Were *your* other activities, such as work, job search, or education, restricted because you needed to constantly be watching over [CHILD] after school?

In table 8.3, we present results on some of these parental monitoring measures for children aged 6–15. About 57% of household heads reported that they closely monitor outdoor activities. The sign of the difference was negative for the Experimental group and positive for the Section 8 Comparison group, but both differences were statistically insignificant. Only 31% of household heads in the Control group said that they need to keep a constant eye on their children after school because of safety concerns. The level of this parental monitoring was roughly 25% lower in the Experimental group and 15% lower in the Section 8 Comparison group. However, the difference in the overall mean between the Experimental and Control groups was only marginally statistically significant, with a *p*-value of .106, and the difference for the Section 8 Comparison group was statistically insignificant. To examine changes in the more problematic situations, we also analyzed the outcome where household heads indicated that

Table 8.3. Parental Monitoring from the MTO-Boston Follow-up Survey

	Control mean (1)	Intent-to-treat difference	
		Exp. − Control (2)	Sec. 8 − Control (3)
Needed to closely monitor child's activities outdoors (or no activities outdoors)	0.574	−0.059 (0.054)	0.014 (0.062)
Needed someone keeping a constant eye on child after school because of safety concerns	0.314	−0.076~ (0.048)	−0.043 (0.061)
Needed someone keeping a constant eye on child after school because of safety concerns AND needed to closely monitor child's activities outdoors (or no activities outdoors)	0.260	−0.084* (0.045)	−0.087~ (0.054)
Needed someone keeping a constant eye on child after school because of safety concerns AND this restricted own activities, such as work, job search, or education	0.150	−0.037 (0.038)	−0.018 (0.047)

Note: Standard errors are reported in parentheses, adjusted for household level clustering; ~ = p-value < .15; * = p-value < .1. Sample sizes for the Experimental, Section 8 Comparison, and Control groups were 248, 125, and 194.

they need to both "closely monitor" and "keep a constant eye on" the child. This was true of 26% of the Control group. The decline in this condition for both groups receiving housing vouchers through MTO was about 8–9 percentage points, with p-values on the differences of .059 in the Experimental group and .101 in the Section 8 Comparison group. If the offer of housing vouchers affected only those who used the vouchers to move to new locations, then the magnitude of these differences is 2.1 times larger for the Experimental group and 1.6 times larger for the Section 8 Comparison group, as described above. Thus, there is some tentative evidence that moves to safer neighborhoods may have reduced the need for parents to closely monitor their children, but our statistical power to detect effects of even quite large magnitude is limited by the size of the samples used in this analysis.

The decline in parental monitoring intensity among the groups receiving housing vouchers, however, did not translate into detectable changes in perceptions that the household head's own activities were restricted. The overall control mean for activity restriction was 15% in the Control group. The percentages were lower among both groups receiving housing vouchers, but the differences were statistically insignificant. In other work, we found no significant effects of either MTO treatment on the employment rates, education, or job training of household heads (Katz, Kling, and Liebman 2001).

One reason that increased safety might not alleviate restrictions on household head activities induced by parental monitoring may be that families moving to new neighborhoods using housing vouchers had more difficulty finding childcare. We find, for example, that after school (and after any school-related activities) on a typical weekday, 75% of children aged 6–15 in the Control group go home as opposed to some other place. Children are 7–8 percentage points more likely to be reported to come home in the Experimental group (p-value = .099) and in the Section 8 Comparison group (p-value = .197). We do note, however, that similar data collected at the Los Angeles site of the MTO demonstration do not indicate any significant differences between groups in the location children go after school (Hanratty, McLanahan, and Pettit 1998).

We investigated the arrangements for after-school supervision of children aged 6–15. In general, we hypothesized that younger children would be more likely to be supervised by an adult after school, so we report results separately in table 8.4 for children aged 6–9 and 10–15.[10] Note that the trend over time for the Control group indicates a decline in parental supervision after school, most likely due to rising employment rates for the mothers. According to the Baseline Survey, 75% of children aged 6–9 in the Control group were supervised after school by their parents. One to three years later at the Follow-up Survey, 67% of children aged 6–9 received after-school parental supervision.

In the Control group, it turns out that the adult supervision pattern is quite similar for younger and older children (although the younger children are often at home with older siblings). Almost no child is alone after school, but about 13% of the Control group are not supervised by an adult and about 20% are supervised by an adult other than a parent. Among younger children in particular, the fraction supervised by an adult other than a parent is lower in the Section 8 Comparison group (p-value = .042), and there is also a statistically insignificant decline in the Experimental group (p-value = .224). The sign of the difference for parental supervision of younger children after school for the two groups is positive but statistically insignificant. On net, relatively more parents are supervising children after school among the families offered housing vouchers (which could be restricting

Table 8.4. After-School Supervision from the MTO-Boston Follow-up Survey

After school (and after any school-related activities) on a typical weekday:	Control mean (1)	Intent-to-treat difference	
		Exp. − Control (2)	Sec. 8 − Control (3)
Ages 6–9			
Parent is with the child	0.665	0.058 (0.071)	0.027 (0.087)
An adult (but not a parent) is with the child	0.215	−0.086 (0.063)	−0.138** (0.068)
No parent or adult is with the child	0.120	0.027 (0.043)	0.111* (0.059)
Ages 10–15			
Parent is with the child	0.684	−0.054 (0.074)	−0.037 (0.084)
An adult (but not a parent) is with the child	0.180	0.024 (0.063)	−0.018 (0.077)
No parent or adult is with the child	0.136	0.030 (0.055)	0.055 (0.066)

Note: Standard errors are reported in parentheses, adjusted for household level clustering; * = p-value < .1; ** = p-value < .05. Sample sizes for the Experimental, Section 8 Comparison, and Control groups for ages 6–9 were 120, 70, and 105; for ages 10–15 they were 127, 56, and 89.

their own work, job search, or education), but these differences are not large in magnitude and are statistically insignificant.

The results also suggest that there are more children without either a parent or an adult supervising them after school especially for the Section 8 Comparison group (p-value = .062). Nearly all of these children not supervised by an adult in the Section 8 Comparison group have mothers who are working, and most are reported to be with other youth or child family members. It is not clear whether these circumstances result from difficulty in arranging for alternative supervision in the new neighborhoods or from a feeling of increased safety that makes mothers less fearful of leaving children unsupervised.

Using Qualitative Data to Place Quantitative Results in Context

During the course of our fieldwork, including both our observation of program operations and our dozen qualitative interviews, we learned many institutional details which were valuable in giving context to our quantitative results. In particular, the fieldwork has helped us to make judgments concerning the external validity of our MTO findings and has prevented us from making some significant errors in interpreting our quantitative results.

The External Validity of Our MTO Findings

One of the most important questions that arises in interpreting results from MTO involves the external validity of the findings — that is, assessing their usefulness in forecasting the results of other potential implementations of housing mobility policies.[11] One might want to use the results about the Section 8 Comparison group from MTO, for example, to make inferences about what would happen if the regular Section 8 voucher program were to be expanded. One concern might arise if the applicants for MTO thought that they had to move to the suburbs and therefore were not representative of the applicants to the regular Section 8 program. Our qualitative work suggests that most MTO applicants essentially thought that they were applying for regular Section 8 assistance. There was little awareness of the special restrictions for those assigned to the Experimental group, except for those actually assigned to that group, who then indicated that they were surprised and often upset about the limitations on their relocation choices. From the point of view of the external validity of MTO for Section 8 expansion, these reports suggest that MTO applicants are likely to be similar to other voluntary Section 8 applicants from public housing.

Avoiding Errors in Interpreting Our Quantitative Results

There are a number of examples where our qualitative research prevented us from making some significant errors in interpreting our quantitative results. We discussed one of these examples above: the possibility that responses to the Baseline Survey were affected by the fact that some respondents erroneously believed that their survey responses would determine whether they received a Section 8 voucher.

Another example involves racial and ethnic differences in location choices. We observed that black families tended to move farther out of the city of Boston than Hispanic families did. Had we not done the fieldwork we would almost certainly have attributed this to language barriers that intensify as one moves farther away from the city. However, our fieldwork suggested that another explanation was at least as important. Spanish-speaking MTO families were assigned to the one Spanish-speaking counselor, and this counselor believed that families were better off staying close to the city. By default the non-Spanish-speaking families were typically assigned to the other counselor, who urged families to move as far from the city as possible. Thus, the variation in geographic location by race and ethnicity was likely due at least as much to counselor attitudes as it was to language issues.

A similar counselor effect appears to have been partially responsible for the decline over time in the lease-up rates of families offered vouchers. While rising rents due to the strong economy appear to have been the major cause of this pattern, it is also the case that we observed some significant burnout by the counselors as the program progressed, and this is likely to have contributed as well.

Other Lessons about Housing Assistance

In addition to helping us generate hypotheses and theories and to interpret our quantitative results, our fieldwork provided us with extensive opportunity to listen to public housing residents and Section 8 recipients talk about their housing situations. These conversations taught us many things that we believe are relevant for housing policy. For many of the things we learned, it is hard to imagine any other data collection strategy that would have led us to these insights.

The Importance of Utility Costs

Perhaps the clearest lesson we learned is that in the minds of public housing residents a large difference between project-based assistance and Section 8 is that the tenant is not responsible for paying for utilities such as gas, heat, and electricity in the projects but usually must pay these costs in private rental units. This was given as a reason for not moving by some of the people who were offered vouchers but did not use them, and it was described as a significant drawback of life in the new apartment by those who moved. Indeed, more than three-quarters of the families we interviewed brought up this issue at some point.

For example, Ms. Rodriguez, an Experimental group household head whose family did not use their voucher told us that she looked for apartments in listings in the *Boston Globe*. She said in Spanish that one apartment she found listed in the paper was "too cold." She went on to say that her mobility counselor would call and leave messages about apartments, but that they were "cold" so she was not interested. Puzzled, we asked what she meant by "cold," and she explained that she would have to pay for utilities, including heat, but she knew she could not afford them, so it would be cold in that apartment. "After $300 on rent, and then gas, light, and oil, I can't afford it. . . . That's why I am still here."

Another woman, Ms. Diaz, gave the following explanation for why she did not use her voucher to move: "I was indecisive. I began to think that one would have to pay light, water, and heat in many places and it seemed like it would be more expensive than here. I couldn't find an apartment in which utilities were included. There are few like that . . . I looked but I would have had to pay for utilities. Some had low rent, but I came to see that in the winter, the light, water, and gas would be a lot."

Finally, a woman named Diane Sanchez did manage to move. But she explained to us why some of her friends did not: "Maybe they didn't want to pay light. If you take Section 8 you have to pay bills. That's the good part of the projects, but I prefer to be safe with my kids even if I have to pay the light." She went on to say that when she moves next, "I want to see if I can get an apartment that includes heat and hot water, because it would be less money for me."

Security Deposits

Talking to the MTO housing counselors helped us understand the importance of certain recent housing policy changes. For instance, soon after MTO began, HUD changed its rules and began to allow Section 8 landlords to require security deposits from tenants. The security deposits could be an entire month's gross rent. Since Section 8 families generally pay only a fraction of the total rent (with the government paying the rest), these deposits could equal several months' worth of rent payments. We observed an initial program informational session in which a number of MTO household heads expressed deep concern that this new rule would make it impossible for them to move, and we therefore expected the counselors to receive many complaints about this change as families searched for apartments.

Our qualitative fieldwork yielded mixed evidence on the importance of these security deposits. The counselors reported that the new rules were having little impact. In part, this was because many landlords were not choosing to require the security deposits. However, even when they were required, voucher recipients were quite resourceful in obtaining funds to pay the security deposits, and therefore this was not a major constraint. We viewed this type of evidence as particularly convincing because the counselors' own reputations were based in part on the success of their clients, and it would have been easy for the counselors to use the security deposit regulations as an explanation for the failure of some of their clients to successfully use their vouchers. Our analysis of lease-up rates over time did not show a discrete decline around the time of the HUD policy change, though adjustment to the new regime by landlords might have been gradual.

However, one MTO household head we spoke with, Cynthia Jones, told us that the security deposits greatly constrained her housing choices. She told us that she had taken her current apartment at the last minute because her voucher was about to expire if she did not use it. She said that while the new neighborhood is safer than the old one, there are drug dealers on her street and her apartment is infested with mice. When we asked her why she did not move to a new place, she said, "I can't move now because they don't offer the security deposits, so now you have to pay the first and last months' rent. I tried to move a couple of times but every place wants $1,600. I don't have that to move so I have to stay where I am at. . . . It's probably going to take me a couple of years [to save it.] Every place I've seen that I liked you had to have first and last months' rent."

Perceptions of Marginal Benefit Reduction Rates

In some of our initial interviews, we observed that MTO families knew that if their income increased, their rent would go up by 30% of the increase.[12] We were struck by this awareness of marginal benefit reduction rates because one of us had conducted interviews with Earned Income Tax Credit (EITC) recipients and had found essentially no awareness of the phaseout of the EITC and the marginal tax rates it creates (Liebman 1996). Therefore, in our interviews, we began asking, "If your income goes up, does your rent change?" Most MTO household heads in our qualitative interviews not only said yes but went on without further prompting to explain that the rent went up by 30%. One respondent went on to explain the exact lag between the increase in her income and the annual income recertification that resulted in the increase in rent. Ms. Quinonez described the cumulative impact of taxes and benefit reductions: "That's why I don't want a raise because you have to pay taxes and then the rent. It's not for you the raise, clearly. It's for them."

In our interview with Cynthia Jones, as soon as we had turned on the tape recorder she said:

> You want to know why I hate this program. Let me tell you why I hate this program. I thought it was a program like to help you get up on your feet.

Because I was on welfare but now I work part-time. So I was working full-
time, but then when I told my leasing officer that I was working full-time,
I was making too much money, so then my rent went sky high. Then I
couldn't afford to pay the rent and take care of my light and my gas and
all my other bills, so I had to cut back to part-time. So I think it stinks because if they are there to help you get up on your feet—say if you make
$400 a week and your net pay is like $275 or whatever. Then your rent
goes up from $150 to $600 [a month], then plus your gas and your light
and that's a lot of money.

Ms. Jones went on to explain that the amount she had to pay for childcare also increased when her income went up and that she had concluded
that she was financially better off working part-time (i.e., that her effective
marginal tax rate exceeded 100%). At the end of the interview, we asked
if she had any advice for the people who run the program. She suggested
that the government take the rent increases that occur due to income increases and put them in a savings account for the individual to help them
leave housing assistance altogether:

They need to give more time to look for a suitable place to live and that
if you start working they should say this person should pay this much
money. Give this person a set amount of rent to pay if they start working
full-time, part-time, or whatever and then tell them they got five years
to have a bank account to save x amount of dollars so that they can save
their money, buy them a house, or move out on their own and get off the
program and let somebody else that really needs it.

We suspect that the monthly nature of rent payments makes changes
in rent transparent to housing assistance recipients. In contrast, the EITC
is typically paid once a year, the credit amount depends in a complicated
way on a taxpayer's earnings, and benefit levels have changed significantly
almost every year, making it difficult for recipients to connect their labor
supply decisions with the resulting change in the credit.

In our quantitative survey, we asked a series of questions to explore
whether the awareness of these marginal benefit reduction rates was as
widespread as we had perceived it to be in our qualitative interviews. We
asked, "Does your rent change when your income goes up?" Ninety percent of MTO households still receiving housing subsidies answered "yes,"
4% said "no," and 5% said that they "did not know." For those who said
yes, we asked, "How much does your rent change if your income goes up

by 10 dollars a month?" Fifty-seven percent said that they did not know, while 43% gave a numeric answer. Of those supplying a number, 33% gave the statutorily correct answer of 30% (or $3), and another 15% gave an answer close to this answer (between 20% and 40%). A surprisingly large number of people gave an answer that was significantly higher than 30%. Sixteen percent gave an answer between 40% and 100%, and 22% reported a number that was 100% ($10) or more.

Our interpretation of these quantitative results is that it appears that most housing residents are aware that their rent rises when their income goes up, but only a minority know the exact marginal benefit reduction rate. We speculate that some of the greater knowledge shown by respondents in the qualitative interview was due to the interview format. It is easy to say, "I don't know," and move on to the next question in a long survey, especially over the phone. Moreover, we suspect that some of the outlier responses to this question on the survey reflect errors by the interviewer or coder. In contrast, in our qualitative interviews we were more likely to interpret responses of "I don't know, maybe 30%," as an accurate perception of the incentives and to ask the question again if someone's answer suggested she was confused about the monetary units.

The Impact of Policy Uncertainty

In our dozen interviews, which were occurring at the height of uncertainty over welfare reform, we encountered two respondents who told us that they were concerned that if they moved to a Section 8 apartment, the government would decide to stop funding the program and then they would be unable to pay their rent and become homeless. In contrast, they felt secure that public housing was not going to disappear. One woman gave this reason along with fear of utility costs as her main reasons for not availing herself of the vouchers. Another, Ms. Brown, said that when she was thinking about enrolling in MTO, other people in her neighborhood cautioned her: "'Be careful,' they said, 'There must be a catch in it. You're gonna move and they ain't gonna pay that rent. And you're gonna be stuck there.' But if I'd listened to everybody, I wouldn't be where I'm at today."

The Importance of Access to Health Care

Toward the end of our field research, we sat down with the MTO mobility counselors with a list of all of their clients who had failed to use a voucher to move and had them tell us the story of why each client had not leased an apartment. There was a wide range of circumstances, but we were struck by the number of people who had decided that they did not want to move farther away from the place where they or their children were currently receiving medical care. Many of the housing projects that Boston MTO families came from were located close to academic medical centers, including Children's Hospital, and mothers whose children were being treated for serious cases of asthma or other conditions or who themselves had serious physical or mental health problems were reluctant to move farther away.

In our qualitative interviews, we found that easy access to health care providers was an amenity that was valued highly. It was also the source of the most negative comment we heard anyone make about life in the suburbs. Brenda Hernandez described the health center she visited in her new neighborhood:

> Here they treat you bad. In Boston they treat you fast. But here they are prejudiced in the way that they treat us. They treat us like nothing. I don't like the hospital here. Sometimes I wish I had a plane and could just fly to Boston. In the hospital there are no Spanish-speaking people. My sister feels the same way. Her neck was hurting and she was crying and they made her wait and wait. In Boston they treat you nice and give you the things you need. We have no problems with the welfare office here. Only the hospital. My social worker is a nice guy. He's an American. The people in the stores are fine. They treat you nice. . . . My children are treated well in the school system.

While this may represent a single isolated incident, it does serve to reinforce the impression that health care is perhaps the most important placebased service that these families rely on in their neighborhoods.

The Large Impacts of Small Management Changes in Public Housing

After violent crime, property crime, drugs, and noise, the most common complaints we heard about housing projects were that the stairwells and common areas of the projects were a mess, entryway garbage cans were always overflowing, and the entryway doors did not have functioning locks so that undesirable people could use the stairwells and roofs of the building to do drugs. We also heard people talk about these problems being eliminated simply because a new building supervisor came in who managed things well by fixing the locks and having the trash cans emptied regularly. We take this to be hopeful news. Significant improvements in the quality of life of project residents are possible with fairly small management improvements.

Many people we interviewed also talked about the tremendous effectiveness of recent efforts of the Boston Housing Authority and the Boston Police to keep drug dealers and other undesirable people away from the projects. Indeed, one participant who moved to the suburbs told us that if the improvements in the projects had occurred earlier, she would not have applied for MTO and moved. She added, however, that she was grateful that she had moved and did not at all regret her decision to participate in the program.

Learning about Additional Housing Options by Living in New Neighborhoods

At the end of our interview with Rosa Calderon, we turned off the tape recorder and got up to leave. While we were walking to the door, she said in Spanish, "I'm going to be moving again soon." We were somewhat embarrassed that we had not managed to elicit this important piece of information in 90 minutes of talking with the woman, and we sat down again, turned on the tape recorder, and asked her to explain why she was going to move. She told us that she took this initial apartment in order to make sure she found something within the 90-day time limit. But now that she was in the new neighborhood, she had heard from a neighbor about a better place that was available down the street.

Two other interviewees told us similar stories of planning to move because they learned about better apartments after moving to the new neighborhoods. Another MTO household head, Shelly Brown, had already moved to a second apartment in the same neighborhood by the time we interviewed her. She moved because her prior unit was on the first floor of a two-family unit, and the family on the second floor had three young children: "There were nights I couldn't sleep. . . . When I come home from work, I don't want no 'Boom! Boom! Boom!' over my head." Her second unit was cheaper, more spacious, more attractive, not to mention much quieter. She has no plans to move anytime soon: "I'm comfortable here, and the kids are comfortable."

Relationships with Neighbors

When we initially analyzed the Baseline Survey data, we were surprised to find that 42 % of household heads said that they had no friends living in their neighborhood, and that a further 48 % said that they had only a few friends in the neighborhood. Earlier we discussed the ways in which fear of crime and violence can lead public housing residents to isolate themselves from their surroundings. From our qualitative interviews, we came to believe this was a broader phenomenon. When asked if they had friends in the housing projects or spent time with their neighbors, the women we interviewed gave us responses such as "I keep to myself" or "I don't want their problems to get in my life."

For many of the women, these guarded attitudes toward neighbors continued after their moves. Ms. Quinonez told us, "The woman next door is white and says hello and asks me if I need anything. The street is very tranquil. Most people own their homes. People are friends and not too close. That's good because I don't like to be too friendly with neighbors." Shelly Brown's comments were similar:

> The people are really nice, but everyone keeps to themselves. There's nobody hanging out here. At nighttime it's like a ghost town. You get a lot of skunks and squirrels. When I first moved here, the birds that wake you up in the morning, the crows, they used to get on my nerves. Oh my, at six in the morning you know it's daybreak. That's all you hear. But the people are friendly, and we watch out for one another. In the daytime we'll say, "Hi, how are you?" We'll talk a little bit. And they go in their house and I'll go in my house and that's it.

Mary Jones told us, "One thing I noticed, having my own place. [You don't want to] get to know too many people. 'Cause you get to know too many people, and you get everybody comin' in and want to sit down and talk to you. I just stay to myself, you know."

Conclusion

In general, as the many examples in this chapter indicate, we believe that we have learned a great deal about the impact of neighborhoods on low-income families through our integration of qualitative and quantitative research on the randomized MTO demonstration. Encouraged by this experience, we are collaborating on further MTO research that will include a substantial qualitative component (led by Susan Popkin) of 60 families in five cities, combined with survey data from a universe of 4,250 households. The next stage of research will allow us another iteration in a cycle of hypothesis generation, survey data collection, analysis, and interpretation of results in which qualitative research will play an integral role.

We also found it tremendously valuable to have the principal investigators conduct the interviews themselves. Because we had our theoretical frameworks and tentative hypotheses in mind as we did the interviews and could ask for further elaboration when a respondent expressed something particularly revealing about one of our hypotheses, we believe we were able to develop insights that we would not have discovered if we had delegated the interviewing to research assistants. Our qualitative interviews were instrumental in shaping our later survey development, with increased emphasis on topics such as exposure to violence, mental health, and after-school supervision of children.

The single most important contribution of our qualitative research is that it has led us to develop an overall conceptual framework for thinking about pathways through which MTO moves might affect developmental outcomes and more generally about the ways in which ghetto residents are affected by their surroundings. In particular, we observed that fear of random violence was pervasive and that safety concerns caused mothers in high-poverty urban housing projects to devote an enormous amount of time and energy to ensuring the safety of their children. We believe that the need to live life on the watch has broad implications for the future prospects of these families—including potential impacts on children's learning and behavior and on mothers' mental health and on their ability to engage in activities that would lead them to become economically self-sufficient.

The policy implications of this finding are potentially quite broad. The most obvious implication is that programs like MTO that help families move out of high-poverty neighborhoods can have potentially large impacts on the well-being of the families that move. However, the implications of these moves for child supervision are more complex. Our quantitative results show that after-school supervision by other adults is actually lower among the groups receiving housing vouchers, possibly because parents are less concerned about having their children supervised in the safer neighborhoods or because childcare options are more limited after the moves. Arrangements for child supervision may become easier over time after adjustment to new neighborhoods, but in the short run we find that moving to safer neighborhoods does not appear to enable adults to increase their school enrollment or employment rates as we had hypothesized that it might.

The experiences of MTO families suggest that, beyond traditional calls for more police and fewer guns on the street, there are policy options for families who remain in the ghetto that could help ease the social paralysis induced by fear of crime. For example, one option might be for schools to organize after-school programs that are supervised by parents. Such programs could potentially provide safe havens for children to engage in both educational and social activities while bringing together like-minded parents in an atmosphere that could help promote social trust. Parents could also cooperate to rotate their supervisory schedules to permit more flexibility in their own schedules to help pursue their own education.

In the broader scope of poverty policy, the crime epidemic in the ghetto has implications for reform of the welfare system that have not been acknowledged. The often-recognized danger of welfare reform is that some mothers will not find work in a weak economy, leaving their children in destitute poverty. The unappreciated danger is that children will not have a mother to protect them during the hours that she is working. Our results on child supervision suggest that difficulties in obtaining adult supervision of children are an issue for a substantial fraction of this population, and that over time as employment rates of MTO mothers have increased, there has been a decline in the share of their children who have adult supervision after school.

Unlike middle-class families, many families receiving welfare—and especially the roughly one-quarter who live in assisted housing (Committee on Ways and Means 1994)—live in truly dangerous areas in which children are afraid and are at risk. Those for whom safe childcare or after-school supervision for children is not available may face an excruciating choice between safety and work. A policy that encourages part-time employment may better allow ghetto residents to secure the safety of their older children while promoting work for long-time welfare recipients. If full-time work is required, childcare and after-school policies could be crucial. Otherwise, we speculate that a 12-year-old boy might be worse off after welfare reform if he is exposed to drive-by shootings, drug pushers, and teen gangs—without anyone to look after him. Although having a working mother may have positive effects on children, welfare reform could have the unintended consequence of increasing the intergenerational transmission of poverty if more children are directly exposed to greater violence and crime.

Notes

1. From 1973 to 1992, for instance, the rate of violent victimizations of black males aged 12–24 increased about 25%. The rate at which black males ages 14–17 commit-

ted murder more than quadrupled from 1985 to 1992, with most blacks killing other blacks (see DiIulio 1996). But, it should be noted, crime rates in the MTO cities, including Boston, have fallen substantially since the early 1990s, with noticeable improvements in safety in many of the public housing projects.

2. These statistics on MTO families are based on our tabulations of MTO Baseline Survey data provided by the Department of Housing and Urban Development (HUD). Results from the national public housing survey are reported in Zelon et al. 1994. That study estimated an annual victimization rate of 27.6% for public housing households living in family developments (1994, 15), which we divide by 2 for an estimate over a six-month period.

3. The neighborhoods in which MTO families lived before entering the MTO program were specifically chosen for the demonstration because they had high poverty rates, and there may have well been more crime in these areas than in the average public housing development. Yet there are several reasons why reported MTO victimization rates may overstate the true rates. Despite explicit instructions that the survey was being conducted by outside researchers and that the Boston Housing Authority would not receive copies of individual responses, our interviews revealed that many respondents assumed that their answers to the questions would influence their acceptance into the program — which may have encouraged them to overreport victimization.

Another reason that the reported victimization rates may be too high is the common survey response phenomenon of "telescoping," in which the respondent recalls that an event took place later than it actually did — so that it falls within the reference period (in this case, within the past six months). In our in-depth interviews, we found that many incidents had occurred outside the reference period after we probed more thoroughly for the timing of the events. The MTO survey and the national public housing survey (Zelon et al. 1994) used similar questions, so we might expect this telescoping effect to be similar in the two surveys. However, the MTO questions were more detailed (six questions rather than two), which may have elicited a greater response. In addition, it is likely that the MTO respondents were more rushed in making their responses, which may have exacerbated the telescoping effect. As part of our observation of the MTO program, we answered the same victimization questions as the participants during a regular administration of the Baseline Survey. The questions in this survey were read out loud by the administrator to a group of respondents and were followed by the possible responses. The heads of households marked their responses on copies of the survey. The administrator moved the group through the survey quickly and respondents had little time to consider whether an incident actually took place "within the past six months" as the survey requested. In contrast, the national public housing survey was conducted with individuals over the telephone, and the interviewer would wait for the interviewee to respond.

4. This research began in 1995, but we only later became aware of the methodological literature specifically addressing the relationship between qualitative and quantitative research (e.g., Sieber 1973; Greene, Caracelli, and Graham 1989; Creswell 1994; Tashakkori and Teddlie 1998). Our approach to qualitative research itself was influenced by practitioners Deborah Belle at Boston University and Michael Piore at MIT, and especially by Weiss (1994).

5. Interviews in English were completed by Kling and Liebman, while interviews in Spanish were completed by Liebman and Yvonne Gastulem, then a doctoral candidate in psychology. Although Kling and Liebman are not the same race or gender as those in-

terviewed for the study, we felt it was important for the principal investigators of the study to be directly involved in the qualitative fieldwork rather than rely on reports from research assistants.

6. Specifically, we were provided with the contact information for 40 families equally split between the Experimental and Section 8 treatment groups. Within each group our list of potential interviewees consisted of 6 Hispanic movers, 6 black movers, 4 Hispanic nonmovers, and 4 black nonmovers. We randomly ordered the families within each race by treatment group by move status cell. Then we attempted to contact families within each cell in order until we had completed interviews with 2 Hispanic movers, 2 black movers, 1 Hispanic nonmover, and 1 black nonmover in each of the two treatment groups for a total of 12 interviews. In total, we attempted to contact roughly twice as many families as we interviewed. Only one person declined to be interviewed. Thus, our success in reaching people was largely determined by whether we could obtain a valid phone number for them. It is possible therefore that the people we managed to interview were systematically different from the overall MTO population. However, we suspect that the bias from the nonresponse rate in our qualitative sample is trivial relative to the sampling variability that comes from having such a small sample of interviews.

We excluded Control group members from the sample because given our limited sample size we wanted to maximize the information we could collect per interview. Therefore, people who could tell us about their experience with the MTO program and about either successful moves to new neighborhoods or their reasons for not using the voucher to move were more valuable than people who could simply describe conditions in the original neighborhood. Moreover, while in theory qualitative interviews with Control group members could help us avoid confounding program impacts with changes that would have happened to the families over time even if they had not received housing vouchers from MTO, in practice with only a dozen interviews random variation in the characteristics of the families we happened to interview would render pointless any attempts to examine treatment-control differences.

7. The characteristics known prior to randomization (X) should have the same distribution within the treatment and control groups because they are statistically independent of group assignment. Thus, including them in this regression will not change the coefficient π (unless X happens to differ between groups due to the variability in a small sample). These characteristics may still be included to improve the precision of the treatment effect estimates, however, if they are related to Y and thereby reduce residual variation in the regression. For the empirical work in this chapter, we use the same variables described in detail by Katz, Kling, and Liebman (2001): age, race, sex, marital status, family structure, disability, welfare receipt, education, employment, car ownership, mobility history, social contact, victimization, neighborhood poverty rate, child behavior variables, and child age, as well as additional indicators for whether the child was supervised after school and whether a parent supervised the child.

8. The adjustment factors to convert the simple mean differences of treatment and control groups into estimates of the treatment on the treated are the inverse of the program-move probabilities for each of the treatment groups. Katz, Kling, and Liebman (2001) present a more formal analysis of the derivation of intent-to-treat and treatment-on-the-treated estimates.

9. Later in our interview with Ms. Jones, we repeated the question, "How did you find out about MTO?" This time, she responded more directly. "I first got a letter from

Boston Housing. They was having a meeting. They gave us the location. And I threw it away, because I said, 'I don't want nothing else to do with Boston Housing.' So my neighbor say, 'Why do you do that? They is talking about subsidies, and giving out certificates and vouchers and all that.' So I said, 'Well, I guess I lost out, 'cause I threw it in the trash.' So then, I went to the mailbox a couple of days later. It said, 'Last chance.' I said, 'Wow, I gonna get in on this, right.'"

This struck us as the response that she had initially begun to give in the first moments of the interview, before her response veered off into her description of the overpowering memories of life in Boston Housing.

10. We also performed separate analyses by age-group for the parental monitoring outcomes in table 8.3. While younger children did indeed have higher reported monitoring levels, the effects of receiving housing vouchers were not significantly different between the younger and older age-groups. Differences between boys and girls were also examined but were not found to be significant.

11. The MTO families volunteered to participate in a lottery for housing vouchers. The quantitative findings in Katz, Kling, and Liebman 2001 suggest that offering housing vouchers to families in public housing projects of high-poverty, inner cities improves (at least in the short run) multiple indicators of the well-being of those residents interested in moving out of public housing. But it is not clear the extent to which such findings translate to other residents of public housing projects or to the case of large-scale policies of demolishing public housing.

12. The total effective marginal tax rate on these families can be much higher than this if they pay payroll taxes and possibly income taxes and face reductions in other benefits such as Food Stamps and childcare subsidies as their incomes increase.

References

Canada, G. 1995. *Fist, Stick, Knife, Gun: A Personal History of Violence in America*. Boston: Beacon Press.

Committee on Ways and Means. 1994. *1994 Green Book*. Washington, D.C.: U.S. Government Printing Office.

Creswell, J. W. 1994. *Research Designs: Qualitative and Quantitative Approaches*. Thousand Oaks, CA: Sage Publications.

DiIulio, J. J. 1996. "Help Wanted: Economists, Crime and Public Policy." *Journal of Economic Perspectives* 10 (1): 3–24.

Furstenberg, F. F., T. Cook, J. Eccles, G. H. Elder, and A. Sameroff. 1999. *Managing to Make It: Urban Families and Adolescent Success*. Chicago: University of Chicago Press.

Greene, J. C., V. J. Caracelli, and W. F. Graham. 1989. "Toward a Conceptual Framework for Mixed-Method Designs." *Educational Evaluation and Policy Analysis* 1 (3): 255–274.

Groves, B. M., B. Zuckerman, S. Marans, and D. J. Cohen. 1993. "Silent Victims: Children Who Witness Violence." *Journal of the American Medical Association* 269:262–264.

Hanratty, M. H., S. A. McLanahan, and B. Pettit. 1998. "The Impact of the Los Angeles Moving to Opportunity Program on Residential Mobility, Neighborhood Characteristics, and Early Child and Parent Outcomes." Bendheim-Thoman Center for Research on Child Well-Being Working Paper no. 98-18, Princeton University, April.

Jarrett, R. L. 1997. "Bringing Families Back In: Neighborhood Effects on Child Development." In *Neighborhood Poverty: Policy Implications in Studying Neighborhoods,* vol. 2, ed. J. Brooks-Gunn, G. J. Duncan, and J. L. Aber, 104–138. New York: Russell Sage.

Katz, L. F., J. R. Kling, and J. B. Liebman. 2001. "Moving to Opportunity in Boston: Early Results of a Randomized Mobility Experiment." *Quarterly Journal of Economics* 116 (2): 607–654.

Liebman, J. B. 1996. "The Impact of the Earned Income Tax Credit on Labor Supply and Taxpayer Compliance." PhD diss., Harvard University.

Peroff, K. A., C. L. Davis, and R. Jones. 1979. *Gautreaux Housing Demonstration: An Evaluation of Its Impact on Participating Households.* Washington, DC: U.S. Department of Housing and Urban Development.

Rosenbaum, J. 1995. "Changing the Geography of Opportunity by Expanding Choice: Lessons from the Gautreaux Experiment." *Housing Policy Debate* 6 (1): 231–270.

Sieber, S. D. 1973. "The Integration of Fieldwork and Survey Methods." *American Journal of Sociology* 78 (6): 1335–1359.

Tashakkori, A., and C. Teddlie. 1998. *Mixed Methodology: Combining Qualtitative and Quantitative Approaches.* Thousand Oaks, CA: Sage Publications.

Weiss, R. S. 1994. *Learning from Strangers: The Art and Method of Qualitative Interviews.* New York: Free Press.

Wright, R. J. 1998. "Review of Psychosocial Stress and Asthma: An Integrated Biopsychosocial Approach." *Thorax* 53:1066–1074.

Zelon, H., B. Rohe, S. Leaman, and S. Williams. 1994. *Survey of Public Housing Residents: Crime and Crime Prevention in Public Housing.* Research Triangle Park, NC: Research Triangle Institute.

9

Qualitative/Quantitative Synergies in a Random-Assignment Program Evaluation

Christina M. Gibson-Davis and Greg J. Duncan

"I could not be where I am without New Hope," was how Maria described the impact on her life of the New Hope antipoverty program. She is a bright, articulate mother of two small children living in Milwaukee, Wisconsin. Prior to New Hope, she had wanted to work full-time but had been unable to afford childcare. Through its provision of a childcare subsidy, one of its four financial benefits, New Hope allowed Maria to secure and sustain full-time employment. She quit her part-time job as a cashier in a drug store and launched a career in sales.

What lessons about New Hope can be drawn from qualitative narratives such as Maria's? She was but one of over 1,300 participants in the program, and there is little reason to suspect that her experience was representative of the larger New Hope population. An ethnographic evaluation of the project, limited in case size, cannot identify statistically significant results, nor can it provide an understanding of the likely effects of a large-scale implementation of New Hope. Yet quantitative measures from surveys and administrative data sources not only miss thick descriptions that are provided by the qualitative data but may also fail to identify key circumstances that are critical for understanding program impacts. Perhaps program evaluations need both narratives and numbers to be complete.

The evaluation of New Hope offered both of these elements (Bos et al. 1999). Survey and administrative data about employment, family functioning, and child well-being were gathered from nearly all participants between the point of random assignment and 24 months later. Forty-six families, including Maria and her two sons, were selected at random to participate in a longitudinal ethnographic study. In this chapter, we demonstrate how the combination of these methodologies greatly enhanced the evaluation of New Hope.

This productive synergy between qualitative and quantitative methodologies was facilitated by two key elements of the evaluation design. We randomly selected our 46 qualitative cases from the larger New Hope population, ensuring that our smaller sample was representative of the larger group. The design was also enhanced because several graduate research assistants received intensive training in both methods and took on the highly productive task of reconciling quantitative and qualitative data.

Our mixed methods enabled us to understand program impacts to a degree that would not have been possible had we been relying on one type of data alone. For example, we used the qualitative data to understand some of the "black-box" program impacts emerging from the quantitative data, one of the most important of which was the program's favorable impacts on the teacher-reported academic performance and positive behavior of boys. We also used the qualitative data to identify important subgroups for which New Hope Project impacts were particularly strong. And even with its small sample ($n = 43$; three families had incomplete data for our analyses), the qualitative interviews provided estimates of impacts of factors that are difficult to measure in a conventional survey (e.g., family problems that interfere with work).

Insights from our qualitative work also facilitated future New Hope–based research by improving the design of our five-year follow-up survey and by suggesting topics worthy of exploration with the quantitative data.

At the same time, we discovered limits to this synergy. When considered individually, qualitative cases, no matter how richly explored, do not identify program impacts. Qualitative data can be misused if Procrustean efforts are employed to force participants' stories to fit particular quantitative results. Complex personal experiences should not be manipulated for illustrative purposes.

We begin with a description of the New Hope Project and the key components of its evaluation. We then present the lessons we learned in each phase of the project, from the design of the evaluation, to the analysis of program impacts, to benefits for future work. We conclude with some thoughts on the implications of our findings.

The New Hope Project

Enrolling its first volunteers in August 1994, the New Hope Project offered its participants a comprehensive package of benefits. In exchange for a proven work effort of 30 hours a week over a given month, participants were eligible for four benefits. First, a wage supplement ensured that the net income of families increased as they earned more on the job. The supplement did not phase out until families were at 200% of the poverty line and ensured that nearly all working families had incomes above the official poverty line (currently $14,824 for a family of three). Second, the program offered subsidized health insurance through a health maintenance organization. The third benefit was a childcare subsidy that enabled families with at least one dependent child under age 13 to choose any state-licensed or county-certified childcare provider, including providers of both preschool programs for young children and extended-day program for school-age children.

Fourth, if a private-sector job could not be found, then New Hope participants were entitled to a community service job for two renewable periods of up to six months each. Although paying only the minimum wage, these community service jobs ensured that families could meet their work requirement of at least 30 hours per week and thus qualify for the rest of the New Hope benefits. All told, the benefits package cost about $4,000 per year, which is at the high end of what states are spending to implement the reforms required by 1996 federal welfare-reform legislation. A final, less tangible benefit was that New Hope had competent and caring "project representatives," who offered intensive case management as well as emotional and instrumental support.

Although its designers conceived of New Hope as a permanent package of benefits to which low-income working families should be entitled, budget realities limited its duration to three years. Budget constraints also limited its geographic scope: eligibility for the New Hope Project was confined to two low-income zip-code-defined neighborhoods in Milwaukee. The "north side" neighborhood was predominantly African American; the "south side" neighborhood was primarily Hispanic.

Eligibility for New Hope benefits was restricted to individuals who (1) lived in one of the two targeted zip-code neighborhoods, (2) were over 18, (3) had family income at or below 150% of the poverty line, and (4) were willing to work 30 or more hours a week. Individuals living in the two targeted neighborhoods were informed about the New Hope Project in a number of ways, both formal (e.g., through the recommendation of other social service agencies) and informal (e.g., signs in laundromats). Those interested in the program attended an orientation session at which benefits were explained, but so too was the fact that a lottery would be run and half of them would be assigned to a "control" group that did not receive any of the New Hope benefits. Between August 1994 and December 1995 the New Hope Project enrolled and assigned 1,357 participants.

By all accounts New Hope was well implemented (Brock et al. 1997). The randomization process was carried out successfully; the demographics of New Hope participants matched those of their larger neighborhoods; and the program's wage subsidies, community service jobs, HMO and childcare subsidies were well implemented and readily available.[1] Independent critics have also noted the innovative nature of the program, the widespread local community and political networks supporting New Hope, and the importance to participants of the "case representatives" (Mead 2000).

The New Hope Evaluation

The evaluation of New Hope's impacts on work, family life, and child well-being was based on data gathered from both quantitative and qualitative sources. The quantitative data came from survey and administrative sources, and the qualitative data were gathered as part of a longitudinal ethnography.

New Hope Quantitative Data

The evaluation of New Hope's impacts on work, family life, and child well-being used data from six quantitative sources. First, just prior to random assignment, all volunteer families completed a baseline survey form that provided information on an array of sociodemographic characteristics. Second, an extensive survey administered two years after random as-

Table 9.1. Descriptive Characteristics at Baseline for the Full Sample, the Child and Family Study (CFS) and the New Hope Ethnographic Study (NHES)

	Full sample	CFS	NHES
Black (%)	51.4	55.0	51.2
Hispanic (%)	26.5	29.3	34.9
Parent's average age (yr)	31.8	29.4	29.6
Female heads of households (%)	71.6	89.8	95.3
Married parents (%)	21.8	20.8	20.1
Parents with a GED or high school diploma (%)	57.3	59.4	65.1
Parents working 30 hours or more (%)	37.5	36.5	39.5
Earned less than $5000 in previous year (%)	72.2	76.2	81.4
Families receiving aid (%)	62.9	80.7	83.7
Three or more children in family (%)	31.5	46.0	44.2
Sample size	1,357	745[a]	43

[a] 812 participants qualified for the CFS; 67 Hmong family participants were not included in the CFS due to cultural and language differences.

signment asked members of the control and program groups about their employment experiences and work-related outcomes during the time of the intervention. All 1,357 participants filled out the baseline information form; 1,086 (80%) responded to the two-year survey.

Third, a subset of 812 experimental and control parents also answered additional questions about their family practices and children's well-being for the Child and Family Survey (CFS). Every family who had at least one child between the ages of 1 and 10 at baseline qualified; up to two children were chosen from each family. Of the 812 families, 578 were used in the final analysis.[2] Baseline demographic characteristics of the full and the CFS sample are presented in table 9.1 and show that most families had low incomes, single parents, and income from welfare sources.

Fourth, when parents signed written consent forms, evaluators sent self-enumerated questionnaires to teachers of school-age children (5–12 years old). Teachers were asked to rate the children on a variety of academic behaviors and skills. The teachers were blind to the purpose of the study and informed only that the child was involved in a study about children and their families. Parents of 557 out of the 627 age-eligible children granted permission for teachers to be contacted. Of the 557 possible responses, 418 were returned, for a response rate of 75%.

Fifth, a database maintained by New Hope as part of its management information system provided data on the use of benefits by all program participants. Sixth, again using signed consent forms (in this case obtained just prior to random assignment), evaluators obtained administrative data on receipt of benefits from the state Temporary Assistance for Needy Families (TANF) welfare and Food Stamp programs, earnings data reported by employers to the Social Security system, and, in aggregated form, state Earned Income Tax Credit payments.

New Hope Qualitative Data

The qualitative data come from the New Hope Ethnographic Study (NHES). The NHES is a longitudinal study of 46 families, most of whom were randomly sampled from the 812 program and control families with children aged 1–10 at baseline. While we would have preferred to begin the NHES when families first enrolled in New Hope, we were unable to secure research funding prior to the program's third year of operation. Thus, the NHES began in April 1998 and continued until the spring of 2001. (A follow-up of both the CFS and NHES samples began in the fall of 2003.) Owing to incomplete information, three families were dropped from the study, which left 43 NHES families: 22 experimental and 21 control group members. Baseline demographic characteristics for the NHES are also presented in table 9.1 and are similar to those of the larger set of 745 families in the CFS. During their monthly visits to families, fieldworkers listened to parents tell their stories, conducted participant observation in homes, took families out for lunch and dinner, went with them to church, and also visited children's schools.

To guide the topics of these visits, researchers generated a set of topics that explore a family's daily activities and routine as well as beliefs and values (Weisner 1997). These topics were then organized into a template, which fieldworkers used to structure their notes. In all, there were 20 main headings in the template, as well as additional subheadings (see table 9.2 for a list of main template headings). Examples of main headings are "Beliefs about and use of childcare," "Relationships with partner/spouse," and "Job barriers." An example of a subheading would be "Alcohol/substance abuse," listed under the "Job barriers" main heading. (For further details on the organization of the ethnography, see Weisner et al. 1999, 2002.) If a template area was not covered on a particular visit, fieldworkers raised these issues on subsequent visits and systematically probed for information, ensuring that fieldwork data were as complete as possible and that there were no "false negatives" in the field data.

Table 9.2. Main Template Headings for the New Hope Ethnographic Study

Influences on New Hope take-up	Outcomes of New Hope participation
Family background	Stability in participant's life
Work history/values of participant and relatives	Feelings of success and evidence of planfulness vs. procrastination
Education of participant and relatives	Participant's future orientation, including investments in further training or education
Role of religion and spirituality	
Paths to employment and pattern of work at entry, including role of underground economy	Meaning of work: job vs. career; resource vs. constraint
Number of and relationships with case representatives, W-2 caseworkers, other social services	Equity
	Social networks and community bridging, including involvement in school
Role of ethnicity	Children and child rearing
Beliefs about and use of childcare	Political ideology
Relationships with partner/spouse	Job barriers
Life goals and ambitions, including attitudes or values about work	Daily routine

Design Lessons

Our mixed-methods approach was enhanced by several decisions we made about the design of the evaluation. In this section, we discuss the advantages of two key decisions: randomly sampling our qualitative cases and using the same individuals to analyze both types of data.

The Wisdom of Randomly Sampling Qualitative Cases

Sampling statisticians long ago established the power of sampling at random a very small subset of the population as a basis for obtaining population estimates of interest (e.g., means, correlations, regression relationships). For many purposes, samples as small as 1,000–1,500 cases provide acceptably precise estimates of the attitudes and behavior of national populations.

Random selection is a key element of this power. A useful analogy is the attempt to infer the taste of a pot of soup from one sip. Stirring the soup prior to its sampling ensures that the sip will be representative.

Qualitative researchers rarely adopt this kind of sampling perspective in their case selection, perhaps believing that lessons from large-sample studies do not apply to the much smaller samples typically employed in ethnographic studies, or that attempts to recruit cases randomly will fail more often than not. In some cases, their nonrandom sampling plans are purposeful and based on a theory-driven belief that selecting cases from a design matrix based on combinations of certain attributes (e.g., economic status, race, and neighborhood type) is key for gathering cases that vary along important dimensions (Bernard 1995; Johnson 1990; Pelto and Pelto 1978).

In the case of the New Hope evaluation, we debated at length the wisdom of random versus purposive sampling for the qualitative study. Since we had a complete list of program and control families, it was a simple matter to generate a simple random sample of cases. But some members of the research team argued that since an $n = 43$ sample was too small to detect program impacts and since the experiences of New Hope experimental families were so much more interesting than experiences of control families, the NHES sample should consist only of families in the experimental group. We also considered the wisdom of including "exemplar" cases—participants whom New Hope Project representatives could readily identify as embodying exactly the kinds of experiences that program designers either hoped for or feared.

In the end, we opted for a stratified[3] random sample of cases plus a handful of exemplar cases: 51 randomly sampled cases plus 3 exemplar families. Response rates were not a problem: our intensive recruitment efforts led to success in recruiting 86% of the sampled families that had not moved out of the Greater Milwaukee area.

Experience has repeatedly confirmed the wisdom of our random-sampling decision. The ethnographic sample has proved invaluable for understanding experiences (see, e.g., Romich and Weisner 2000) that were not at all anticipated when the ethnographic study began. It can also correct for false assumptions by offering an invaluable form of insurance in representation of cases. Our a priori theoretical expectations about "interesting" and "uninteresting" situations proved depressingly inaccurate in the light of what subsequent analysis of both quantitative and qualitative data revealed to be truly interesting situations for understanding New Hope Project impacts. All in all, we came away from our experiences believing that most ethnographic studies would profit from serious consideration of random case selection.

Using the Same Individuals to Gather and Analyze Both Kinds of Data

Although hard to prove, our experience suggests that it is vital to integrate the two methods of data collection. For three graduate students who both gathered and analyzed qualitative data and analyzed the survey data, the integration was complete. We cannot imagine achieving the same degree of integration between our two groups of methodologists, each of which specializes in one form of data collection and analysis. Individuals trained and actively engaged in both methods must constantly confront the resulting but productive tensions between the two. The qualitative dimension provides a deeper level of meaning to the quantitative variables and analysis, while the larger quantitative sample provides a needed population perspective on the relatively small and potentially idiosyncratic nature of families in the qualitative study. We document below several instances where the synergy between the two methods deepened our understanding of family process and child development in New Hope families.

Another advantage these students offered was that they were simultaneously qualitative and quantitative researchers. In meetings consisting of only quantitative analysts, for example, they could offer insights into the progress and findings of the qualitative study. This was done at no additional cost to the project (as the students would have attended anyway) but greatly enhanced the knowledge base of the meetings. Other members of the project thus benefited from the students' methodological multitasking, as they were more informed of the findings from the other branch of the project than they might otherwise have been.

Understanding Program Effects

We gained a much richer understanding of New Hope's impacts than we anticipated by relying on the combination of qualitative and quantitative data. Researchers used the insights from one methodology to inform the findings of the other.

Using Qualitative Data to Understand Program Effects

One of the most important—and initially puzzling—findings of the New Hope experiment concerned the teacher-reported achievement and behavior of preadolescent children. In the experimental group, boys, but not girls, were rated by their teachers 0.3–0.5 standard deviations better behaved and higher achieving than their control group counterparts. These are quite large impacts and important to understand. Based on the survey data alone, however, the analysts were unable to understand why the New

Hope Project, focused as it was on the parents' work and income, should have such different impacts for boys and girls.

The qualitative data revealed instances where parents referenced the gender of their children and suggested that mothers believed that gangs and other neighborhood pressures were much more threatening to their elementary school boys than to girls. As a response to these pressures, mothers in the experimental group channeled more of the program's resources (e.g., childcare subsidies for extended-day programs) to their boys. A 35-year-old African American mother of four, quoted in the field notes, observed:

> Not all places have gangs, but [my neighborhood] is infested with gangs and drugs and violence. My son, I worry about him. He may be veering in the wrong direction. . . . it's different for girls. For boys, it's dangerous. [Gangs are] full of older men who want these young ones to do their dirty work. And they'll buy them things and give them money.

These kinds of sentiments appeared consistently in the qualitative data. Further quantitative analyses of both New Hope and national-sample survey data support the interpretation that parents living in bad neighborhoods do indeed devote more time and other resources to their boys than to their girls (Romich 2000). We would not have had this insight, however, had we not had the ethnographic data.

Using Qualitative Data to Isolate Program Effects

Qualitative interviews suggested important heterogeneity among the experimental families. Some, perhaps one-fifth, appeared to have so many problems (e.g., drug dependence, children with severe behavior problems, abusive relationships) that New Hope's package of economic benefits was unlikely to make much of a difference. A second group was at the other end of the spectrum: they had no such apparent problems and were able to sustain employment on their own. In this case, control families in this group might be expected to do so well in Milwaukee's job-rich environment that it would be difficult for comparably unconstrained experimental families to do better.

A third group, however, with only one of the problems of the sort that New Hope might be able to address (e.g., Maria's difficulties in arranging for childcare or a minor criminal record that experience in a community service job could overcome), appeared poised to profit from the New Hope package of benefits. Extensive quantitative work on subgroups defined ac-

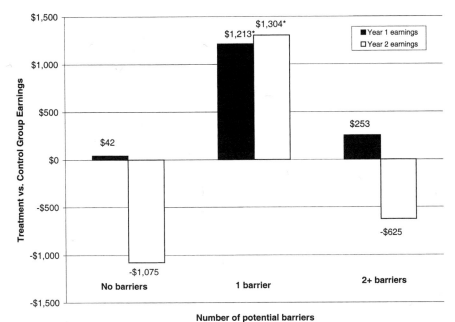

*Treatment/control difference is statistically significant at the .05 level. All other differences are insignificant.

Figure 9.1. Impact of New Hope on earnings, by number of potential employment barriers.

cording to the number of potential employment-related problems they faced at the beginning of the program confirmed the wisdom of these qualitatively derived insights. Using data gathered from the baseline interviews, Magnuson (1999) constructed an index of potential employment barriers based on past history of employment, completed schooling, arrests, and the presence of either many or very young children.[4] She then estimated treatment-control differences for subgroups defined according to whether the family faced zero, one, or two or more barriers to employment. The results are presented in figure 9.1.

This figure confirms what we had suspected based on our qualitative evidence. Experimental members who had either no barriers or multiple barriers did not earn a significantly different amount than their control counterparts. Program impacts on the earnings of families with only one barrier, however, were large and statistically significant in both years.

Promising Quantitative Uses of $n = 43$ Qualitative Data

From a quantitative perspective, a sample of 43 cases seems pitifully inadequate to support inferences about the larger population. But given the qualitative interviews' unique ability to generate measures of important constructs, it is important to ask whether *any* quantitative inferences can be supported by a sample as small as 43 cases.

In statistical terms, a 43-case sample produces large but still informative confidence intervals. Suppose a circumstance (such as drug abuse) is suspected to be nearly universal in a population such as New Hope's and that only extensive qualitative interviews, rather than surveys, will provide valid data on its frequency. Suppose further that reports of drug abuse appeared in only 15% of cases in the qualitative sample. A 43-case sample produces a 95% confidence interval around the 0.15 proportion that spans 0.00 to 0.35. Thus, one cannot reject the hypothesis that there is virtually no drug abuse in the larger population, but one can be confident that the incidence is not as high as was initially suspected.

To take an example from New Hope, one of our interests was in understanding the extent to which children had temperamental, behavioral, or health problems and the links between these problems and their mothers' ability to obtain and keep a job. The survey revealed problems with a relatively small fraction of families. In contrast, the qualitative interviews were able to probe extensively on this topic and found that some 60% of families reported at least one child with one or more significant problems or troubles, that perhaps a third of these were not recognized by service providers, and that parents with children with troubles or disabilities faced greater difficulties in sustaining a daily routine (Bernheimer, Weisner, and Lowe, forthcoming).

Thus, the "stylized facts" that emerge from simple descriptions based on an $n = 43$ sample can be useful for conceptualizing important processes that may be at work, placing anecdotes and stereotypes into perspective, and thinking about policy levers.

A more formal statistical use of a matched qualitative/quantitative design to estimate important parameters in the larger population is based on the conception that a randomly sampled qualitative study is a kind of planned missing-data design (Little and Rubin 1987). Survey measures are available for both the qualitative and the larger survey sample, but qualitative measures are available only for the $n = 43$ qualitative sample. If the qualitative sample is a random subset of the larger survey sample, then it is possible to impute measures uniquely found in the qualitative sample to the larger survey sample.

Suppose that we want to estimate for the larger New Hope sample the mean of Y, a measure (e.g., drug abuse) found in the qualitative sample (number of cases = m) but not in the larger survey sample (number of cases $= n$). Suppose further that both data sets contain a set of predictors of Y ($X_1, \ldots, X_k$). Little and Rubin (1987) show that the mean of Y can be estimated as the average of the observed and predicted values of Y in the survey sample. The variance of this regression estimator is

$$V_{reg} = \frac{\sigma^2}{m} \left(1 - \frac{n - m}{n} \rho^2 \right)$$

where σ^2 is the variance of Y, σ^2/m is the variance of the NHES sample mean, and ρ is the multiple correlation coefficient between Y and $X_1, \ldots,$ X_k (Little and Rubin 1987). If the X's are completely predictive of Y (i.e., $\rho = 1$), then the method is virtually equivalent to measuring Y on the full survey sample. On the other hand, if $\rho = 0$, then there is no information gained from the survey-sample cases that is not included in the qualitative subsample.

Suppose $\rho^2 = 0.20$, $m = 43$, and $n = 800$. The effective sample size for the estimation of the mean of Y increases from 43 to $[43 + (0.2 \times 755)]$ $= 194$, which reduces the standard error by a factor of about 2.1. Analogous methods can be applied to estimation of subgroup and conditional means. Thus, under some circumstances it is possible to use the rich measures only available in the $n = 43$ qualitative sample to estimate their prevalence in the larger population.

The Benefits to Future Work

Even after we had completed the evaluation of two-year New Hope data for the program report (Bos et al. 1999), we used the synthesis between the qualitative and quantitative data in additional ways. We were able to improve the five-year follow-up survey based on knowledge gleaned in the ethnography, and we were able to generate additional quantitative research from the qualitative data.

Using Qualitative Data to Generate Survey Measures

As our ethnographic work began, we discovered that certain aspects of family functioning were measured poorly in the two-year follow-up survey. This is because the NHES did not begin until just after the two-year survey data collection was completed. In contrast, the five-year survey will profit greatly from lessons learned from the ongoing qualitative interviewing. In particular, by listening to how New Hope families understand their daily routines, we constructed quantitative measures that will offer a more complete account of family well-being. Some items that are included in the five-year follow-up that were not part of the two-year survey include the role of male partners, beliefs about the welfare system, budget questions, and the role of family support.

For example, our ethnographic work revealed that the presence of troubled children and inflexible jobs account for some of the variance in labor force participation. Neither dimension was listed as a possible job impediment on the two-year survey. On the five-year survey, however, we expanded the section that measures job attitudes by including two new items. Participants are now asked to rate the influence of "having a child with a serious health, emotional, or behavioral problem" and "being allowed to deal with family problems or emergencies that may come up while you're at work or school." Neither of these items would have been included had it not been for the ethnographic research.

Exploring Quantitative Data Generated from the Qualitative Data

The beauty of ethnographic work is that the data provide detail on topics that cannot be fully explored by survey data. If, however, there is no larger data set on which to test a hypothesis, then findings from an analysis of ethnographic data are limited in their generalizability and replicability. However, if both types of data are present, then one can use the qualitative data to explore program dimensions, which can then be analyzed in the larger survey data.

An example is the use of New Hope benefits by program participants. The intent of New Hope was to centralize assistance for participants, so that they did not have to deal with several different agencies to receive the services that they needed (Brock et al. 1997). Soon after the qualitative study began, however, fieldworkers noticed great differences in how the New Hope families used the benefits. Very few used the program as was intended (as a continuously used bundle of benefits); most used individual benefits selectively and intermittently. Both New Hope evaluators and designers were puzzled by this disconnect between program intent and program use.

A systematic qualitative analysis of benefit usage by experimental members of the NHES revealed that participants evaluated the usefulness of New Hope according to different standards (Gibson and Weisner 2002). Some saw its usefulness in cost-benefit terms (the advantages of receiving the supplements vs. the demands of working full-time), while others measured its usefulness by how well the program coincided with personal and cultural-ecological concerns (not accepting a community service job because it was considered too demeaning; not using childcare vouchers because kin /family assistance was preferred and in place [Lowe and Weisner 2003]). As these standards varied, so too did service use. Gibson (2003) analyzed the larger survey data and confirmed the great heterogeneity in program use among experimental members. Not only was this heterogeneity related to sociodemographic characteristics at baseline, as fieldworkers had suspected, but it also shaped the effect that the program had on individual families.[5] These quantitative analyses, however, were undertaken only after the rich qualitative data revealed their likely potential value.

The Limits of Qualitative Data

Until now, we have described only the advantages of our mixed-methods approach. We also discovered some limits to this approach.

The Limits of $n = 43$ Qualitative Data for Understanding Experimental Impacts

An important goal for the New Hope evaluation is to estimate program impacts on family and child outcomes of interest. These take the form of differences in means and proportions between the experimental and control groups. Is an $n = 43$ sample, evenly divided between experimental and control families, helpful for this purpose? It would be extremely useful if this were indeed the case, given that important measures such as the sustainability of family routines were gathered only for the qualitative subsample. But the task of estimating subgroup differences with a mere 43 cases is much more difficult than an estimation of a mean or proportion for the entire population.

To illustrate the power of an $n = 43$ sample to estimate program impacts, we coded several of the template themes from the NHES and converted the measures into a 0–8 scale.[6] We then standardized and regressed each on the experimental /control status of each case. The standard errors for the estimated coefficients were around 0.30, indicating that the $n = 43$ NHES sample is capable of detecting a program impact of about 0.6 of a standard deviation at a 95 % confidence level. This is a very large effect size, and larger than any of the impacts actually estimated from the quantitative data. Thus, the $n = 43$ sample has a very limited ability to

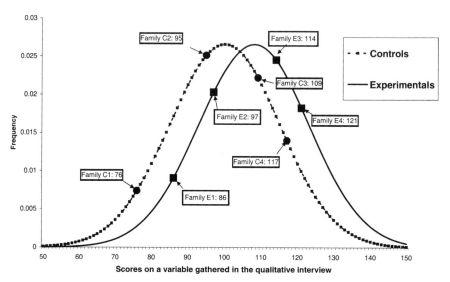

Figure 9.2. Four experimental (E) and control (C) cases drawn from populations with an experimental impact of 0.5 standard deviations. For controls, mean = 100; standard deviation = 15. For experimentals, mean = 108; standard deviation = 15.

identify any but the largest program impacts for the quantitative measures derived from the qualitative interviews.

A different, more person-centered question is whether there is some way in which *individual* experimental cases in the qualitative sample can somehow represent the more general set of experimental families and be contrasted with *individual* control families in the qualitative sample who somehow represent the larger set of control families. We see no way in which this might be done. Imagine two normal distributions for an outcome of interest—say, sustainability of family routines—one for the experimental and the other for the control group (fig. 9.2). Suppose further that the bundle of New Hope benefits has a fairly large positive impact on sustainability. In figure 9.2, this is illustrated by the fact that the experimental group's distribution is shifted to the right of the control group's distribution by 8 points on a normal distribution with a (control) mean of 100 and a common standard deviation of 15.

But now consider some of the individual cases in the two groups. While the average sustainability of program group members will exceed that of control group members, there will be many instances of low-sustainability program families and high-sustainability control families. For example, experimental family E1's score of 86 is well below the control group average of 100, while control group family C4, with a score of 117, is well above the program group average of 108.

It is clear from figure 9.2 that even a large program impact leaves a great deal of overlap between the treatment and control groups. The task of assessing program effects amounts to discovering the nature of these shifts, a task that no amount of intensive analysis of or reflection about individual cases can accomplish. Having hundreds of sample points along these two distributions is key; a richer description of a small number of sample points cannot help. Thus, there is simply no way of using the detailed data gathered from individual cases in the $n = 43$ ethnographic sample to assess overall program effects.

Proper and Improper Uses of Qualitative Data to Illustrate Quantitative Findings

For reasons related to the timing of its funding, the qualitative evaluation of New Hope was not launched until the final year of New Hope's operation. As a result, the quantitative evaluation of the two-year effects was completed long before the qualitative evaluation. Nevertheless, when preparing the two-year report, the NHES provided participant narratives that exemplified and crystallized the statistical program effects of New Hope. Such narratives presented the context and dynamics of our families in a way that mere survey data could not.

These vignettes added an important dimension to the report by providing readers with vivid descriptions of families in the program. We were aware, however, that selective case description might not do justice to the subtleties of the cases and might also confirm the quantitative research community's suspicion that qualitative data are merely anecdotes. This is why we opted for page-long, rather than one- or two-sentence, descriptions of family circumstances when selecting individual families and constructing their vignettes. No family fits a "simple" story, and we believed that a too-brief description of any given family would fail to provide a realistic picture of family circumstances.

To illustrate our point, the following is part of a vignette that was used in the evaluation report:

> Janet is a single mother who lives on the south side of Milwaukee with her two young ones. . . . She used the New Hope medical benefits supplement for only a year, and during that year she had her son's tonsils removed. The premiums were over $400 a month for her and her sons, so after the surgery was completed, she discontinued the care. She says she almost

never takes her boys to the doctor. They are very healthy and her point of view is that paying so much money for a service she never uses is unreasonable. (Bos et al. 1999, 74)

A simple telling of this story might indicate that the New Hope medical benefits were very useful, as they allowed parents to have medical procedures performed on their children that they otherwise could not afford. However, that would ignore the interesting detail that Janet stopped using the New Hope health insurance, even though she did not have other health care coverage. With this fact, Janet's story becomes more complex, but it is also likely to be more representative of the complicated response people had to the New Hope benefits (Gibson and Weisner 2002). We also included cases in the report that did not fit predicted program impacts or that showed control group families benefiting from non–New Hope services.

Conclusion

We have delineated the advantages of using a mixture of qualitative and quantitative methodologies for evaluation projects. For the New Hope Project, the use of both was critical, as the interplay between the two enhanced the evaluation effort throughout the process. Our evaluation benefited by randomly sampling our ethnographic cases and using the same graduate students to work with the quantitative and qualitative data. As we progressed in the assessment of the New Hope Project, other advantages of using mixed methods emerged. We used the qualitative data to isolate and identify quantitative program effects and explored ways in which it might be possible to make quantitative inferences with a very small number of cases. Finally, once the evaluation of the two-year findings was completed, we used our qualitative work to better inform the construction of our five-year follow-up survey.

We have skirted some of the hard questions regarding the balance between the two methods. Given that evaluation efforts have limited resources, issues of the scope of the two types of data collection are quite important. For example, we had initially planned to use 60 families for the NHES, but budget constraints reduced that number to 46. What was the cost of forgoing those 14 families? Should those families have been kept, even if that had meant fewer resources to maximize our surveys' response rates or fewer minutes of interviewing time? We have not made these kinds of cost-benefit comparisons across methods and cannot say if we have correctly allocated resources between the quantitative and qualitative arms of the project.

We also know that we benefited from fortuitous circumstances, which may not apply in all situations. New Hope's directors and researchers in the evaluation team all embraced the idea of a mixed-methods evaluation. Quantitative researchers, many of whom had had no prior experience with qualitative data, quickly grasped its potential importance. We also benefited from having excellent research assistants who were willing and able to be trained in both methodologies. This cross-training proved invaluable, as most of the productive synergy between the two methods was either generated or first noticed by this group of graduate students. And, as noted above, New Hope was well implemented, making our task as evaluators that much easier.

It is unfortunate that project evaluations rarely involve both quantitative and qualitative methodologies. But this lack of interaction could stem from the perception that these methods are antithetical rather than complementary. Quantitative methodologists are skeptical that reliable conclusions can be gathered from the traditionally small sample sizes involved in qualitative work; and qualitative methodologists believe that survey data may oversimplify complex realities. However, one need not be employed at the expense of the other. A combination of the two, as we saw in our assessment of New Hope, can be used to greatly enrich evaluation efforts.

Acknowledgments

This paper summarizes an evaluation conducted by MDRC under a contract with the New Hope Project, Inc., and in collaboration with the John D. and Catherine T. MacArthur Foundation Research Network on Successful Pathways through Middle Childhood. It was supported by the John D. and Catherine T. MacArthur Foundation, the Helen Bader Foundation, the Ford Foundation, the State of Wisconsin Department of Workforce Development, the William T. Grant Foundation, the Annie E. Casey Foundation, and the U.S. Department of Health and Human Services. We are grateful to the MacArthur Foundation and the National Institute of Child Health and Human Development (1 R01 HD360-38) for supporting the child and family portion of this research.

Notes

1. The Manpower Demonstration Research Corporation (MDRC) oversaw all aspect of the evaluation efforts and coordinated the efforts of the other researchers involved. Hans Bos, Aletha Huston, Robert Granger, Greg Duncan, and Vonnie McLoyd codirected the quantitative study of the child and family portion of the evaluation. Tom Weisner and Lucinda Bernheimer codirected the qualitative study.

2. Sixty-seven Hmong participants in the program were not included in the CFS because of cultural and language differences. If we disregard this portion of the sample, the final response rate was 78%.

3. Stratification is a method used by sampling statisticians that involves ordering the population by group prior to sampling. To ensure that we had an even balance of program and control cases, we randomly sampled within these two groups. We also stratified by race/ethnicity and residential location prior to the random sampling of the program and control groups.

4. Although the qualitative interviews pointed to an additional set of maternal mental health and child behavior problems, the baseline interview did not ask the kinds of questions that would have provided this kind of information.

5. Community service job users, for example, tended to have poor employment histories at baseline but were the only group of participants who showed increases in emotional well-being after two years. Other participants may have had stronger labor market connections at the time of random assignment, and they did not show any emotional health benefits.

6. For example, we coded the adequacy of a family's income to meet basic needs, where 0 indicates that the family had no income, and an 8 indicates that the family is able to meet basic needs every month. This is part of a much larger coding project in the NHES; see Weisner, Coots, and Bernheimer 1996 and Weisner and Bernheimer 1998 for further details.

References

Bernard, H. R. 1995. *Research Methods in Anthropology, Qualitative and Quantitative Approaches.* 2nd ed. Walnut Creek, CA: Alta Mira Press.

Bernheimer, L., T. S. Weisner, and T. Lowe. Forthcoming. "Impacts of Children with Troubles on Working Poor Families: Experimental and Mixed-Method Evidence." *Mental Retardation.*

Bos, J., A. Huston, R. Granger, G. J. Duncan, T. Brock, and V. McLoyd. 1999. *New Hope for People with Low Incomes: Two-Year Results of a Program to Reduce Poverty and Reform Welfare.* New York: Manpower Demonstration Research Corporation.

Brock, T., F. Doolittle, V. Fellerath, and M. Wiseman. 1997. *Creating New Hope: Implementation of a Program to Reduce Poverty and Reform Welfare.* New York: Manpower Demonstration Research Corporation.

Gibson, C. M. 2003. "Privileging the Participant: The Importance of Sub-group Analysis in Social Welfare Evaluations." *American Journal of Evaluation* 24 (4): 443–469.

Gibson, C. M., and T. S. Weisner. 2002. "'Rational' and Ecocultural Circumstances of Program Take-up among Low-Income Working Parents." *Human Organization: Journal of the Society for Applied Anthropology* 61 (2): 154–166.

Johnson, J. C. 1990. *Selecting Ethnographic Informants: Qualitative Research Methods.* Series no. 22. Newbury Park, CA: Sage Publications.

Little, R. J. A., and D. B. Rubin. 1987. *Statistical Analysis with Missing Data.* New York: John Wiley and Sons.

Lowe, E., and T. S. Weisner. 2003. "'You have to push it—who's gonna raise your kids?' Situating Child Care in the Daily Routines of Low-Income Families." *Children and Youth Services Review* 25 (3): 225–261.

Magnuson, K. 1999. "Appendix K—The Barrier Indicator Index." In *New Hope for People with Low Incomes: Two-Year Results of a Program to Reduce Poverty and Reform Welfare,* ed. J. Bos, A. Huston, R. Granger, G. J. Duncan, T. Brock, and V. McLoyd, 346–355. New York: Manpower Demonstration Research Corporation.

Mead, L. M. 2000. "The Twilight of Liberal Welfare Reform." *Public Interest* 139:22–34.

Pelto, P. J., and G. Pelto. 1978. *Anthropological Inquiry: The Structure of Inquiry.* 2nd ed. New York: Cambridge University Press.

Romich, J. L. 2000. "To Sons and Daughters: Gender, Neighborhood Quality, and Resource Allocation in Families." Unpublished manuscript, Joint Center for Poverty Research, Northwestern University, Evanston, IL.

Romich, J. L., and T. S. Weisner. 2000. "How Families View and Use the EITC: Advance Payment versus Lump Sum Delivery." Special Issue, *National Tax Journal,* Fall.

Weisner, T. S. 1997. "The Ecocultural Project of Human Development: Why Ethnography and Its Findings Matter." *Ethos* 25 (2): 177-190.

Weisner, T. S., and L. Bernheimer. 1998. "The New Hope Ecocultural Family Interview for Working Poor Families." Unpublished Field Manual, Center for Culture and Health, University of California—Los Angeles.

Weisner, T. S., L. Bernheimer, C. Gibson, E. Howard, K. Magnuson, J. Romich, and E. Lieber. 1999. "From the Living Rooms and Daily Routines of the Economically Poor: An Ethnographic Study of the New Hope Effects on Families and Children." Paper presented at biennial meeting of the Society for Research in Child Development, Albuquerque, NM, April.

Weisner, T. S., J. Coots, and L. Bernheimer. 1996. "Ecocultural Family Interview Field Manual." Unpublished manuscript, Center for Culture and Health, University of California—Los Angeles.

Weisner, T. S., C. Gibson, E. D. Lowe, and J. Romich. 2002. "Understanding Working Poor Families in the New Hope Program." *Poverty Research Newsletter* 6 (4): 3–5.

Mixed Methods in Studies of Social Experiments for Parents in Poverty

Aletha C. Huston

Chapters 8 and 9 address the following question: What does qualitative research contribute to studies using conventional surveys? The studies reported in the chapters are both random-assignment experiments testing social programs designed to improve the circumstances of families living in poverty.

Chapter 8, by Jeffrey Kling, Jeffrey Liebman, and Lawrence Katz, contains a description of how qualitative interviews enriched survey design and interpretation in the Moving to Opportunity experiment. The experimental program offered housing vouchers to public housing residents that allowed them to move to low-poverty neighborhoods. Before designing the survey, the investigators interviewed potential participants about their concerns. The authors describe four ways in which these qualitative interviews were useful.

First, qualitative data helped to identify important topics for quantitative surveys. Second, qualitative data influenced their conceptual framework by pinpointing parents' major concerns and motivations for changing housing circumstances. Although the authors had intended to emphasize the economic advantages associated with better neighborhoods, the parents stressed their fear of violence and their interest in increased safety. This construct, in turn, suggested outcomes to be measured (e.g., the frequency with which children were victims of violence).

Third, qualitative interviews helped in understanding the institutional details of a program, providing information about why different groups respond differently. The examples refer to differences in preferences of particular counselors. This seems to be an instance of the more general issue of implementation of programs. The attitudes and beliefs of the people administering the program and the group climate in organizations administering it can have a considerable impact on the actual services delivered.

Finally, interviews helped in understanding the realities of policy from the participants' perspectives, showing how they weighed costs and benefits for themselves and the extent to which they trusted public systems.

In chapter 9, Christina Gibson and Greg Duncan describe an ongoing ethnographic study of 43 families who are part of a larger evaluation of Milwaukee's New Hope Project. They point out how qualitative data have been used to understand quantitative findings, such as the different program impacts for boys and girls in the sample. It is noteworthy that this also illustrates how quantitative data can guide the qualitative method. After sex differences appeared in the quantitative findings, the ethnographers were alerted to include this issue in their interviews. This two-way influence, qualitative to quantitative and quantitative to qualitative, is relatively unusual; it results from a continuing integration and interaction between researchers using the two approaches.

Gibson and Duncan illustrate how qualitative data can suggest fruitful analysis strategies for quantitative data and inform future survey development. For example, subgroups based on barriers to employment were identified as a result of information obtained in ethnographic interviews. Questions about these barriers were pursued in the subsequent survey. These authors also propose an ingenious strategy for estimating parameters in a larger group from quantitative analysis of qualitative data.

In the sections that follow, I describe another example of integrating data from ethnographic interviews with survey information to understand parents' use of childcare subsidies. Then I will offer some general observations about qualitative, quantitative, and mixed methods.

Childcare Subsidies

I begin with an example of an analysis combining quantitative and ethnographic data to understand the role of childcare subsidies in parents' lives in the New Hope study. We are trying, not just to interpret our quantitative data, but to use each source to inform analyses of the other toward a common set of conclusions or interpretations. Ted Lowe and Tom Weisner of the University of California at Los Angeles, Danielle Crosby of the University of Texas, Christina Gibson of Northwestern University, and I are collaborating in this work. As Gibson and Duncan noted, one component of the New Hope package of benefits was a childcare subsidy, available to all program participants who met the 30-hour-per-week work requirement. The subsidy could be used for any child under the age of 13 and for any state-licensed or county-certified childcare provider. It paid the entire cost except for a small copayment from families based on income level and household size. Eligibility for the subsidy was contingent on full-time employment, which participants had to document each month by delivering earnings records to the New Hope office. Parents in both the program and the control group were also entitled to public childcare subsidies associated with the welfare system or the Child Care Block Grant funds if they qualified. Eligibility was contingent on some employment and on income; these subsidies paid the entire cost of care up to a specific limit, and eligibility was recertified less frequently than in New Hope.

Within the first 24 months of the program, approximately 47% of the program group with children aged 1–12 received the New Hope subsidy for an average of about 11.5 months. The average monthly benefit was $686. Overall, almost 60% of the New Hope sample and 41% of the control sample received any subsidy, New Hope or other (Bos et al. 1999). Although the New Hope childcare subsidy represented a substantial financial benefit for many families, about half of the sample never used it. On average, families had three spells of using benefits, indicating that, for many, use was not continuous.

These figures led us to ask: For whom were different subsidies useful and under what circumstances? What factors were related to longer and shorter periods of subsidy use? And how did subsidies affect the types of care chosen by parents and experienced by children?

Questions like these are being asked on a national level as well. Childcare subsidies have become a key policy consideration for those interested in supporting the employment efforts of low-income parents. Yet there is currently little understanding of how subsidies play out on the ground, and the information that is available is often conflicting. There are widespread reports of low take-up rates by parents leaving welfare, leading some policy makers to infer that most parents do not need or want subsidized care. In the New Hope survey, parents were asked why they did not use the childcare benefit; the majority of those not using it said they did not need it. At the same time, there are long waiting lists for childcare benefits in many states because of insufficient federal and state funding.

Parents' decisions about childcare arrangements and childcare subsidies are the result of a complex set of factors, including personal beliefs, quality, cost, convenience, and availability. Recent studies, including an analysis of the National Survey of American Families, and several state studies of families leaving welfare indicate that those most likely to use subsidies are between the ages of 25 and 34, have an infant or toddler as well as an older child, and have had some previous experience with the welfare system. Our analyses of data from the New Hope sample (Huston, Chang, and Gennetian 2002) show that parents with large families in which the youngest child is beyond infancy are most likely to use subsidies. Parents with lower levels of prior earnings and work experience and those with a longer history of welfare receipt were also more likely than other parents to use subsidies. These analyses of the quantitative data suggest that subsidies are more useful to parents whose children are beyond infancy and who are less "work ready," although the latter finding may result from the fact that people leaving welfare are given priority for public subsidies. These findings are consistent with Gibson and Duncan's report that New Hope was most useful to people with one barrier to work that could be addressed by New Hope benefits. These findings do not tell us, however, much about how subsidy policies operate in people's lives.

We are currently analyzing the New Hope ethnographic data to expand our understanding of why parents did or did not use the childcare subsidies available from New Hope or from other public agencies. One goal is to identify ways in which policies could be designed to make subsidies more helpful to parents trying to support their families. Preliminary results suggest that parents fall into four groups.

First, although most of the 43 participants in our sample preferred to take care of their own children or to leave them in the care of a trusted family member or close friend, a few parents indicated that leaving children in the care of paid service providers was simply out of the question. Many were distrustful of paid strangers, worrying about potential abuse or neglect of their children. Most parents, however, would and did use childcare and liked having subsidized childcare even if paid care was not their first preference.

Second, some parents were willing to use subsidies, but the nature of their employment made it difficult for them to find paid care. Many parents worked the second or third shift, when childcare centers and childcare homes are unlikely to be open for business. Parents who knew of paid home providers available at night often viewed them with suspicion and distrust.

Third, the conditions required for obtaining and retaining subsidies facilitated or obstructed access and continued use. Indeed, this theme was parents' most common explanation for not using subsidies. For example, subsidy programs require a great deal of effort to meet bureaucratic demands such as filling out paperwork and spending several hours, if not days, waiting to be serviced by case workers. New Hope had fewer bureaucratic barriers and did a much better job of facilitating subsidy receipt than does the state welfare program, but rules in both effectively limited parents' use of childcare subsidies. In particular, the fact that parents had to meet the 30-hour-per-week work requirement each month in order to receive the New Hope subsidy posed difficulties for many families. In the ebb and flow of the lives of low-income employed parents, they often failed to meet these requirements as a result of temporary perturbations in their or their partner's work effort. Parents lost their benefits when their circumstances changed and then had to go through the process of reapplying for subsidies. Moreover, they could not maintain stable childcare arrangements under these circumstances.

Families who found subsidies most useful were those for whom regular paid care fit their stable daily routine. They had relatively stable employment that enabled them to maintain eligibility and to plan on regular paychecks. Most paid childcare settings require that children attend on a regular schedule and for a planned number of hours. Families whose routines were more chaotic and uncertain found it more difficult to maintain the use of subsidies for childcare mainly because it was difficult for them to plan their work schedules and childcare needs, as well as the financial resources to make their copayment.

Our next step in this work will be to create new variables from the New Hope surveys based on the patterns we are finding in the ethnographic analyses. We will then test models that include these variables to predict childcare subsidy use. Examples are parents' attitudes about formal childcare, work schedules and employment stability, stability of residence and family composition, respondents' perceptions of the New Hope Project, and whether respondents' household circumstances fit those assumed by the program design.

Qualitative, Quantitative, and Mixed Methods

Using these three examples, I turn now to some more general points with respect to qualitative, quantitative, and mixed methods. I begin by deconstructing the terms "qualitative" and "quantitative." These terms are used to encompass a vast array of theoretical and methodological approaches. They are often posed as a dichotomy. Scientists sometimes align themselves at one end or the other, rejecting research representing the opposite pole as trivial, anecdotal, or superficial.

Continuum rather than Dichotomy

What do "qualitative" and "quantitative" mean in the contexts of chapter 8 and 9? The principal qualitative method used in both of the programs discussed, as well as the one I described above, is an open-ended interview in which interviewees are asked general questions and there is wide latitude for a range of responses. This technique can be contrasted with a closed-ended interview, in which the range of responses is highly restricted, usually by "yes/no" or numerical-response scales (e.g., 1 = never; 5 = always).

In fact, however, open-ended and closed-ended methods are not dichotomous categories but two ends of a continuum. Many interview techniques and questions fall somewhere between these two extremes. For example, in the New Hope survey, there were open-ended questions about parents' reasons for stress and about their goals for the future. These were useful in understanding their responses to closed-ended questions about how much stress they were experiencing or how well they were meeting their goals (Bos et al. 1999).

In the mailed teacher surveys administered at 24 months in the New Hope Project, there were open-ended questions asking why the teacher thought the child did or did not achieve at a level commensurate with ability. We devised a coding scheme that captured many of the reasons teachers offered for children's performance. In order of frequency they were the child's motivation and personal characteristics (e.g., attitude, interest, self-esteem); the child's classroom behavior (e.g., attendance, attention span, work habits); the child's home environment (e.g., parental interest, peers, neighborhood); the child's intellectual ability; and physical problems (e.g., disability, attention deficit disorder, problems with medication). The absence of certain categories of response can be as instructive as those that do occur. For example, teachers almost never mentioned factors in the school environment as possible positive or negative causes of children's achievement.

These open-ended answers were informative but did not lend themselves to statistical analysis because some teachers answered the questions in detail and others wrote nothing. There was no way to compare children across teachers. We used this information, however, to create closed-ended questions for the 60-month survey asking teachers to rate each of the five "causes" as obstacles, supports, or neither for a child's achievement.

Although there is clearly a continuum between open- and closed-ended, these two approaches do represent some of the differences in approach between investigators who identify their work as qualitative and those who fall in the quantitative camp. One difference is the focus on allowing important content to emerge from the research participant versus selecting content to which the participant can respond.

Who Sets the Content Agenda?

Qualitative, open-ended interviews and other techniques are based on the assumption that the respondent should be given maximum opportunity to set the agenda of topics. The researcher tries to impose as little structure as possible so that the perspectives, concerns, and frameworks of the participant can emerge. There are usually general guidelines (e.g., talk about your housing decision, your experiences with a social program, your children), but the philosophy guiding the method is to discover rather than impose, to allow information to emerge, to be inductive rather than deductive.

Closed-ended techniques, by contrast, are designed to obtain information from each respondent that is as comparable as possible. One means of doing so is to present each participant with a standard "stimulus" in the form of a question with a restricted set of answers. The philosophy guiding the method is to elicit information about preselected topics, to reduce the effects of variability in responsivity and verbal fluency across people, and to be deductive rather than inductive.

Analysis of Persons rather than Variables

Qualitative studies usually emphasize understanding a few individuals in depth rather than a large number superficially. They often emphasize complexity and the interrelations among an individual's circumstances and actions. As a result, they lend themselves to person-oriented analyses like the one described in our work on childcare subsidies. Groups of people are selected because they have a similar constellation of attributes. Closed-ended approaches lend themselves to variable-oriented analyses in which the groupings consist of one or more variables on which all participants are compared. We should note, however, that both types of data can be used to do either person-oriented or variable-oriented analyses.

Data Collection versus Data Analysis

The discussion of person-oriented versus variable-oriented analysis illustrates the more general point that we should separate data collection and data analysis when discussing qualitative and quantitative methods. For example, there is nothing inherent in data collected by open-ended methods that precludes quantitative analysis, a point that is illustrated by many of the studies presented in this volume. Open-ended responses can be coded, quantified, and subjected to statistical analysis. Similarly, closed-ended data can be subjected to person-oriented analyses using such techniques as cluster analysis in order to identify people who share a set of attributes or conditions. It is even possible, though less frequently attempted, to examine individual patterns of responses across a range of closed-ended measures to draw inferences about that individual.

Beyond Interviews

The discussion thus far has focused primarily on open-ended and closed-ended interviews, the primary method used in the studies reported in chapters 8 and 9 and in much of the literature. By definition, interviews rely almost exclusively on verbal report. The advantages of mixed methods go well beyond using different forms of verbal report. Combining verbal reports with observation, for example, is much more powerful than using one or the other, especially when studying children. Few ethnographic studies include open-ended interviews with children, probably because children are less articulate than adults. When ethnography is combined with close observation by a talented researcher, a rich picture of children's lives can emerge (e.g., Thorne 1994).

Observation is particularly useful for measuring characteristics that are strongly influenced by social desirability, such as parenting practices. For example, in two large-scale evaluations of welfare-to-work interventions

(New Chance and the National Evaluation of Welfare to Work Study), parents were interviewed about their child-rearing practices, and a short version of the Home Observation Measure of the Environment (HOME) was administered. A subsample of families also participated in structured mother-child interaction tasks that were videotaped. The three methods provide a much richer picture of parenting behavior than any one of them would (Zaslow and Eldred 1998). Comparisons indicated that parents' responses to closed-ended interview questions were virtually unrelated to their behavior in the videotaped observations; both types of measure were moderately associated with the HOME score, which combines open-ended verbal report and observer ratings.

Conclusion

The mixed methods used in the studies described chapters 8 and 9 offer some insights into children's developmental pathways, primarily by describing important features of the contexts that shape development. In chapter 8, the methods helped to shed light on the ways in which threats of violence lead parents to constrain their children's involvement with much of the outside world. Seeing the world from their perspectives enables us to understand the priorities that guide their actions and to draw some inferences about policies that might be helpful to them.

In my own experience of collaboration in New Hope and in another project, the Next Generation, mixing ethnographic and survey methods adds value to the research enterprise in many ways: by helping to understand quantitative findings, by suggesting content and topics for surveys, and by providing different points of view about the same questions. The most critical lesson from this collaboration has been the importance of continuing collaboration and communication between people conducting different parts of the study. This communication enables the research team to go beyond using ethnographic data as interesting "stories" or as illustrative case studies. It comes about when people regularly share their ideas and tentative findings and when they participate jointly in the design of survey questions and ethnographic methods.

There are also some interesting disciplinary differences. As a developmental psychologist, I have always used combinations of open- and closed-ended measures and combinations of observation and verbal report routinely in my research. I find it surprising to hear my colleagues in other disciplines talk about qualitative and quantitative approaches as though they were alien methods. I also find it somewhat frustrating that, with some notable exceptions (e.g., the Children 5–16 Research Programme in Great Britain), both ethnographies and surveys tend to use adults as informants rather than gathering data directly from children, particularly young children. If we are to understand pathways of children's development, we need the child's perspective, using multiple methods. Two dissertations being completed at the University of Texas exemplify the value of going directly to the children with both open- and closed-ended methods. As a follow-up to our finding that children in New Hope families increased their participation in organized out-of-school activities (Huston et al. 2001), David Casey (2001) interviewed a subsample of the children in New Hope about their time use and activities during the summer. Similarly, Marika Ripke (2001) pursued our finding that boys in New Hope families had higher occupational aspirations than boys in control group families. She did in-depth interviews with seventh graders about their aspirations and expectations for the future and found that many of them were remarkably focused and knowledgeable. Both studies contain rich information shedding light on children's developmental pathways.

We have just begun to consider the possibilities for using multiple methods to attack the thorny questions of human behavior. The virtues of using different methods have been known for a long time, but that typically meant separate studies testing the same question with different methods (e.g., experiments and naturalistic studies of childcare quality). The approaches represented in this volume strive for true integration of methods; to the extent that they succeed, they will provide richer and more powerful understanding of complex social processes.

References

Bos, J. M., A. C. Huston, R. C. Granger, G. J. Duncan, T. Brock, and V. C. McLoyd. 1999. *New Hope for People with Low Incomes: Two-Year Results of a Program to Reduce Poverty and Reform Welfare.* New York: MDRC.

Casey, D. M. 2001. "Summer Activities and Social Competence of Adolescents from Low-Income Families Individual, Family, and Neighborhood Factors." PhD diss., University of Texas at Austin.

Huston, A. C., Y. E. Chang, and L. A. Gennetian. 2002. "Family and Individual Predictors of Child Care Use by Low-Income Families in Different Policy Contexts." *Early Childhood Research Quarterly* 17: 441–69.

Huston, A. C., G. J. Duncan, R. C. Granger, J. M. Bos, V. C. McLoyd, R. S. Mistry, D. Crosby, C. Gibson, K. Magnuson, J. Romich, and A. Ventura. 2001. "Work-Based

Anti-poverty Programs for Parents Can Enhance the School Performance and Social Behavior of Children." *Child Development* 72:318–336.

Ripke, M. N. 2001. "Middle-School Children's Perceptions and Motivation regarding Work and Their Future: Simple or Complex? Optimistic or Realistic?" PhD diss., University of Texas at Austin.

Thorne, B. 1994. *Gender Play: Girls and Boys in School.* New Brunswick, NJ: Rutgers University Press.

Zaslow, M. J., and C. A. Eldred. 1998. *Parenting Behavior in a Sample of Young Mothers in Poverty: Results of the New Chance Observational Study.* New York: MDRC.

Commentary

Viewing Mixed Methods through an Implementation Research Lens: A Response to the New Hope and Moving to Opportunity Evaluations

Thomas Brock

Like men from Mars and women from Venus, qualitative and quantitative researchers often do not communicate well. If one group pays attention to what the other is doing, it is to point out flaws in the other's methods or interpretations. Thanks to the chapters on the Moving to Opportunity (MTO) demonstration by Jeffrey Kling, Jeffrey Liebman, and Lawrence Katz and on the New Hope Project by Christina Gibson and Greg Duncan, we see that qualitative and quantitative researchers not only can work together but can profit from one another's tools and perspectives. The chapters show how qualitative methods — specifically, intensive interviews with research sample members — help explain impact findings and identify important themes and outcomes for further investigation. Both chapters describe how the qualitative research led to improvements in the design of follow-up surveys. In chapter 9, we learn how the qualitative research helped the impact researchers identify subgroups that benefited most and least from the program intervention.

My own interest in the chapters is as one who studies the implementation of social programs within the context of impact

evaluations. I come favorably disposed to the topic, as I try to blend qualitative and quantitative methods to understand how programs are operated, used, and perceived by providers and clients. Most of my work has
focused on welfare reform and antipoverty initiatives, including the New
Hope Project. I have two main comments: first, that intensive interviews of
program target groups can play as valuable a role in implementation as in
impact research; and second, that the evaluation community may need to
make a stronger case for the *practical* benefits of mixed-methods designs
if such designs are to gain greater support among the people who fund and
use evaluation research. I conclude with some thoughts on how to manage
mixed-methods evaluations so that researchers work together effectively
and produce findings that might strengthen the policies and programs that
they study, including services that target low-income children and families.

The Role of Intensive Interviews in Implementation Research

In a seminal essay on the policy implementation process, Van Meter and
Van Horn (1975) describe the study of policy implementation and impact
as distinct, though clearly related, undertakings. The study of impact
searches for the consequences of a policy; the study of implementation examines the forces that determine policy impact. Stated differently, impact
studies typically ask, "what happened?" while implementation studies ask,
"why did it happen this way?"

Implementation researchers look at the process whereby social policies
are translated into practice. They typically investigate a broad range of topics, including the following:

- The interpretation of policies by program administrators and staff.
- The ways that staff explain program policies and offerings to clients.
- The mechanisms by which program benefits and services are delivered
  to clients.
- The goals of administrators, staff, and clients vis-à-vis the program.
- The use of program benefits and services by clients.
- The enforcement of program rules.
- The perceived quality, helpfulness, and effectiveness of the program by
  staff and clients.
- The factors that distinguish a program from others operating in its
  environment.

This wide range of topics pushes implementation researchers to collect a variety of qualitative and quantitative data. Common strategies include interviews or focus groups with staff and clients, observations of program activities, reviews of program documents, surveys of staff and clients, and analyses of program participation data.

As evidenced above, implementation research is heavily (if not exclusively) program focused. This is both its strength and its weakness. On the one hand, a program *as* operated—not just as described in policy—must be well documented and understood. Evaluators have to say what intervention occurred, determine whether the experience of program group members differed from that of control group members, and examine what features of the program influenced people's behavior. On the other hand, the "program centrism" that predominates in the implementation literature overlooks or oversimplifies the complex relationships that clients often have with programs.

The intensive-interview strategy used in the MTO and New Hope studies offers a solution to this problem. By allowing clients to speak in their own terms about their experiences—including, but not limited to, their interactions with the programs under study—researchers acquire a much richer understanding of clients' goals, use of benefits and services, and other topics. They also gain a truer sense of the relative importance that programs play in clients' lives. Although the intensive-interview strategy does not eliminate the need for more traditional ways of investigating program structures and processes, it adds an important body of evidence that is missing from most impact evaluations.[1]

It is worth noting that the value added of an intensive-interview component is proportional to the rigor of its design. Both the MTO and New Hope interview samples were randomly selected,[2] providing greater confidence that the major themes identified by researchers were representative of other people in the study. Larger samples, as seen in the New Hope study, bolster this confidence further. Had the researchers paid less attention to whom they interviewed—choosing only cases recommended by program staff, for example, or those that showed up at the program office—they could not have generalized their findings to the larger sample. The inclusion of control group members in the New Hope interview sample is worth special note, in that it gave researchers an appreciation for the surprising *similarity* between program and control group members' experiences. Implementation and impact research normally concentrate on explaining how they are different.

One of the findings that emerged from the intensive client interviewing in the MTO and New Hope studies was that the goals clients were trying to achieve differed in subtle but important ways from the goals advocated by program designers or staff. For the MTO participants, for example, the program's promise of helping to find better apartments or move closer to employment opportunities seemed secondary to participants' interest in bringing up their children in less violent neighborhoods. This raises interesting questions for the implementation study. For instance, to what extent were neighborhood safety issues addressed in the marketing of the program? Did program applications go up after violent incidents occurred? Was there stronger interest in the program among residents living in housing projects with the highest levels of violence?

Similarly, in the New Hope chapter, researchers provided an illustration of a woman who used the program's health insurance only temporarily. She had an immediate objective of paying for a tonsillectomy for her son but did not believe that continuous health coverage was important—at least not enough to justify the copayment that the program required of her every month. Her story no doubt frustrated program staff, who worked hard to maximize benefit usage. It may, however, help explain why implementation researchers found that intermittent use of benefits and services was the modal pattern in New Hope (Brock et al. 1997; Bos et al. 1999).

Another finding that emerged from the MTO and New Hope intensive interviews was that clients drew on extensive personal networks and resources to meet their goals. For example, clients accessed a number of social service programs besides the ones being evaluated (e.g., general equivalency diploma and day care programs in the MTO study). While implementation researchers are usually aware of the existence of such providers, they have tended not to explore how other providers may complement or compete with the program they are studying. They are even less likely to pay attention to clients' informal networks, including family, friends, employers, and acquaintances. An area ripe for further study is the extent to which these networks support or hinder clients' participation in programs and the ways that program staff respond. For example, do programs define eligibility rules in a way that includes or excludes other family members? Do program staff ever contact clients' family members, friends, or employers, and if so, for what reasons?

In sum, chapters 8 and 9 suggest that intensive client interviews offer as much benefit to implementation research as to impact research. The findings generated by intensive client interviews challenge the program centrism that characterizes so much implementation research and provide greater insight into why and how clients use programs.

Making a Practical Case for Mixed-Methods Designs

One of the goals of implementation research is to provide feedback that will help policy makers and administrators meet their program objectives. Chapters 8 and 9 describe the *research* benefits of a mixed-methods approach, but I see *practical* benefits as well. Among the payoffs suggested by these chapters were the following.

Improved program operations. Once policy makers and administrators hear about a program's impacts, they usually want to know what they should have done differently or, phrased another way, how might they have done better. Qualitative research focused on program operations and client experiences is often the best means for identifying the unintended consequences of policies and possible areas for improvement. In the MTO study, for instance, researchers found that Spanish-speaking clients were less likely to move out to the suburbs than black clients. They initially assumed that this was due to clients' own preferences, but they learned through their fieldwork that counselors heavily influenced clients' decisions. For program administrators, such findings might suggest the need for more staff training and supervision to lessen the probability that clients are treated differently on the basis of race or ethnicity.

Better program targeting. Given limited resources, most policy makers and program administrators would choose to target people who will derive the maximum benefit from the intervention. In the New Hope study, Gibson and Duncan showed how the qualitative research helped identify subgroups defined by barriers to employment. Operating on a hunch from the ethnographic team, the quantitative researchers discovered that clients with just one barrier to employment derived the greatest benefit from New Hope's benefits and services. If the program were to be replicated, administrators and staff could use such information to refine their recruitment and screening procedures.

Identification of service gaps. Policy makers and program administrators are often interested in knowing what additional services might be needed to help clients succeed. The fact that New Hope did not prove effective for clients with multiple barriers to employment, for instance, might suggest the need for more intensive case management or other services. In the

MTO study, the findings on the difficulties low-income single mothers faced in arranging child supervision underscored the importance of expanded and improved-quality day care to help mothers go to work.

Improved fiscal planning. Among other things, policy makers and program administrators need to understand program participation trends in order to estimate how many staff and other resources a program needs in the future. New Hope greatly overestimated demand and miscalculated how much money it needed to raise. This was not a trivial issue, as fundraising proceeded slowly and consumed significant staff time (Brock et al. 1997). Intensive client interviews can shed light on participation patterns and suggest whether they are likely to change or remain constant.

Evaluators are most useful to policy makers and program operators when they can provide quick feedback on program performance. Unfortunately, estimating program impacts is slow business, due to the elapsed time needed for clients to go through program activities and for researchers to collect and analyze follow-up data. Qualitative research has the potential to provide useful information sooner. Each round of intensive interviews, for example, can offer insights into topics such as why clients applied to a program (or not), how well they understand the benefits and services offered, and what needed program elements may be missing. By sharing such findings as they emerge—rather than holding out for the impact results—evaluators may demonstrate their usefulness to policy makers and administrators in the short term and hence build greater support for mixed-methods designs in the long term.

Conclusion: Managing Mixed-Methods Research Projects for Success

If mixed-methods research yields so many benefits, why isn't it done more often? One answer is that it tends to increase costs, although researchers who emphasize the practical applications—as outlined above—may have greater success in raising financial support. A second answer, often forgotten once the results are in, is that mixed-methods evaluations are more difficult to manage, if for no other reason than they usually involve more players than single-method designs. As Pressman and Wildavsky (1984) concluded after studying the implementation of an economic development program in Oakland, California, each person who is added to a project increases the number of perspectives and reduces the odds of reaching agreement on major decisions. Large research teams also pose greater challenges in sharing information, tracking progress, and managing relationships with external stakeholders, including research funders and program representatives.

While there are no magic formulas, I have found that the most successful mixed-methods projects tend to have several features in common. The first is strong leadership of the qualitative and quantitative components. Occasionally one person can manage both equally well, but more often, co–principal investigators or task leaders are needed to ensure that qualitative and quantitative research activities receive sufficient attention and resources. Project leaders also need to build a common vision for the evaluation among all team members. This requires frequent communication with staff at all levels and from both sides of the methodological aisle. Team meetings are an obvious strategy, but less formal mechanisms, such as e-mail, are often just as beneficial and sometimes more efficient for planning data collection, debating alternative courses of action, making sense of puzzling findings, and the like.

A second characteristic of successful mixed-methods projects is that staff are willing (or encouraged) to blend roles and adopt new tools. Although it is common for researchers to divide along methodological lines — one group carrying out qualitative data collection and analysis, another doing the same for quantitative data — there are numerous ways that they can cross traditional boundaries and collaborate. Participant observers, for example, might think about developing scales to rate the social settings or interactions that they study. Survey researchers and ethnographers can work together to develop questions and protocols for structured and open-ended interviews. As Gibson and Duncan note in chapter 9, some of the most productive synergy in the New Hope evaluation involved graduate students who participated in both qualitative and quantitative data analysis.

A third feature of successful mixed-methods projects is that the quantitative and qualitative research activities are designed and carried out concurrently. This is not always feasible; in New Hope, for instance, the intensive client interviews were not funded until relatively late in the project. Without question, late was better than never, but the delay came at a cost: first, in the steep learning curve that intensive interviewers faced when they joined the project; and, later, in the missed opportunities to use the intensive-interview findings (which provided insights into clients' family lives and program experiences, among other things) to generate questions for the implementation research and the structured client survey. Such problems are avoided when mixed methods are part of the design from the beginning.

Management challenges notwithstanding, we are past the point where qualitative or quantitative methods are an either/or debate. The New Hope and MTO studies — along with others in this volume — provide too strong a case for blending the two approaches. In traditional experimental evaluations, impact analysts examine program effects through quantitative methods, and implementation researchers study program operations through a combination of field research and structured data gathering. The New Hope and MTO evaluations delved further by conducting intensive interviews with clients, thus gaining a better understanding of clients' motivations and experiences inside and outside the programs. These data greatly enhanced the researchers' ability to explain why the programs produced the effects they did on participating families and children.

Combining quantitative and qualitative methods also provides researchers with greater opportunities to address the needs of policy makers and program administrators. While it often takes time for quantitative researchers to determine a program's "bottom line," qualitative researchers — through interviews and observations — may pick up early signs that a program is on or off track. Prompt feedback can help policy makers and program administrators correct obvious flaws even before the final results are tabulated. In an evaluation context, the value of mixed-methods research ultimately lies in its ability to strengthen programs that serve populations in need, including low-income children and families. This suggests that the challenge of mixed-methods research lies not only in adopting new approaches to data collection and analysis but in communication of findings as well.

Notes

1. I am aware of three impact evaluations that included intensive client interviews comparable to what was done in the MTO and New Hope studies. Quint and Musick (1994) conducted interviews with 50 teen mothers in the New Chance demonstration. Johnson conducted interviews with 32 noncustodial fathers in the Fathers' Fair Share program (Johnson, Levine, and Doolittle 1999). Edin is leading a team of ethnographers in conducting interviews with approximately 120 families, subject to time limits and other rules introduced under welfare reform, in the Project on Devolution and Urban Change (see Quint et al. 1999).

2. The New Hope ethnographic sample ($n = 43$) included 3 "exemplars" recommended by program staff.

References

Bos, J., A. Huston, R. Granger, G. Duncan, T. Brock, and V. McLoyd. 1999. *New Hope for People with Low Incomes: Two-Year Results of a Program to Reduce Poverty and Reform Welfare.* New York: MDRC.

Brock, T., F. Doolittle, V. Fellerath, and M. Wiseman. 1997. *Creating New Hope: Implementation of a Program to Reduce Poverty and Reform Welfare.* New York: MDRC.

Johnson, E., A. Levine, and F. C. Doolittle. 1999. *Fathers' Fair Share: Helping Poor Men Manage Child Support and Fatherhood.* New York: Russell Sage Foundation.

Pressman, J. L., and A. Wildavsky. 1984. *Implementation: How Great Expectations Are Dashed in Oakland.* 3rd ed. Berkeley and Los Angeles: University of California Press.

Quint, J., K. Edin, M. L. Buck, B. Fink, Y. C. Padilla, O. Simmons-Hewitt, and M. E. Valmont. 1999. *Big Cities and Welfare Reform: Early Implementation and Ethnographic Findings from the Project on Devolution and Urban Change.* New York: MDRC.

Quint, J., and J. Musick. 1994. *Lives of Promise, Lives of Pain: Young Mothers after New Chance.* New York: MDRC.

Van Meter, D. S., and C. E. Van Horn. 1975. "The Policy Implementation Process: A Conceptual Framework." *Administration and Society* 6 (4): 445–487.

PART V

Family Intervention Studies:
Inclusion and "Multiple
Worlds" in Research
and Practice

10

Entering the Developmental Niche: Mixed Methods in an Intervention Program for Inner-City Children

Sara Harkness, Marcia Hughes, Beth Muller, and Charles M. Super

In children's developmental journey through middle childhood, no pathway is more important for success than the one that connects home and school. Trod on a daily basis by children, that pathway may appear either short and straight or long and tortuous; a friendly stroll from one familiar place to another, to be taken together with parents, teachers, and others; or a lonely enterprise upon which children are expected to embark by themselves. Understanding how this pathway is formed has become a central concern for developmental research in recent years. Building on this understanding in order to enhance children's successful development has, in parallel, become a focus for intervention programs with schools and families.

This chapter will review several theoretical frameworks for understanding the nature and significance of home-school relations, the "pathways" that link them to each other. A central premise to be developed here is that intervention efforts are based on the designer's conceptualization of the relevant variables. Conceptual models, in turn, are instantiated through the methods available to their authors. Thus, we argue that mixed-methods approaches, which have long been an accepted tenet of interdisciplinary research on children's environments of development, offer a fuller and more accurate base of knowledge for improving the circumstances and outcomes of children's development than do models drawn from one disciplinary method alone. We illustrate our approach with preliminary data from an intervention project with inner-city school children that is based on the "developmental niche" framework of Super and Harkness (1997, 1999).

Models of Home-School Relations

Theoretical frameworks for understanding home-school relations have been influenced by close ties between policy and research in this area: as Epstein comments: "More than for most topics, researchers, educators, and parents have been working together to identify the goals, problems, and potential solutions to create more successful partnerships to assist more students. These cross-connections of university researchers, educators, and policy makers have transformed how some research is designed, conducted, and interpreted" (1996, 213). Epstein's own model of "overlapping spheres of influence" (Epstein 1987, 1996) is illustrative. In Epstein's model, the overlapping spheres are viewed from the perspective of the school, with an eye to policies and practices that may enhance family-school partnerships for the benefit of students. Six types of involvement that fall within the areas of overlap between home and school are identified. First are basic parenting and child-rearing skills, knowledge about child development, and the creation of optimal settings for children's learning at home. Second is communication with families about school programs and student progress. Third is parent involvement in school-based activities, such as attending children's performances and volunteering in the classroom. Fourth are learning activities at home, including help with homework and decision making about extracurricular activities. Fifth is parent participation in decision making about school, including governance and parent-teacher organizations. Sixth and last is collaboration with community organizations in order to strengthen school programs as well as support positive family practices. This model of home-school relations identifies the many different forms that "overlapping spheres of influence" can take, from actual parent-teacher interactions in the classroom to parenting practices that may have been established before the child even entered school. The inclusion of community relations, a later addition to the model, reflects awareness that neither home nor school is independent of the larger social context.

Epstein's model is comprehensive in its inclusion of various home-school linkages, but it does not attempt to organize them into a dynamic system. Eccles and Harold's (1996) model of parental involvement does just this, drawing in part from work by Epstein and others. Eccles and Harold, like Epstein, are motivated by immediate practical and policy considerations, notably the need to understand what limits parental involvement in schools in order to increase such involvement. Their model links a series of variables through presumed causative relationships. First are "exogenous variables" (parental characteristics, neighborhood and community influences, and characteristics of the child, the teacher, and the school) that have indirect or global effects on parental involvement. Teacher and parent beliefs follow in the model, and they are conceptualized as influencing each other as well as affecting practices in each setting. Practices at home and at school, the next components of the model, can similarly influence each other. Child outcomes, the last part of the model, are influenced by practices at home and at school, as well as by parent and teacher beliefs. Eccles and Harold have used this model to analyze relationships between parental beliefs and involvement with their children's education in a large longitudinal study of elementary school children. Some empirical support for the model emerges from their analysis: for example, parent involvement at several grade levels is predicted by parents' confidence in their own intellectual abilities, achievement motivation, and perception of the child's level of interest. Interestingly, parental characteristics such as education correlated only weakly with parent-school involvement in this sample.

Although both these models include domains that could be studied using a variety of methods, these researchers have relied primarily on structured questionnaires and existing information such as students' grades in school. Many of the instruments used in these investigations have been derived from extensive field research and in partnership with teachers. Given the multifaceted nature of home-school relations, it is useful to have a portfolio of variables shown to be related to children's success in school, at least in the kinds of communities studied so far. Further, the variables can be manipulated in a variety of different configurations representing hypothesized causal pathways. For example, Grolnick and Slowiaczek (1994) have tested a multidimensional model of parental involvement in children's schooling as it relates to children's experience. They propose that children experience parental involvement related to their education in three ways. First, parents manifest involvement through behavior, such as attending school events; the child may experience this behavior either directly (as when the parent helps in the classroom) or indirectly (e.g., if a parent-teacher contact influences the teacher's interactions with the child). Second, parents can provide children with an experience of personal involvement in which they express a sense of caring about the child in relation to school matters. The third kind of parental involvement is cognitive/intellectual and includes parents' provision of experiences that may enhance the child's knowledge base and cognitive skill for school—for example, by encouraging reading or taking the child to visit a local museum. Grolnick and Slowiaczek's conceptualization corresponds partially to Epstein's six types of overlapping spheres, but it is distinctive in differentiating the affective and cognitive elements of parental input at home and also in considering various types of parent-school contact as a single category. Factor analysis of a set of parent involvement measures supported this multidimensional model, and the idea of the child's perceptions as mediators of parental involvement also received partial support from a path analysis.

Models based on predefined variables can be successfully used to identify causes and consequences of parental involvement in children's education, but they have two important limitations. First, there is no guarantee—indeed, it is highly unlikely—that the same variables will be equally valid in cultural settings that differ from the ones in which they were first conceptualized. In our cross-cultural research on parents, children, and schools, we have found a variety of different ideas, shared by both parents and teachers, about how parents can best help their children be successful in school. For example, we have found that Dutch parents and teachers emphasize the importance of a regular and restful schedule, free of excessive stimulation by after-school activities; Italian parents and teachers, on the other hand, stress the central role of emotional closeness both within the family and between teacher and child. These culturally shared ideas are not just different views on the same issue but are qualitatively different "takes" on a universally recognized challenge of child rearing. We have also found that there are basic differences across cultural groups in ideas about how parents and schools ought to relate to each other: whereas Dutch parents are frequently present in their children's schools, Spanish parents and teachers assume that parents should stay out of the school unless specifically invited. It is clear that research based on predefined measures that leave little room for the introduction of unexpected answers, might produce results of limited meaning and usefulness when carried out in new cultural settings.

Ethnographic Studies

In contrast to research rooted in mainstream psychology, ethnographic research on home-school relations has sought structure and meaning through understanding particular communities in a holistic manner. Such research also provides depth to findings on relationships between family and parental background variables and parental involvement. For example, Graue (1993) interviewed and observed parents of children entering kindergarten in two nearby but socioeconomically contrasting communities: rural, working-class "Fulton" and suburban, middle-class "Norwood." She found that mothers in Fulton were hopeful but not very knowledgeable about what to expect in kindergarten. Without previous preschool experience, they had little basis for comparing their children's readiness with that of peers. They accepted the teacher's opinion about their children's progress, although this meant adjusting their perceptions of the children's intelligence downward as the year progressed. They took a more passive role in communications with the school, such as parent-teacher conferences, in which they expected the teacher to tell them what was important for them to know. Contacts with the school were limited, since the mothers worked and therefore could not volunteer in the classroom. Norwood parents, in contrast, approached their children's entry into kindergarten with an informed and assertive attitude. Unlike the Fulton parents, who automatically signed their children up for kindergarten as soon as they met the minimal age requirement, many parents in Norwood kept their children out for an extra year in order to give them a competitive advantage in academics and sports. These parents had active social networks centered on children's activities and preschool and thus felt well-informed about the school even before their children entered. Their knowledge base was further developed through volunteering in the classroom (most of the mothers were not employed outside the home). In contrast to the Fulton parents, the Norwood parents felt that they themselves were the experts on their children's needs and development and actively sought to shape the school's programs to benefit their child. Graue concludes that the different approaches of these two groups of parents were shaped by the conceptualizations of parenthood that they learned as members of community-based networks.

Graue's findings are consistent with the conclusions of Lareau's classic study of parental involvement in two classrooms located in different socioeconomic milieux (2000). Like the two contrasting groups of parents in

Graue's study, Lareau's samples differed in terms of parents' involvement in the school and advocacy on behalf of their children. Lareau used Bourdieu's concept of "cultural capital" to explain socioeconomic-status differences in parental behavior: with more education, status, and income than working-class parents, the middle-class parents in her study had more resources—knowledge, social contacts, and self-assurance—to use in their interactions with the school. The result was that the middle-class parents had much closer connections to the school than the working-class parents, even though, ironically, the working-class parents were willing to grant the teachers higher status and expertise than were their middle-class peers.

Differences in beliefs and expectations, both about the family and about children in school, also have been presented in ethnographic studies of Mexican American immigrant families. For example, Valdes's (1996) study of Mexican immigrant families in a Texas border town vividly illustrates the widely differing ideas about the family, the child, and the goals of schooling held by these parents and their children's teachers. Based on her understanding of these differences, Valdes suggests that no simple school-based intervention programs are likely to help in addressing the widespread problem of school failure by Mexican immigrant children.

Ethnographic studies such as the ones described here deal with particular children and families in interaction with their schools at a given historical moment. Samples are small: 10–12 families in the studies mentioned above. The process of data analysis is lengthy and recursive, as the same pieces of text or observation are studied and restudied in relation to different emerging themes. Lareau's account of putting her interview material on 5 × 8 cards, arraying them in different configurations, and deriving the possible themes illustrates how intensive and time-consuming this process can be. The results are presented in narrative form, with commentaries and interpretation interwoven, in contrast to the results of quantitative research, which are presented explicitly or implicitly in formulas showing how abstract variables (e.g., "social support") relate to other variables (e.g., "child's perceived competence"). Each type of research offers understanding but also presents challenges to generalization, an especially important issue for research with such clear implications for intervention. With narratives, the question for generalizability to another school is how that story fits the story of one's own situation; if there are obvious differences, how much do they matter for the whole story and its outcome? With formulas, the question is whether the variables as defined by the researcher would correspond accurately to the same kinds of things that one is dealing with in another situation; if there are differences, how much do they matter for the way the whole formula fits together?

Theoretical Frameworks for Integrative and Mixed-Methods Research on Home-School Relations

Methods are closely tied to theoretical frameworks as well as to disciplinary traditions. Thus, in order to develop integrative studies of home-school relationships, it is important to have a theoretical framework that has "places" for the array of information and issues one wishes to consider. One model that has been widely influential for both research and policy is Bronfenbrenner's ecological model for the study of child development (Bronfenbrenner 1979). The part of this model most directly relevant for the study of home-school relations is the "mesosystems," which are links among the child's various "microsystems" that constitute the environments of daily life. In order to understand the environmental forces affecting developmental outcomes for children, Bronfenbrenner argues, it is necessary to take these links into account. As an example, Bronfenbrenner (1979) has described the young child who goes alone to school on the first day. In this case, the child herself is the only link between home and school. Stronger links—including shared beliefs and practices as well as increased contact—should thus lead to higher success in school. Bronfenbrenner's ecological model has helped identify the multiple settings and levels of influence that must be included in contextualized research on child development, but the model does not differentiate their various components—for example, beliefs and values of parents or teachers as opposed to social relationships or activities. The role of culture is also indeterminate in the model: on the one hand, culture is represented as the macrosystem, separated from the child by the intermediate microsystem, mesosystems, and exosystems; on the other hand, systems at all levels are characterized in terms of the shared values and beliefs that shape them.

More recent conceptual models draw from research traditions in anthropology, psychology, and ecology to create theoretical frameworks that enable the integrated analysis of individual child development and family functioning in cultural context (see Super and Harkness 1999; also Weisner, Introduction to this volume). These models draw primarily, but not exclusively, from a long tradition of mixed-methods theorizing and research in anthropology; today they are most evident in the sub- or interdisciplines of psychological anthropology and, increasingly, developmental science. The intellectual genealogy is worth tracing.

Franz Boas, the founder of anthropology as an empirical discipline in the United States, was initially trained in Wilhelm Wundt's experimental psychology laboratory in Leipzig, where he learned to measure "elementary sensations" in conditions assumed to be environmentally neutral; this same tradition inspired the initial but short-lived forays of cross-cultural psychology as European scientists and explorers took their brass instruments around the world (Jahoda 1993). Convinced that no psychological phenomenon exists free of context, however, Boas devoted much of his career to studying the sociocultural and environmental features that shape human experience, focusing on Native American groups of North America. Margaret Mead, one of Boas's students, was sent to Samoa with a similar mission: to understand whether the "storm and stress" of adolescence so notable in the United States would be found in a different cultural milieu. Mead's research — typical of the contemporary zeitgeist that produced the interdisciplinary Society for Research in Child Development — used a mixture of methods from psychology and anthropology. For example, her data on Samoan girls included demographic information on their families, their own personal histories, psychological tests, and many naturalistic behavior observations as well as general ethnographic information (see Harkness and Super 1987). In this same tradition, research by John Whiting and Beatrice Whiting, who trained several generations of psychological anthropologists up to the present, has also been based on mixed methods and cross-disciplinary theories. Among their pioneering methodological contributions was the use of qualitative naturalistic observations made by trained local observers for quantitative analyses of the determinants of children's social behavior across multiple settings (Whiting and Edwards 1988; Whiting and Whiting 1975). Robert A. LeVine, an anthropologist who was a member of the Whitings' research team in the Children of Six Cultures project, has included methods and ideas from a wide variety of disciplines, including psychoanalytic theory, child development, pediatrics, and demography, in research over the course of several decades; recent work, carried out in collaboration with a multidisciplinary team, is a virtual compendium of mixed-methods research organized around a central question (LeVine et al. 1994).

It is noteworthy for the present discussion that significant contributions to this evolving tradition have come from scientists whose primary training was not in anthropology, and access to innovative methods came through scholars who had received significant exposure to other disciplines during their intellectually formative years. Perhaps the most prominent of these is the social psychologist Donald T. Campbell (see Campbell and Overman 1988). Campbell, whose initial work was in psychology's tradition of measurement and analysis, became interested in the biases introduced by single-measure or single-method approaches, and he developed a specific epistemology that came to be known as "convergent operationalism" or "methodological triangulation," which was itself operationalized in the "multitrait-multimethod matrix" (Campbell and Fiske 1959). The core idea is that every measurement device, by the nature of its refinement, ignores nonfocal information and therefore introduces a kind of bias; the truth is best seen when viewed from several perspectives, or through several methods, so that a diversification of biases overcomes the fallibility of any single device. Having studied briefly with the Boasian anthropologists Alfred Kroeber and Robert Lowie, Campbell connected easily with faculty colleagues Melville Herskovits and Robert LeVine in anthropology when he moved to Northwestern University in 1953, and the issue of "key informants" soon became a topic of common interest (see Campbell 1955). Campbell's work in subsequent decades contributed significantly to the mixture of methods in anthropological fieldwork (Campbell 1961; LeVine 1981) and, more generally, initiated a constructive approach to understanding the similarities and differences between "qualitative" and "quantitative" research (see Kidder 1981).

The Developmental Niche: Theory and Applications

As we have detailed elsewhere (Harkness and Super 1995; Super and Harkness 1997, 1999), the concept of the developmental niche draws on three distinctive but complementary conceptualizations of the child, each represented in the research literature. In the first, culture is seen to provide an array of settings for daily life, each characterized by particular kinds of actors and tasks. This perspective has been elaborated in the research of the Whitings, especially Beatrice Whiting's idea of parents as "providers of settings" that offer the child practice in different kinds of social behavior. In the second conceptualization, culture is seen as a collection of customary practices that convey messages and provide systematically different learning experiences to the child. This perspective can be traced back to early studies in the "culture and personality" school of anthropology, as evidenced in the work of Ruth Benedict and Margaret Mead; it has reemerged in research on the developmental role of children's participation in culturally organized practices. The third perspective focuses on the psychological reality of culture, as constructed by caretakers' shared beliefs about children, the family, and child development. This approach, interwoven in early anthropological accounts of parenting in other cultures, has emerged more recently as a distinctive focus in the developmental, as well as anthropological, literature, drawing from psychological research on parents' ideas as a force in children's development and on the anthropological construct of "cultural models." Each of these three lines of research provides a critical perspective on culture as a developmental environment, but none of them accommodate sufficiently two core issues that are well articulated in the broader disciplines of social anthropology and developmental psychology. These are, respectively, the integration of various elements in the child's culturally structured environment and endogenous aspects of individual development that alter the specifics of individual-environment interactions. The developmental niche is a theoretical framework that attempts to acknowledge and integrate this set of considerations.

At the center of this model is the individual child, and the primary view is to take the place of the child and look outward to the everyday world, which is conceptualized in terms of three components or subsystems. First are the child's physical and social settings of daily life. Second are the customs and practices of care that children experience in these settings, including, for example, childcare arrangements and bedtime routines. Third is the psychology of the caretakers, in particular the cultural belief systems that parents, teachers, and others bring to their interactions with children. Three corollaries govern the operation of the developmental niche as a system. First, the three subsystems interact with each other as part of a larger system: customs and practices instantiate ethnotheories and can be observed in the settings of daily life. Second, each subsystem of the niche interacts independently with the larger cultural environment: settings of daily life may be affected by changes in parental employment, for example, thus initiating a reworking of customary practices of care. Third, children contribute actively to the construction of their own niches, both through their own individual characteristics and over the course of development.

The developmental niche framework has been used by its authors and others for research in a number of domains, including motor development, emotional expression, sleep and arousal, cognitive development, language development, literacy and numeracy, temperament, and health (see Super and Harkness 1999). This approach lends itself easily to studies of culture and human development, as cultural themes are expressed in multiple domains that can be accessed in a variety of ways. For example, in recent research on differences in sleep patterns between Dutch and U.S. infants and children, parental diaries of children's daily routines, parent interviews, and observations of the children's behavior were all used to understand the expression and consequences of parents' cultural beliefs about the importance of rest and regularity for early development (Super et al. 1996).

Although the developmental niche framework was originally constructed for the analysis of children's home environments, it is well adapted to the study of other settings, including school. Indeed, this framework, by conceptualizing culture as present in the immediate settings of children's daily lives, can accommodate studies of children who must move between different cultural worlds as they make the transition between home and school, an increasingly common phenomenon in many countries (Meyers 1992). In this case, it is useful to identify settings, customs, and ethnotheories both at home and at school in order to study how they may relate to each other. Harkness and Super (1999) have discussed the usefulness of the developmental niche framework for early-intervention programs; they suggest that in order for interventions to be effective, teachers and other educators not only must be familiar with relevant practices at home (e.g., book reading at bedtime) but also need to understand parental concepts of the child and goals for development as they are instantiated in such practices.

Although research by ourselves and others has demonstrated the relevance of the developmental niche framework for interventions with children and families, we ourselves had not until recently been directly involved in any such interventions. The opportunity to do so was presented through the University of Connecticut's GEAR UP project, a federally funded program to help children complete high school and continue their education (the acronym stands for Gaining Early Awareness and Readiness for Undergraduate Programs). Under the leadership of Principal Investigator John Bennett, the project was to follow two cohorts of children who were in the sixth and seventh grades (a total of about 120 children) at a prekindergarten through eighth-grade school in Hartford; the project was designed to provide these children, and their teachers, with a range of educational and social services throughout middle and secondary school. The school services were to be provided by faculty and students at the University of Connecticut's Neag School of Education, and outreach to children and families would be accomplished by faculty and students at the university's School of Family Studies.

The developmental niche framework was not initially part of our conceptualization for the role of the School of Family Studies in the GEAR UP project; rather, we planned simply to match undergraduate "mentors" with individual children and their families, in order to strengthen home-school links and offer socioemotional support to the children. Over the course of our first year in the GEAR UP project, however, our involvement grew to a more broad-ranging set of explorations and activities with not only the children but also their families and teachers. In the process, we found that we were using familiar research methods such as parent interviews and participant observation and applying the results not only to understand the children's situations but also to involve their families more effectively in the intervention. In crossing the divide between research and practice, we ourselves had become active participants in the daily lives of the children, their families, and their school: in essence, we had entered their developmental niches. The resulting approach to intervention is distinctive in several regards:

1. The program is school based but family oriented. We have an ongoing presence in the school through a variety of activities, but we are centrally concerned with the child in the family, and by extension with the family as a whole. We assume that the child's success in school is closely connected to the child's developmental niche at home.

2. We approach families in an ethnographic mode: we seek to understand how each family perceives their child and their situation as a family, as well as how they perceive the school. Parental ethnotheories, along with family practices and routines, are a special focus of our attention, as these shape the child's experience at home and beyond.

3. Within this framework, we seek to understand each child's strengths and needs individually.

4. We conceptualize home-school relations in terms of two interactive developmental niches, each with its own physical and social settings, customs of care, and psychology of the caretakers.

At the level of intervention, our approach has led us to a greater emphasis on parents' developmental issues than is typical of school improvement programs. Likewise, our focus on the family leads us to include younger siblings in clubs and activities for the intervention group. Using the framework of the developmental niche has led to efforts to tailor the intervention to the child and family's needs, working in a holistic rather than service-based mode. Awareness of the family and school as interacting developmental niches results in attention to linkages between them: How do home and school schedules and settings support or detract from each other? How do parents and teachers perceive the children's strengths and needs? How do customs of adult-child communication and children's responsibilities complement or conflict with each other? How do parents' and teachers' expectations for the children, and for each other, fit or not fit? The core feature of this approach, which differs from other well-known school improvement programs such as the Comer schools (Finn-Stevenson and Stern 1997), is that it puts primary focus on understanding each child within the context of his or her culturally constructed environment, with the goal of identifying those aspects of the environment that may be available and effective for intervention. Although it might be argued that learning about the developmental niche of each child is too time-consuming to be practical for large-scale intervention programs, we suggest that this process can save a great deal of time and resources by targeting the most relevant areas for investment in extra services. Furthermore, just as cross-cultural studies using the developmental niche framework have identified commonalities among children in particular environments, so can this framework help to shape programs that are relevant to a number of children in a given setting. Finally, the research process itself, which involves conversation and consultation with parents, teachers, and children, can serve as a means of self-discovery and empowerment.

We present here some preliminary results from home interviews with parents that were carried out as a means of getting to know the GEAR UP families and gaining some understanding of parents' background and concerns. Two case studies of children in the GEAR UP cohort are then described to illustrate the insights that can be gained through a person-centered ethnographic approach. We conclude with a discussion of how the developmental niche, as a mixed-methods research paradigm, has been used in an intervention context.

The Batchelder School Community

The Batchelder School, a prekindergarten through eighth-grade public school in the Hartford school system, serves approximately 600 students. At the time the intervention began, 64% of the students were Hispanic, 22% were African American, and the remaining 14% were Caucasian, Asian, or Native American. Seventy percent of these young people received free or reduced-price lunches, 67% came from non-English-speaking homes, and about one-quarter of the students moved in or out of the school each year. Almost half the children were enrolled in special programs for students needing extra academic support, such as Special Education or Bilingual Education. Scores of sixth-grade students on the Connecticut Mastery Tests indicated low rates of students meeting state goals: 15% in reading, 9% in writing, and 22% in mathematics. Levels of instruction at the Batchelder School were consistent with the students' low achievement, with no algebra and no foreign languages offered at the upper grades.

Although these figures depict a poor inner-city school and community, Batchelder School and the surrounding neighborhood present a decidedly more favorable impression. The school itself is a pleasant, modern two-story building with spacious and airy classrooms, set in ample green space. Much of the immediately surrounding area looks like a prototypical 1950s middle-class neighborhood, with small single-family homes set prettily in fenced yards, many with flower gardens and decorative shrubs. In fact, this area was just that until fairly recently—within memory of many of the teachers at the school. The changes in the school community reflect larger trends in the city of Hartford, which has hosted a new influx of immigrants (mostly Hispanic) while also suffering an economic downturn.

The GEAR UP Families

To get to know the families in the GEAR UP project, we interviewed parents in their homes about their backgrounds, their involvement with their children's education, and their perceptions of their children. Table 10.1 provides a demographic profile of these children and their families, based on the first 55 families (almost half the entire cohort in the GEAR UP program) that we interviewed when the children were in sixth and seventh grades. As shown in table 10.1, both mother and father (or stepfather) were present in almost half the families, while most of the others were mother-headed households. The majority of the parents, especially the fathers, were immigrants, having arrived mainly from Puerto Rico. Of those who had grown up in the United States, most had lived only in Hartford: there seemed to be little mobility within the new country of residence. English was reported to be the primary language spoken in almost half the homes, with most of the remainder speaking both English or Spanish, or exclusively Spanish. The level of education of these parents varied from some high school to completion of a four-year college, but two-thirds of the mothers and three-fourths of the fathers had only a high school education or less.

Table 10.1. GEAR UP Children's Families

Child lives with:	
Mother and father	36%
Parent and stepparent	11%
Mother only	43%
Father only	2%
Other relatives/friends	19%
Number of people in household:	
2	4%
3–5	82%
6–7	14%
Mother's place of origin:	
Puerto Rico	47%
Other Latin American country	8%
Other country outside Latin America	6%
Hartford	32%
Other place in United States	8%
Father's place of origin:	
Puerto Rico	45%
Other Latin American country	10%
Other country outside Latin America	15%
Hartford	21%
Other place in United States	9%
Language spoken at home:	
English	45%
English and Spanish	24%
Spanish	29%
Other	2%
Mother's education:	
Less than completed high school	34%
Completed high school	32%
Some college/technical school	30%
Four-year college or more	4%
Father's education:	
Less than completed high school	34%
Completed high school	41%
Some college/technical school	25%

Parental Involvement with Their Children's Education

Since a central mission of the GEAR UP project was to promote children's success in school and eventual continuation on to postsecondary education, we were interested to learn about how these parents communicated with their children and with their children's schools regarding academic progress and educational goals. As shown in table 10.2, over one-third of these parents of middle-school children said they had emphasized the importance of continuing their education beyond high school, and parents reported in equal measure that they had initiated conversation on the subject. In addition, the same proportion of parents said that their children had initiated conversations with them about going to college. Only one-fifth of the parents said that they had not talked about college with their children. Almost all the parents reported supporting their children's homework—whether by actual helping, checking it over, or simply asking whether it was done. Despite their involvement with children's education at home, however, frequency of parental contact with the school was low: over half the families said they had contact only once or twice a year. Forty percent of the parents did report having contact with teachers once a month or more, but this was mainly related to children's problems at school. Consistent with this pattern, the nature of parent-school contacts was also quite limited, consisting mainly of formal parent-teacher conferences (the school had recently introduced a new policy whereby parents were required to go to the school to pick up their child's report card from the teacher). About one-fifth of the parents reported having informal contacts with the teachers in school, but none said they had such contacts outside the school. About one-fifth of the parents also reported having phone contacts with teachers and an equal proportion said they were in contact with teachers "as needed"—in order to deal with their child's academic or behavioral problems in school. Only a few parents were involved with the Parent-Teacher Association and few reported coming to school events. It should be added, however, that school events had been largely cut back in response to the new demands of the central administration for more effort on preparation for the standardized tests. Finally, it appears that the great majority of parents at this school had little or no contact with one another.

In summary, these families did not look very different from middle-class families in some respects: although there were many single-parent households, there was also a strong constituency of two-parent families. Al-

Table 10.2. Parental Involvement in Children's Education

Parent-child communication about college:	
Parent emphasizes importance	39%
Parent initiates conversation	35%
Child initiates conversation	37%
No parent-child communication	20%
Involvement with homework:	
Helps	25%
Looks at /reviews	37%
Asks if homework is done	26%
Does not monitor	12%
Frequency of contact with school:	
Once or twice a year	60%
Once a month	25%
Once a week or more	15%
Type of contacts with school:	
Parent-Teacher Association	6%
School events	10%
Formal meetings with teacher	90%
Other meetings/phone conversations	50%
Informally with teacher at school	15%
Contact with other parents at school:	
Little to no contact	84%
Familiar with 2 – 4 other families	12%
Familiar with more than 4 families	4%

though the parents' own educational backgrounds were limited mostly to high school, they professed to be involved in monitoring their children's homework, and some were in frequent contact with teachers concerning their children's current issues at school. The most striking difference between these parents and middle-class parents was evident in the low rates of communication *not* related to problems at school, as well as little contact with other parents. In combination with language barriers between some families and teachers, it appeared that there had not been enough opportunity to build a sense of community around the school. Parents and teachers had not had a context of ongoing interaction within which to form constructive, trusting, and mutually respectful relationships. Without such relationships between the developmental niches of home and school, the children lacked support for developing and maintaining appropriate behavior in school and being academically successful.

Parents' Perceptions of Their Children's Strengths and Needs

The home-school issues that are evident in the parent interviews are also reflected in parents' perceptions of their children's strengths and needs as they described them to us. An analysis of the free descriptions provided by the parents shows an interesting pattern, as suggested in tables 10.3 and 10.4. Few parents described their children as having specific academic strengths such as math, reading, and writing; in contrast, almost half the parents mentioned their children's need for improvement in math, and one-third mentioned problems in reading. The proportion of children described as being well-behaved in school was balanced by an equal number who seemed to be having behavior problems or difficulty with particular teachers. Parents' mentions of good motivation for school were also balanced by negative assessments. Interestingly, however, many parents de-

Table 10.3. Child Strengths Mentioned by Parents

Domain	Percent of parents mentioning
Good academics:	
Math	13%
Reading	4%
Writing	2%
Science	6%
Arts	16%
Good grades	11%
Good school behavior:	
Well-behaved in school	13%
Likes school	18%
Athletic	31%
Good aptitude/motivation:	
Smart	22%
Works hard	22%
Motivated to learn	13%
Learns quickly	5%
Calm, focused	13%
Good social behavior:	
Gets along well with others	11%
Helpful	20%
Caring	27%
Good manners	27%
Cooperative/obedient	11%

Table 10.4. Child Problems Mentioned by Parents

Domain	Percent of parents mentioning
Academic problems:	
Math	47%
Reading	33%
Writing	15%
Science	16%
Social studies	7%
Poor grades	11%
School behavior problems:	
Behavior problems in school	18%
Difficulty with teachers	15%
Motivation problems:	
Lacks motivation for school	22%
Problems with concentration	5%
Disorganized	9%
Social behavior problems:	
Behavior problems at home	9%
Withdrawn	5%
Affected by family issues	11%
Anger/temper	9%

scribed their children as having good aptitude and motivation for learning, including being smart, being motivated to learn, working hard, learning quickly, or being calm and focused. Parents also described their children more in terms of positive social behavior at home, such as getting along well with others, being helpful or caring, having good manners, and being compliant, than in negative terms related to interpersonal behavior or issues. In general, it is evident that academic problems far exceed academic success, and school problems are mentioned slightly more often than good behavior at school. Nevertheless, parents' attributions regarding their children's aptitudes and motivation are high in comparison with motivation problems; and the great majority of the children were described as having positive social qualities.

Thus, the GEAR UP parents perceived their children—accurately—as having problems at school; but they also saw them in general as having good aptitudes and motivation and as being positive members of the family and community outside the school. One unfortunate consequence of the lack of communication between home and school was that teachers rarely had the opportunity to see the children in this more favorable light. Using the developmental niche framework, it becomes clear that the GEAR UP children were experiencing sharp discontinuities between their home and school environments, including notably the psychologies of the caretakers as exemplified in how their parents and teachers perceived them. The physical and social settings of the children's daily lives, as we came to know, lacked the variety of organized after-school activities typical of suburban children today, and in addition their access to informal play with friends in the neighborhood was curtailed by their parents' well-founded apprehensions about the dangers of drugs and gangs. Finally, the customs of care for many of these children included being in charge of younger siblings or being cared for in turn by relatives; family routines such as dinnertime were often affected by parents' work schedules, which in many cases also curtailed children's time with their parents. Even when parents were present, the limitations of their own educational backgrounds made it difficult to provide these children with effective academic support. Without a strong partnership role for parents within the school, the children's education was limited—not as strong or as full as it should be (Fuller and Olsen 1998).

Interventions in the Developmental Niche

A major assumption underlying the family-centered approach derived from the developmental niche framework was that the child and family must be viewed as interactive parts of a system (or unit), such that an effect on one would affect the other (McWilliam, Maxwell, and Sloper 1999). As the family is the main context for a child's learning and development, we predicted that interventions for both the family and the child would have a larger impact than those focused on only the child. As McWilliam, Maxwell, and Sloper suggest, "Although people often think of school readiness in terms of children being ready for the school, it also means that schools should be ready for children and their families" (1999, 378).

The purposes of child and family mentoring and the related activities of the GEAR UP project were thus to work with the subsystems of the developmental niche relevant to the production of the child's skills for succeeding in school. We hypothesized that children's performance in school would be best supported by being exposed to consistent, stable adults who were emotionally invested in them; to a physical environment that was safe and predictable; to regular routines and rhythms of activity; to competent peers; and to materials that would stimulate their exploration and enjoyment of the object world (Pianta and Walsh 1996). As Pianta (1999) has suggested, for children who are exposed to social stressors such as lack of supervision, family stress, divorce, unpredictable or unstimulating environments, or poor childcare or maltreatment, the quality of social experiences—specifically relationships with adults—has accounted for links between these social stressors and poor school outcomes. Relationships with adults form the foundation that supports nearly all of what a child is asked to do in school: be persistent and focused, stay motivated to perform, be compliant or assertive, communicate, and explore the world. In this view, child competence is often embedded in and a property of relationships with adults.

Mentored youth, in addition to showing positive change in grades, in perceived scholastic competence, truancy rates, and substance use, are also more likely to report improved parent and peer relationships (Rhodes, Grossman, and Resch 2000). Through the experience of a trusting and consistently supportive mentor relationship, adolescents are able to modify or "correct" their perceptions of other relationships (i.e., challenge a negative view) and gradually build more trusting, caring bonds with a parent as well as with their peer group. Rhodes, Grossman, and Resch (2000) emphasize that to the extent that mentors and parents can work together (i.e., parents feel involved in, rather than supplanted by, the mentoring relationship), adolescents are more likely to show improvements in multiple domains. Childhood friendships are also critical, as they provide an important source of companionship, personal guidance, and emotional support (Doll 1996). Interventions designed to facilitate satisfying friendships can insulate students against deleterious effects. Many developmental researchers insist that social competence (i.e., within peer groups and friendships) needs to be recognized as a core responsibility of schooling (Doll 1996).

It is through these relationships with mentors, parents, and peers that the social behavior, self-control, and achievement motivation of a child can be improved and also through which an intervention can be delivered. Pianta (1999) has suggested that parallel or integrated efforts to improve or develop a relationship between an adult and a child will almost always have the added benefit of improving the child's response to any intervention or enrichment program. Similarly, Styles and Morrow (1995) concluded in their examination of mentoring relationships that it was the experience of the supportive relationship as opposed to a mentor's focus on specific goals that predicted better outcomes among youth.

A first priority for the Family Studies component of the GEAR UP project, thus, was to help improve relationships between the children and the school, to provide them with opportunities for more interesting after-school activities, and to offer them new opportunities for meaningful relationships with other adults. In pursuit of these goals, the GEAR UP project provided a number of after-school, weekend, and summer school interests clubs and activities. The school-based clubs, organized by University of Connecticut undergraduates who became interns in the GEAR UP project, included a wide range of different activities: drama, drumming, cooking, world cultures, chess, and gardening, to name only a few. Saturday activities featured a hiking club and a bird-watching club as well as sports. During the summer, GEAR UP supplemented a morning academic program with recreation and field trips in the afternoons. Special activities included a jobs club and a Red Cross babysitting course. Participation in the activities was voluntary, but approximately two-thirds of the children in both cohorts were involved on a regular basis. The group activities provided an opportunity for GEAR UP leaders to get to know the children better, resulting in other small-group or individual activities such as going out to lunch or the movies or attending a college basketball game.

Families also became involved through participation of younger siblings in the activities and through parents helping as chaperones on field trips or with the Saturday sports activities. Furthermore, the parent interviews described above turned out to be an important intervention in and of themselves. Through the interviews, parents learned at firsthand about our interest in building a partnership with them. By showing care and interest in both the child and the family, and by taking the initiative to establish an egalitarian relationship, the interviewers were able to create a comfortable exchange of information and ideas. The children also appeared quite impressed with the presence of an adult from the school context in their homes. A typical result of the interview was increased participation of the child—and often siblings—in the various GEAR UP activities. The interviews also paved the way for further informal parent communication with GEAR UP leaders.

The positive socioemotional climate created by these activities and contacts laid the groundwork for more focused academic interventions, including activities to raise awareness of college, and an ongoing mentoring program in which students meet regularly with GEAR UP leaders to talk about their experience in school, to assess progress, and to address problems in consultation with teachers and parents.

Entering the Developmental Niches of Children in Need: Two Case Studies

As we came to know the GEAR UP children, it became apparent that there was a wide range of needs. Some children were doing well both at home and at school, while others were struggling in one or both contexts (interestingly, we found examples of both in the same families). Two children, Rosa and Rafael (not their real names), were of special concern to us during our first two years, and we present the stories of our involvement with them as illustrations of what can be learned through intervention in the developmental niche.

Rosa: Creating a "Walking Milieu" for a Child in Crisis

Rosa was referred to us for individual help when she was in the seventh grade, the second year of her involvement in the GEAR UP project. The second of three children, Rosa lived with her mother, an older teenage sister, her sister's baby, and her younger brother. Rosa, an attractive but unruly child, had been a challenge both at home and at school. Her mother's previous struggle with drug addiction had interfered with parenting at times, and the teachers already were familiar with Rosa as a child who sometimes arrived in school unkempt and hungry. By the time we met the family, Rosa's mother was doing better and things seemed more hopeful for the children. This all changed when Rosa was raped by an older acquaintance in their neighborhood. At this point, Rosa's behavior in school became dramatically more provocative to the point that it was interfering with her academic performance as well as putting a strain on the rest of the class. At home, she was losing her temper, threatening family members with a knife, staying out late without permission, and hurting herself.

The third author, a psychiatric nurse, took responsibility for arranging help through the GEAR UP project's holistic approach as framed by the developmental niche. This strategy fit well with the nursing discipline's concept of creating a "walking milieu," analogous to outreach in ambulatory pediatric care. In this context, the goals were to engage the child and her family in their own space and family context, to begin to explore the difficult issues, and to support the family's areas of strength to create movement toward healthy outcomes. Specifically, the approach was oriented to assist Rosa and her family to make changes in their settings and customs of daily life that could enhance and speed their ability to develop new ways of dealing with life events. This intervention—an adjunct to formal mental health services—had the flexibility to meet the family's needs as they arose and to provide helping relationships apart from institutions that might be problematic for the family.

Rosa, suffering from post–traumatic stress disorder, needed a stabilizing therapeutic relationship. An additional need for GEAR UP was to make a positive connection with Rosa's mother and help her advocate for her daughter with the health care system and the Hartford school system—a change in psychology of the caretaker, the third component of the niche. A psychiatric nursing student was assigned as a mentor to work with both Rosa and her mother, becoming a trusted member of the household through her frequent informal contacts and activities. Events moved rapidly, alternating between hopeful developments for Rosa and times when she became suicidal; at one point she disappeared altogether for a night. The mentor and her supervisor became directly involved in helping to arrange hospitalization for Rosa on three occasions and were also involved in conferences with the school to arrange an appropriate placement for Rosa. The mentor assisted the family in managing an emergency when an acquaintance broke into their home and beat a cousin severely in front of two younger children. The mentor, who had arrived home with the family to find the cousin unconscious and bleeding, called the police, helped the family to safety from a threatened return attack, and facilitated follow-up with Rosa, who was hospitalized at the time.

As participants in Rosa's developmental niche during this time, we became aware of the issues raised by recent cutbacks in psychiatric care, a situation that would have left Rosa and her family on their own at moments of great vulnerability had it not been for our intervention. As it was, the mentor helped Rosa to achieve periods of stabilization and helped her mother to advocate more effectively for her care and education. At the end of the academic year, Rosa's family moved out of the school district to seek a safer living environment.

Rafael: Mentoring a Multiply Challenged Child and His Family

To his teachers, sixth-grade Rafael was both a favorite and a constant source of irritation. An academically gifted child as indicated by his performance on standardized tests, Rafael nonetheless seemed unable to concentrate effectively in class, choosing instead to entertain his classmates by clowning around, teasing, and being markedly inattentive. He presented the kind of behavioral profile that demanded medication for attention deficit/hyperactivity disorder (ADHD), and his teachers were frustrated that Rafael's mother had refused to follow their advice in requesting medication from the family doctor. What the teachers did not know—but as we learned in a short time—was that Rafael was also the "man of the house" at home, a primary source of emotional support to his mother at a time of family crisis. Rafael's father was one of the Connecticut prisoners who had recently been transferred to a notorious high-security prison in Virginia due to overcrowding in local state prisons. When we first met Rafael's mother in the context of a family interview, it quickly became apparent that Rafael's family exemplified the kind of multiproblem situation that has been noted in studies of families in economic distress. In addition to coping with their father's removal from a nearby family-friendly prison to a distant and dangerous one, both Rafael and his younger sister Elena were having behavioral problems at school. Having resisted putting Rafael on drugs for ADHD, their mother was now under intense pressure from Elena's teacher to do the same for her. The mother, an intelligent and sensitive woman, was effective in advocating for her husband and her children but lacked confidence in her ability to pursue her own educational and career goals. Their extended family, who lived between Puerto Rico and Hartford, was a source of both support and stress on a daily basis.

It seemed to us that in order to help Rafael, we needed to help his family and particularly his mother. Within a short period of time, the first author had become a family mentor who, with the family's encouragement, attempted to address issues across several domains. She helped Rafael to write a statement that would be read in front of television cameras at a rally on behalf of prisoners sent to Virginia. She arranged for Elena to be assessed for ADHD at a local teaching hospital and watched the process (the evaluators recommended changes in her school environment but not medication). She organized support at her church for bringing attention to the problem of prisoners such as Rafael's father and worked with a state senator to press for his return to Connecticut. She helped Rafael's mother enroll in courses at the University of Connecticut and coached her through term papers and test preparations. She spent time as a mentor with Rafael in school and out and invited the whole family to her home. She and Rafael's mother had frequent conversations on the phone and in person about all the issues surrounding the family.

Eventually, Rafael's father was brought back to a nearby prison where the family could visit him regularly. The first author also went to visit him and learned at firsthand why he was the anchor of the family despite his prisoner status. Rafael's father was by now taking several college courses, and as Rafael told the first author, "All my dad asks is that I do well in school and stay out of trouble." Rafael's behavior in school had improved considerably and he was now an honor roll student, though there were still lapses. Rafael's mother arranged for Elena to attend a new magnet school in their area, where she was happier and more appreciated by her teacher. At home, family routines were becoming more stable and the family developed a new evening activity of reading from the Bible and praying together. Rafael, now in eighth grade, decided to run for president of the class and planned, if elected, to give a speech at graduation that his father had written but never had a chance to deliver for a graduation ceremony in prison.

Being at the same time an ethnographer and mentor for Rafael and his family gave us a sense of immediacy about the many issues confronting families at risk. Using the developmental niche framework enabled us to locate these issues in different parts of a dynamic system. Features of the larger environment, including the Connecticut prison system, had a major impact on Rafael's physical and social settings of daily life (not having his father at home) and also through the changes wrought in family routines without a father present. Customs of care were also disrupted by the absence of a father who had been (and in fact continued to be) closely involved in the care and education of the children. A key component of Rafael's developmental niche, the psychology of the caretakers, was also negatively affected by the impact of his father's continued absence on his mother's ability to cope with multiple challenges on her own. The school, as a developmental niche, also presented challenges in each domain: strict routines unsuited to active and distractible children; rigid disciplinary practices; and teachers' perceptions of Rafael as hyperactive and in need of medication. The poor communication between Rafael's home and school, evident in teachers' surprising ignorance of Rafael's efforts on behalf of his father, made it difficult for Rafael's mother and his teachers to work together in creating the kind of environmental redundancy that characterizes effective developmental niches. In this situation, we chose to address several areas of the developmental niches of home and school concurrently, in hopes of tipping the balance toward a more positive developmental outcome. Whether through our efforts, through natural developmental change, or through other changes in Rafael's environment, it appears that this goal was accomplished at least in part.

Conclusions: Mixed Methods in an Intervention Study with Children at Risk

During our early involvement in the GEAR UP project, as documented here, we had many different opportunities to learn about the children, their school, and their families. The family interviews provided quantitative and qualitative indicators of the children's cultural and educational backgrounds, their parents' concerns, and the relationships between home and school. The most salient finding from these interviews was the apparent lack of connection between home and school, and our experiences with Rosa, Rafael, and other children provided cases in point to illustrate this reality. It was striking to us, for example, that although Rafael was featured in the evening news on television and was quoted in the local newspaper, his teachers were unaware and, more surprisingly, seemed uninterested in his activities on behalf of his father and other prisoners. Our experiences with particular children also led us to observe that although their parents' ideas might not be so different from those of middle-class parents, the differences in outcome for the family and the children seemed to be attributable to the myriad of challenges, both external and internal, that confronted these families on a daily basis. The strength of our method for making such interpretations lay in exploring multiple aspects of the children's developmental niches both at home and at school. As participant observers and actors in multiple contexts, we were able to derive a fuller picture of the children's life circumstances than any of the participants in the niche had themselves.

Using the developmental niche framework for this project has allowed us to conceptualize children's pathways of development as they are determined by the culturally structured landscape. In this framework, basic processes such as cognitive and physical changes in early adolescence set the developmental agenda for all children; and individual differences in such areas as temperament and intelligence provide different possibilities of interaction with the environment. A focus on the environment itself, however, illustrates that it too functions in developmental time. In this regard, aspects of the children's developmental niches at school need to be examined carefully to discern whether the messages that children are receiving as they move from one grade or teacher to the next are basically encouraging and supportive, as well as developmentally appropriate. In addition, disparities between the developmental niches of home and school need to be addressed continuously so that the niches can operate in a harmonious and developmentally supportive manner. Our experience in entering the developmental niches of children, families, and classrooms through the GEAR UP project took us a considerable distance from our home base in academic cross-cultural studies. Becoming involved so closely in the lives of a few children and families in need was an experience that involved us emotionally as fellow human beings as well as scientists and practitioners. Obviously, it would be impossible for us to become involved at that level with all families in the project; but our experiences underlined the importance of a holistic approach to intervention, one that must rely on a variety of methods from different disciplines. The developmental niche provided a framework that was sufficiently encompassing and flexible to incorporate approaches drawn from other disciplinary traditions such as nursing and education.

Our central finding on the lack of communication and "fit" between the worlds of home and school for this population is consistent with the results of other studies carried out in several disciplinary traditions, as we have described above. The developmental niche framework has allowed us to parse these problems into their component parts: physical and social settings of daily life at home and at school, customary practices related to education and development in each place, and ideas of parents and teachers that give both settings and customs meaning. Structuring knowledge of the children's environments of learning and development this way provides, in turn, a blueprint for how and where to intervene. Like the theory itself, intervention based on the developmental niche framework includes many different kinds of activities in a variety of contexts—a mixed-methods intervention reflecting the characteristics and needs of the children, their families, and their schools rather than the traditions of any single discipline.

References

Bronfenbrenner, U. 1979. "Contexts of Child Rearing: Problems and Prospects." *American Psychologist* 34:844–850.

Campbell, D. T. 1955. "The Informant in Quantitative Research." *American Journal of Sociology* 60:339–342.

———. 1961. "The Mutual Methodological Relevance of Anthropology and Psychology." In *Psychological Anthropology: Approaches to Culture and Personality,* ed. F. L. K. Hsu. Homewood, IL: Dorsey Press.

Campbell, D. T., and D. W. Fiske. 1959. "Convergent and Discriminant Validation by the Multitrait-Multimethod Matrix." *Psychological Bulletin* 56:81–105.

Campbell, D. T., and E. S. Overman, eds. 1988. *Methodology and Epistemology for Social Science: Selected Papers.* Chicago: University of Chicago Press.

Doll, B. 1996. "Children without Friends: Implications for Practice and Policy." *School Psychology Review* 25:165–183.

Eccles, J., and R. D. Harold. 1996. "Family Involvement in Children's and Adolescents' Schooling." In *Family-School Links: How Do They Affect Educational Outcomes?* ed. A. Booth and J. F. Dunn, 3–34. Mahwah, NJ: Erlbaum.

Epstein, J. L. 1987. "What Principals Should Know about Parent Involvement." *Principal* 66 (3): 6–9.

———. 1996. "Perspectives and Previews on Research and Policy for School, Family, and Community Partnerships." In *Family-School Links: How Do They Affect Educational Outcomes?* Ed. A. Booth and J. F. Dunn, 209–246. Mahwah, NJ: Erlbaum.

Finn-Stevenson, M., and B. M. Stern. 1997. "Integrating Early-Childhood and Family-Support Services with a School Improvement Process: The Comer-Zigler Initiative." *Elementary School Journal* 98:51–66.

Fuller, M. L., and G. Olsen. 1998. *Home-School Relations.* Boston: Allyn and Bacon.

Graue, M. E. 1993. "Social Networks and Home-School Relations." *Educational Policy* 7:466–490.

Grolnick, W. S., and M. L. Slowiaczek. 1994. "Parents' Involvement in Children's Schooling: A Multidimensional Conceptualization and Motivational Model." *Child Development* 65:237–252.

Harkness, S., and C. M. Super. 1987. "The Uses of Cross-cultural Research in Child Development." *Annals of Child Development* 4:209–244.

———. 1995. "Culture and Parenting." In *Handbook of Parenting,* vol. 2, *Biology and Ecology of Parenting,* ed. M. H. Bornstein, 211–234. Hillsdale, NJ: Erlbaum.

———. 1999. "From Parents' Cultural Belief Systems to Behavior: Implications for the Development of Early Intervention Programs." In *Effective Early Education: Cross-cultural Perspectives,* ed. L. Eldering and P. Leseman, 67–90. New York: Falmer Press.

Jahoda, G. 1993. *Crossroads between Culture and Mind: Continuities and Change in Theories of Human Nature.* Cambridge: Harvard University Press.

Kidder, L. H. 1981. "Qualitative Research and Quasi-experimental Frameworks." In *Scientific Inquiry and the Social Sciences: A Volume in Honor of Donald T. Campbell,* ed. M. B. Brewer and B. E. Collins, 226–256. San Francisco: Jossey-Bass.

Lareau, A. 2000. *Home Advantage: Social Class and Parental Intervention in Elementary Education.* 2nd ed. New York: Rowman and Littlefield.

LeVine, R. A., S. Dixon, S. LeVine, A. Richman, P. H. Leiderman, C. H. Keefer, and T. B. Brazelton. 1994. *Child Care and Culture: Lessons from Africa.* New York: Cambridge University Press.

LeVine, R. E. 1981. "Knowledge and Fallibility in Anthropological Field Research." In *Scientific Inquiry and the Social Sciences: A Volume in Honor of Donald T. Campbell,* ed. M. B. Brewer and B. E. Collins, 172–193. San Francisco: Jossey-Bass.

McWilliam, R. A., K. L. Maxwell, and K. M. Sloper. 1999. "Beyond 'Involvement': Are Elementary Schools Ready to Be Family-Centered?" *School Psychology Review* 28:378–394.

Meyers, R. 1992. *The Twelve Who Survive: Strengthening Programmes of Early Childhood Development in the Third World.* New York: Routledge.

Pianta, R. C. 1999. *High-Risk Children in Schools.* New York: Routledge.

Pianta, R. C., and D. Walsh. 1996. *High-Risk Children in the Schools: Creating Sustaining Relationships.* New York: Routledge.

Rhodes, J. E., J. B. Grossman, and N. Resch. 2000. "Agents to Change: Pathways through Which Mentoring Relationships Influence Adolescents' Academic Adjustment." *Child Development* 71:1662–1671.

Styles, M. B., and K. V. Morrow. 1995. *Understanding How Youth and Elders Form Relationships: A Study of Four Linking Lifetimes Programs.* Philadelphia: Public/Private Ventures.

Super, C. M., and S. Harkness. 1997. "The Cultural Structuring of Child Development." In *Handbook of Cross-cultural Psychology,* vol. 2, *Basic Processes and Developmental Psychology,* 2nd ed., ed. J. Berry, P. Dasen, and T. S. Saraswathi, 1–39. Boston: Allyn and Bacon.

———. 1999. "The Environment as Culture in Developmental Research." In *Measuring Environment across the Life Span: Emerging Methods and Concepts,* ed. S. L. Friedman and T. D. Wachs, 279–323. Washington, DC: American Psychological Association.

Super, C. M., S. Harkness, N. van Tijen, and E. van der Vlugt. 1996. "The Three R's of Dutch Child Rearing and the Socialization of Infant State." In *Parents' Cultural Belief Systems: Their Origins, Expressions, and Consequences,* ed. S. Harkness and C. M. Super, 447–466. New York: Guilford Press.

Valdes, G. 1996. *Con Respeto: Bridging the Distances between Culturally Diverse Families and Schools.* New York: Teachers' College.

Whiting, B. B., and C. P. Edwards. 1988. *Children of Different Worlds: The Formation of Social Behavior.* Cambridge: Harvard University Press.

Whiting, B. B., and J. W. M. Whiting. 1975. *Children of Six Cultures: A Psychocultural Analysis.* Cambridge: Harvard University Press.

11

Including Latino Immigrant Families, Schools, and Community Programs as Research Partners on the Good Path of Life (*El Buen Camino de la Vida*)

Catherine R. Cooper, Jane Brown, Margarita Azmitia, and Gabriela Chavira

In industrialized countries, students' pathways through school to work have been described as an academic pipeline. Many democracies have laws regarding equal access to education, and each class of 5-year-olds begins school representing their community's demographics. But so many low-income, ethnic-minority, and immigrant youth — especially males — leave school and its career opportunities that as 20-year-olds, they are less likely to be in college and more likely to be in prison than middle-income, ethnic-majority youth. As immigrant and ethnic-minority youth make up growing segments of school enrollments and populations in many nations, the *academic pipeline problem* has emerged as immigrants, refugees, and guest workers remain in host countries and try sending their children through school. A college education is not the only definition of success in life, but in all ethnic groups education is strongly linked to income, and youth who leave school with low skills face lives of poverty that may lead them toward illegal work. Most programs to address the academic pipeline problem focus on early childhood or the years from high school to college, with only a few focusing on childhood. Still, after years of civil rights laws, programs, and policies, progress has stalled, so new coalitions are working on the academic pipeline problem, and scholars are rethinking theories, research methods, and their relationships with research participants.

Rethinking Theories: Capital, Alienation, Ecocultural, and Challenge Models

Debates on ethnic diversity, inclusion, and schooling reach across the social sciences, with scholars participating actively in these interdisciplinary coalitions around the pipeline problem (Cooper and Denner 1998). *Capital* models suggest that children with college-educated parents develop college-based career identities and achieve at higher levels than those whose parents have less education, thereby reproducing social hierarchies from one generation to the next (Coleman 1988). *Alienation* models (Fordham and Ogbu 1986) argue that racial and economic barriers dim ethnic-minority parents' high hopes for their children's future and their families' upward mobility. These barriers also foster their children's oppositional identities that affirm ties with peers and buffer against failure in school and work. *Ecocultural* models, based on Vygotsky's sociohistorical analysis of cultural continuity and change, suggest that all families have tools for adaptation and well-being for children that foster change or continuity across contexts (Reese et al. 1995; Weisner, Gallimore, and Jordan 1993). Variations in families' circumstances, goals, and adaptation strategies are associated with variations in school performance. And *challenge* models, such as the Bridging Multiple Worlds Model (Cooper 1999), suggest that challenges such as immigration, poverty, or racism can motivate children and youth to succeed on behalf of families and communities and prove gatekeepers wrong, and that challenges in the context of support foster career and college identity formation.

The Bridging Multiple Worlds Model links concepts from anthropology, psychology, sociology, economics, and education to discover how youth navigate their worlds of families, peers, schools, and communities in identity development and pathways to adulthood. This multilevel model maps how individuals, relationships, institutions, and cultural communities can each serve as a bridge across worlds as students move along these pathways. Although past research on ethnic diversity and the pipeline problem has focused on dropouts, new research asks under what conditions immigrant, low-income, and ethnic-minority students persist and succeed in school. This model predicts that students who coordinate resources with challenges will be more successful navigating their personal, relational, institutional, and cultural pathways to college and adult work and family roles. Five key elements are highlighted in the model:

1. *Demographics along the academic pipeline*—of families' national origin, ethnicity, home languages, education, and occupation—reflect diversity and equity in access to education from childhood to college.
2. *Children's identity pathways* to college, careers, and family roles start in childhood and link generations.
3. *Children's math and language academic pathways* to college and careers start in childhood and emerge in five patterns: consistently high, declining, "back on track" (declining, then increasing), increasing, and persisting with low grades.
4. *Challenges and resources exist across children's worlds* of families, peers, schools, and communities.
5. *Cultural research partnerships* reach across lines of national origin, ethnicity, social class, and gender; they can boost resources across worlds for pathways to college and connect children, families, schools, community programs, and university staff all as researchers.

In collaboration with colleagues and students, we have conducted a series of studies to test, clarify, and apply the Bridging Multiple Worlds Model in communities with diverse cultural and ethnic groups, including American youth of African, Chinese, Filipino, Latino, European, Japanese, and Vietnamese descent as well as Japanese youth (Cooper 1999; Cooper et al. 2002). We traced math pathways from three samples (academically *inclusive* school-based samples, *selective* programs, and *competitive* programs) and mapped variation within cultural groups and similarities and differences across groups (Cooper 2001).

This chapter focuses on two of these studies. Study 1 involves an *inclusive* school-based sample of 100 low-income Mexican American and European American children whom we followed as they moved from elementary to middle school (Azmitia and Brown 2002; Azmitia et al. 1996; Azmitia and Cooper 2001). We traced continuity and change in the aspirations of the parents and children as well as parents' guidance toward attaining these goals. Study 2, part of the MacArthur Foundation California Childhoods Project, involves over 500 youth in the Cabrillo Advancement

Program (CAP), a *selective* community college outreach program that awards scholarships to sixth-grade students from low-income families and offers activities to help students stay on track to college (Cooper, Denner, and Lopez 1999). In this chapter we draw from these two studies to show how mixed-methods research advances science, policy, practice, and inclusiveness for successful pathways through childhood.

Inclusion and Mixed Methods: Two Approaches

In studying inclusion in educational opportunities among ethnically diverse youth and families, we have found two mixed-methods approaches especially valuable: linking longitudinal case studies to quantitative variable-based analysis and building *interpretive cycles* in cultural research partnerships. These partnerships reach across lines between community insiders and outsiders and among science, policy, and practice and across levels of analysis from cultural communities to institutions, relationships, and individuals over time (Cooper 1997; Denner et al. 1999). These two approaches not only build pathways to college for youth and families but, by using them together, strengthen *ecological validity* by considering local meanings and *external validity* by comparing within and across groups through statistical analyses.

Linking Variable- to Case-Based Analyses over Time

In comparing models of pathways through childhood, we have assessed group patterns through variable-based longitudinal analyses and developed longitudinal case studies to map configurations of demographics, identities, resources, and challenges across worlds in predicting each child's academic pathway. We draw on qualitative case study methods (Mertens 1994) to conduct theory-based work, in which scholars develop research questions from theoretical models; derive hypotheses from models; specify units of analysis; map the logic linking hypotheses to data and criteria to interpret findings; specify methods, including samples, measures, and data analysis; report results by mapping data in terms of hypotheses or questions; and discuss findings by linking data to the original model, refining the model, and comparing findings with other models. These steps are typical of quantitative analyses but are not always applied in case studies. We also use Qualitative Comparative Analysis (QCA; Ragin 1994) in Study 2.

Cultural Research Partnerships and the Interpretive Cycle

We conducted individual and group interviews to develop surveys that include open-ended questions, and we used multivariate statistical analyses with Prediction Analysis (von Eye and Brandtstadter 1988) and QCA (Ragin 1994) to examine students and families as cases. This cycle includes participants' and researchers' insights about both quantitative and qualitative findings. Participants' reflections deepen our understanding of poverty, immigration, racism, early parenting, incarceration, physical disability, and gender, and how, paradoxically, such obstacles are also resources for some youth when they operate—in the words of one program director—as "good burdens" that motivate students to succeed. We use these reflections in analyzing our initial qualitative and quantitative results. These mixed-methods strategies have led to productive revisions of our model, measures, and applications. Getting quantitative methods to capture what we know qualitatively as part of traditional science is usually not discussed in published articles. Although scholars have done this for years as pilot work, formalizing and presenting this cycle strengthen our science, policy, and practice (Greene and Caracelli 1997).

Study 1, Latino Immigrant Parents' Beliefs about and Guidance for Their Children's Good Path of Life

A recent study by members of our Study 1 research team focused on parents' concepts of the "good path of life (*el buen camino de la vida*)—first studied by Reese et al. (1995). (The following discussion draws extensively on Azmitia and Brown 2002.) The concept of the "good path of life" is common across many cultural communities. Reese and colleagues found that Latino parents spontaneously offered beliefs about the path of life when answering questions about their hopes and dreams for their children's futures. Parents mentioned challenges children faced staying on the good path of life and guidance they used to help them. They also held high aspirations for their children's education (Cooper et al. 1994; Goldenberg and Gallimore 1995; Henderson 1997) that were part of their beliefs about moral development (Delgado-Gaitán 1992; Reese et al. 1995; Valdés 1996). In particular, immigrant Latino parents articulated a concept of *educación* that was broader than what the English word "education" conveys, with moral development as its central component and school achievement only one element. Parents used the metaphor of following the good path of life, *el buen camino de la vida,* to explain their goals as a set of beliefs that related moral development to schooling and more general positive and negative development. In figure 1.1, Goldenberg, Gallimore, and Reese (chap. 1, this volume) show the embedded nature of moral and academic well-being in the concept of the good path of life.

We built on the work of Reese and her colleagues to investigate two key questions. First, we examined parents' *descriptions and definitions* of the good and bad paths of life for their own children as they moved from childhood to early adolescence, parents' *explanations* for where and how they placed their children on the path of life, the *challenges* they saw ahead for their children, and what *guidance* they used along the path, through crossroads, or to help their children get back on the path. In contrast to Reese et al.'s interviews with parents of younger children, we focused on parents of older children in the transition to adolescence. This time is especially salient for immigrant Latino parents, who have expressed concern that in the United States, older children spend more time outside the family and under the influence of "malas compañías" (bad influences, typically peers) than in their home countries (Kroesen, Reese, and Gallimore 1998).

Second, we examined to what extent parents' beliefs and practices showed variation and change within a cultural community. Do parents' beliefs about the good path of life change over time? Previous research shows that parents' beliefs about development influence their guidance (Goodnow 1988; Sigel and McGillicuddy-Delisi 1992) and that shared values and beliefs also organize and motivate practices of cultural communities (Strauss 1992). Immigration, schooling, and knowledge about parenting can change parents' and communities' beliefs and practices (Harkness, Super, and Keefer 1992; Sabogal et al. 1987). Rather than assume uniformity across a community, we explored variation among Latino families (Leyendecker and Lamb 1999; Romo and Falbo 1996).

To do so, we asked to what extent parents held different beliefs for different children in the family. We anticipated similarities across parents in their general ideas about the path of life but variation in views of their own children, including where they saw each child on the path, challenges they saw ahead, and ways parents guided them. For example, if siblings had different peers or academic profiles, parents' beliefs about challenges their children faced and guidance to help them stay on the good path might also differ. We considered whether parents saw different challenges for their younger and older children and whether their guidance strategies changed when one child strayed off the good path or was at a crossroads. Just as parents' expectations for their children's achievement may change to reflect changes in their school performance (Goldenberg et al. 2001), parents may also reexamine other beliefs about development when problems arise. In sum, we elicited immigrant Latino parents' descriptions and definitions of the good and bad paths and asked them to explain where each child was on the path, challenges the child faced, and guidance the parent used. We examined parents' beliefs about younger and older siblings to assess whether children's age, gender, or experiences influenced parents' beliefs.

Methods

Research participants. Participating families were drawn from a larger study of the transition from elementary to middle school among 100 low-income Latino and European American families (Azmitia et al. 1996; Azmitia and Cooper 2001; Cooper et al. 1994). The 27 Latino families who are the focus of this report each had two siblings, the younger in the first year of middle school (the target child in the larger study) and the older also in school. The younger children were 11 or 12 years old at the beginning of the study, and older siblings ranged from 12 to 18. All but three fathers and all but two mothers were born in Mexico, with fathers averaging 7.6 years of education and mothers, 7.4 years. Most parents worked in semiskilled or unskilled occupations, typically in hotels, restaurants, factories, or canneries. All but three families had annual incomes of $40,000 or less, and children were receiving free or reduced-price lunches at school.

The path of life interview. Parents were interviewed at home in their language of choice, typically Spanish. Interviews were audiotaped and parents' answers transcribed and coded in the language of the interview. The interviewer showed parents two diagrams: (1) a straight path with lines showing crossroads and challenges and (2) a path forking into *el buen camino* (the good path) and *el mal camino* (the bad path), with the fork labeled *encrucijadas* (crossroads) and *retos* (challenges) and connecting paths between the forks to show that a person might stray from the good path but return to it (see fig. 11.1). Parents were asked to choose the path diagram that best fit their idea of the good path (*el buen camino*) for the interview. Most Latino parents chose the forked path.

Parents were then asked the following open-ended questions:

What does "the good path of life" mean to you? (¿Qué significa para usted "el buen camino de la vida"?) What does the "bad path of life" mean to you? (¿Qué significa para usted "el mal camino de la vida"?)

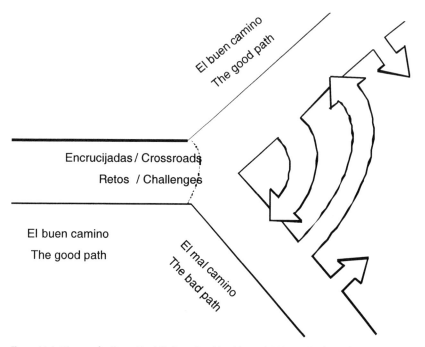

Figure 11.1. Diagram for the path of life interview (Azmitia et al. 1994, revised 1998)

Each of the following questions was asked about the younger and older siblings:

Thinking about your child and this idea of the good and the bad paths, could you point to the place where you would put him/her at this time? Why would you choose this place? (Pensando en su hijo/a y en esta idea del buen y el mal camino: ¿Podría usted decirme donde pondría a su hijo/a? ¿Por qué escogería usted ese lugar?) (The parent wrote the child's name on the diagram at the identified location.)

Has there been a time in the past that you thought that your child was on the bad path or at a crossroads? If yes, how old was he or she? Why do you think that he or she was there? (¿Ha habido alguna vez en el pasado que ud. penso que su hijo/a estaba en el mal camino o en las encrucijadas? Si es así, ¿qué edad tenía? ¿Porqué piensa que su hijo/a estaba allí?)

What do you think the challenges of staying on or choosing the good path might be for your child? (¿Cuáles piensa usted que son los retos que va a encontrar su hijo/a para que siga el buen camino o sobrepase las encrucijadas?)

Is there anything you are doing to keep your child on the good path?

(¿Está usted haciendo algo para que su hijo/a siga en el buen camino [o escoja el buen camino]?)

Inductive thematic coding of interviews. Themes from parents' responses were derived inductively from transcripts on four topics: parents' *descriptions* of the good and bad paths of life, their *explanations* for where each child stood relative to the good path, *challenges* parents anticipated for their children's progress along the good path, and *guidance* parents used to encourage their children to stay on the good path or return to it if they strayed.

Parents' descriptions of the good path included four themes: (1) respect for values and morals reflecting aspects of the concept of *educación,* included showing proper demeanor, living a moral and responsible life, behaving as parents had taught, being responsible to home and family, being a respectful person, and developing oneself spiritually; (2) avoiding bad influences, drugs, vices, and bad companions; (3) education and work, including realizing one's goals and performing well in school and work; and (4) marriage and family, without mentioning family values or obligations.

Parents' descriptions of the bad path included six themes: (1) alcohol and drug use; (2) bad companions; (3) poor character; (4) being estranged from home; (5) illegal activities; and (6) abandoning goals.

Explanations for why parents placed their children at a particular place on the path included four themes: (1) peer influence, (2) developmental stage, (3) behavior, and (4) character or attitude.

Up to three themes were coded in parents' answers concerning the challenges they anticipated for each child: (1) peer influence, including boyfriends or girlfriends; (2) school-related, including academic and social challenges and violence or gang activity at schools; (3) adolescence; (4) drugs; and (5) personal character (including mood or attitude).

Up to three themes were coded for each parent's response to the forms of guidance they used, with five themes emerging: (1) *consejos* (advise and teach values); (2) role model; (3) emotional support; (4) monitor or restrict; and (5) involve outside assistance, including school, therapists, or church.

Coders made global ratings of whether or not parents expressed concern about each child's progress on the good path, with particular attention to where parents indicated the child was on the path diagram and whether they believed the child had ever strayed off the good path or been at a crossroads. Parents were also asked explicitly how often each child made them proud, whether always, often, occasionally, or never.

The two coders who developed the coding system coded all transcripts and resolved differences by consensus. Reliability was established using transcripts from nine families. The percent agreement and modified kappa for each code were Good Path (0.89, 0.83), Bad Path (0.95, 0.94), Explanations (0.94, 0.93), Challenges (0.88, 0.87), Guidance (0.88, 0.87), and Concern (0.95, 0.90).

Key Findings

Latino parents' beliefs and guidance about their children's life pathways, consistent with the ecocultural models of Reese and her colleagues, emphasized the encompassing moral qualities of these pathways. In addition, consistent with the Bridging Multiple Worlds Model, although parents saw peers as the greatest challenge for children staying on the good path, most indicated their fears had not yet been realized. For children at a crossroads or on the bad path, peers were a major factor in parents' views of what had derailed them. Parents were more concerned about older than younger siblings. *Consejos* (advice) was the most frequently used guidance strategy, although parents experiencing difficulties with their children also restricted and monitored their activities.

The good and the bad paths. Table 11.1 presents themes parents most frequently expressed in defining the good and bad paths of life. The most frequent concerned being respectful and maintaining high morals and values and avoiding bad influences, or *malas compañías* (bad company), typi-

Table 11.1. Themes from Parents' Descriptions of the Good and Bad Paths of Life Following Child's Transition to Junior High School

Theme	Percent (frequency)
Good path:	
Respect, morals, and values	81 (22)
Avoiding bad influences	33 (9)
Education and work	33 (9)
Marriage and family	11 (3)
Bad path:	
Alcohol and drug use	56 (15)
Bad companions	33 (9)
Poor character	26 (7)
Being estranged from home	15 (4)
Illegal activities	19 (5)
Abandoning goals	14 (4)

Source: Azmitia and Brown 2002.
Note: The sum of percentages exceeds 100 because parents could cite more than one theme. No parent's descriptions included more than two themes.

cally peers. Education and work were always associated with morality. Some parents emphasized studying or working hard, while others stressed achievement. Several parents linked education with moral development, as when one explained that without an education one was more likely to follow a bad path. Marriage and family themes were cited by parents of both girls and boys. Descriptions of the bad path were more specific behaviors and activities, with alcohol and drug use most frequent. Multiple activities were often cited, including *andar en la calle* (hanging out in the streets), associating with *malas compañías* (bad company), and engaging in gang activity.

To explain where their children were on the path, parents cited their children's behavior, their peers, and children's character or attitude; parents cited peers as challenges for their children more than three times as often as school. Parents gave *consejos* about three times as often as monitoring or restricting children's activities. Interestingly, emotional support was less frequently cited as a strategy for keeping children on the good path, and seeking outside assistance was rare.

Age and gender patterns. Table 11.2 compares the patterns of parents' explanations, challenges, and guidance on the good path for the younger and older siblings. When the number of parents citing different themes in explanations, challenges, and guidance was compared with McNemar's chi-square test for related samples (Siegel and Castellan 1988), more parents cited peers' influence on older than younger siblings in their explanations (40% vs. 14%, $z = 2.83$, $p < .01$) and as challenges for daughters (37% vs. 22%, $z = 2.64$, $p < .01$). Parents of daughters more often said they monitored or restricted activities than did parents of sons (35% vs. 19%, $z = -3.18$, $p < .01$).

Similarities and variation in parents' concern and pride. Similarities in parents' beliefs about the good path, challenges, and guidance may reflect enduring cultural belief systems (D'Andrade and Strauss 1992) or more universal concerns that children live a moral life and avoid bad peers. Among our sample of 27 families, 5 expressed concern about younger and 16 about older siblings. Parents who did not express concern were more likely to report using advice (*consejos*) (73% vs. 62%, $z = -2.56$, $p < .05$), but parents who did so were more likely to monitor or restrict their children (43% vs. 13%, $z = -2.00$, $p < .05$). Thus, parents used more direct interventions when their children were already engaging in behaviors that concerned them.

To look more closely at similarities and variation within families, we used Prediction Analysis (von Eye and Brandtstadter 1988). Prediction

Table 11.2. Themes in Parents' Explanations for Placement of Younger and Older
            Siblings on the Path of Life, Child's Challenges in Staying on the Good
            Path, and Parents' Guidance

Theme	Percent (frequency)		
	Younger	Older	Total
Explanations:			
Behavior	71 (15)	44 (11)	56 (26)
Peer	14 (3)	40 (10)	28 (13)
Personal character or attitude	33 (7)	24 (6)	28 (13)
Developmental stage	24 (5)	12 (3)	17 (8)
Other	9 (2)	16 (4)	13 (6)
Challenges:			
Peers	74 (18)	73 (19)	74 (37)
School related	17 (4)	32 (8)	24 (12)
Drugs	13 (3)	4 (1)	8 (4)
Personal character or attitude	13 (3)	2 (1)	8 (4)
No challenges	8 (2)	4 (1)	6 (3)
Adolescence	4 (1)	0	2 (1)
Other	17 (4)	15 (4)	16 (8)
Guidance:			
Consejos (advice)	64 (16)	73 (19)	69 (35)
Monitor or restrict	28 (7)	23 (6)	25 (13)
Emotional support	20 (5)	19 (5)	19 (10)
Role model	16 (4)	4 (1)	10 (5)
Outside assistance	9 (2)	8 (2)	8 (4)
Other	4 (1)	15 (4)	10 (5)

Source: Azmitia and Brown 2002.
Note: The sum of percentages exceeds 100 because parents could give more than one response; up to three were coded
per parent.

Analysis tests specified relations among cross-classified categorical data to
assess hypothesized associations between two or more categorical variables or attributes. Like chi-square analysis, computation is based on cross-
classifying predictors with criteria and tests the difference between observed and expected frequencies, but unlike standard chi-squares,
prediction analysis compares estimated with observed cell frequencies
only for particular cells specified a priori rather than across all cells. These
"hit cells" contain events confirming the prediction. The success of a prediction is defined by a proportional reduction in errors, represented by
"del" (von Eye 1990; von Eye and Brandtstadter 1988). Del is a descriptive
statistic that indicates "strong" or "weak" support for a hypothesis evident
in a data matrix and hit cell pattern. Prediction Analysis can generate a

measure of statistical probability (z), but because z depends on sample sizes (power), strong descriptive evidence can support a particular hypothesis yet not be statistically significant.

We used Prediction Analysis to examine parents' concerns about one or both children, expressed during their path-of-life interview, in relation to pride in their younger child. Parents' interviews were rated as not concerned about either child, concerned about the older sibling only, or about both. Parents' reported pride in their younger child was coded as "always," "often," or "occasional-to-rare." We tested the hypothesis that those parents not concerned about either child would be more likely to report they were always proud of their younger child, those concerned about the sibling would be more likely to report they were often proud of the younger child, and those concerned about both children would be more likely to be occasionally-to-rarely proud of their younger child. Prediction Analysis (see table 11.3) yielded strong support for the hypothesis that parents' pride in their younger child was tempered by concern about both children on the path of life ($z = 2.75$, del $= .38$). As part of our interpretive cycle, we continue to learn about interrelations of feedback about one child for parents' views of other children and how the family as well as individual children may be key units of analysis for understanding successful pathways through childhood.

Longitudinal case studies. When we conducted follow-up case studies, parents who saw their children on the bad path or crossroads saw school

Table 11.3. Prediction Analysis: Is Parents' Pride in the Younger Child Tempered by Concern about One or Both Children on the Path of Life?

Concern on path interview	Make you proud?		
	Always	Often	Occasional-to-rare
Neither	6*	2	3
	3.67	4.07	3.26
Sibling only	2	7*	2
	3.67	4.07	3.26
Both	1	1	3*
	1.67	1.85	1.48

Note: Asterisks (*) represent the "hit cell" pattern for this hypothesis, and expected frequencies are shown in italics in each cell. Prediction Analysis indicated "strong support" for this hypothesis (del = .38, z = 2.75), with a 35% reduction in the proportion of errors observed by applying the prediction to the model. These findings point to how feedback and adaptation regarding one child are linked to parents' views of others, with the family a key unit of analysis in successful pathways.

as key to children's protection and safety, while parents of children more clearly on good paths saw greater continuity across families and schools in promoting longer-term moral, school, and career goals. Although there were not enough European American families in the sample with two adolescent children to conduct the analyses reported in this chapter, we still asked these families to place their adolescent children on the path and answer the same questions as we asked the Latino parents.

The interpretive cycle in cultural research partnerships. In the bilingual newsletter from this project to participating families, Azmitia conveyed findings by combining quantitative and qualitative insights about the path of life:

> We asked parents to tell us where on the path of life they saw their children and what challenges they might face in the future. Here's what they said: 84% believed their children were on the good path; 15% placed their children at the crossroads of the path of life and one parent thought her child was already on the bad path; 19% reported they believed their children had been on the bad path . . . because they were hanging out with the wrong crowd of friends, doing poorly in school or ditching school, or had been caught using drugs (typically boys) or shoplifting (typically girls); and 70% said bad friendships and peer pressure were the most serious challenges their children would face. Ways parents keep children on the good path or help them through the crossroads included talking, giving advice, and teaching values about right from wrong, monitoring their activities, praising them or doing something special when they behaved well, and keeping them busy so they wouldn't have time to stray.

Following the distribution of the newsletter, Azmitia conducted workshops for parents and teachers at the participating schools to discuss these findings, where parents expressed concern about their children's safety at school with peers and asked for greater supervision by teachers on the playground. The concordance of parents' and teachers' concerns about peers led us to continue our work with them and with the children on peers as challenges and resources on the path of life.

Thus, longitudinal case studies and the interpretive cycle of interviewing parents as cultural insiders, inductive coding and statistical analyses by researchers, and continued exchanges with families and youth helped us understand how immigrant parents guide their children as they adapt to a new country. This work strengthens partnerships with families and schools by illuminating both similarities and differences in guidance strategies in other ethnic-minority and ethnic-majority families.

Study 2, Sixth-Grade Summers: A Cultural Research Partnership with a Community College Outreach Program

In this partnership, which began in 1995, we trained ethnically diverse college students working in community programs as researcher-practitioners, enhancing their mentoring skills, educational leadership, and university studies. We built on their roles as front-line staff of programs and as students. In the project, we embedded Bridging Multiple Worlds measures in program activities and interviewed youth, young adults, parents, teachers, program executives, and funders to map factors that create resources for students as they move across their worlds of families, peers, and school and along the academic pipeline.

We helped the program in monitoring indicators of success with research tools and data analysis systems to foster students' progress, gain feedback about program effectiveness, and sustain program funding. With the director, we set up a longitudinal database for children's program attendance, grades, and demographic data as well as program essays so staff could ask questions useful to them, such as: What "kind of kid" participated and who did not? Who attended particular activities such as tutoring? Did students' grades rise and fall or were they stable? What did graduating students believe were the most valuable program components and what did they suggest for improvement? The database also included responses to the annual Summer Institute activities based on the Bridging Multiple Worlds surveys (Domínguez et al. 2001).

Methods

Research participants. In one analysis from this larger study (Denner et al., in press) we traced the experiences of 116 students, 76 girls and 40 boys (typical for college outreach programs, girls outnumbered boys), who entered the program from 1995 to 1997. Students were mostly Latino and almost all of Mexican descent. As part of selection, students were considered low-income by their eligibility for free and reduced-price school lunch programs. Participants were chosen by teachers and the program director based on application essays as well as their potential, motivation, and grades. Among those chosen, parents' formal education, usually in Mexico, was typically less than high school, and for many was at the elementary (*primaria*) level. They primarily worked picking strawberries or lettuce, on factory lines, or cleaning houses and hotels.

Measures. In this study we used indicators occurring naturally in the community, such as application essays, attendance records, and school transcripts, as well as measures tapping the five dimensions of the Bridging Multiple Worlds Model: demographic portraits, identity pathways, math and English pathways, challenges and resources across worlds, and cultural research partnerships.

Key Findings

Children's identity pathways linked generations. When we analyzed 116 children's essays written when they were in the sixth grade (Denner et al., in press), we found they described dreams of college-based careers: becoming doctors, lawyers, nurses, and teachers as well as secretaries, police officers, firefighters, and mechanics. Like children in the low-income Mexican immigrant families in Study 1, children in the program dreamed about college and college-based careers rather than following their parents' careers of physical labor and about contributing to their communities and families.

One case can be traced over time in the reflections of Soledad Rosas, a student in the program. At age 12, she wrote on her application:

> I would like to be a writer for children's stories that will teach children many things, like becoming interested in reading. I want to help my community by finding economical resources so that the children don't leave their studies. . . . With my determination and effort I will successfully accomplish my goal to obtain these careers. My obstacles are that I have cerebral palsy. Another obstacle is the English language.

At age 13, during the career exploration activities of the program's Summer Institute, she wrote:

> I want to be a writer and a DJ [disc jockey] at a radio station. I have decided to go to [the University of California at] Berkeley because it has a program for disabled people and I have problems like that. The college is close but not that close. I want to live on campus. The subjects I want to take are the ones I need for my career. . . . My challenges are my disabil-

ity, working to pay for college, and having problems in college. . . . My resources are my teachers, college, books, and DJ's of other radio stations.

At age 17, she celebrated the second anniversary of her own radio
show and still retained her dream of becoming a DJ (although she had begun to think of television as well) and of college studies in broadcasting.

When we interviewed young adult tutors and mentors in the program,
we found they bridged across generations and from home to college. Like
the Latino parents in Study 1, these young adults defined success in life in
terms of morality and schooling. They helped children with homework and
linked families, schools, and communities with their dreams and fears for
the future. The young adults also gave children a chance to talk and write
about their dreams for careers, education, families, and communities
(Cooper, Denner, and Lopez 1999). They valued children's home communities and many shared home languages and, sometimes, family histories.
Many had learned to be bicultural and could help children understand how
to retain community traditions while succeeding in school, college, and
community.

The program director, Elizabeth Domínguez, was also a cultural broker,
linking families, schools, peers, and communities. She explained her own
theory of how Latina godmothers (*comadres*) promote children's pathways
to success by describing her own family history, in which her parents' *co-
madre* was a bridge between her family and school:

> My parents immigrated from Mexico to Los Angeles in search of a better
> life for their children. They made sure we did our homework and main-
> tained frequent contact with school, and nine of their thirteen children
> completed college. Most of my peers dropped out before they reached
> high school. Their parents also came to the U.S. to give their children a
> better life, with dreams for their children to obtain a college degree. But
> like many non-educated immigrant parents, they did not feel comfortable
> helping their children with school because they did not understand the
> system. My parents had a *comadre* [godmother] who took them under her
> wing, explained how U.S. schools function, and reassured them their par-
> ticipation was demanded for us to be successful. (Domínguez 1995, cited
> in Cooper, Denner, and Lopez 1999)

Thus, in helping children and youth find pathways to success in the eyes of
their families, communities, and schools, the program's young adult staff

and director forged links across generations, including senior staff, young adults, and the families and children they served. These intergenerational pathways appeared to foster skills children need if they are to succeed in their increasingly diverse worlds along their pathways to college, careers, and adult family and community roles.

Challenges and resources across worlds. Children's family, peer, and school worlds were both challenges and resources. In the yearly activities based on the Bridging Multiple Worlds Model (the materials are entitled *It's All about Choices/Se Trata de Todas las Decisiones;* Domínguez et al. 2001), the most frequently named resource was the family, and the most controversial (both resources and challenges) was peers. Children saw peers, families, and teachers as both challenges and resources in reaching their dreams. Both in 1997 (when we heard from 77 children) and 1998 (84 children), students listed peers as challenges and resources at comparable rates (30% vs. 40% of the students in 1997 and 50% vs. 55% in 1998). For example, students described their challenges by listing boyfriends, girlfriends, peer pressure, "temptation of friends dropping out," "friends as bad examples," gangs, "bad friends," "bigger students," "illegal friends" (i.e., friends engaged in illegal activities), and "enemies." Many also listed "drugs," "sex," "having babies," or "pregnancies." As resources, students also listed friends, boyfriends, "bigger students," girlfriends, and "leave your boyfriend if he takes too much time." In contrast, students were much more likely to list their families as resources than as challenges (70% vs. 10% in 1997 and 73% vs. 10% in 1998).

These findings replicate other research on the challenges peers pose for students' school engagement and also point to how central families are to children on their pathways to college even though many parents had completed only elementary school.

A closer look with longitudinal case studies: The regulars. We followed 28 students from the year they entered the program at sixth grade through ninth grade (Azmitia and Cooper 2001). Many were immigrants, learning English during these years. When we analyzed their school transcripts, we found that their math and English pathways to college diverged early but some got back on track. We found math pathways ranged from consistently high to slowly declining, rapidly declining (and dropping out, including youth becoming incarcerated or becoming parents), moving into remedial math, and delaying taking any math. By ninth grade, more than half had taken and passed Algebra, a key step to eligibility for four-year colleges and universities. Of the remaining students, each was eligible for community college, where Algebra 1 is the only math required for an associate arts degree. These pathways diverged early: students who passed Algebra 1 at ninth grade had made higher grades in sixth grade than students who failed Algebra or took remedial classes. But some students moved back on track after challenging personal events, and others moved up from remedial math to Algebra, sometimes retaking Algebra before more advanced classes in high school. These findings go beyond group differences in school achievement toward understanding variation and change within groups as well as similarities across them. Tracing more than one pathway to more than one kind of college helps build inclusive opportunities for college and college-based careers.

To examine these issues over time with longitudinal case studies, we wanted to see if family and peer resources and challenges predicted who among the regulars was on a math pathway to Algebra. Capital models would predict that children with more resources would do better, and challenge models, that those with challenges who also had resources would do better.

Qualitative Comparative Analysis (QCA; Ragin 1989) is a statistical software program designed to analyze and link case- and variable-based data in order to build theory. Its goal is to "find patterns or configurations of variables within cases and show how, across many cases, such patterns are associated with a given outcome of interest." Based on Boolean logic, in which each variable within each case is coded as present or absent, the QCA analysis program sorts cases with similar configurations of predictors into "families," thereby testing the possibility of multiple pathways to the same outcome. For our work on how demographic portraits, career identities, challenges, and resources across children's worlds of families, schools, peers, and communities may interact in pathways to college, we have used QCA to build our model by preserving the cases of individual students while testing the Bridging Multiple Worlds Model in the context of capital, ecocultural, and alienation models.

For example, when we conducted a QCA analysis of the challenges and resources from families and peers of the 28 regulars, we found two patterns that predicted students who took and passed Algebra 1 in ninth grade. One group reported only resources: one subgroup reporting a family resource and the other subgroup reporting a peer resource. The second group, consistent with the challenge hypothesis from the Bridging Multiple Worlds Model, indicated that a subgroup of students not only had resources but also challenges. We have more to learn about the kinds of challenges students find motivating and those challenges that derail their pathways. We have also begun to consider how different students may exemplify different models (e.g., "challenge cases" and "capital cases") rather than that all cases exemplify only one model. These findings indicate that the models may offer complementary accounts of children's pathways through school.

The interpretive cycle: Sustaining cultural research partnerships. Coordinating cultural research partnerships—both with the families in Study 1 and the families, schools, and program in Study 2—reflects vulnerabilities and institutional fragility of key participants and partnerships, but long-term, sustained engagement—instead of a "project" mentality—fosters ongoing partnerships. For example, in our ongoing partnership with the community program, the economic downturn motivated our collaborating on a grant proposal that stimulated us to write a Memorandum of Understanding about the next phase of the work. We use the term "program analysis" to distinguish our research activities from formal program evaluations, which are valuable but can also trigger worries, particularly in new or small programs. And we built on these findings in developing the Bridging Multiple Worlds Tool Kit as a no-cost, multi-user resource in Spanish and English that allows families, schools, and community programs to help children map assets across their worlds and pathways through school. For example, it helps them write about their dreams for the future and see if they are off track in math, and it shows them how to get back on track and find and use resources across their worlds. These activities for elementary, middle, and high school students are being used for teacher training, in school classrooms, and in statewide evaluations of outreach programs. They also help researchers to understand what factors support and impede youth pathways to college and to design further research.

Conclusions and Implications

Intergenerational Research Partnerships as Assets

As policies involving diversity, immigration, and inclusion continuously change, stakeholders value monitoring diverse children's pathways in both quantitative and qualitative terms. Analyses of programs deemed effective appear to sustain parents' and other adults' beliefs that schooling will benefit children (Adger 2001). We have observed partnerships with students, families, community organizations, schools, districts, and universities at local, regional, state, and national levels. Some partnerships build "vertical teams" to support ethnically diverse children and youth navigating from kindergarten through college. We have seen partners become increasingly interested and sophisticated in thinking about longitudinal analyses of qualitative and quantitative data.

This work has involved building innovative partnerships among youth, families, schools, and community organizations. Children and youth have commented that the activities help them think about the future. Families may hold high educational values and goals but may be less familiar with the language and practices of schools and need ways to become involved. They find these activities useful not only for helping their children but also for developing their own understanding of the U.S. educational system, community support systems, and relationships with other families, researchers, and program staff. Community organizations often seek partnerships with families and schools and can provide academic skills, information, high expectations, and a sense of moral goals to achieve on behalf of families and communities, but changes in funding pressure them for program evaluation. School staff tell us they are seeking ways to include families with diverse literacy and linguistic backgrounds but often lack tools to use in this endeavor. Our work with intergenerational partnerships and our attending to the feedback and concerns of all our constituents led to our developing the Bridging Multiple Worlds Tool Kit, which includes activities for schools and programs which tap the elements of the model, graphing templates for quantitative work, and materials for longitudinal case studies so partners can link qualitative and quantitative methods. Our tool kit is available on the Web and has also been incorporated in printed workbooks used by schools and community agencies.

Reaching across Disciplines: Capital, Alienation, Ecocultural, and Challenge Models

These two studies reveal how families, schools, peers, and community programs can bridge to careers for youth entering university and community college. These patterns indicate that families, peers, schools, and programs can support both college-bound and remedial students, whom scholars often find to be increasingly pessimistic, disengaged, and alienated as they move through school (Fordham and Ogbu 1986; Gibson 1997). Selective programs may help keep these students engaged in school and continuing through the academic pipeline. Although some of the students we studied were not initially eligible for a four-year university, with few exceptions they all graduated from high school and were eligible for community colleges. Many of these students aimed to transfer to four-year institutions after completing their degree in community college.

These findings indicate that future studies of capital, alienation, ecocultural, and challenge models will benefit from probing the configurations of students' lives over time with families, peers, schools, and community programs. That is, rather than a "one-model-fits-all" approach, researchers will benefit from understanding and explaining the links between each model and particular subgroups of families and youth.

Immigrant children and families who are new to a nation's schools and who had limited formal education in their home countries face similar challenges. Our studies of Mexican immigrant families (the largest immigrant group in the United States) show that parents hold high hopes that their children will move up from their parents' lives of physical labor picking strawberries or lettuce, standing on factory assembly lines, or cleaning houses and hotels to technical or professional careers (Azmitia et al. 1996). In essence, we found that they seek to "beat the odds" and disprove theories of social reproduction—that each society's social-class hierarchy tends to be reproduced from generation to generation. However, we also found that each cultural group experiences unique challenges and resources and that how they adapt to their circumstances can lead to variation in students' educational and career pathways.

Linking the International and the Local for Inclusion in Multicultural Democracies

With colleagues in several nations, we are working to coordinate concepts of families, peers, schools, programs, and community organizations; link demographic, institutional, relational, and individual levels of analysis; and thereby unify our writings and recommendations. This has engaged local, state, national, and international partners on ethnic diversity and inclusion. For example, the Bridging Multiple Worlds Model and tools are being used by the federal GEAR UP program (Gaining Early Awareness and Readiness for Undergraduate Programs) serving all middle school students in Watsonville, California, to enhance access to college.

Our common goal is to enhance access to college and legal employment for children of diverse ethnic, racial, economic, and geographic communities. And our capacity to be nations "where diversity works" rests on customizing programs for communities while staying attuned to common goals and collaborating among diverse stakeholders: students, families, schools, community programs, legislators, the business sector, and media. Achieving these goals is fostered by building clear models of change, testing them with evidence, and sustaining partnerships among stakeholders as intergenerational research partnerships.

Reflections on Mixed Methods

This partnership with families and community programs created intergenerational pathways through which children became tutors, undergraduates became staff, staff returned to college, and partners of all ages, including undergraduate and pre- and postdoctoral students, played key research roles. We include children and youth as members of the research team, and their insights can benefit the work. For example, when children were learning to graph their math pathways toward their career dreams in the community college outreach program, one 12-year-old girl, the daughter of Mexican immigrants, looked up at her peers and exclaimed, "So these are the beginnings of our math roads!" She later told us her career goal is to become a psychologist.

Longitudinal case studies and interpretive cycles are, in our view, essential for work on including families in multicultural democracies. We do not regard any single data analysis technique as essential and use Prediction Analysis, QCA, and other qualitative and quantitative approaches (Miles and Huberman 1994). Prediction Analysis, a variation on categorical analyses, allows specifying target patterns and testing longitudinal models with small samples with inferential statistical tests. Although QCA can be cumbersome and must be linked to other programs for inferential statistical tests, we agree with Weitzman and Miles:

> [QCA's] real strength is in helping you think clearly about a few key variables and their configural relationships within cases—but seen across as large a number of cases as you have. In qualitative research, it is no longer rare to have multiple cases, sometimes ranging up to 20, 30, or more. But your mind usually goes blooey when it's faced with the patterns within more than a dozen or so cases. QCA successfully combines "case-oriented" and variable-oriented views of your data, enabling a coherent understanding: you can both build and test theory. It achieves this power

at some costs, of course: forcing the values of your case-level variables into a present/absent mode or at best, a high-medium-low mode. Still you can learn a lot that way. (1995: 265)

Mixed-Methods Tools for Science, Policy, and Practice in Multicultural Nations

We see a five-element cycle valuable in mixed-methods work: linking guiding questions from local questions to general models; using demographic data to compare local with representative samples; using interview, survey, and group activity formats to link career and college dreams across generations for research, schools, and programs; making math and English pathway graphs linked to students' career goals for youth and other stakeholders; and developing longitudinal databases, codebooks, and graphing templates to link cases and variables over time for regular stakeholder conferences and communication. Taken together, these activities help youth navigate to college and careers while adults in families, schools, and programs learn about students' realities. Materials for them appear in the Bridging Multiple Worlds Tool Kit, available at no cost via our Web site http://www.bridgingworlds.org. More generally, we see longitudinal case studies and interpretive cycles, more than particular data analysis methods, as helping cultural research partnerships engage and sustain science, policy, and practice toward diversity and equity in multicultural nations.

Acknowledgments

Study 1 and Study 2 were supported by grants to Margarita Azmitia and Catherine R. Cooper from the U.S. Department of Education Office of Educational Research and Improvement through the Center for Research on Education, Diversity, and Excellence, Santa Cruz, California. Study 2 was supported as well by grants to Catherine R. Cooper and Barrie Thorne from the John D. and Catherine T. MacArthur Foundation Research Network on Successful Pathways through Middle Childhood. The authors thank the students, families, schools, and community program for participating and Gregory Thrush for assisting with data for Study 1, as well as Elizabeth Domínguez, Jill Denner, Edward M. Lopez, Nora Dunbar, and Wendy Rivera for their many contributions to Study 2.

References

Adger, C. T. 2001. "School-Community-Based Organization Partnerships for Language Minority Students' School Success." *Journal for the Education of Students Placed at Risk* 6:7–26.

Azmitia, M., and J. R. Brown. 2002. "Latino Immigrant Parents' Beliefs about the 'Path of Life' for Their Adolescent Children." In *Latino Children and Families in the United States,* ed. J. M. Contreras, K. A. Kerns, and A. M. Neal-Barnet, 77–10. Westbrook, CT: Praeger.

Azmitia, M., and C. R. Cooper. 2001. "Good or Bad? Peers and Academic Pathways of Latino and European American Youth in Schools and Community Programs." *Journal for the Education of Students Placed at Risk* 6:45–71.

Azmitia, M., C. R. Cooper, E. E. García, and N. Dunbar. 1996. "The Ecology of Family Guidance in Low-Income Mexican-American and European-American Families." *Social Development* 5:1–23.

Azmitia, M., C. R. Cooper, L. Rivera, E. M. Lopez, A. Ittel, and N. Dunbar. 1994. *The Path of Life Interview.* Santa Cruz: University of California. (Revised 1998.)

Coleman, J. S. 1988. "Social Capital in the Creation of Human Capital." *American Journal of Sociology Supplement* 94:95–120.

Cooper, C. R. 1997. "When Diversity Works: Cultural Partnerships for Science, Policy, and Youth in Democracies." *Society for Research in Adolescence Newsletter,* pp. 1–7.

———. 1999. "Multiple Selves, Multiple Worlds: Cultural Perspectives on Individuality and Connectedness in Adolescent Development." In *Minnesota Symposia on Child Psychology: Cultural Processes in Child Development,* ed. A. Masten, 25–57. Hillsdale, NJ: Erlbaum.

———. 2001. "Bridging Multiple Worlds: Inclusive, Selective, and Competitive Programs, Latino Youth, and Pathways to College; Affirmative Development of Ethnic Minority Students." *CEIC Review: A Catalyst for Merging Research, Policy, and Practice* 10:14–15, 22.

Cooper, C. R., M. Azmitia, E. E. Garcia, A. Ittel, E. M. Lopez, L. Rivera, and R. Martínez-Chávez. 1994. "Aspirations of Low-Income Mexican American and European American Parents for Their Children and Adolescents." *New Directions in Child Development* 63:65–81.

Cooper, C. R., R. G. Cooper, M. Azmitia, G. Chavira, and Y. Gullatt. 2002. "Bridging Multiple Worlds: How African American and Latino Youth in Academic Outreach Programs Navigate Math Pathways to College." *Applied Developmental Science* 6:73–87.

Cooper, C. R., and J. Denner. 1998. "Theories Linking Culture and Psychology: Universal and Community-Specific Processes." *Annual Review of Psychology* 49:559–584.

Cooper, C. R., J. Denner, and E. M. Lopez. 1999. "Cultural Brokers: Helping Latino Children on Pathways to Success." *When School Is Out: The Future of Children* 9:51–57.

D'Andrade, R., and C. Strauss, eds. 1992. *Human Motives and Cultural Models.* Cambridge: Cambridge University Press.

Delgado-Gaitán, C. 1992. "School Matters in the Mexican-American Home: Socializing Children to Education." *American Educational Research Journal* 29:495–513.

Denner, J., C. R. Cooper, N. Dunbar, and E. M. Lopez. In press. "Access to Opportunity: How Latino Students in a College Outreach Program Think about Obstacles and Resources." *Journal of Latinos and Education.*

Denner, J., C. R. Cooper, E. M. Lopez, and N. Dunbar. 1999. "Beyond 'Giving Science Away': How University-Community Partnerships Inform Youth Programs, Research, and Policy." *Society for Research in Child Development Social Policy Report* 13:1–17.

Domínguez, E., C. R. Cooper, G. Chavira, D. Mena, E. M. Lopez, N. Dunbar, J. Denner, and R. Marshall. 2001. "It's All about Choices/Se Trata de Todas las Decisiones: Leadership and Career Development." In Bridging Multiple Worlds Toolkit, ed. C. R. Cooper. Available online: http://www.bridgingworlds.org.

Fordham, S., and J. U. Ogbu. 1986. "Black Students' School Success: Coping with the 'Burden of Acting White.'" Urban Review 18:176–206.

Gibson, M. A. 1997. "Exploring and Explaining the Variability: Cross-National Perspectives on the School Performance of Minority Students." Anthropology and Education Quarterly 28:318–329.

Goldenberg, C., and R. Gallimore. 1995. "Immigrant Latino Parents' Values and Beliefs about their Children's Education: Continuities and Discontinuities across Cultures and Generations." In Advances in Motivation and Achievement: Culture, Ethnicity, and Motivation, vol. 9, ed. P. R. Pintrich and M. Maehr, 183–228. Greenwich, CT: JAI Press.

Goldenberg, C., R. Gallimore, L. Reese, and H. Garnier. 2001. "Cause or Effect? A Longitudinal Study of Immigrant Latino Parents' Aspirations and Expectations and Their Children's School Performance." American Educational Research Journal 38 (3): 547–582.

Goodnow, J. J. 1988. "Parents' Ideas, Actions, and Feelings: Models and Methods from Developmental and Social Psychology." Child Development 59:286–320.

Greene, J. C., and D. J. Caracelli. 1997. "Crafting Mixed-Method Evaluation Designs." In Advances in Mixed-Method Evaluation: The Challenges and Benefits of Integrating Diverse Paradigms, ed. J. C. Greene and V. J. Caracelli, 19–32. New Directions for Evaluation, vol. 74. San Francisco: Jossey-Bass.

Harkness, S., C. M. Super, and C. H. Keefer. 1992. "Learning to Be an American Parent: How Cultural Models Gain Directive Force." In Human Motives and Cultural Models, ed. R. D'Andrade and C. Strauss, 163–178. Cambridge: Cambridge University Press.

Henderson, R. W. 1997. "Educational and Occupational Aspirations and Expectations among Parents of Middle School Students of Mexican Descent: Family Resources for Academic Development and Mathematics Learning." In Social and Emotional Adjustment and Family Relations in Ethnic Minority Families, ed. R. D. Taylor and M. C. Wang, 99–131. Mahwah, NJ: Erlbaum.

Kroesen, K., L. Reese, and R. Gallimore. 1998. "Navigating Multiple Worlds: Latino Children Becoming Adolescents in Los Angeles." In Diasporic Identity, ed. C. A. Mortland, 197–223. Selected Papers on Refugee and Immigrant Issues, vol. 6. Washington, DC: American Anthropological Association.

Leyendecker, B., and M. E. Lamb. 1999. "Latino Families." In Parenting and Child Development in "Nontraditional" Families, ed. M. E. Lamb, 247–262. Mahwah, NJ: Erlbaum.

Mertens, D. M. 1994. Research Methods in Education and Psychology: Integrating Diversity with Quantitative and Qualitative Approaches. Newbury Park, CA: Sage.

Miles, M. B., and A. M. Huberman. 1994. Qualitative Data Analysis: An Expanded Sourcebook. Thousand Oaks, CA: Sage.

Ragin, C. C. 1989. The Comparative Method: Moving beyond Qualitative and Quantitative Strategies. Berkeley and Los Angeles: University of California Press.

————. 1994. "Introduction to Qualitative Comparative Analysis." In *The Comparative Political Economy of the Welfare State,* ed. T. Janoski and A. M. Hicks, 299–319. Cambridge: Cambridge University Press.

Reese, L., S. Balzano, R. Gallimore, and C. Goldenberg. 1995. "The Concept of *Educación:* Latino Family Values and American Schooling." *International Journal of Educational Research* 23:57–81.

Romo, H. D., and T. Falbo. 1996. *Latino High School Graduation: Defying the Odds.* Austin: University of Texas Press.

Sabogal, F., G. Marin, R. Otero-Sabogal, B. VanOss Marin, and E. J. Perez-Stable. 1987. "Hispanic Familism and Acculturation: What Changes and What Doesn't?" *Hispanic Journal of Behavioral Sciences* 9:397–412.

Siegel, S., and N. J. Castellan. 1988. *Nonparametric Statistics.* 2nd ed. New York: McGraw-Hill.

Sigel, I. E., and A. V. McGillicuddy-Delisi, eds. 1992. *Parental Belief Systems: The Psychological Consequences for Families.* 2nd ed. Hillsdale, NJ: Lawrence Erlbaum.

Strauss, C. 1992. "What Makes Tony Run? Schemas as Motives Reconsidered." In *Human Motives and Cultural Models,* ed. R. D'Andrade and C. Strauss, 197–224. Cambridge: Cambridge University Press.

Valdés, G. 1996. *Con Respeto: Bridging the Distances between Culturally Diverse Families and Schools: An Ethnographic Portrait.* New York: Teachers College Press.

von Eye, A., ed. 1990. *Statistical Methods in Longitudinal Research.* Vol. 2. New York: Academic Press.

von Eye, A., and Brandtstadter, J. 1988. "Application of Prediction Analysis to Cross Classifications of Ordinal Data." *Journal of Biometrics* 30:651–665.

Weisner, T., R. Gallimore, and C. Jordan. 1993. "Unpackaging Cultural Effects on Classroom Learning: Native Hawaiian Peer Assistance and Child-Generated Activity." *Anthropology and Education Quarterly* 19:327–351.

Weitzman, E. A., and M. B. Miles. 1995. *Computer Programs for Qualitative Data Analysis: A Software Sourcebook.* Thousand Oaks, CA: Sage.

12

Civil Rights and Academic Development: Mixed Methods and the Task of Ensuring Educational Equality

Mica Pollock

I am an anthropologist with expertise in race analysis and an "Anthropology of Education" degree who was hired out of graduate school as an "educational expert" to do civil rights policy analysis for lawyers. I have since joined the faculty at a school of education as an anthropologist who studies race, youth, and inequality ethnographically. My daily life, thus (like most other lives in the education profession), has long required thinking about young people and the systems that serve them through multiple methodological and analytic lenses simultaneously. I believe that my thinking about racial inequality has benefited particularly from this necessary enforcement of mixed methods. As many of the other race- and inequality-focused chapters in this volume suggest, analyzing well the inequality systems in which our nation's children are embedded is itself a mixed-methods task. Yet while we laud the importance of mixed methods for understanding inequality systems in our research, more explicitly engaging mixed methods for understanding these systems is also necessary in practice. That is, people who work *with* children, and who work directly to protect them, also need to be thinking through multiple analytic lenses about the inequality systems affecting both children and themselves. Both researchers and "practitioners" need to think hard about the various ways we might analyze children's lives and needs—and the various ways in which we currently are. And to do so, as I want to argue here, we need to struggle to understand the other thinkers—to engage directly the analytic habits and analytic disputes (Nader 2002) of this mixed-methods profession.

One particular methodological, intellectual, and practical way of thinking that I would argue is not developed nearly enough in research and practice regarding equality for young people is that of thinking like a civil rights lawyer. I learned what I know of civil rights law by working at the U.S. Department of Education's Office for Civil Rights (OCR) for a year and a half after finishing my PhD (note well: no longer an OCR employee, I do not represent OCR in any way in this chapter or any other work). This experience in working firsthand with civil rights analyses of inequality, and with the various players in the U.S. educational system who are themselves wrestling with the definitions, requirements, and logic of civil rights laws and regulations, taught me that attempting to ensure educational equality in the United States is and *should* be a continual exercise in mixed-methods work. That is, we would do best to employ not only multiple social science methods but also other professions' methods—particularly legal methods—for understanding (and equalizing) opportunities for young people. To do so, however, both researchers and practitioners must learn to navigate and merge a vast existing diversity of professional and everyday methods for defining what inequitable practice actually looks like.

Before I went to work on race in the civil rights field, I conducted a research project that explored racial inequality through a completely different analytic and methodological lens: I studied, ethnographically, how people throughout three years of life in a California school and district struggled in everyday ways with using racial labels to describe school people and school orders. People struggled daily with the basic question of when and how it would be helpful or harmful to talk about people racially in school, I found, and in doing so they were really struggling with the reality that they themselves were (often unwillingly) helping to reproduce a racial inequality system through both talk and silence (see Pollock 2004). In this study of race talk and "colormuteness" (as I came to call the daily American act of deleting race labels from talk), I was not interested in racial "identity" in young people's lives, as are most of the race research contributors to this volume (see, e.g., the chapters in part 2). Rather, I was interested in a more basic and less-often-studied issue of racial practice affecting children and youth: that is, our communal, everyday processes of racial labeling, what I called racial "identification" (see Pollock 2004). The basic process of labeling others and selves racially, of course, is a core part *of* constructing racialized identities, as Rumbaut's chapter (chap. 5) demonstrates in this volume; yet as Rumbaut's work itself suggests, racialized labeling is a communal action involving both adults and young people, not one solely of personal, individual, or internal struggle by the young.[1] In particular, the institution of *school* plays a key role in having us label and frame each other racially and thus actually "*make each other* racial" (Olsen 1997, emphasis mine); my work demonstrated that people also reinforce the relevance of race when we actively refuse to mention race in schools (Pollock 2004). Rather than asking how children from different "cultural"/ "ethnic"/"racial" groups think about themselves (as do a number of chapters in this volume), then, my work has asked how and when young people and adults across the American schooling system frame one another as race group members, and when they resist doing so (Pollock 2004). Moreover, as opposed to the analytically atomized "cultures" (e.g., "Latinos" or "blacks") more typically studied by analysts (see chaps. 4 and 11 in this volume; this is a far more methodologically normalized way of framing "culture[s]"), culture for me was a national unit of analysis (see, similarly, Henry 1963; see also Varenne and McDermott 1998). That is, I was interested in shared American dilemmas of racialization—in particular, the paradoxical, often inequality-increasing consequences of the basic American act of *refusing* to label people racially (here, in the daily life of schools). In this version of "cultural" analysis, then, I took into account the various players—including researchers like myself—using, struggling with, and deleting race words in a shared, though conflicted, choreography called American culture (I use "American" in this analysis for its ideological resonance, but more precisely I mean "the United States").

Methodologically, this first project was ethnographic in part because it accepted as data the unprompted discourse interactions of everyday life; this is a research strategy far too little used in educational research, which more typically has researchers either measuring subjects from afar or sitting respondents down in artificial situations to talk about their lives as if such packaging of discourse is more "valid" than naturally occurring talk (see Briggs 1986). I used only a fraction of my own interview data in the end, for example, because I decided that I really wanted to see how race labels appeared spontaneously in the private and informal talk of classrooms and hallways as well as in the more public talk of staff or school board meetings. That is, I wanted to actually study a subset of the "thousands of [racialized] daily interactions" (Johnson, chap. 4, this volume) taking place between the multiple players in a young person's life—interactions that we all know pile up to create racial patterns in schools and elsewhere but that few analysts study directly. In this ethnographic research, everybody's language was fair game, and I listened and talked for three years to the students, teachers, and administrators of this California high school; I also dissected the words of administrators and judges and newspapers in the school's district. As the district was under a desegregation order, I started getting interested in education lawyers and their role in educational systems. Then I went to work with them.

From 1999 until 2001, I worked as an "equal opportunity specialist" at OCR. OCR—a federal agency that looms large to many educators in the nation's schools and districts yet is oddly unknown to others—enforces federal civil rights laws outlawing discrimination in any federally funded public educational institution on the bases of race, national origin, gender, and disability. As an equal opportunity specialist at OCR, my task was to investigate and analyze claims of discrimination brought to the office by "complainants"—typically parents, teachers, and advocates with their own analyses of inequality. I was hired, in addition, to coordinate a new research project on "early learning," an effort to look closely at educational opportunity in the early grades and see how legal analysis defining racial and national-origin discrimination could be extended to analysis of children's earliest school opportunities to learn.

In this early-learning project, we were interested, as are Harkness and Cooper and their colleagues in this volume (chaps. 10 and 11), in the racial "pipeline" problem: the dwindled numbers of high school graduates of color that emerge from the limitless pool of child potential. We were interested, however, far more in the role schools played in creating such racial patterns in children's academic development than in the developmental or academic beliefs of children's parents or of children themselves. Civil rights lawyers think very differently from most developmental researchers about analyzing the location of responsibility for educational patterns. As a regulatory organization operating under the logic and methods of education law and federal bureaucracy, OCR investigates the actions of schools and districts, and secondarily the responsive actions of the children and parents who attend them. Since it is schools that receive federal funds, federal lawyers cannot regulate the at-home actions of children or parents: by statute, they keep their analysis focused primarily on the practices of school and district people (and on those of parents and children when they are interacting with school and district people). In thinking about the obvious role of parenting in students' academic development, then, as I will discuss below, we ended up thinking about how schools and districts engaged parents in monitoring children's academic progress—an important counterpart to social science analysis focusing on children and their parents as the primary populations of interest/fault.

As both Johnson and Rumbaut (chaps. 4 and 5, this volume) argue explicitly, parents are only one set of players constructing a child's racialized life. In consequence, any study of the development of children is enhanced when we examine simultaneously other factors of the child's ecology. While neither Johnson nor Rumbaut actually studies schools directly, both authors argue for analyzing the particular role schools play in creating racialized contexts for children and youth—a conclusion I share, and one lawyers would find particularly welcome analytically. Yet research on the pipeline—or, indeed, on any racialized "achievement gap"—rarely focuses on the full ecology of children's lives. Rather, research (albeit often apologetically) typically selects one set of players in one setting and analyzes how they participate in creating racialized patterns. Further, such research reveals (often unwittingly) that various players in the education system *themselves* also isolate other players to hold primarily responsible for racialized patterns, rather than themselves looking more systematically at how various such players together create such patterns and thus can work together to eliminate them (Pollock 2001; for a nice example of more systemic analysis, see Valencia 1991; see also Payne 1984). That is, everyday analysts, just like researchers, typically find particular players on whom to lay the brunt of any analysis of racialized inequality. Cooper's informants, for example, were Latino parents themselves routinely blamed by a school/societal deficit analysis denigrating nonwhite parenting; in turn, they blamed their children's peers for getting their children off track in school (see chap. 11, this volume). The latter analysis, blaming children's peers, is a habitual location of blame in educational research and practice, just as is blaming children's parents (see Ogbu 1974; for counterarguments, see Carter, forthcoming; O'Connor 1997). These kinds of revolving blame analyses tend simply to clash, both in educational research and in "on-the-ground" attempts to actually assist children better. Far more rarely do players get together to think through the analytic clashes that keep them blaming one another and get busy figuring out how each set of players can assist in the project of achieving educational equality for children.

It was while I was working at OCR that I became convinced that this equality project itself requires mixed methods—and that solving educational problems requires confronting analytic disagreements directly. In an attempt to think more systematically about eliminating the American racial achievement gap in its earliest (kindergarten through third grade [K–3]) stages, in February 2000 OCR convened an early learning symposium that I organized for education researchers, elementary school practitioners, and OCR lawyers and investigators entitled "Isolating Key Spheres of Elementary Equity: Defining Equal Access to Early Learning Opportunities."[2] Immediately—and purposefully—this early learning symposium sparked fundamental analytic disputes between invitees and hosts over how to think about the beginning of the "pipeline." At the symposium, lawyers came into contact with educational researchers, advocates, principals, teachers, and superintendents. As "legal" modes of thinking met "educational" modes of thinking (a binary opposition quickly delineated, in the symposium, in the casual banter of both the lawyers and the "educators" in attendance), we experienced the ultimate mixing of method. Up for debate came the very process of *defining equal opportunity*—the appropriate analyses, methods, and territory for evaluating the educational opportunities afforded American children.

Some key questions of territory and methodology raised over the two days of our symposium are useful for thinking about how the analytic methods of social science, educational research, educational practice, and law interact, intertwine, and clash in the analysis of educational inequality. Such ways of thinking actually already interface every day in our schools: research thinking about the "causes" of educational inequality infuses (and complicates) educators' plans for educational improvement, while legal thinking about individuals and groups with "rights" infuses (and complicates) popular definitions of a "fair" distribution of educational opportunities (Minow 1990). Despite this daily intertwining of logics, however, lawyers and educators (both academics and practitioners) who come into direct contact with one another can butt heads remarkably on how to measure the educational opportunities offered the young. The following questions raised in our symposium demonstrate as much:

- Which players' roles should be analyzed when evaluating the opportunities made available in a child's educational life?
- How do we measure the opportunities available in a child's educational life in a way understandable to both lawyers and educators?
- What counts as "evidence" when evaluating equal opportunity?
- When can educational opportunity be quantified?

- How does one measure and observe educational opportunities that are not so easily quantified, like the opportunity to be taught by a teacher with "high expectations" for one's success?
- Can lawyers get involved in demanding fairness in the "qualitative" aspects of schooling?
- Does this necessitate that civil rights lawyers practice "educational judgment"? If so, are civil rights lawyers allowed to think like educators? Or must civil rights lawyers avoid altogether the more "qualitative" aspects of schooling?
- When do lawyers have the authority to comment on anything that happens inside a classroom?
- Conversely, when do educators have the right to question the equality definitions of the law?
- How many "expert" opinions from educational research and social science are necessary to create a new standard of equal opportunity for lawyers to consider?
- What does the law consider illegal rather than simply unfair?
- What do educators consider unfair rather than technically illegal?
- Most basic, what aspects of schooling, or spaces in a child's life, can and should these different players get involved in analyzing and improving?

Talking to our practitioner and academic researcher invitees in the months before the conference, it had become immediately clear to me that many of them measured elementary school opportunity very differently from how civil rights lawyers needed it measured. (By the way, "expert" is a term often bandied about by lawyers as if it refers only to academic researchers: at our symposium, exemplary elementary teachers and principals and superintendents too were treated as educational experts.) For the educator and academic experts, fundamentally, not all necessary K–3 opportunities were obviously "countable." Many educators and academics were arguing for the necessity of creating intellectually inspiring classrooms or fostering in young children an innate joy of learning or developing curricula that built upon communities' localized knowledge. In contrast, the lawyers needed opportunities to be basic, standardized, and explicitly measurable for the purposes of comparison: opportunities, like books or computers, had to be present or absent in countable amounts in order to make inequality claims. And federal policy makers, finally, needed opportunities to be politically intelligible. (For example, the idea that states or districts should assist schools serving poor students of color by matching the money wealthy white PTAs could donate to their own neighborhood elementary schools seemed only fair to many educators, but to policy makers the idea sounded politically impossible.)

Beginning to realize this impending clash of measurement methods in my conversations with attendees-to-be *before* the symposium, I decided to enforce a mixed-methods task for the symposium itself. I asked every educational expert—scholars and school practitioners alike—to bring OCR an "early elementary equity checklist" listing the specific kinds of educational opportunity they thought were essential for all students to experience in the K–3 years. This, in a sense, prepared us *to* argue over defining equal opportunity, by concretizing invitees' analyses of what educational opportunities actually were. Each item on the checklist had to be something that lawyers and investigators could at least attempt to investigate as available or not available to students in a district, school, or classroom.

Some of the experts found the assignment useful for organizing their own thinking. Others (particularly the academics) grumbled repeatedly that their work was far too complex to be summarized into a bullet-pointed list. However, all obligingly made the checklist a central piece of their participation in the symposium. Their checklists, which ranged in the end from 1 spare page to 10 dense pages, themselves functioned as mixed-methods documents that made it possible for lawyers and educators to speak concretely to one another throughout the symposium about what actually might constitute an essential early elementary educational opportunity. Scholars and educators could no longer speak vaguely about "high-quality teaching"; neither could lawyers speak sweepingly about "equal treatment." Making the checklists and talking to one another about them also prompted usefully self-conscious *conflict* between "legal" and "educational" ways of measuring unfairness in school—it enforced an explicit battle of analytic methods, if you will. At times, these methods clashed explicitly in our discussions (such as when a scholar who had spent a career trying to define equitable pedagogical interactions met a lawyer who argued that pedagogical practice could not be part of an equity conversation at all because it was neither measurable nor a subject area for lawyers). The issue of *what aspects* of schooling life to analyze and measure, and *how* to do this analysis and measurement, became the core subject of debate at the conference. In the end this forced clash of analytic habits—which was really a purposeful exercise in arguing self-consciously over *a definition of equality*—sparked a vision of an explicitly legal-educational way of analyzing equal elementary opportunity. I shall describe this vision momentarily.

Such basic questions about how to analyze schooling—and about what, in the school world, is to be analyzed when considering how to improve education for children—have been central to recent national battles over measurement and validity in educational research (see the recent National Research Council report entitled *Scientific Research in Education*). Like educational researchers these days, education civil rights lawyers are concerned constantly with the eventual public scrutiny of their analyses and methods in potentially hostile situations. As lawyers, however, they also need the educational opportunities to which they promote access to appear both concrete and undebatable. The final early learning analysis would ultimately have to pass legal muster, of course, and having been urged to think like a worried civil rights lawyer myself in anticipation of arguments from higher-ups working within the additional constraints of federal politics, as I processed all of the checklists over the subsequent months I found myself deleting a few K–3 requirements suggested by our experts that seemed either too "subjective" or too "educational" for lawyers to handle. "Subjective" items were those that seemed too tied to individual experts or too explicitly "opinionated" ("*creative* curriculum" seemed a rather vague "subjective" requirement, for example). In turn, detailed pedagogical recommendations, such as those about teacher-student interaction, often did seem too "educational" for a lawyer to evaluate or mandate. Still, the majority of the experts' "educational" recommendations found their way into the summative document I finally produced, such that the lawyers soon had a template suggesting how they could begin to actually look at what children were learning and doing in classrooms as well as at the tangible, obvious resources children were holding (books) or the crucial resource (the teacher) standing credentialed in front of them. This merging of "legal" and "educational" analysis was possible because each side had worked to frame their field's insights about educational opportunity so that the other audience could use them. Had the scholars and schools simply come to speak generally about educational opportunity in ways that assumed lawyers could simply appropriate any "expert" commentary about what constituted "good schooling"—or had the lawyers come prepared only to accept the obviously quantifiable aspects of school opportunity (numbers of computers available per child) rather than also remaining open to thinking about how to analyze the various learning opportunities offered or denied children in schools and classrooms—I think a vast majority of the "educational" knowledge may have appeared "nonlegal" to lawyers, and the lawyers would have seemed like bean-counters to the educators. To really think through how to analyze K–3 equality, it was necessary for educational experts to try to think like lawyers, and vice versa—

for everyone to try to analyze equal opportunity through a distinctly unfamiliar methodological lens.

The final early learning analysis that I produced from the symposium — which was, more specifically, a first attempt at figuring out how to assess whether academic racial discrimination was occurring in the early years of elementary school—was an explicitly mixed-methods analysis of academic opportunity because it explicitly combined legal ways and educator ways of thinking about equal opportunity. For one, it utilized the basic notion of a common academic standard (an educator concept) against which to measure the provision of equal opportunities to meet that standard (a legal concept). Besides combining the opportunities deemed essential by the educational experts into a set of K–3 "standards," the early learning analysis framed the existing academic standards of districts and states as potential blueprints for actively measuring and enforcing equal access to opportunities to learn. That is, we reasoned that if states and districts were increasingly articulating what students were supposed to know and be able to do in the early grades — and if they were penalizing or advancing students based on the demonstration of such standards-based knowledge and skills — these standards were a concrete benchmark against which both equity-minded educators and equity-minded lawyers could measure whether students actually received equal or adequate opportunities to learn the fundamental skills, content, and concepts for which they were being held accountable. Measuring the availability of such academic opportunities to learn was a mixed-methods task both "qualitative" and "quantitative" in nature, since one had to understand the full web of opportunities constituting an "adequate" education when measuring whether specific opportunities to learn specific skills, content, or concepts were present or lacking.

A lawyer-plus-educator way of thinking about providing equal opportunity in the K–3 grades also boiled down to thinking about the task as a matter of protecting both *groups* (the civil rights way of thinking) and *individuals* (more typically the educator way of thinking). Civil rights law worries about whether people are treated unequally because they are members of particular (socially produced) groups, be they "racial," gendered, or "disabled" (Minow 1990); civil rights work in education thus proceeds by monitoring the treatment of such groups (or group representatives) in school. School-level educators, in contrast, tend to worry more openly about the academic progress of individual students than about the progress of groups within their classrooms, though seeing individual students as representatives *of* racialized groups is the quiet reality of U.S. educational logic (see Steele 1992). The early learning analysis went a step further in combining group- and individual-level analysis. To combine the concerns and expertise of both equity-minded lawyers and equity-minded educators, the analysis called for treating *members of racialized groups*—in this case, kids of color—as *academic individuals* who had the civil right to be systematically afforded up-to-standards opportunities to learn.

Rather than monitoring proactively whether children of color (as groups *or* as individuals) are afforded equal or even adequate learning opportunities, U.S. educational habit is typically to leave it to school-level educators to monitor the academic progress of racialized individuals unsystematically and in private—often with problematic consequences (Pollock 2001). With educators implicitly advised to only think privately about race, routine racial discrimination in school often involves educators quietly treating even tiny kids of color as less able or less likely to achieve as a consequence of presumed racialized "inability" (Steele 1992; Ferguson 1998) or low "motivation" (O'Connor 1997; Carter, forthcoming), often without recognizing that they are doing so. Conversely, paradoxically, educational racial discrimination also involves national-, state-, district-, or school-level people actively *refusing* to label kids of color (as individuals or in the aggregate) in racial terms, and thus doing nothing to point out local examples of educational opportunities denied: kids of color overrepresented in "Special Education," for example, or underrepresented in "Gifted and Talented," or denied adequate educational resources in segregated schools and in tracked classrooms. This is why antidiscrimination lawyers must monitor both how school people actively treat students unequally *as race group members* (e.g., placing students of color in low-track classes despite high test scores, while placing white students in high-track classes despite low test scores; Oakes et al. 1990) and how they *ignore* racialized patterns harming students (e.g., by doing nothing about known racial disparities in achievement; Pollock 2004). The early learning analysis suggested that rather than ignoring student race in school *or* evaluating student potential in racialized terms, achieving racial equality even in the first years of elementary school necessitates getting educators *and* lawyers to monitor, explicitly and proactively, whether children of color are systematically being provided adequate foundational learning opportunities in the districts, schools, and classrooms in which they are placed.

This is really an analytic and practical tactic of analyzing *opportunities* in racial terms, rather than children. This leads me to an important aside on the use of a race lens in research on pathways in child and youth development, especially that concerned with analyzing academic pathways. Such work might be served well, I think, by researchers becoming a bit more self-conscious about when and how and whether and why we suggest that race is relevant to the developmental pathways we describe. As chapters throughout this volume demonstrate, developmental scholarship seems much more comfortable with labeling children and families as racial than with describing the systems that serve them in racial terms. In contrast, civil rights lawyers concerned with protecting low-income kids of color in schools self-consciously keep evaluating the role race plays in *institutions* in order to be able to call for equity remedies — and, as stated earlier, they also analyze in racial terms, not just children themselves, but more precisely the opportunities afforded by the people *serving* children. In order to get equality work done, further, lawyers must also avoid shifting vaguely between race analysis and other analytic frames. This has to do with the analytic constraints of the law itself: federal civil rights laws do not protect "the poor" or "the poorly educated," but they do protect members of racialized groups from being discriminated against in racialized ways. In contrast, scholarship on child/youth developmental pathways routinely moves back and forth between framing and not framing research subjects in racial terms. Often, it shifts somewhat blithely between explicitly racial categories ("black," "low-income Mexican American") and more subtly racialized analytic categories like "less educated," "disadvantaged," "inner city," or "the poor." Such an unsystematic shifting to and from explicitly racial analysis often facilitates an analytic vagueness about the role race plays in the phenomenon described — and about who precisely is acting in racialized ways (Pollock 2004). In contrast, civil rights lawyers cannot, for example, casually intertwine poverty and race in their analyses of schooling, for other analysts stand by always ready to argue that inequalities are "because of poverty" rather than "because of race" and are thus irremediable by federal law (although some state constitutions, luckily, do allow lawyers to protect children from the educational ravages of economic inequality).

Inconsistent ways of claiming race's relevance in educational research can have serious consequences too. In scholarly analyses of phenomena such as the achievement gap (Pollock 2001), the *children failing* are relentlessly described in racial terms, but the opportunity systems *serving* children are only sporadically described racially. Confronted with inconsistently racialized analyses of institutions and consistently racialized analyses of children, the public is just as likely to conclude that race no longer "really matters" in the distribution of opportunities to children (a dangerous assumption for children) as to conclude that race will always matter to how children from certain groups achieve (a dangerous assumption for children). If not conducted and presented with a self-consciousness about analyzing race's relevance, child development research that tackles questions of racial inequality is especially prone to the risk of blaming racialized children rather than adequately analyzing the racialized systems that serve them.

Similarly, when scholars proactively examine racialized groups of parents as players implicated in children's academic and life success (as do many of the chapters in this volume), it seems similarly important to make clear why we are utilizing racialized lenses at all, in order to avoid unwittingly fueling the racialized blame game endemic to American education (Pollock 2001). In the first version of her important paper on the role of Latino families in the pipeline phenomenon, for example (which I read as a discussant for the January 2001 conference), Cooper made race her variable of interest without explaining exactly why: *why* was she interested in *"Latino"* families? In response to this question, Cooper stated the obvious: Latino kids, of course, are particular victims of the pipeline phenomenon. The presentation problem in this instance was more precisely the unexplained focus on Latino *families* rather than on the systems and people that serve Latino children in schools. That is, *many* American readers would find it dangerously unremarkable that Latino families would be the unit of analysis in a pipeline inquiry, since a typical American way of "explaining" racial patterns in achievement is to argue that such patterns exist because *parents of color, as* race or ethnic group members, have certain habits or "beliefs" about schooling (Valdés 1996). Acknowledging this national habit of racialized blaming, researchers might beware any matter-of-fact or unexplained focus on racialized parents' or children's beliefs or habits when discussing the academic pipeline, as such a focus always threatens to reinforce a preexisting American assumption that racial patterns in achievement exist because kids and parents of color alone, not schools and institutions in tandem, make it so.

More than most American research or educational discourse, as suggested earlier, education law includes in the analysis of responsibility for racialized patterns racialized schooling systems, not just racialized kids. That is, education civil rights lawyers proactively use race analysis to analyze whether *districts and schools* provide racialized students equal access to the benefits of schooling. Of course, the placement of responsibility for social problems is often a reductive requirement of U.S. law, just as it is for research; producing simplified assessments of "fault" is central to the legal profession (Minow 1990), and *school* people often come off in legal analysis as actors who are bluntly discriminatory rather than conflicted or well-meaning or overburdened.

Far better than any reductive investigation of racial inequality, it seems, is a mixed-methods investigation that attempts to integrate in a solution the *various* players, systems, and practices involved in creating racialized patterns. Coming up with such a distributed analysis requires thinking outside the analytic boxes of each discipline. As I tried to think about equal elementary educational opportunity in such an explicitly mixed-methods way while at OCR, the various players' arguments, taken together, came to suggest the following.

In U.S. schools, young students of color are routinely denied adequate academic opportunity and systematic, individualized academic attention. Not only are young students of color routinely viewed by educators as less capable of timely, sustained academic development than their white peers, but the resources available in these students' schools and classrooms systematically do not afford *adult educators* the time, staffing, or equipment to address children's academic development (as a group or as individuals) sufficiently. Further, racialized demographic patterns in teacher hiring, placement, and retention mean that the teachers serving young students of color are often not sufficiently trained to teach them the foundational skills and knowledge assumed by common standards, a situation that handicaps teachers and students alike. Finally, the outdated classrooms and watereddown curricula that are often set up for young students of color deny them the intellectual stimulation educational experts deem necessary for healthy K–3 academic development. K–3 educational racial discrimination, thus, often takes shape as the denial of essential academic attention and resources to young children of color (as groups and as individuals) along race group lines. Remedying such discrimination requires entitling systematically underresourced students of color to such resources both as groups and as individuals—in a sense, entitling them to adequate academic attention, monitoring, and stimulation.

Prescribing such academic attention is quite possibly the most powerful education civil rights action known. Currently, the law prescribes such attention explicitly only for certain populations. Educational civil rights law, for example, prescribes attention to the academic development of "the disabled": "Disabled" students' "individual education plans," required and supported by federal and state regulations since the 1970s (with the help of an ever-expanding arsenal of medical and psychological tests), hold educators accountable for providing the specific academic assistance deemed necessary to meet students' individually assessed academic needs. Civil rights law since the 1970s has also given "language minority" students (protected under laws prohibiting discrimination based on national origin) an entitlement to academic attention. By law, schools cannot throw English-language learners into English-only classrooms without making specific provisions for their language development needs. This legal standard is being tested by antibilingual education millionaire Ron Unz, who argues in his spreading state referenda that to throw students of various ages and languages into English-only classrooms *is* a form of academic attention.

The law's prescribed academic attention, of course, is still denied routinely to the disabled and to English-language learners (Olsen 1995): civil rights lawyers spend a good deal of time enforcing attention to the academic needs of both populations, who are often left to "sink or swim" in "mainstream" or English-only classrooms despite the law. Still, the very legal entitlement to academic attention means that accusations of academic negligence toward these two populations must be taken seriously under law. In contrast, English-fluent, non-"disabled" students of color are protected generally from racial discrimination in schools by earlier education civil rights law (the Civil Rights Act of 1964), yet the need for equal academic attention to such students as learners is not spelled out in detail. Thus, remedying even egregious denials of academic opportunity to students of color often seems to require legal debate — such that these students' access to fully adequate academic opportunities has long been considered by some to be optional rather than required and legally enforceable. While many educators are held by law and bureaucracy to give "disabled" students the systematic, individualized education they are deemed entitled to, then, and while advocates for English-learning students can at least fight for entitled attention to such students' academic development (as a group and as individuals), advocates for other students of color must seemingly convince skeptics that such students deserve academic attention at all.

The mixed-methods, legal/educational model for analyzing equal elementary opportunity that began to emerge from our symposium quickly came to focus on this very need to use existing civil rights law to monitor whether children of color were receiving adequate attention (as groups and as individuals) to their academic development. In their various ways, it became clear, various legal and educational players had to be analyzing the basic educational opportunities available to K–3 students of color and determining whether these students were receiving equal opportunities in their districts, schools, and classrooms to learn the material required by common standards. Legal and educational adults had to be asking regularly whether students of color had equal access to sufficiently trained teachers, whether these teachers themselves had access to adequate professional development, and whether students of color had equal and adequate access at the classroom, school, and district levels to the basic resources assumed present by common standards (such as science materials, libraries, desks, curricula, teachers, aides, specialists, and books)—in sum, whether classroom life actually demonstrated the availability of adequate learning opportunities for each small child. They also had to be making sure that people in classrooms, schools, and districts were monitoring the progress of students of color (as groups and as individuals) on a systematic basis. To this end, it was also necessary that schools involved the parents and guardians of students of color in detailed analysis of their individual children's academic growth.

This last issue—addressing the role of families in the opportunity ecology—required viewing families analytically not as actors "socializing" children in isolation at home but rather as players interacting *with* school personnel in providing learning opportunities to children. All symposium participants agreed that equitable schools and districts keep the parents and guardians of students of color continually aware of the external (state/ national) and internal (school-level) academic standards against which their children's individual progress will be measured. At equitable schools, parents and guardians are given examples of student work that has met common standards, and they get the opportunity to discuss with school personnel the specific skills and concepts on which their individual children still need to improve. Equitable schools keep families fully informed of the various assessments being given their children, the stakes and consequences tied to those assessments, and the results of the assessments. Equitable schools and districts also keep families informed of enrichment opportunities and of the academic interventions available if their children fall behind. They make families aware of the academic programs available in schools and districts, such as academic acceleration and intervention programs; and they inform families about school and district retention and promotion policies. Most important, equitable schools keep parents and guardians continually informed of their individual children's progress toward common academic goals. Personnel in equitable schools also keep an eye out for how children of color are doing *as groups*—that is, they make sure to check proactively whether achievement gaps are patterning out racially, and they work proactively to dismantle those patterns that are racial (Pollock 2001). In sum, both families and school personnel in equitable schools are kept informed of what K–3 students are expected to know and be able to do—and what children of color as individuals and in the aggregate are currently knowing and doing.

Without this intertwining of relevant players in a child's life and without explicit monitoring of whether necessary academic opportunities are available *to* children of color as individual learners and in the aggregate, K–3 children of color in U.S. schools are at particular risk of being left behind in the academic dust. This is the "pipeline's" origin, and remedying it requires the meeting of methods and minds in a common analytic and practical quest to make academic opportunities equal. Such analytic and practical work, unsurprisingly, is a job for both lawyers and educators, and for educational researchers as well as people in district and government offices. Monitoring whether young children of color (as groups and as individual learners) truly have equal access to adequate learning opportunities — and whether they are being adequately steered as individuals toward reaching common academic standards — necessitates the eyes of teachers and principals for monitoring the learning opportunities actually being offered in classrooms and schools on a daily basis. It also necessitates the eyes of superintendents and civil rights lawyers and investigators, for analyzing more structurally whether students have equal access to adequate resources in the districts, schools, and classrooms in which they are placed. It even necessitates the eyes of researchers, watchful for various players' roles in the opportunity ecology.

Ideally, in sum, all adults responsible for young American children's development (including civil rights lawyers) would be put in the role of systematically ensuring *el buen camino,* or successful academic "pathway," for each small child. Mapping, planning, and monitoring the academic paths of children of color (as groups and as individuals) toward universal academic goals is a task for researchers, school folks, lawyers, and parents alike. Indeed, perhaps *only* such mixed-methods inequality analysis and equality practice can challenge and counteract the prevalent "pipeline" assumption that only some kids, of some colors and classes and groups, make it to the end of the line.

Notes

1. Rumbaut's hypothesis about anti-immigrant Proposition 187 increasing the "racial" self-labeling practices of California youth is a good example of framing race labeling as a shared cultural practice.

2. Academics at the symposium included Jeannie Oakes, UCLA; James Patton, the College of William and Mary; Eugene Garcia, UC Berkeley; Catherine Cooper and Roland Tharp, UC Santa Cruz; Gloria Ladson Billings, University of Wisconsin at Madison; David Ramirez, UC Long Beach; and Linda Darling Hammond, Stanford University.

References

Briggs, C. L. 1986. *Learning How to Ask: A Sociolinguistic Appraisal of the Role of the Interview in Social Science Research.* Cambridge: Cambridge University Press.

Carter, P. Forthcoming. *Not in the "White" Way: Aspirations, Achievement and Culture among Low-Income African American and Latino Youth.* Oxford: Oxford University Press.

Ferguson, R. F. 1998. "Teachers' Perceptions and Expectations and the Black-White Test Score Gap." In *The Black-White Test Score Gap,* ed. C. Jencks and M. Phillips, 273–317. Washington, DC: Brookings Institution Press.

Henry, J. 1963. *Culture against Man.* New York: Vintage Books.

Jordan, W. D. 1974. *The White Man's Burden: Historical Origins of Racism in the United States.* London: Oxford University Press.

Minow, M. 1990. *Making All the Difference: Inclusion, Exclusion, and American Law.* Ithaca: Cornell University Press.

Nader, L. 2002. *The Life of the Law: Anthropological Projects.* Berkeley and Los Angeles: University of California Press.

Oakes, J., with T. Ormseth, R. Bell, and P. Camp. 1990. *Multiplying Inequalities: The Effects of Race, Social Class, and Tracking on Opportunities to Learn Mathematics and Science.* Santa Monica: Rand Corp.

O'Connor, C. 1997. "Dispositions toward (Collective) Struggle and Educational Resilience in the Inner City: A Case Analysis of Six African-American High School Students." *American Educational Research Journal* 34 (Winter): 593–629.

Ogbu, J. 1974. *The Next Generation: An Ethnography of Education in an Urban Neighborhood.* New York: Academic Press.

Olsen, L. 1995. "School Restructuring and the Needs of Immigrant Students." In *California's Immigrant Children: Theory, Research, and Implications for Educational Policy,* ed. R. G. Rumbaut and W. A. Cornelius, 209–233. San Diego: Center for U.S.-Mexican Studies, University of California San Diego.

———. 1997. *Made in America: Immigrant Students in Our Public Schools.* New York: New Press.

Payne, C. 1984. *Getting What We Ask For.* Westport, CT: Greenwood.

Pollock, M. 2001. "How the Question We Ask Most about Race in Education Is the Very Question We Most Suppress." *Educational Researcher,* December, pp. 2–12.

———. 2004. *Colormute: Race Talk Dilemmas in an American School.* Princeton: Princeton University Press.

Steele, C. 1992. "Race and the Schooling of Black Americans." *Atlantic Monthly,* April, 68–78.

Valdés, G. 1996. *Con Respeto: Bridging the Distances between Culturally Diverse Families and Schools.* New York: Teachers College Press.

Valencia, R. 1991. "The Plight of Chicano Students: An Overview of Schooling Conditions and Outcomes." In *Chicano School Failure and Success: Research and Policy Agendas for the 1990s,* ed. R. Valencia, 3–26. London and New York: Falmer Press.

Varenne, H., and R. McDermott. 1998. *Successful Failure: The School America Builds.* Boulder: Westview Press.

Synthesis

A Reprise on Mixing Methods

Jennifer C. Greene

In this chapter, I share a set of reflective interpretations of the papers presented at the January 2001 conference "Discovering Successful Pathways in Children's Development: Mixed Methods in the Study of Childhood and Family Life," with a focus on those included in this volume. I arrived at these interpretations by listening keenly throughout the several days of the conference, listening with my antennae finely tuned to hear novel ideas, perceptive insights, and creative entwinements of diverse perspectives. I took notes on what I heard. I then inductively organized these notes into themes that captured some of the strands of meaning that were being woven at the conference. (I have also since enhanced my notes by reading some of the full papers.) My intentions were largely to reconstruct emic meaning—or the ways the conference engaged its participants in the moment. Yet I fully acknowledge that my renderings of meaning are my own, filtered by my own ways of making sense of the mixing of social inquiry methods. And these ways, my ways, are those of an applied methodologist and program evaluator who has spent more than a decade pondering the theory and the practice of mixing methods.[1] So, this concluding discussion about mixing methods in social inquiry itself represents a mix — of interpretations grounded in our collective experiences at this conference and ideas imported from other times and places.

These interpretive reflections are offered in three parts:

1. *Why* are we interested in the mixing of methods in social inquiry? What visions accompany this way of conducting research? Why do we consider mixed-methods work of potential value? What value?
2. *How* do we creatively and meaningfully mix methods in social inquiry? In particular, what contributions to mixed-methods practice are offered in this volume?
3. What are important *future directions* for advancing the theory and practice of mixed-methods inquiry?

Voices of Conference Participants

Here are some of the voices I heard at the conference, some of what participants said about their reasons for mixing methods in their work. Conference participants said we mix methods

- to be inclusive;
- to hear both inside and outside voices, to honor both emic and etic lenses, to attend to both micro- and macroperspectives;
- to develop better hypotheses or better instruments;
- to provide a rich context for our empirical findings, to broaden our interpretations of our findings;
- to triangulate and thereby attain synergy or convergence;
- to challenge dominant viewpoints or stances;
- to honor or to create a rich mosaic that fully represents the multifaceted complexity of lived experience;
- to deconstruct and then reconstruct an interpretation of a social practice;
- to capture the ways in which culture and self are mutually constitutive;
- to unsettle what is seemingly settled;
- to find jagged, not smooth, models;
- to get it right;
- to contest established notions of "rightness";
- to understand what is really going on;

- to come to terms with the inevitable uncertainty, contingency, and ambiguity of the human condition;
- to tell the (untold) story — because it needs to be told;
- to pursue unexpected and surprising findings;
- to generate unexpected and surprising findings;
- to pursue with an agenda of discovery;
- to take a journey through the data;
- to get closer to the truth;
- to reduce errors of nonobservation or to reduce biases of observation;
- to enhance the plausibility of our findings;
- to be better connected, less dislocated in our work, to find and experience a better sense of place.

These various claims that inquirers made about their purposes or intentions for mixing methods can be clustered into four distinct, albeit overlapping frames.

Frame 1: Enhancing the Validity or Credibility of Findings

We mix methods to *get it right*, to enhance the validity or credibility of our findings. Convergent results from different methods accomplish this purpose.

Christina Gibson and Greg Duncan's chapter on the New Hope antipoverty program evaluation has some instances of mixing methods to get it right. Ethnographic data, for example, enabled better, more complete understanding of differential program effects observed for boys' and girls' school behavior and achievement. "Researchers used the insights from one methodology to inform the findings of the other" (chap. 9). Gibson and Duncan describe their mixed-methods design as a "productive synergy," and they highlight the importance of having evaluation team members be involved in both qualitative and quantitative data collection and analysis. "Individuals trained and actively engaged in both methods must constantly confront the resulting but productive tensions between the two."

Chapter 4, by Deborah Johnson, recounts a series of three studies, all intended to better understand the ecology of African American children's ability to cope with racial discrimination and prejudice. Her studies probe diverse standpoints within an ecological framework, including those of (a) family, school, and community, (b) micro- and macrosocialization processes, and (c) the child's daily life as well as the institutional practices he/she encounters. These different standpoints invoke different methods, both within and across studies. Moreover, the series of studies was designed to employ a variety of methods that *triangulate* on a single construct, children's racial coping. Different standpoints and different methods were used in the interest of "convergence" in understanding children's racial coping more deeply, more contextually, and thus more accurately.

Rubén Rumbaut's expansive study (chap. 5) on historical shifts in the cultural and ethnic identities of adolescent children of immigrants—and how such shifts are themselves reconstituting the meaning of American identity—also uses a mix of methods to try to "get it right." Large-scale surveys of immigrant children that tracked changes in language usage, psychosocial adjustment, and other markers of cultural identity were supplemented with in-depth interviews of a sample of their parents *and* with a sociopolitical analysis of related cultural events, for example, the passage of Proposition 187 in California (which denied social, health, and educational services to undocumented immigrants and their children). This particular mix of methods underscored the potential power of combining relatively value-neutral methods like surveys with more value-committed methods like interviews and historical documentation and analysis. For example, while survey results showed a rapid decline in native-language proficiency and use, indicating a possible "thinning" of ethnic identity, the reactions of young people to events like Proposition 187 suggested otherwise. Youths such as Stephanie Bernal joined with each other and with adults of Mexican heritage to strongly oppose this ballot initiative with political activism. Although "Proposition 187 won in a landslide, getting 59% of the statewide vote . . . Stephanie's Mexican ethnic self-identity was 'thickened' in the process, a sense of belonging made more salient than ever as she came to define who she was and where she came from *in opposition to* who and what she was not" (chap. 5, emphasis added).

Finally, a conference participant representing the policy-making lens on social issues remarked during one discussion, "our purpose as social scientists should be to get closer to the truth."

This frame of "getting it right" assumes a realist view of social reality, that there is an "it" out there to get right, to understand accurately and comprehensively. The phenomena of interest may well be complex, multi-layered, contextual, and temporal, and our understanding of them may well be constrained by such complexities. But these phenomena do exist independently of our knowledge or experience of them. And our knowledge of them can in fact be enhanced though a mix of methods, pragmatically selected as those best suited to our questions about the phenomena and contexts at hand. And thus, in this frame, methods importantly differ by their location on the same set of continua, for example, open-ended or closed-ended, inductive or deductive, emergent or a priori. Other continua and dimensions of mixed-methods social inquiry—philosophical-epistemological, disciplinary, political, representational, moral-ethical dimensions—are not centrally invoked or considered in this view.

Frame 2: Developing Broader, Deeper, and More Inclusive Understandings

We mix methods to *do our work better,* to develop understandings that are broader, deeper, more inclusive and that more centrally honor the complexity and contingency of human development. Arguably, this is the most common frame. Chapter 8, on research by Jeffrey Kling, Jeffrey Liebman, and Lawrence Katz on the Boston site of the Moving to Opportunity (MTO) housing demonstration project, provides several considered examples. In one, the researchers' qualitative fieldwork, consisting of on-site observations and program participant interviews, refocused their "quantitative data collection strategy on a substantially different set of outcomes." In addition to the "outcomes most familiar to labor economists: the earnings and job-training patterns of MTO parents and the school experiences of MTO children," the researchers included outcomes related to "safety and health" that were revealed as participant priorities in the qualitative interviews. That is, a mix of methods focused attention on participants' concerns about safety and health, *in addition to* inquirers' concerns about self-sufficiency. More broadly, these researchers' iterative and sequential mix of methods helped "develop an overall conceptual framework for thinking about pathways through which MTO moves might affect developmental outcomes." The researchers found "that fear of random violence was pervasive and that safety concerns caused mothers in high-poverty urban housing projects to devote an enormous amount of time and energy to ensuring the safety of their children. . . . [Moreover, this] need to live life on the watch has broad implications for . . . mothers' mental health and on their ability to engage in activities that would lead them to become economically self-sufficient" (chap. 8). This broader framework for understanding what difference MTO might make in the lives of its participants well illustrates the deeper and more complex results that can come from mixing methods.

In Gibson and Duncan's New Hope study (chap. 9), one key finding concerned the relationship between the number of problems a family faced and the family's ability to benefit from the New Hope package. Analysis of qualitative data suggested broad heterogeneity in family problems. In quantitative analysis then, an index of "potential employment-related problems," or barriers, was created and used to sort the families into three groups: no barriers, one important barrier, or two or more barriers. Separate analyses of program effects on earnings for these three groups yielded significant benefits only for the middle group, a group perhaps well "poised to profit from the New Hope package of benefits." This more fine-grained disaggregation of program effects is a clear instance of using mixed methods to generate deeper, more contingent understanding.

In an additional example, Southern California researchers Claude Goldenberg, Ronald Gallimore, and Leslie Reese argued in chapter 1 that a mix of inquiry methods is needed to understand the complexities of contextual influences on Latino children's literacy development. Among the several examples in their chapter is an extended discussion of the contributions made by a mix of qualitative and quantitative methods to a rich understanding of how parents' cultural view of reading significantly affected their use of literacy materials and their literacy interactions and engagements with their children in the home. The central role played by parents' cultural models on home literacy practices surfaced in qualitative data and was refined and extended via further qualitative work and larger-scale quantitative analyses.

In chapter 2, by Heather Weiss and collaborators at the Harvard Family Research Project, and in chapter 3, by Lois-ellin Datta, the central argument was that a mix of methods generated a more complete, contextual, contingent, and complex understanding of the phenomena of interest than would have a single-method study. Through a mix of methods, Weiss and colleagues were able to understand not just the role of work in family involvement in education—obstacle or facilitator—but its varied and contextualized meanings. Examples of these meanings included the possible centrality of parental efficacy to both work and involvement and the personalized and relational—rather than formal or institutional—character of parents' balancing of work and family responsibilities. Similarly, Datta argued that a mix of methods and data was essential to a comprehensive understanding of the important effects of a major school reform initiative *in context*. While quantitative data alone indicated no program effects, qualitative data enabled analyses that clearly demonstrated positive effects when the program was fully implemented. The mix of data further indicated that the overall context (the city of Detroit) had itself moved toward greater adoption of the reform's principles. Fully understanding context through a mix of methods was thus critical in this evaluation study.

In short, many, if not most, mixed-methods studies are undertaken, in significant part, to "do our work better," to develop a more complex, nuanced, contextual, and contingent understanding of the phenomena of interest. While in the first frame, a mix of methods is used to pinpoint findings with greater precision and accuracy, in this frame diverse methods are mixed to add breadth, depth, and complexity to findings. This frame thus rests on a philosophical stance of fallible realism with perhaps a strand of interpretive or constructivist thinking. That is, social reality is assumed to be complex and contextual and, at least in part, constructed via interpretation. So, neither distanced observation and measurement nor up-close engagement and interaction alone can capture the complexities of social reality; rather, both, and more, are needed. The point in this frame is specifically to honor complexity rather than to get it right. Therefore, methods are chosen in large part for their diversity of perspective, and multiple dimensions of methodological diversity are considered: epistemological, disciplinary, representational, political, and moral-ethical dimensions, among others. Sometimes, the inclusion of diverse methods intentionally introduces new dimensions into a study, as in Tom Fricke's addition of ethnographic methods to a survey study (chap. 6). With these added methods, the study needed to "take culture seriously," as culture is the central preoccupation of ethnography.

Often underlying or motivating this mixed-methods frame of honoring complexity is a substantive theory or lens that is itself complex and multidimensional and that therefore demands or requires a mix of methods to fully address. In fact, a complex, multifaceted theory of children's developmental pathways probably underlies most of the chapters in this volume, providing direction and guidance for the mixing of methods. For example, the Goldenberg et al. research on Latino children's literacy development rests on pivotal claims that important "influences on children's development . . . are embedded in the routines of family life that themselves are embedded in a larger ecological and cultural . . . niche." This perspective leads to an inquiry focus on "activity settings [which] are regular scenes ... that represent the playing out of the family's ecocultural milieu. They represent the way families can and do structure their time based on the traditions handed down to them, the orientations provided by culture, and the strictures of the socioeconomic system within which they live" (chap. 1). Clearly, this multilayered, multifaceted perspective on child development can be meaningfully addressed only with a diverse set of multiple methods. Similarly, in their urban ethnographic study (chap. 7), Debra Skinner, Stephen Matthews, and Linda Burton understood development as a multilayered, contextual sociocultural process and were able to generate a richer and more complete representation of this process with the combined use of traditional fieldwork and Geographic Information Systems technology than was possible with fieldwork alone. Deborah Johnson's image of the mosaic or the puzzle is a good metaphor for this mixed-methods frame, as is Leslie Reese's shared comment from a participant in one of her studies: "Lo que no mata se engorda." Let us indeed seek to mix methods that are both friendly and nonfattening.

Frame 3: Challenging Conventional Wisdom

We mix methods to *unsettle the settled,* to probe the contested, to challenge the given, to engage multiple, often discordant perspectives and lenses. This third mixed-methods frame is intentionally *dialectic* (Greene and Caracelli 1997b) in that it seeks out tensions and discord as potentially generative locations for new insights. Diverse methods are mixed specifically to provoke and challenge what is accepted as common wisdom or shared understandings. This third frame is also sometimes explicitly value engaged, as the tensions it provokes are often imbued with value or political dissonance.

In his commentary on the chapters in part 4, on social experiments, Tom Brock discussed participant interviewing as offering a clear challenge to the "program-centrism" of much implementation research on demonstration programs. Participant interviewing brings in not only the program perspectives of participants but also their values and interests, which may well be at odds with those advanced by program and policy designers. In Deborah Johnson's work on the ecology of African American children's racial coping (chap. 4), her third study intentionally focused on understanding racial coping in its community context entirely from the perspective of the child, invoking issues of child agency and child values. More broadly, the lenses of childhood often challenge adult understandings and stances.

In their study on the interconnections between parental work and parental involvement in their children's education, Weiss and colleagues intentionally adopted a dialectic stance in their mixed-methods analysis, with fruitful results.

Our contrasting findings about maternal work as a barrier and an opportunity for family involvement underscored the value of mixing methods, specifically its potential to expand and make more complex our understanding of phenomena of interest. The contrast led to new learning be-

yond what "everyone knows"—that work poses obstacles to involvement—to an understanding that work can also facilitate some involvement. Specifically, this led to learning about conditions under which work
can support involvement at school, open up new avenues for family involvement, and contribute to children's learning beyond school walls.
(Chap. 2)

This frame for mixing social inquiry methods thus actively courts difference, not only of method and perspective but also of ways of knowing,
meanings of knowledge, views of social reality, disciplinary traditions and
values, representational styles, political alliances, value commitments, sociocultural standpoints, and many other dimensions of our methodologies.
Our methods in this mixed-methods frame differ in multiple ways. In this
frame, we seek questions in addition to answers and we aim to both deconstruct and reconstruct understandings. In this frame, we value paradox,
complexity, and intrigue, and we build not smooth but "jagged" models of
social understanding, models where all components are not fully aligned,
models with irritating squeaks and rattles, models that invite further work.[2]
We do so by valuing difference, such that difference becomes constitutive
of understanding, and inquiry becomes iterative, with each new understanding generating its own discord and thus invitation for further inquiry.

Frame 4: Engaging Politics and Values

We mix methods to foreground the political and value dimensions of
our work, to *engage with each other about our differences,* to advance our di-
alogues. In frame 4, that is, we mix methods not only to illuminate and understand difference but also to engage with the politics and values that
define its contours and meanings.

Several conference discussions displayed strands of frame 4 in participants' attention to issues such as the construction of gender over time, the
ways in which immigrants are assimilated and discriminated against, and
the role of science in society. Leslie Reese challenged conference participants to privilege the overall goal of social betterment in our work, arguing
that social science becomes legitimate and valuable only if it contributes to
social betterment. And throughout the conference, many participants renewed commitments to understanding the viewpoints of children themselves on the challenges and possibilities of development—*and children's
accompanying interests and values.*

Frame 4 thus centrally features questions about the nature of politics and values in science and about the role of science in society. Whose interests do we advance in our work? What views, values, and assumptions about "healthy" child development and social change are we promoting in our research? What views, values, and assumptions about the important contributions of social science to society are we advocating in our work as researchers? And in frame 4, we intentionally mix methods—along multiple, diverse dimensions—to engage our differences, to insist that we attend to them. Conference participant William Cross eloquently argued that there are some stories we as researchers simply "must tell"—stories about silenced voices, unseen events, muffled experiences. Methods that disrupt and that demand attention to untold tales are the methods of frame 4.[3]

Ideas for Mixing Methods: What to Mix and How

Conference participants also offered many rich and varied examples of what to mix in mixed-methods social inquiry (i.e., what dimensions of our methodologies to mix) and how to mix them, or what procedures and creativity can be enjoined in the process of mixing.

What to Mix

Conference participants were particularly thoughtful in considering and experimenting with mixes of methodological dimensions that included but also extended well beyond the technical. The technical level of mixing methods—the mixing of different kinds of data gathering and analysis techniques—is neither problematic nor problematized in the literature (Greene and Caracelli 1997b). Far more interesting precisely because it is more problematic is the mixing of other dimensions of our methodologies. To describe the myriad ways in which conference participants mixed methods, I will use Van Maanen's (1995) useful trilogy of "interpretive moments" in contemporary ethnography. According to Van Maanen, the work of ethnographers, and here by extension other social researchers, is mediated by interpretation, (1) first, as we offer our own interpretations of what we have learned, (2) second, as we offer particular representations of these interpretations, and (3) third, as our readers/listeners/viewers make their own meanings of our interpreted representations of social understandings.

Mixing in generating our own interpretations. Participants mixed many dimensions of methodology in their inquiry studies, importantly including

- what questions to ask;[4]
- at the technical level, what design, methods, and samples to employ,[5] and what analyses to conduct;[6]
- underlying philosophical assumptions—about the nature of social reality, the nature of lived experience, the nature of our social knowing and what is possible and desirable to know, and the relationship of knower to known;[7]
- disciplinary traditions, norms, and domains of understanding;
- ecological levels or spheres of inquiry, for example, micro- *and* macrolevels or the individual *and* the community spheres; and
- location of the observer or the viewer, for example, inside *and* outside the context of study.

Mixing in representing our interpretations. The value of mixing representational forms was more of a theme in conference discussions than in conference papers and presentations. Discussed, with occasional support from papers and presentations (see especially chap. 7), was the importance of moving beyond text-based, formalized language for conveying what we learn in our research. We now have many other alternatives, including other forms of texts for representation—notably, such literary forms as stories, poems, plays, and performances—and other media as well, such as film, computer-generated imagery, and the geography of GIS technology. The contributions of mixed-methods inquiry can be further enhanced if we extend our mixed-methods thinking to our representational responsibilities (Goodyear 2001).

Audience mixing in interpreting our work. Although there was little opportunity at the conference to involve a mix of audiences in making their own sense of our findings, some of the conference discussions did note how mixed-methods work could meaningfully invite or welcome diverse audiences, interpretations, and actions.[8] Datta (chap. 3) specifically observed that mixed-methods inquiry can politically engage multiple levels and forms of policy influence through the inclusion of diverse voices and perspectives. Many conference participants noted that mixed-methods inquiry can speak more persuasively to diverse audiences. Mixed-methods inquiry characteristically broadens the role of social science in society beyond knowledge generation to also address policy influence, reeducation, and social change and thereby also broadens the audience mix for our work.

How to Mix

As a whole, the research in this volume suggests an iterative, interactive, dialogic agenda for mixed-methods social inquiry, where the mixing of "methods" implies a commitment to and engagement with multiple ways of seeing, knowing, and valuing. This agenda rests on several conditions:

1. The methods that are mixed have relatively equal status (Creswell 1994; Greene, Caracelli, and Graham 1989).
2. There is reciprocal, respectful understanding of each methodology by all involved. Not everyone needs equal expertise in each methodology, but all need to accept and respect all methodologies.
3. There is an openness to the possibility, even desirability, of dissonance emanating from the mix. There is an acceptance of "jagged models" for our inquiry understandings.
4. There is also a valuing of practicality and pragmatism in our work. Extended dialogue is rarely possible and even more rarely instrumental in making policy decisions. While interaction and inclusion are the ideal, many practical inquiry contexts can necessarily only aspire to this ideal.

Iterative, dialogic, mixed-methods inquiry involves back-and-forth interactions between the diverse methodologies included in the study, interactions that are conversational and collaborative and are intentionally generative of new insights and understandings. The process of mixed-methods inquiry relies not so much on a set of codified procedures but rather on making room for these back-and-forth conversations, planning pauses in the inquiry for the sharing and mixing of lenses, and allocating analytic time and space for the ongoing dialogue about difference. Such pauses or places for mixing can and probably should occur throughout the inquiry (Tashakkori and Teddlie 1998), but particularly during the phases of (a) determining what questions to ask, (b) developing the inquiry design and methods, (c) conducting the analysis and interpretation of data, and (d) representing and promoting the understandings reached in the outside world. Numerous examples of mixed-methods thinking and engagement during all but the last of these inquiry phases were evident at the conference, many of which have been presented and discussed above.

What Comes Next?

This volume offers substantial and thoughtful testimony to the wisdom of adopting a mixed-methods way of thinking in applied social inquiry. The chapters add much richness to the mixed-methods literature—richness of inquiry examples, of creative imaginings of possibilities, and of the inclusion of diversity and difference.

My words for the future are to carry on. Carry on the work of thinking dialogically in social inquiry, of inviting difference into our work, of welcoming the jagged edges, the untold stories, the puzzles and mosaics. We need to continue to educate ourselves about other ways of navigating and making sense of our social world, continue to enlarge our own perspectives and horizons, keep learning about new methods, and dare to try out alternative ways of representing social knowledge. And we need to continue to educate our colleagues and our audiences about the importance of iterative, interactive, dialogic social inquiry, about the value of adopting a mixed-methods way of thinking and acting. The complexity and urgency of the social issues we strive to understand demand no less.

Notes

1. See, for example, the following conceptual and practical ideas about the mixing of methods in social and educational program evaluation: Greene and McClintock 1985; Greene, Caracelli, and Graham 1989; Caracelli and Greene 1993; Greene and Caracelli 1997a; Greene, Benjamin, and Goodyear 2001; Mathie and Greene 2002; Greene and Caracelli 2003.

2. Thanks to Michael Zuckerman for this image of "jagged models."

3. Hood similarly argues for attention to "the experiences of pain and abandonment [that] have led to a search for roots and on occasion, for a revision of recorded history" (2001, 33; quoted from Greene 1993, 17) Hood's specific argument is for a recovery of the work of early African American educational evaluators, for a restoration of their place in our recorded history and honored legends.

4. As one example of mixing methods in asking questions, in her work on the racial coping of African American children, Johnson (chap. 4) intentionally planned three different studies, each addressing the issues from a different ecological niche, thus enabling study of both the proximal influences of family processes and more distal factors of social stratification.

5. Most conference papers illustrated the mixing of methods in social inquiry design. These include the social interventionist, policy-oriented evaluations of GEAR UP (chap. 10), New Hope (chap. 9), Moving to Opportunity (chap. 8), and the Comer school reform program in Detroit (chap. 3). These also include the knowledge generation research studies of African American children's racial coping (chap. 4), Latino children's

literacy (chap. 1), "school transitions" and the place of parent work therein (chap. 2), and studies on child development in the context of urban poverty (chap. 7) and immigration (chap. 5).

6. This is also a familiar location for mixed-methods thinking, although examples of thoughtful and creative mixed-methods analysis are underdeveloped in the literature. Chapter 2 in this volume emphasizes analytic attention to different ways of knowing and valuing by featuring the highly innovative and creative analytic conversation between qualitative and quantitative data.

7. Conference studies included mixes of postpositivist, interpretivist, constructivist, and critical social science stances on these underlying assumptions.

8. Goodyear's work in the domain of evaluation demonstrated that use of mixed representational forms in mixed-methods inquiry is especially valuable in welcoming diverse audiences to participate in interpreting and acting upon inquiry findings (Goodyear 2001).

References

Caracelli, V. J., and J. C. Greene. 1993. "Data Analysis Strategies for Mixed-Method Evaluation Designs." *Educational Evaluation and Policy Analysis* 15:195–207.

Creswell, J. W. 1994. *Research Designs: Qualitative and Quantitative Approaches.* Thousand Oaks, CA: Sage.

Goodyear, L. K. 2001. "Representational Form and Audience Understanding in Evaluation: Advancing Use and Engaging Postmodern Pluralism." PhD diss., Cornell University, Ithaca, NY.

Greene, J. C. 2001. "Mixing Social Inquiry Methodologies." In *Handbook of Research on Teaching,* 4th ed., ed. V. Richardson, 251–258. Washington, DC: American Educational Research Association.

Greene, J. C., L. Benjamin, and L. Goodyear. 2001. "The Merits of Mixing Methods in Evaluation." *Evaluation* 7 (1): 25–44.

Greene, J. C., and V. J. Caracelli. 2003. "Making Paradigmatic Sense of Mixed-Method Practice." In *Handbook of Mixed Methods in the Social and Behavioral Sciences,* ed. A. Tashakkori and C. Teddlie, 91–110. Thousand Oaks, CA: Sage.

———, eds. 1997a. *Advances in Mixed-Method Evaluation: The Challenges and Benefits of Integrating Diverse Paradigms.* New Directions for Evaluation, vol. 74. San Francisco: Jossey-Bass.

———. 1997b. "Defining and Describing the Paradigm Issue in Mixed-Method Evaluation." In *Advances in Mixed-Method Evaluation: The Challenges and Benefits of Integrating Diverse Paradigms,* ed. J. C. Greene and V. J. Caracelli, 5–17. New Directions for Evaluation, vol. 74. San Francisco: Jossey Bass.

Greene, J. C., V. J. Caracelli, and W. F. Graham. 1989. "Toward a Conceptual Framework for Mixed-Method Evaluation Designs." *Educational Evaluation and Policy Analysis* 11:255–274.

Greene, J. C., and C. McClintock. 1985. "Triangulation in Evaluation: Design and Analysis Issues." *Evaluation Review* 9 (5): 523–545.

Greene, M. 1993. "The Passions of Pluralism: Multiculturalism and the Expanding Community." *Educational Researcher* 22 (1): 13–18.

Hood, S. 2001. "Nobody Knows My Name: In Praise of African American Evaluators Who Were Responsive." In *Responsive Evaluation,* ed. J. C. Greene and T. A. Abma, 31–43. New Directions for Evaluation, vol. 92. San Francisco: Jossey-Bass.

Mathie, A., and J. C. Greene. 2002. "Honoring Difference and Dialogue in International Education and Development: Mixed-Methods Frameworks for Research." In *Multiple Paradigms for International Research in Education: Experience, Theory and Practice,* ed. L. Bresler and A. Ardichvili, 139–154. New York: Peter Lang.

Tashakkori, A., and C. Teddlie. 1998. *Mixed Methodology: Combining Qualitative and Quantitative Approaches.* Thousand Oaks, CA: Sage.

Van Maanen, J. 1995. "An End to Innocence: The Ethnography of Ethnography." In *Representation in Ethnography,* ed. J. Van Maanen, 1–35. Thousand Oaks, CA: Sage.

Contributors

Margarita Azmitia is a professor of developmental psychology at the University of California, Santa Cruz. Her research focuses on the role of family, peers, and schools in helping ethnically diverse adolescents manage their life and school transitions.

Thomas Brock is a senior research associate at MDRC, a nonprofit social policy research organization with offices in New York City and Oakland, California. He uses qualitative and quantitative methods to study the implementation of education, employment, and social service programs for youth and adults.

Jane R. Brown is a developmental psychologist affiliated with the University of California, Santa Cruz, and California State University, Monterey Bay, where she works in program evaluation. Now writing a Web-based child development text, Brown's research focuses on children's emotion regulation.

Linda M. Burton is currently director of the Center for Human Development and Family Research in Diverse Contexts and professor of Human Development and Sociology at Pennsylvania State University. Using ethnographic methods, her research explores the relationship between community contexts, poverty, intergenerational family structure and processes, and developmental outcomes across the life course in ethnic/racial-minority populations.

Gabriela Chavira is assistant professor of psychology at California State University, Northridge. Her research focuses on identity development and family relations of ethnically diverse youth.

Catherine R. Cooper is professor of psychology and education at the University of California, Santa Cruz. She builds theories and mixed-methods tools to link science, policy, and practice involving diversity, youth identity, and pathways through school in multicultural societies.

William E. Cross, Jr., is professor and coordinator of the Doctoral Program in Social-Personality Psychology at the Graduate Center, City University of New York. He is an expert on racial/cultural identity theory and research.

Lois-ellin Datta has served as director of Evaluation in Human Service Areas for the U.S. General Accounting Office, as director of the Teaching, Learning, and Assessment Division of the National Institute of Education, and as director of the National Head Start Evaluation and of Children's Bureau Research. In association with the Kohala Center and with Datta Analysis, she is an international consultant and writes, teaches, and speaks on the intersections among policy, programs, practice, and research in health, education, income and work, and community development areas.

Greg J. Duncan is the Edwina S. Tarry Professor of Education and Social Policy and a Faculty Fellow at the Institute for Policy Research at Northwestern University. His research interests include the impacts of welfare reform and residential mobility programs on children.

Tom Fricke is professor of anthropology and director of the Center for the Ethnography of Everyday Life at the University of Michigan. His research, teaching, and publications from fieldwork in Nepal and the rural United States are in the areas of family and kinship, the intersection of work and family relations, and cultural moralities.

Ronald Gallimore is professor of psychiatry and biobehavioral science at the University of California, Los Angeles. He teaches and conducts research on culture, education, and the improvement of teaching.

Christina M. Gibson-Davis is assistant professor of public policy at the Terry Sanford Institute of Public Policy and a faculty affiliate of the Center for Child and Family Policy, Duke University. Her research interests include the effects of poverty on children, family formation decisions among low-income populations, and the effectiveness of social welfare policy.

Claude Goldenberg is professor of teacher education and associate dean of the College of Education, California State University, Long Beach. His research focuses on improving literacy achievement for children from Spanish-speaking homes.

Jennifer C. Greene is professor of educational psychology, with a specialty in educational and social program evaluation, at the University of Illinois, Urbana-Champaign. Her evaluation scholarship addresses the intersections of social science method and political discourse and includes work in the domains of qualitative, mixed-methods, and participatory approaches to evaluation.

Sara Harkness is a professor in the School of Family Studies, University of Connecticut, and director of the university's Center for the Study of Culture, Health, and Human Development. She directs the International Study of Parents, Children, and Schools, a collaborative project in seven Western countries, and is a principal investigator in an NIH-supported research project investigating relationships between culturally organized customs of child care and infants' patterns of arousal and emotion in the United States and the Netherlands. She is a principal investigator in a federally funded intervention project (GEAR UP) to help youth in Hartford succeed in school and continue on to postsecondary education.

Rebecca Hencke is an independent scholar in the Boston area, with a background in early childhood education. She is currently pursuing her research interests in socioemotional development while working as a statistical consultant.

Marcia Hughes is a doctoral student in the School of Family Studies at the University of Connecticut. She is the project director of the university's GEAR UP project, a federally funded intervention to help children from disadvantaged backgrounds succeed in school and prepare for postsecondary education. Her research and teaching interests are families and schools and their joint role in childhood socialization. She is particularly interested in student relationships with adults as they mediate developmental outcomes, including social behavior, emotional regulation, and achievement motivation.

Aletha C. Huston is the Priscilla Pond Flawn Regents Professor of Child Development at the University of Texas at Austin. She teaches and does research on the effects of poverty on children and the impact of childcare and income support policies on children's development.

Deborah J. Johnson is professor in Family and Child Ecology and associated with the Institute for Children, Youth, and Families at Michigan State University, East Lansing. Her research interests include parental ethnic/racial socialization, ethnic identity development, and racial coping among children and families of color in the United States and internationally, including Zimbabwean children, Sudanese refugee children, and Indigenous Australian children.

Lawrence Katz is the Elisabeth Allison Professor of Economics at Harvard University and a research associate of the National Bureau of Economic Research. His research focuses on a broad range of issues in the general areas of labor economics and the economics of social problems.

Jeffrey R. Kling is assistant professor of economics and public affairs at Princeton University and a faculty research fellow of the National Bureau of Economic Research. His research and teaching are in the fields of public sector economics, labor economics, and econometrics.

Holly Kreider is a research associate at the Harvard Family Research Project, Harvard Graduate School of Education. She conducts applied research in the areas of family educational involvement and teacher education.

Jeffrey Liebman is associate professor of public policy at Harvard's John F. Kennedy School of Government and a faculty research fellow at the National Bureau of Economic Research. His research focuses on tax and budget policy, social insurance, and labor markets.

Stephen A. Matthews is associate professor of geography, demography, and sociology; senior research associate; and director of the Geographic Information Analysis Core at the Population Research Institute, Pennsylvania State University. His research interests focus on different dimensions of health and well-being, particularly among low-income and minority families, as well as ecological and neighborhood studies.

Ellen Mayer is a research associate at the Harvard Family Research Project, Harvard Graduate School of Education. She conducts research in family educational involvement and develops research-based practitioner tools.

Beth Muller, MSN, RN, is a doctoral candidate at the University of Connecticut School of Family Studies in Storrs. She is a psychiatric nurse practitioner who works with children, adolescents, and families and is a co-investigator on several studies examining cultural values, parenting practices, and children's development. Her teaching and research interests include ADHD, cross-cultural psychiatric models, and cultural practices.

Mica Pollock is an assistant professor at the Harvard University Graduate School of Education. She examines the everyday struggles over inequality and diversity occupying adults and youth in schools and communities. Her first book, *Colormute: Race Talk Dilemmas in an American School,* pinpoints six basic dilemmas of race-label use and deletion plaguing people in U.S. schools. She is currently analyzing everyday battles over defining educational discrimination in the United States.

Leslie Reese is a professor in the Department of Teacher Education at California State University, Long Beach. She is a co-investigator on two longitudinal studies of children's literacy development and home-school connections among Spanish-speaking families. Her research and teaching interests include immigration, multicultural education, instruction of English learners, and community contexts of literacy development.

Rubén G. Rumbaut is professor of sociology at the University of California, Irvine, and codirector of its Center for Research on Immigration, Population, and Public Policy. His work on immigrants and refugees in the United States has focused on their intergenerational mobility, educational achievement, and aspirations, bilingualism and language loss, ethnic identity, depression and self-esteem, infant health, and paradoxes of assimilation.

Diane Scott-Jones is professor of psychology at Boston College. A developmental psychologist, she studies social development and family processes in children and adolescents from a variety of ethnic backgrounds.

Debra G. Skinner is a senior scientist at the Frank Porter Graham Child Development Institute at the University of North Carolina, Chapel Hill. She is an anthropologist whose current work focuses on cultural and family issues relevant to poverty and disability and to genetic knowledge and technologies.

Charles M. Super is professor and dean in the School of Family Studies at the University of Connecticut. As a developmental and clinical psychologist, he does research on the cultural regulation of early development and on interventions to promote the physical and mental health of children and families. He is currently involved in comparative and collaborative projects in the United States and several European countries concerning school-family relations and the early regulation of children's attention, arousal, and affect.

Margaret (Peggy) Vaughan is a doctoral candidate in the Eliot Pearson Department of Child Development at Tufts University. Her research interests include early intervention, childhood disability, and foster care.

Thomas S. Weisner is professor of anthropology, Departments of Psychiatry (NPI Center for Culture and Health) and Anthropology, at the University of California, Los Angeles. He studies culture and human development, family adaptation, and children and families at risk.

Heather B. Weiss is founder and director of the Harvard Family Research Project, Harvard Graduate School of Education. She writes, teaches, speaks, and advises on child and family policy, family and community involvement in children's education, and innovative evaluation strategies.

Author Index

Subject Index

Abt evaluation of Comer schools: child development improvement results, 73–74; evaluation design, 69, 71–72t; evaluators' role, 75–76; implementation findings, 70; importance of, 76, 77, 78–79; merging of approaches, 75–76; methodologies integration, 80t; possible improvements to evaluation, 79, 81; qualitative knowledge addition, 73

academic pipeline problem: challenge model (*see* Bridging Multiple Worlds Model); described, 359–60; experienced by Latino immigrants (*see* Latino children's literacy development); inequality of academic opportunity (*see* civil rights and academic development); reasons for focus on Latino families, 399; research partnership study (*see* outreach program for low-income sixth-graders); types of models applicable to, 360

acculturation: association between family structure and youth's level of, 120; graphical representation of acculturation and discrimination, 167; index of, 121–22; interaction with discrimination, 151; language and, 140–42, 153–54; parent-child acculturation types, 118. *See also* ethnic identity determinants; ethnic identity formation

ADHD (attention deficit/hyperactivity disorder), 353

adolescents: benefits from a mentor relationship, 349; ethnic identity formation (*see* ethnic identity formation); mechanism for coping with racialization (*see* racial coping by children); myth associated with black oppositional stance, 180–81; outreach program effectiveness (*see* outreach program for low-income sixth-graders)

African Americans: historical reliance on single-method study measures, 179–

433